SOCIAL JUSTICE IN ACTION

Models for Campus and Community

SOCIAL JUSTICE IN ACTION

Models for Campus and Community

Edited by

NEAL A. LESTER

The Modern Language Association of America
New York 2024

85 Broad Street, New York, New York 10004
www.mla.org

To order MLA publications, visit www.mla.org/books. For wholesale and international orders, see www.mla.org/bookstore-orders.

The MLA office is located on the island known as Mannahatta (Manhattan) in Lenapehoking, the homeland of the Lenape people. The MLA pays respect to the original stewards of this land and to the diverse and vibrant Native communities that continue to thrive in New York City.

Library of Congress Cataloging-in-Publication Data

Names: Lester, Neal A., editor.
Title: Social justice in action : models for campus and community / edited by Neal A. Lester.
Description: New York : The Modern Language Association of America, 2024. | Includes bibliographical references.
Identifiers: LCCN 2024010790 (print) | LCCN 2024010791 (ebook) | ISBN 9781603296571 (hardcover) | ISBN 9781603296588 (paperback) | ISBN 9781603296595 (EPUB)
Subjects: LCSH: Education, Higher—Social aspects—United States. | Social justice and education—United States. | Educational equalization—United States.
Classification: LCC LC191.94 .S64 2024 (print) | LCC LC191.94 (ebook) | DDC 378/.0150973—dc23/eng/20240619
LC record available at https://lccn.loc.gov/2024010790
LC ebook record available at https://lccn.loc.gov/2024010791

FIRE . . . flaming, burning, searing, and penetrating far beneath the superficial items of the flesh to boil the sluggish blood.

FIRE . . . a cry of conquest in the night, warning those who sleep and revitalizing those who linger in the quiet places dozing.

FIRE . . . melting steel and iron bars, poking livid tongues between stone apertures and burning wooden opposition with a cackling chuckle of contempt.

FIRE . . . weaving vivid, hot designs upon an ebon bordered loom and satisfying pagan thirst for beauty unadorned . . . the flesh is sweet and real . . . the soul an inward flush of fire. . . . Beauty? . . . flesh on fire—on fire in the furnace of life blazing. . . .

> "Fy-ah,
> Fy-ah, Lawd,
> Fy-ah gonna burn ma soul!"

Wallace Thurman
Foreword to *FIRE!!* (1926)

Contents

Confronting Privilege

Building Connections

Introduction

Neal A. Lester

At best, "social justice" is an ideal realized variously by some individuals and communities. This ideal is based on individuals' intersecting identities and acknowledges that every individual is a member of multiple communities simultaneously. While social justice embodies the ideal of "full participation in society and the balancing of benefits and burdens by all citizens, resulting in equitable living and a just ordering of society" (Buettner-Schmidt and Lobo 948), what is problematic about this particular framework is that it imagines a kind of "universal" truth and experience. My experience socially, personally, professionally, and historically is that no such "universal" truth exists here in the United States or elsewhere on the planet. This volume, then, is not a history of social justice; nor an overtheorized account of what constitutes "social justice." Rather, it raises critical questions about larger and inherently intersecting efforts to imagine, realize, and witness justice—whether environmental justice, racial and criminal justice, menstrual justice, reproductive justice, climate justice, economic justice, or food justice (to name but a few). Each of these areas of perceived and lived experiences of injustice denies dignity and life, disenfranchises, delegitimizes, minoritizes, and marginalizes. The volume is thus both an exploration of "justice" and "injustice" and a blueprint of sorts of the many diverse ways that individuals and communities conceptually and practically are disrupting the status quo. The very existence of this volume aligns with what Martin Luther King, Jr., highlights in his speech "The Other America," at Stanford University, wherein he warns against what he sees as "America's postponing of justice": "Large segments of . . . society are more concerned about tranquility and the status quo than about justice and humanity." In yet another declaration of urgency to America and Americans to make good on the promise and "promissory note" invoked in his "I Have a Dream" speech—the pledge "that all . . . would be guaranteed the unalienable rights of life, liberty and the pursuit of happiness"—King frames social justice within the realm of economics, race, prosperity, social neglect, and humanity, both individual and shared. Such a lens connects all social justice work to these binaries: "the milk of prosperity and the honey of opportunity" versus "the ebullience of hope [that transforms] into the fatigue of despair" ("Other America"). King proclaims boldly that the United States has had a historically persistent and morally corrosive challenge from its founding to the present: "to make America one nation, Indivisible, with liberty and justice for all." He articulates a commitment to social justice as a call to action for those of "good will" who embrace the ideals of diversity, inclusion, and equity: "With this faith, we will be able to hew out of the mountain of despair a stone of hope" ("Other America").

The historical context of questioning ideals lies in the very birthing of this nation, full of contradictions, hypocrisies, and shortfalls. The author Toni Morrison reminds us of this complex US history:

> I have often wished that Jefferson had not used that phrase, "the pursuit of happiness," as the third right—although I understand in the first draft was "life, liberty and the pursuit of property." Of course, I would have been one of those properties one had the right to pursue, so I suppose happiness is an ethical improvement over a life devoted to the acquisition of land; acquisition of resources; acquisition of slaves. Still, I would rather he had written life, liberty and the pursuit of meaningfulness or integrity or truth.

Morrison, commenting on this still evolving USA experiment, aligns justice with "meaningfulness," "integrity," and "truth." This sentiment is like that of Frederick Douglass, who as an enslaved person questions the meaning and mockery of America's Independence Day in his 5 July 1852 address to the Rochester Anti-Slavery Society, framing his critique around America's "high lessons of wisdom, of justice, and of truth":

> Are the great principles of political freedom and of natural justice, embodied in that Declaration of Independence, extended to us? . . . I say it with a sad sense of the disparity between us. I am not included within the pale of glorious anniversary! Your high independence only reveals the immeasurable distance between us. The blessings in which you, this day, rejoice, are not enjoyed in common. The rich inheritance of justice, liberty, prosperity and independence, bequeathed by your fathers, is shared by you, not by me. The sunlight that brought light and healing to you, has brought stripes and death to me. This Fourth of July is yours, not mine. You may rejoice, I must mourn.

Like those of so many others in history, Douglass's life calls out the bold hypocrisies of "liberty and justice for all." As the United States reckons with racial justice following the murder of George Floyd in May 2020, it is imperative to declare the hypocrisy, bias, and cisheteropatriarchal privilege that the "founding fathers" did not acknowledge in their grand pronouncements. Clarifies Lisa M. O'Neill, "These laws were made by white, cisgender men who enslaved other human beings and never intended to include a vast sum of Americans—like women and people of color—in their quest for equal rights." Audre Lorde furthers this inherent connection between justice, authority, authoring, and othering and the potential complicity of all Americans in upholding and benefiting from systems that simultaneously advantage and disadvantage individuals and groups:

> In america, this norm is usually defined as white, thin, male, young, heterosexual, christian, and financially secure. It is with this mythical norm that the trappings of power reside within this society. Those of us who stand outside that power often identify one way in which we are different, and we assume that to be the primary cause of all oppression, forgetting other distortions around difference, some of which we ourselves may be practicing. ("Age" 106)

This complicated and complex ideal of "justice," then, demands a lens through which to see intersecting identities and looks to a faith in human potential and possibility, not just for a select few but for one and all. Indeed, the urgency of this challenge does not come from complacency or gradualism but from a persistent pressure for intentional and focused action.

Impetus

The impetus for this volume comes from my own personal frustration, weariness, and, yes, despair, as someone engaged in social justice work as a university teacher, a scholar of US race relations, and an African American cishetero middle-aged male in the United States. Having written, published, taught, and lectured extensively on US race and gender from antebellum to the present, I continually find that well-meaning, potentially progressive, and typically white people, immediately after hearing my diversity, equity, inclusion, and justice (DEIJ) talks or participating in my DEIJ workshops, ask me this rather loaded question: "What can I do?" While I understand the place of well-intentioned innocence and the sincere desire for guidance and instruction from which this particular question or one similar emerges, I am always struck by the fact that this question has yet to come from a person of color in any of my audiences or classes over thirty years of being in the academy. I have a similarly visceral response to news media interviewers whenever I, as their Rolodex expert on US race relations, am called in to talk in a two-minute segment about the latest Black American race incident and to give a quick answer to complex social problems. Lorde, in her essay "The Uses of Anger: Women Responding to Racism," reaffirms this all too familiar feeling of "equity fatigue" (see Le) that results from the reality that "[o]ppressed peoples are always being asked to stretch a little more, to bridge the gap between blindness and humanity" (Lorde, "Uses" 123). Ableist language aside, Lorde captures my "blue funk," especially after the August 2017 Charlottesville white supremacy / white nationalism march. While not in KKK robes this time, the young white males with their tiki torches and chants made historical parallels uncanny. The filmmaker Ava DuVernay visualizes this mirroring in her powerful documentary *Thirteenth*, on Black criminality, racial injustice, and mass incarceration of Black and Brown men and boys in the United States; the marching University of Virginia white males remind viewers that "[t]he past is the present. It's the future too and life won't let us lie out of that" (E. O'Neill). Rather than retreat from the challenge of answering the question, for which I do not have a single answer or a readily available menu of easy-fix options to recommend or boxes to check off, I envision this volume as an opportunity for me to respond more constructively and patiently to those who approach me and similarly frustrated Others for whom this work is at the core of our existence within and beyond the academy with this same question about predicting the future of race and other systemic oppressions nationally and globally. This volume then, for me, is also a reprieve of sorts. It's what I hope will be like no other existing volume—MLA or otherwise—in that it will be more holistic, more practical, and more thoughtful about what those around the globe are thinking about and doing as social justice work and about the scope and nuance of that work. This volume is meant for those who are veterans of this justice work as well as those who are newcomers and novices. The range of perspectives rendered here represents the diversity and commitment of those doing this work. My hope is that this volume will be useful to everyone who seeks to better understand and practice living their best lives knowing that they are engaged in work that is bigger than ourselves and the comfort of our immediate geographical, social, and political circles. Social justice work, then, embodies Booker T. Washington's notion in *Up from Slavery* that "we can be as separate as the fingers yet one as the hand in all things essential to mutual progress." For those with agency and privilege to act, thrive, and move more freely than others who are targets of oppression, disenfranchisement, and social neglect, this work constitutes civic engagement wherein "[c]ivic engagement includes more than just involvement with the political process; it also includes how we as individuals participate in the life of a community and how we come together for a public purpose that is not solely self-serving" (*Report* 2).

I have found the enthusiasm of this volume's contributors and anonymous reviewers energizing, hopeful, and inspiring. The process of editing the volume has already opened my eyes to the exhaustive range of work by everyday people taking risks to act and make change on behalf of a greater social good. Each act has challenged me to see daily that framing and understanding social justice work as manifestations of our individual and shared humanity means that there is a role for everyone in addressing inequality, inequity, and the myriad injustices that plague and define a shared human condition.

Context and Structure

This is not the only volume that extensively addresses social justice theory and praxis. There are also lots of critical essays in scholarly journals on various dimensions of social justice. Yet this is one of the only volumes that takes pedagogy beyond the walls of high school and college classrooms to underscore social embeddedness, civic engagement, and community-building at their most fundamental levels. For those engaged in this life work, the personal, political, and professional have always converged quite seamlessly. This volume is premised on the assumptions about "social justice" outlined by Lee Anne Bell in the third edition of *Teaching for Diversity and Social Justice*:

> "Social justice" connotes both a process and a goal. The goal is full and equal participation of all groups in a society that is mutually shaped to meet their needs. The vision of such a society promotes (a) equitable distribution of resources, (b) physical and psychological safety and security, (c) self-determination and independent agency, and (d) a sense of self and responsibility to society as a whole. The vision of a socially just process includes practices and procedures that are democratic and participatory, inclusive and affirming of human capacities for working collaboratively to create change. (3)

Other ways of practicing and creating social justice involve understanding social justice as a "redistribution of resources from those who have unjustly gained them to those who justly deserve them, and it also means creating and ensuring the processes of truly democratic participation in decision-making" (Feagin 5). The National Association of Social Workers defines "social justice" as "the view that everyone deserves equal economic, political and social rights and opportunities" (Dolan-Reilly). To address and effect change that humanizes, legitimizes, and levels the proverbial playing field, social justice work must consider questions of individual and communal agency and positionality as well as notions of privilege and unconscious bias. Further, this volume foregrounds social justice work within the context of what Project Humanities—the initiative I founded and direct at Arizona State University—calls Humanity 101, a social justice tool kit with a programmatic focus on these seven principles of all and any success and progress: compassion, empathy, forgiveness, integrity, kindness, respect, and self-reflection. The tools for students, teachers, and community members offered in this new volume complement the following resources. *Teaching for Diversity and Social Justice*, edited by Maurianne Adams and colleagues, is a textbook for educators and workshop facilitators. Comprehensive in its multidisciplinary approach, this volume of essays by a "community of social justice educators" supports those seeking to "develop a more thoughtful understanding of diversity and group interaction, . . . to critically evaluate inequitable social patterns and institutions, . . . and to work in coalition with diverse others to create more social justice and inclusive relationships, practices, and social structures" (ix). Kim A. Case's volume *Intersectionality Pedagogy: Complicating Identity and Social Justice*, a text for college teachers, includes essays from different disciplinary perspectives—critical race and gender studies, psychology, and education—exploring intersectionality in theory, classroom applications, and social justice pedagogy. Thandeka K. Chapman and Nikola Hobbel's *Social Justice Pedagogy across the Curriculum* is aimed at K–12 educators seeking to implement social justice practices in their classrooms. The case studies in Katy M. Swalwell's single-authored volume *Educating Activist Allies: Social Justice Pedagogy with the Suburban and Urban Elite* aim to foster social responsibility among students and to connect them more empathetically with minoritized individuals and communities. *Revolutionizing Pedagogy: Education for Social Justice with and beyond Global Neo-Liberalism*, edited by Sheila Macrine and colleagues, is part of Palgrave's Marx and Education series. This volume specifically explores capitalism and its roots as foundational to social injustice and oppressions. The eight essays in Tracy Davis and Laura M. Harrison's *Advancing Social Justice: Tools, Pedagogies, and Strategies to Transform Your Campus* offer practical suggestions about making social justice work more robust and meaningful for college and university students as well as for the educators themselves. John Smyth's volume *Critical Pedagogy for Social Justice* looks at social justice through the lens of Paulo Freire's notion of "critical hope" in *Pedagogy of Freedom*, encouraging teachers to embrace their roles as intellectuals, students to embrace their roles as activists, and communities to engage not just socially but also critically.

Arguably, since the 2016 US presidential election, a growing number of marginalized groups fighting against white supremacy and systemic racism prompted new scholarly strategies to address and explore social justice. The realities of racial, class, economic, age, and gender disparities that the COVID-19 pandemic laid bare, and then George Floyd's May 2020 murder and the global social unrest and protest that followed, have led to a bevy of new social justice volumes—some focused on niche audiences, others more generally focused. Among them are these:

Adams, Maurianne, et al., editors, *Readings for Diversity and Social Justice*

Baker-Bell, April, *Linguistic Justice*

Benedict, Cathy, et al., editors, *The Oxford Handbook of Social Justice in Music Education*

Boyd, Ashley S., and Janine J. Darragh, *Reading for Action: Engaging Youth in Social Justice through Young Adult Literature*

Davids, Nuraan, and Yusef Waghid, *Academic Activism in Higher Education: A Living Philosophy for Social Justice*

Eklund, Hillary, and Wendy Beth Hyman, editors, *Teaching Social Justice through Shakespeare: Why Renaissance Literature Matters Now*

Eliason, Michele J., et al., *Social Justice Pedagogy Plus: Transforming Undergraduate Research Methods Courses*

Freebody, Kelly, et al., editors, *Higher Education, Pedagogy and Social Justice: Politics and Practice*

Godley, Amanda J., and Jeffrey Reaser, *Critical Language Pedagogy: Interrogating Language, Dialects, and Power in Teacher Education*

Gorski, Paul C., and Seema G. Pothini, *Case Studies on Diversity and Social Justice Education*

Irby, Decoteau J., et al., editors, *Dignity-Affirming Education: Cultivating the Somebodiness of Students and Educators*

Kafele, Baruti K., *The Equity and Social Justice Education Fifty: Critical Questions for Improving Opportunities and Outcomes for Black Students*

Kay, Matthew R., *Not Light, but Fire: How to Lead Meaningful Race Conversations in the Classroom*

Kezar, Adrianna, and Julie Posselt, editors, *Higher Education Administration for Social Justice and Equity: Critical Perspectives for Leadership*

Kinloch, Valerie, et al., *Where Is the Justice? Engaged Pedagogies in Schools and Communities*

Lawless, Brandi, and Yea-Wen Chen, *Teaching Social Justice: Critical Tools for the Intercultural Communication Classroom*

Leung, Sofia Y., and Jorge R. Lopez-McKnight, editors, *Knowledge Justice: Disrupting Library and Information Studies through Critical Race Theory*

Lynch, Shrehan, et al., *Pedagogies of Social Justice in Physical Education and Youth Sport*

Marine, Susan B., and Chelsea Gilbert, editors, *Critical Praxis in Student Affairs: Social Justice in Action*

Marshall, Catherine, et al., *Educational Politics for Social Justice*

McNair, Tia Brown, et al., *From Equity Talk to Equity Walk: Expanding Practitioner Knowledge for Racial Justice in Higher Education*

Mink, John, editor, *Teaching Resistance: Radicals, Revolutionaries, and Cultural Subversives in the Classroom*

Muhammad, Anthony, and Luis F. Cruz, *Time for Change: Four Essential Skills for Transformational School and District Leaders*

Murff, Dennisha, *Culturally Responsive Pedagogy: Promising Practices for African American Male Students*

Parker, Kimberly N., *Literacy Is Liberation: Working toward Justice through Culturally Relevant Teaching*

Reagan, Timothy G., and Terry A. Osborn, *World Language Education as Critical Pedagogy: The Promise of Social Justice*

Reece, Bryan, *Social Justice and Community College Education*

Safir, Shane, and Jamila Dugan, *Street Data: A Next-Generation Model for Equity, Pedagogy, and School Transformation*

Sims, Jeremiah J., *Revolutionary STEM Education: Critical-Reality Pedagogy and Social Justice in STEM for Black Males*

Strunk, Kamden K., and Leslie Anne Locke, editors, *Research Methods for Social Justice and Equity in Education*

Trzak, Agnes, editor, *Teaching Liberation: Essays on Social Justice, Animals, Veganism, and Education*

Unlike volumes geared specifically toward students or teachers, this volume intentionally expands to reach wider and more diverse audiences. It also centers transdisciplinarity, including areas not always acknowledged in typical public discourse, such as evolutionary science and justice, acting and activism, and architectural design and justice. Shorter works in varied formats speak to the importance and urgency of justice work from still other activists' unique perspectives.

As the editor of this volume, I know that some, if not many, will expect this to be a very different kind of pedagogy volume. For some, this assembly of perspectives will resemble a "kitchen sink" with all manner of dishes stacked inside. I suggest, however, that these essays come together to make a statement about the who, what, when, where, why, and how of social justice work today. I trust each reader to think of this volume as an open buffet of critical commentaries to sample, taste, digest, and share. What amaze me still as I reflect on the process of putting this volume together are the robust energies that emerge from each and every one of these pieces by individuals whose lives have been inextricably touched by this call of duty.

As the World Turns in Search of Justice

Bringing this volume to fruition has been a rather long haul. While preparing this manuscript for submission in its first stages in late 2018, I thought that I fully and clearly understood its direction and the vision that I had for it. I knew that it needed to be significantly different from the existing volumes that address aspects of social justice and even social justice pedagogy. I knew that I wasn't necessarily trying to arrive at a single definition for social justice. I knew that I was less interested in how to teach a text per se and more interested in exploring how ideas about social justice translate into action more broadly. I knew that I wanted to showcase examples of what others were doing personally, professionally, organizationally, and communally to effect positive change toward equity, equality, and the dignity of all. I knew that this volume, like its subject, would cross boundaries of discipline and genre. I also knew that the volume must have diverse representation of thought and appeal to diverse audiences. The resulting collection reinforces my belief as expressed by Juanita, an African American female character, as she responds to Parnell, a "progressive" white male character playing both sides of the racial justice fence at the end of James Baldwin's play *Blues for Mister Charlie*:

> *Parnell:* Can I join you on this march, Juanita? Can I walk with you?
> *Juanita:* Well, we can walk in the same direction, Parnell. Come. Don't look like that. Let's go on. (313)

As I read the final moment of this play, which I have taught many times over thirty years, it is without closure or, rather, absolute clarity regarding how precisely to get to the destination of racial justice and sexual equality desired in the 1960s. Its questions resonated in the summer of 2020, when racial unrest boiled over in US streets, sending cities and properties up in flames, because of decades and centuries of racial and economic injustices entrenched and institutionalized in complex systems of oppression. Likewise, in the scene that opens Baldwin's play, mostly young, Black male protesters prepare to gather in the streets in demonstration against the murder of Richard, a young Black man, presumably by a respected white man, Lyle, with no legal accountability or consequence, in the segregated Deep South. Loosely based on the tragic story of Emmett Till, *Blues for Mister Charlie* captures in its staging and its set design the surreal, segregated Black/white living spaces, Black/white communal lived experiences, and Black/white communal responses to Black deaths that catalyzed the US civil rights movement. The play, by a writer who at the time was widely considered "militant lite" rather than a powerful voice for change, seemed to many to excuse the white presumed murderer Lyle, asking viewers to see US racism as a plague that negatively affects everyone, though differently. In "Notes for Blues," the introduction to the play, Baldwin offers a conciliatory challenge to audiences not to point fingers at one villainous race or another but rather to examine the deeply intertwined and embedded roots of US racism psychologically and spiritually:

> But if it is true, and I believe it is, that all men are brothers, then we have the duty to try to understand this wretched man; and while we cannot hope to liberate him, begin working toward the liberation of his children. For we, the American people, have created him, he is our servant. . . . It is we who have locked him in the prison of his color. It is we who have persuaded him that Negroes are worthless human beings, and that it is his sacred duty, as a white man, to protect the honor and purity of his tribe. (243)

Baldwin is clearly onto something about humanity even amid the most horrific and tragic actions of Black people's deaths and suffering. Here he is boldly and unapologetically walking the road less traveled among his contemporaries by calling for an acknowledgment of everyone's humanity. The same occurred when the activist Angela Y. Davis visited my university, Arizona State University (ASU), in 2011, just after the death of Osama bin Laden. While the nation and the world cheered Bin Laden's death and the cruelty he knowingly inflicted upon others, Davis preceded her speech to the packed audience of over four hundred faculty members, administrators, students, and community members with this question: "What is it about us that allows us to cheer the death of any human being?" The audience was silenced, challenged to reflect and to self-reflect. Importantly, then, these brief final lines of Baldwin's play become for me an affirmation that walking toward justice, however practiced and imagined, is a walk toward each person's humanity. It means walking together in the same direction but perhaps along different trails.

The pieces in this volume are different lanes of the highway converging toward justice in its many manifestations. These texts, for me, come together in critical conversations about the denial or the affirmation of the life and dignity of all living beings. As the US and the world witness this great disruption of the status quo that has resulted from death, power grabs, unchecked privilege, and all manner of inequities, I see some protesting in the streets, others challenging injustices through the written word. I see allies, accomplices, and coconspirators calling in and calling out family, colleagues, neighbors, and strangers. I see white people asking what they can do to advance real change in systems that oppress, and I see folks responding with prescribed lists of resources and action items. I see a reaching across boundaries and communities to support and to chastise. I see folks coming together to talk within and beyond their group memberships. So many see this post–George Floyd moment as the storm that destroys in order to rebuild, the fire that burns down in order to regrow, hence the Wallace Thurman epigraph that opens this volume, underscoring my scholarly efforts to create and re-create communities that do not shy away from risk-taking through a kind of necessary destruction that can lead to a reimagining of what individual and communal social transformation and evolution can look like.[1] Perhaps these are indeed the "fires next time" after the floods of national and global injustice (Baldwin, *Fire*). Perhaps this action, this cosmic pause and unrest, will indeed lead to living and coexisting in this world where *all lives really do matter*. This volume and this moment in our US and world history beckon all to join this march toward justice, as pronounced as the final sentiment in the Negro National Anthem, "Lift Every Voice and Sing": "Let us march on, 'til victory is won" (Johnson).

Still, the social upheaval that has derived from the attacks on immigrants, on Black and Brown folks, on transgender folks, on women, on reproductive rights, on poor people, on old people—and the proverbial beat goes on—has taken its toll of those of us who have been intimately living and doing social justice most, if not all, of our lives. My decision to teach African American literature and culture thirty-plus years ago as an assistant professor was an effort to promote and interrogate racial and social injustice. As I have written about, lectured on, workshopped, and keynoted on US race relations and African American culture, I have become somewhat disillusioned by the actions, the inactions, and the seeming disconnect of too many white people from the centuries-old US struggle against racial injustice and anti-Blackness. I cannot, of late, count the number of phone calls and emails I have received from news media and others asking for interviews, guidance, and help—all without compensation for or even an awareness of my emotional labor and the personal, emotional, and psychological toll that watching the replays of Black people's deaths exacts from me (and others like me) as a Black male here in this country right now. These frequent requests come as though I have personally not been impacted by what is happening and has happened historically in the world around me. They come as though I am not personally trying to process individual and communal trauma. They come with an implied though more often than not explicit expectation that I possess some magic solution to this country's centuries-old systemic racism and its accompanying social injustices. They come as though I am sitting idly waiting to teach and guide those who are not my students. And yes, most of these requests are from white people leading predominantly white, reputable organizations. Too often, what is being asked of me as an "expert" is typically not anything that the askers can't google. It makes me wonder how committed these progressive white allies really are if they aren't taking the time to reflect on the trauma that I and so many Black Americans I know are experiencing right now. Newcomers to racial and social justice work must travel a substantial distance from awareness to acceptance to action, and the expectation that those with professional and lived experience will educate those who haven't done any of the foundational work is absolutely exhausting and discouraging.

Here is a glimpse into some of the many local requests I received in the immediate wake of George Floyd's murder, mostly from folks in professional leadership positions who were just then waking up to the deeply systemic roots of US racism and its many manifestations and who were now tasked with responding to the local, national, and global racial upheaval from an organizational perspective. These individuals and organizations allegedly wanted to do something, and the something for many was to immediately reach out to me—or someone like me—to answer sometimes seemingly random questions or questions that required far more than a simple and reductive answer from a one-off talk or presentation. For instance, such requests asked me to explain the rationale and goals of Black folks protesting in the streets and destroying their own neighborhoods, to explain why their white colleagues were more committed to "law and order" than to fighting for social justice, to explain the social media popularity of the African American political conservative pundit Candice Owens, to explain the benefits of DEI work and how to engage in that work, to explain the present and historical tensions in US race relations, and to explain the overall importance of diversity and equity.

One request from an attorney group asked that I help them plan an open forum on the "tragedy of George Floyd." Such requests came mostly from non-Black individuals inviting me to speak to groups of judges, attorneys, and other community organizations. Not only did such requests register a kind of cultural insensitivity to the fact that I, as a Black person in this country who through media replays had experienced the trauma of watching another Black male being suffocated by police holding him down, was not in a position to give anyone advice about how to fix racism in this country, but apparently, my role as a race relations "expert" trumped my humanity as a person who had witnessed the murder of a person who looked like me. When a white *Arizona Republic* reporter, Karina Bland, reached out to me to ask what white people could do in the wake of George Floyd's murder, my response to her resonated in a way that she only then understood and acknowledged. Her published account, "What Should We Do to Fight Racism? We Are Asking the Wrong People," summarized our conversation and captured my repeated sentiment at the time:

> When one of my friends posted on Facebook, "All lives matter," the other day, I did something I hadn't done before. I responded with, "All lives do matter, but black lives are in danger." . . . I hadn't done that before because it was easier to ignore it. Scroll by. Pretend I didn't hear what was said. These are people I like, and that makes it harder. But sometimes, the things they say, or post on social media, are not nice. Sometimes, they are racist.
>
> I had let them get away with it, though I knew it wasn't right. Now I say so.
>
> I didn't think of doing that on my own. I had called Neal Lester for help on a story. . . . He has done extensive research on race and society. And he's black.
>
> When I reached him, he said he did not have the emotional or psychological energy to talk about what is happening in the aftermath of the killing of George Floyd. I was the third person who had called him that morning. . . .
>
> Lester sounded tired, and he is. Tired of talking about race, of saying the same thing every time this happens. He's tired of answering the questions. . . . It's not a single incident but decades of having his humanity denied.
>
> He's grappling with the horror of that, and people like me ask him again and again, "What should we do?" . . . I'm asking the wrong questions of the wrong people. I should be asking questions of other white people, the ones decrying looting but not the loss of human life, those insisting "all lives matter." I should ask, "How are you OK? If you are paying attention, how are you not outraged?" I shouldn't have to ask what to do, Lester said. If someone was drowning, would I wait for someone to tell me what to do? "People are drowning," Lester said. If people ask what to do, I should ask, "What did you do the last time it happened?" If the answer is "nothing," that's telling." . . .
>
> He's right.

> We shouldn't ask what to do. We know what to do, and if we don't, there's plenty of information out there.

Says Natalie Morris about this moment of awakening to systemic injustices, "Many Black people and ethnic minorities are tentatively hopeful that this could be the beginning of monumental change. But, witnessing this change happen in real-time can also feel incredibly draining and triggering for people who have experienced racism their whole lives."

Still, appeals to me to fix the complex and systemic US race problem with a simple forty-five-minute lecture, or something equally reductive, have not come just from white people. Black community members also sought out my expert guidance that likely could have been derived from a number of sources independent of me. One group's administrator asked me to provide resources on race-based trauma, not really an area of my expertise, as I am not a psychologist or a psychiatrist. I could have pulled together something respectable, but not anything more than a quick *Google* search could quickly and easily yield. Another administrator asked that I come in to share resources on K–12 African American history for their teachers. Again, this is nothing that a *Google* search couldn't yield. A Black judge invited me to conduct a virtual session for their judges' group on implicit bias. The invite came with a time and date and no mention of compensation for my expertise, another aspect of social justice work that continues to elude those allegedly committed to doing this equity work. This request expressed an interest in having me talk from my personal experience and not just from a scholarly and professional perspective, a request that, for me, flirts with poverty porn and reliving or re-creating one's racial trauma. Hence, cultural insensitivities and the desire for quick fixes to centuries-old US systemic racism and white supremacy came in furiously and frantically, so much so that it was emotionally and psychologically dizzying.

I know well from various conversations and social media posts that I am not the only person being asked to comment on social justice and DEI by individuals and organizations. The fact that I am being asked seems not to acknowledge my own humanity and need to process what is happening around and to me as an African American scholar, as an African American faculty member, as an African American father with two African American adult children, and as an African American spouse. I spoke to this point in my much-shared and circulating op-ed piece, "No, I Am Not Okay, but Thanks for Asking." That, however, did not give these askers pause in reaching out to get what they needed or wanted from me. I hope, then, that this volume will be such a resource that readers will consult before asking another person of color or other marginalized individual for help without demonstrating a record of commitment to acknowledging and then changing their learned behaviors and the oppressive systems which they have been complicit in perpetuating and sustaining.

In the aftermath of George Floyd's death—and sadly too many other deaths before and since—I have gladly unfriended *Facebook* "friends" whose commitment to and responses to this national pulling the scab off the wounds of US racism I question and am exhausted by. Now I know I have, for them, become the "angry Black man" for being impatient with police apologists and those more focused on property damage than the loss of human lives, for declining requests to give advice on television about how to racially heal our society when the truth is that I don't have a solution to a problem I didn't create. Plus, the tenets of systemic racism and social justice are intersectional and so far-reaching that no single answer or solution can possibly address this all. The struggles for justice are indeed ongoing and more nuanced. To acknowledge this reality is not to give in or to give up but to recognize that this work is communal and demands commitment for the long haul. So I have had to refocus my thinking and take deep breaths as I walk through my own predominantly white suburban neighborhood, observing not a few US flags proudly waving where not long ago Trump campaign signs decorated well-manicured lawns. I also have to remind myself that my personal frustration, anger, grief, confusion, and disappointment come from not knowing "the answer" to this hard question of how to achieve justice for all. As I move daily through these roller-coaster emotions and responses, I take solace in Lorde's profoundly encouraging words for self-preservation:

> Whenever the need for some pretense of communication arises, those who profit from our oppression call upon us to share our knowledge with them. In other words, it is the responsibility of the oppressed to teach the oppressors their mistakes. I am responsible for educating teachers who dismiss my children's culture in school. Black and Third World people are expected to educate white people as to our humanity. Women are expected to educate men. Lesbians and gay men are expected to educate the heterosexual world. The oppressors maintain their position and evade their responsibility for their own actions. There is a constant drain of energy which might be better used in redefining ourselves and devising realistic scenarios for altering the present and constructing the future. ("Age" 104–05)

The filmmaker Ava DuVernay echoes Lorde in this assertion about allyship, in this sense relative to race. To the *CBS News* anchor Gayle King's question "So what action can white people who see themselves as allies, what can they do?" DuVernay responds:

> [T]hat's not a question that people who are not white should answer. . . . We take on the emotional labor of racism. And it is not our job to explain to white folk how to fix their broken selves in this context. . . . There are many educated Caucasian folk who are talking to each other about it. They need

> to continue to do that, so that we can save our energy for survival and thriving. ("Ava DuVernay")

While engagement in justice work is both life-giving and life-affirming, it is also life-draining. Indeed, this volume offers a reprieve of sorts for me. For now, I will continue to decline requests for media interviews seeking a sound bite rather than a deep systemic analysis of social injustices. This volume itself and these essays individually are a step toward showing that social justice is not a hobby and not simply an intellectual exercise. This work is my life. In this sense, the volume engages with the past, the present, and the future.

Challenging Ourselves as Humans and as Humanists

"Close your eyes," I tell my privilege and bias workshop participants. "Imagine Cinderella. See her. Look at her. Now open your eyes and describe her." They uniformly respond with words that describe what she looks like—blonde, thin, hair in updo, wearing a blue dress. When these responses emerge—and they always do, no matter the group—my focus is on the fact that no one has to think about their Cinderella image because it comes immediately as something we have absorbed through the ubiquity of Disney films directed at us as children. Thus emerges an easy foray into unconscious bias, that which we accept and presume as true and truth without having to pause and think about it. Such biases are devoid of critical thinking. Occasionally, a lone responder will reference the African American pop singer Brandy, the first Black actor to play this role in a movie in the 1997 adaptation of Rodgers and Hammerstein's *Cinderella*.

Responders to this exercise rarely describe what Cinderella is doing—cleaning, dancing, trying on a glass slipper, riding in a carriage, cleaning the house, or being mistreated by stepsisters and a stepmother. Such responses often lead to gender discussions of how women and girls are socially defined by and valued based on what they look like rather than on what they do. Such a gendered discussion is underscored by the prevalence of anti-aging products directed disproportionately toward women or even traditional heterosexual wedding ceremonies, where marriage is an accomplishment for women and the wedding is all about what the bride looks like, or the fancy celebrity galas where the post-event buzz is about what the women wore. In contrast, men and boys are most often judged on what they have accomplished and can do rather than on what they look like.

Too many of us humanists suffer from a sheer lack of imagination. This is not to say that we are not creative; we are. We have not, though, given ourselves permission to imagine possibilities, especially in the academic work that we do, beyond what we have always done and thought. In part, this lack of imagination explains the persistent alarmist refrain, mostly from white cis, hetero, male academics, about a "crisis in the humanities." Having served as department chair, dean, and vice president at my current university, whose focus in humanities is consistently on growing majors and on increasing overall student numbers and "research" dollars through grants, I know that these concerns about enrollment are real. Yet I do not consistently hear administrative conversations engaging creatively with the quality of the experiences of those we try to recruit and retain, especially those from minoritized groups. In focusing on metrics over experience, this crisis language serves only to highlight the academy's failure to encourage, support, or reward those teachers, scholars, students, and professionals who dare to think beyond the campus classroom, beyond the illusory rigidity of disciplines or even pedagogy. Such alarmist language highlights the extent to which "tradition" reared its head even as this new MLA volume on global social justice began to take shape.

I contend—as do others in this volume—that the academy as a whole suffers from a lack of imagination even as we race toward and proclaim our innovations and cutting-edginess. Attachment to old ways of thinking—academic and scholarly biases that create and sustain hierarchies of what constitutes excellence and what is valued as learning—has kept many a teacher and scholar from creating and embracing new ways of educating and connecting with our students and even entertaining new subjects for our research. It also potentially limits our students, who seem not to value imaginative risk-taking. When students respond to an assignment with the question "What is it that you want?" I am reminded that their education has minimized the value and reward of intellectual and creative risks. New ways of thinking and doing are indeed riskier for faculty members in that tenure and promotion at some institutions are based not on the newest and most provocative demonstrations of knowledge creation but rather on ways that things have always been done, paying homage to the often static white cisheteropatriarchal hierarchy of scholarly journals and presses as well as our profession's preoccupation with book publishing over other creative expressions. Such parochial thinking persists as many academic discussions still consider artificial binaries, such as critical versus creative, service versus teaching, online versus print—and, yes, one I acknowledge having used earlier in this introduction, theory versus praxis—as though these ideas are not intricately connected and fundamentally interdependent. This binary thinking is deeply entrenched in our sustained teaching and learning; while it is not without value, it can restrain us from opening ourselves to more intellectual, creative, and pedagogical possibilities, and deliberate and intentional pressures are needed to break us out of them. The "historical imagination" is precisely what allows teachers, students, and scholars to unveil the complicity of university elitism in creating traditions of alleged excellence at the expense of those who literally built these institutions yet were denied access to them as education and learning spaces: "From their very beginning, the American university and American slavery have been intertwined, but only recently are we beginning to understand how deeply" (Carp). These are the systems in systemic racism, for instance, that plague our classrooms, our assignments, our pedagogies, and our limited imaginations. A prevailing academic lack of imagination leads to what the Nigerian author Chimamanda Adichie calls the "danger of a single story": "It is impossible to talk about the single story without talking about power. . . . How [stories] are told, who tells them, when they're told, how many stories are told, are really dependent on power. . . . Power is the ability not just to tell the story of another person, but to make it the definitive story of that person." Liberating our imaginations frees us to experience the realities of Others' stories that offer and invite more complete, more nuanced, and more complicated narratives of who we are as humans continually engaged in meaning-making that both challenges and sustains us individually and communally. Adichie's commentary situates this volume's central goals and objectives—to challenge the academy's "single narratives": "The consequence of the single story is this: It robs people of dignity. It makes our recognition of our equal humanity difficult. . . . Stories matter. Many stories matter. Stories have been used to dispossess and to malign. But stories can also be used to empower, and to humanize. Stories can break the dignity of a people. But stories can also repair that broken dignity." Imagine this volume and its diverse perspectives as a narrative of what justice and humanity look, taste, feel, sound, and smell like.

As this volume was proposed and conceptualized, a prospectus reviewer specifically questioned how this new volume would align with the MLA publishing program and with other MLA volumes. Even the framing of this question, to me, demonstrates a limited thinking rather than looking at new ways that the proposed volume might very well challenge our thinking beyond what the MLA publishing program has already done and what readers of MLA volumes have already seen. Such a question signaled for me some homage to the past rather than an embrace of new possibilities in this humanities publishing space. While there are indeed essays in the volume on literature, theater, museum studies, public libraries, AP English essays, and language studies—more "traditional" humanities topics of study—my approach really is to reimagine our humanist thinking and practices and to move beyond the boundaries and binary constructions of "traditional" MLA volumes. As a professor of English with specific teaching and research experience in African American literary and cultural studies who has served as chair of one of the largest English departments in the United States, encompassing English education, film and media studies, linguistics, applied linguistics, creative writing, literature, and writing programs—and later as dean of humanities for the School of International Letters and Cultures (which at the time offered some nineteen international languages), the Department of English, and the School of Historical, Philosophical and Religious Studies—I understand the value of and need for transdisciplinary approaches to what we humanities teachers and students do in our classrooms and what "public-facing" scholars do in our research. (As an aside, I was doing this "public-facing" work thirty years ago, but it was not acknowledged as "legitimate." My, how times have changed . . . for some inside the academy.) In the same way that people are not single-identity individuals, as Audre Lorde and so many other mostly women "radical" thinkers of color remind us—"There is no such thing as a single-issue struggle because we don't live single-issue lives" ("Learning" 138)—I create this volume as an intentional disruption of more static and even restrictive "traditional" ways of understanding, engaging, and experiencing humanities. The very nature of the question that opens this paragraph underscores the artificial and sadly too persistent belief that the humanities exist in a space separated from the rest of the world and life, as though the humanities aren't really the air that we breathe but are rather peculiarly apart from the everyday. Further, as founding director of the multiple-award-winning initiative Project Humanities—whose annual multidisciplinary, intergenerational, multiprofessional, and multicommunal event Hacks for Humanity: Hacking for the Social Good was called out in ASU's 2015 annual report as an example of innovation after ASU was ranked first in innovation by *US News and World Report,* a ranking the university has upheld now for nine years in a row (*Learn to Thrive* 6; Faller)—I understand the need and desire for open dialogues and engagements beyond the seemingly intellectually stuffy confines of disciplinary restrictions and campus classrooms. As an award-winning public scholar fundamentally committed to demystifying and thus engaging a model of public humanities that includes rather than excludes, I have created this volume as an extension and manifestation of my life work as a teacher-scholar-professional.

In inviting humanists to step outside our disciplinary and scholarly silos, this volume challenges standard definitions of pedagogy. Because I do not subscribe to a restrictive view of what constitutes "teaching," when a prospectus reviewer questioned how this proposed volume connects with teaching and learning, I was again baffled at the lack of creative possibility embedded in the question. This questioning, for me, emerges from a place of skepticism rather than a place of openness to something that the MLA publishing program has not seen in this precise configuration and with this broad and multidisciplinary focus. Following the premise that teaching and learning are as diverse as students and educators who teach and learn, this volume positions pedagogy more broadly than typical MLA pedagogy volumes, showcasing nontraditional and even nonclassroom models.

My experience in creating this volume relative to the reviewers' comments is not unlike the skepticism the poet-playwright ntozake shange received with her choreopoem *for colored girls who have considered suicide/ when the rainbow is enuf* premiered on Broadway in 1976. The "new" format of improvisational movement on the stage, the conjoining of poetry and dance, and the nontraditional characters all made for a challenging experience for theater traditionalists, as the work broke from and challenged aesthetically and artistically their expectation of what a Broadway play was and could be. Rather than accept the production on its own terms, as a new structure bending itself to new experiences and new subjects, for what it had to offer, the critic John Simon, in *The New Leader,* sought to attack and diminish: "Is this poetry? Drama? Or simply tripe? Would it have been staged if written by a white?" Others not wedded to Simon's limited and culturally biased thinking saw in this choreopoem (a term coined by shange [*for colored girls* xx]) bold connections to non-Western traditions that shange contends speak more fully to the complexities and realities of human experience:

> as a poet in american theater/ I find most activity that takes place on our stages overwhelmingly shallow/ stilted & imitative. . . . for too long now afro-americans in theater have been duped by the same artificial aesthetics that plague our white counterparts/ "the perfect play," as we know it to be/ a truly european framework for european psychology/ cannot function efficiently for those of us from this hemisphere. . . .
>
> the fact that we [black folks] are an interdisciplinary culture/ that we understand more than verbal communication/ lays a weight on afro-american writers that few others are lucky enough to have been born into. We can use with some skill virtually all our physical senses/ as writers committed to bringing the world as we remember it/ *imagine it*/ & know it to be to the stage/ we must use everything we've got. (shange, *lost* 13, 16; emphasis added)

Simon's classist, elitist, racist, and sexist response is echoed in recent mainstreamed voices perpetuating cultural sirens around "the crisis in humanities" narrative, such as Frank Bruni's "The End of College as We Knew It?" and Bruce Abramson's "The Humanities Are Dead." Both opinion pieces share similar laments for similar reasons, using similar examples of what constitutes learning and authority. Abramson unapologetically registers his intellectual and creative panic and concern: "The humanities are indeed dead in America. It's long past time to stop funding the institutions that pretend to study them, subsidizing students who pretend to study them and paying the faculties who've failed to teach them. Once we have cleared away the detritus, perhaps we can invest in a humanities education that teaches the value of *our rich cultural legacy*" (emphasis added). Bruni's references to "we" and Abramson's to "ours" code in no uncertain times the absolute need to perpetuate a racialized and gendered ivory tower way of thinking that deliberately excludes and clamors to hang onto a dying way of thinking and being for too many academics. In this volume, as elsewhere, I offer a response to the crisis narrative: "We [humanists have] to reframe how we [are] talking about the work that we do. We have to talk about intersectionality. Even though somebody may be a business major or a kinesiology major doesn't mean that they can't engage in these conversations about humanist principles and about how we are human" (Lester, "Are the Humanities Really in Crisis?").

Humanities teachers and students experience, read, and engage pedagogies beyond disciplinary boundaries, and I offer this volume as innovative and entrepreneurial in its varied disciplinary approaches and strategies of imagining and practicing social justice around the globe. Contributors include scholars writing in Spanish and German alongside a stage and screen actor writing about actors and social justice, a choreographer commenting on dance and justice, an HBCU (Historically Black Colleges and Universities) president commenting on systemic racism, a prison educator offering mediation as resistance for incarcerated persons, an evolutionary biologist connecting science and social protest, a rhetorician writing about antispeciesism, Advanced Placement teachers revealing unacknowledged and unaddressed bias in scoring, and a transgender faculty member highlighting exclusion within higher education diversity and inclusion. Not restricted or necessarily tailored to my MLA colleague readership, this volume is for everyone, including those outside and perhaps excluded from formal academic settings. Having served on the board of directors of the Arizona Humanities Council for six years—two as chair—and before that as a speaker for the Alabama Humanities Council, I know the value of public humanities work (now trending as "public-facing" humanities), that is, engaging and being more intentionally inclusive in spaces beyond campus classrooms. In this spirit of affirmation, this volume is created for and offered to a wider audience readership.

No, I personally and professionally do not subscribe to the notion that this volume can speak to humanists in a way that it will not speak to social scientists or natural scientists, hence my efforts to provide a wide range of social justice approaches and topics. I offer up this volume in the hope that scholars, students, community members, teachers, and so many others will find something in it for their personal and professional enrichment and guidance. To imagine that this volume can speak to humanists and nonhumanists, to scholars and nonscholars, to educators and noneducators, and to students and nonstudents is to challenge the lack of imagination that essentially prompted this effort: white folks—alleged allies—asking me and other Black, Indigenous, and People of Color (BIPOC) educators and scholars what they can do rather than looking at their own circles of influence and their own resources to communicate what they are already doing or can do before approaching those most affected intersectionally and directly by injustice.

It is also to remind the proverbial justice choir members that there is a reason choirs rehearse weekly, learn new songs, and sometimes go over the same songs over and over until most choir members get it right. To imagine real interventions necessary in dismantling white supremacy and systemic racism and in disrupting the status quo requires true imagination and a recognition that racism—in all its oppressive and systemic manifestations—affects everyone in one way or another. The philosopher Martha C. Nussbaum, in *Not for Profit: Why Democracy Needs the Humanities*, underscores the centrality of radical imagination in both survival as a species and in the humanities as a field of sustained and evolving critical inquiry:

> [T]he faculties of thought and imagination . . . make us human and make our relationships rich. . . . [D]emocracy is built upon respect and concern, and these are built upon the ability to see other people as human beings, not simply as objects. . . . [T]he spirit of humanities [is experienced] by searching

> critical thought, daring imagination, empathetic understanding of human experiences of many different kinds, and understanding of the complexity of the world we live in. (6–7)[2]

In this case, then, it is no stretch to see how the academy as we come to understand it and to absorb its white supremacist, conservative values, even in the face of anti-intellectual attacks and accusations of neoliberalism gone awry, is the reason we humanists can't give ourselves permission to imagine, to create, and to act in ways that challenge the race, gender, and class status quo that is our US education system. The film director Kasi Lemmons takes to task the individuals and systems that perpetuate American racism and racial injustice in all its various forms because of its serviceability. For me, it is also no stretch to see in her assessment a challenge to all systems that support white supremacy, including classrooms specifically and higher education more generally:

> White people have never needed to exercise [a certain] kind of curiosity. You've never had to. You can live your whole lives without really considering how [minoritized groups and individuals] live ours. . . . *Can you imagine* what it has taken for [Black folks in this country] to come so far? To survive a historical journey this arduous, and to not merely be standing, but to turn the pain of that voyage into a culture that defines style, music and art around the world? To have used our ingenuity to invent, or contribute to the invention of everything from the cotton gin to the cellphone? (emphasis added)[3]

This volume, then, is an exercise in ingenuity and imagined possibilities for discovery, for new connections, new perspectives, and for new teaching and learning. This volume is an invitation to engage our imaginations in seeing new connections and arriving at new understandings of relationships between peoples, ideas, and perspectives. The University of Wisconsin chancellor Biddy Martin explains the necessity of humanists' liberating our imaginations:

> [I]magine that you have only memory and can do nothing more than mimic the past, robotically, or that you have no capacity for reflection or analysis, and no tools for developing your individuality. What about a society or societies of people who cannot think for themselves, transform their experiences and cultural heritage, or *imagine more than they have already seen?* . . . . Science and technology are essential to our well-being and economic prosperity, but science and technology cannot explain the world or help us live in it wisely. We are, by nature, cultural beings. We are learners. Our cultural environment shapes us. If we fail to understand how it shapes us, we forfeit our freedom and our responsibility to think about what we learn and who we are. The humanities help us understand how value is established, why some things are valued and others are not. They show us how dependent we can be on ingrained

> patterns of behavior, unexamined assumptions, ideological biases. That understanding allows us to find balance between preservation and innovation, tradition and change. ("Chancellor Martin's Remarks"; emphasis added)

This volume and these voices are offered in the spirit of imagining possibilities in an ongoing search for justice and Truth. It is also offered in the spirit of identifying my allies, accomplices, and coconspirators; perhaps even making a case for empathy from those who now see our interconnecting oppressions and oppressings:

> You do not have to be me in order for us to fight alongside each other. I do not have to be you to recognize that our wars are the same. What we must do is commit ourselves to some future that can include each other and to work toward that future with the particular strengths of our individual identities. And in order for us to do this, we must allow each other our differences at the same time as we recognize our sameness. (Lorde, "Learning" 134)

I fully understand the skepticism that many humanists and others bring to any conversation championing a litany of ideas deemed "new." Newness is certainly relative and depends on one's perspective and access to resources. The context for my thinking about "newness," however, is tempered by Lorde's sobering sentiment:

> Sometimes we drug ourselves with the dreams of new ideas. The head will save us. The brain alone will set us free. But there are no new ideas still waiting in the wings to save us as . . . human. There are only old and forgotten ones, new combinations, extrapolations and recognitions from within ourselves—along with the renewed courage to try them out. And we must constantly encourage ourselves and each other to attempt the heretical actions that our dreams imply, and so many of our old ideas disparage. . . .
>
> For there are no new ideas. There are only new ways of making them felt—of examining what those ideas feel like . . . while we suffer the old longings, battle the old warnings and fears of being silent and impotent and alone, while we taste new possibilities and strengths. ("Poetry" 26–27)

Now, "let us march on 'til victory is won" (Johnson). The absolute urgency of now is upon us all to be and to do, for, as Martin Luther King, Jr., declared in "The Other America," "Somewhere we must come to see that social progress never rolls in on the wheels of inevitability. It comes through the tireless efforts and the persistent work of dedicated individuals. And without this hard work, time itself becomes an ally of the primitive forces of social stagnation. And so, we must help time, and we must realize that the time is always right to do right."

NOTES

1. The poem was published in a 1926 volume featuring poetry, short stories, visual art, essays, and drama—representing a range of new Black art and artists. The sad irony of the quarterly is that it burned in a basement and no other issues subsequently appeared. The present multidisciplinary, multiprofessional, and multicommunal volume aligns conceptually, organizationally, and philosophically with this strategy and energy of challenging, disrupting, and burning down in order to renew and rebuild something that is new and more just.

2. Nussbaum elaborates the connection between democracy, humanity, and the imagination: "If a nation wants to promote this type of humane, people-sensitive democracy dedicated to promoting opportunities for 'life, liberty and the pursuit of happiness' to each and every person, what abilities will it need to produce? At least the following seem crucial: The ability to recognize . . . people with equal rights, even though they may be different in race, religion, gender, and sexuality: to look at them with respect, as ends, not just as tools to be manipulated for one's own profit. . . . The *ability to imagine* well a variety of complex issues affecting the story of a human life as it unfolds: to think about childhood, adolescence, family relationships, illness, death, and much more in a way informed by an understanding of a wide range of human stories, not just by aggregate data" (25–26; emphasis added)

3. Lemmons's comment echoes to some extent the need for imagination to effect real change when those who practice white supremacy realize that white supremacy impacts them negatively as well. The imagination exercise the defense attorney Jake, played by Matthew McConaughey, presents as his closing argument in the movie *A Time to Kill*, in which he asks his mostly white jurors not to convict a Black man for killing two white supremacists who have raped, beaten, defiled, and hung a ten-year-old Black girl—Hollywood white saviorism aside—is one example: "I want to tell you a story. I'm going to ask you all to close your eyes while I tell you a story. I want you to listen to me. I want you to listen to yourselves. Go ahead. Close your eyes, please. This is a story about a little girl walking home from the grocery store one sunny afternoon. I want you to picture this little girl." The attorney then details the barbaric way in which this little girl was beaten and violated. He concludes the exercise: "Can you see her? Her raped, beaten, broken body soaked in their urine, soaked in their semen, soaked in her blood, left to die. Can you see her? I want you to picture that little girl. *Now imagine* she's white" (emphasis added). This scene is both an emotional and intellectual exercise in bias, empathy, humanity, justice, and imagination, or the lack thereof. Clearly, empathy alone will not necessarily effect justice.

WORKS CITED

Abramson, Bruce. "The Humanities Are Dead." *Newsweek*, 2 July 2020, www.newsweek.com/humanities-are-dead-opinion-1514862.

Adams, Maurianne, et al., editors. *Readings for Diversity and Social Justice*. 4th ed., Routledge, 2018.

Adams, Maurianne, et al., editors. *Teaching for Diversity and Social Justice*. 3rd ed., Routledge, 2016.

Adichie, Chimamanda Ngozi. "The Danger of a Single Narrative." *TED*, July 2009, www.ted.com/talks/chimamanda_ngozi_adichie_the_danger_of_a_single_story?language=en.

"Ava DuVernay: 'Not Our Job to Explain to White Folk' How to Combat Racism." *CBS News*, 28 May 2020, www.cbsnews.com/news/ava-duvernay-array-101-when-they-see-us/.

Baker-Bell, April. *Linguistic Justice: Black Language, Literacy, Identity, and Pedagogy*. Routledge, 2020.

Baldwin, James. *Blues for Mister Charlie*. 1964. *Contemporary Black Drama from* A Raisin in the Sun *to* No Place to Be Somebody, edited by Clinton F. Oliver and Stephanie Sills, Charles Scribner's Sons, 1971, pp. 233–313.

———. *The Fire Next Time*. Dial Press, 1963.

Bell, Lee Anne. "Theoretical Foundations for Social Justice Education." Adams et al., *Teaching*, pp. 3–26.

Benedict, Cathy, et al., editors. *The Oxford Handbook of Social Justice in Music Education*. Oxford UP, 2018.

Bland, Karina. "What Should We Do to Fight Racism? We Are Asking the Wrong People." *The Arizona Republic*, 4 June 2020, www.azcentral.com/story/news/local/karinabland/2020/06/04/white-people-asking-wrong-people-help-right-now-fight-racism/3137073001/.

Boyd, Ashley S., and Janine J. Darragh. *Reading for Action: Engaging Youth in Social Justice through Young Adult Literature*. Rowman and Littlefield, 2019.

Bruni, Frank. "The End of College as We Knew It?" *The New York Times*, 7 June 2020, www.nytimes.com/2020/06/04/opinion/sunday/coronavirus-college-humanities.html.

Buettner-Schmidt, Kelly, and Marie L. Lobo. "Social Justice: A Concept Analysis." *Journal of Advanced Nursing*, vol. 68, no. 4, Apr. 2012, pp. 948–58, https://doi.org/10.1111/j.1365-2648.2011.05856.x.

Carp, Alex. "Slavery and the American University." *The New York Review of Books*, 7 Feb. 2018, www.nybooks.com/online/2018/02/07/slavery-and-the-american-university/.

Case, Kim A., editor. *Intersectionality Pedagogy: Complicating Identity and Social Justice*. Routledge, 2017.

"Chancellor Martin's Remarks at Humanities Grant Announcement." U of Wisconsin-Madison, 20 Dec. 2010, news.wisc.edu/chancellor-martins-remarks-at-humanities-grant-announcement/.

Chapman, Thandeka K., and Nikola Hobbel, editors. *Social Justice Pedagogy across the Curriculum*. Routledge, 2010.

Cinderella. Walt Disney Productions, 1950.

Cinderella. Written by Robert L. Freedman, directed by Robert Iscove, performance by Brandy Norwood, Walt Disney Television, 1997.

Davids, Nuraan, and Yusef Waghid. *Academic Activism in Higher Education: A Living Philosophy for Social Justice*. Springer, 2021.

Davis, Tracy, and Laura M. Harrison. *Advancing Social Justice: Tools, Pedagogies, and Strategies to Transform Your Campus*. Jossey-Bass, 2013.

Dolan-Reilly, Georgianna. "The Definition of Social Justice." *Social Justice Solutions*, 15 Jan. 2013, www.socialjusticesolutions.org/2013/01/15/the-definition-of-social-justice/.

Douglass, Frederick. "What to the Slave Is the Fourth of July?" 1852. www.owleyes.org/text/what-to-the-slave-is-the-fourth-of-july/read/text-of-douglasss-speech#root-2.

Eklund, Hillary, and Wendy Beth Hyman, editors. *Teaching Social Justice through Shakespeare: Why Renaissance Literature Matters Now*. Edinburgh UP, 2021.

Eliason, Michele J., et al. *Social Justice Pedagogy Plus: Transforming Undergraduate Research Methods Courses*. San Francisco State U, 2019.

Faller, Mary Beth. "ASU Ranked No. 1 in Innovation for Ninth Straight Year." *ASU News*, 17 Sept. 2023, news.asu.edu/20230917-university-news-asu-no-1-innovation-nine-years-us-news-world-report.

Feagin, Joe R. "Social Justice and Sociology: Agendas for the Twenty-First Century." *American Sociological Review*, vol. 66, no. 1, Feb. 2001, www.asanet.org/wp-content/uploads/savvy/images/members/docs/pdf/featured/feagin.pdf.

Freebody, Kelly, et al., editors. *Higher Education, Pedagogy and Social Justice: Politics and Practice*. Palgrave Macmillan, 2019.

Freire, Paulo. *Pedagogy of Freedom: Ethics, Democracy, and Civic Courage*. Translated by Patrick Clarke, Rowman and Littlefield, 1998.

Godley, Amanda J., and Jeffrey Reaser. *Critical Language Pedagogy: Interrogating Language, Dialects, and Power in Teacher Education*. Peter Lang, 2018.

Gorski, Paul C., and Seema G. Pothini. *Case Studies on Diversity and Social Justice Education*. Routledge, 2018.

Irby, Decoteau J., et al., editors. *Dignity-Affirming Education: Cultivating the Somebodiness of Students and Educators*. Teachers College Press, 2022.

Johnson, James Weldon. "Lift Every Voice and Sing." 1926. *Poetry Foundation*, 2024, www.poetryfoundation.org/poems/46549/lift-every-voice-and-sing.

Kafele, Baruti K. *The Equity and Social Justice Education Fifty: Critical Questions for Improving Opportunities and Outcomes for Black Students*. ASCD, 2021.

Kay, Matthew R. *Not Light, but Fire: How to Lead Meaningful Race Conversations in the Classroom*. Stenhouse Publishers, 2018.

Kezar, Adrianna, and Julie Posselt, editors. *Higher Education Administration for Social Justice and Equity: Critical Perspectives for Leadership*. Routledge, 2019.

King, Martin Luther, Jr. "I Have a Dream." 29 Aug. 1963, www.americanrhetoric.com/speeches/mlkihaveadream.htm.

———. "The Other America." 1967. *Civil Rights Movement Archive*, www.crmvet.org/docs/otheram.htm. Accessed 13 Oct. 2020.

Kinloch, Valerie, et al. *Where Is the Justice? Engaged Pedagogies in Schools and Communities*. Teachers College Press, 2021.

Lawless, Brandi, and Yea-Wen Chen. *Teaching Social Justice: Critical Tools for the Intercultural Communication Classroom*. Rowman and Littlefield, 2021.

Learn to Thrive. Arizona State U, 2015, live-asu-edu.ws.asu.edu/sites/default/files/2022-01/151229_asu_2015_year_in_review_single_pages_0.pdf.

Le, Vu. "Equity Fatigue and How It Affects Leaders of Color." *Changemakers Blog*, RVC, 2 Aug. 2017, rvcseattle.org/2017/08/02/equity-fatigue-affects-leaders-color/.

Lemmons, Kasi. "White Americans, Your Lack of Imagination Is Killing Us." *The Washington Post*, 1 June 2020, www.washingtonpost.com/opinions/2020/06/01/white-americans-your-lack-imagination-is-killing-us/.

Lester, Neal A. "Are the Humanities Really in Crisis?" Interview by Emma Pettit. *The Chronicle of Higher Education*, 9 Feb. 2020, www.chronicle.com/article/are-the-humanities-really-in-crisis/.

———. "No, I Am Not Okay, but Thanks for Asking." *Ahwatukee Foothills News*, 3 June 2020, p. 23.

Leung, Sofia Y., and Jorge R. Lopez-McKnight, editors. *Knowledge Justice: Disrupting Library and Information Studies through Critical Race Theory*. MIT Press, 2021.

Lorde, Audre. "Age, Race, Class, and Sex: Women Redefining Difference." Lorde, *Sister Outsider*, pp. 104–14.

———. "Learning from the Sixties." Lorde, *Sister Outsider*, pp. 134–44.

———. "Poetry Is Not a Luxury." Lorde, *Sister Outsider*, pp. 36–39.

———. *Sister Outsider*. Crossing Press, 1984.

———. "The Uses of Anger: Women Responding to Racism." Lorde, *Sister Outsider*, pp. 124–33.

Lynch, Shrehan, et al. *Pedagogies of Social Justice in Physical Education and Youth Sport*. Routledge, 2021.

Macrine, Sheila, et al., editors. *Revolutionizing Pedagogy: Education for Social Justice within and beyond Global Neo-liberalism*. Palgrave Macmillan, 2010.

Marine, Susan B., and Chelsea Gilbert, editors. *Critical Praxis in Student Affairs: Social Justice in Action*. Routledge, 2021.

Marshall, Catherine, et al. *Educational Politics for Social Justice*. Teachers College Press, 2020.

McNair, Tia Brown, et al. *From Equity Talk to Equity Walk: Expanding Practitioner Knowledge for Racial Justice in Higher Education*. Jossey-Bass, 2020.

Mink, John, editor. *Teaching Resistance: Radicals, Revolutionaries, and Cultural Subversives in the Classroom*. PM Press, 2019.

Morris, Natalie. "The Emotional Impact of Watching White People Wake Up to Racism in Real-Time." *Metro*, 12 June 2020, metro.co.uk/2020/06/12/emotional-impact-watching-white-people-wake-racism-real-time-12839920/.

Morrison, Toni. "Toni Morrison's Commencement Address to Rutgers University Class of 2011." *Llanor Alleyne*, www.llanoralleyne.com/news/2014/5/toni-morrisons-commencement-address-to-rutgers-university-class-of-2011.

Muhammad, Anthony, and Luis F. Cruz. *Time for Change: Four Essential Skills for Transformational School and District Leaders*. Solution Tree Press, 2019.

Murff, Dennisha. *Culturally Responsive Pedagogy: Promising Practices for African American Male Students*. Information Age Publishing, 2020.

Nussbaum, Martha C. *Not for Profit: Why Democracy Needs the Humanities*. Princeton UP, 2010.

O'Neill, Eugene. *Long Day's Journey into Night*. Yale UP, 1956.

O'Neill, Lisa M. "Amy Coney Barrett Went to My All-Girls High School. I Hope She's Not Confirmed." *The Guardian*, 12 Oct. 2020, www.theguardian.com/commentisfree/2020/oct/12/amy-coney-barrett-bad-choice-women.

Parker, Kimberly N. *Literacy Is Liberation: Working toward Justice through Culturally Relevant Teaching*. ASCD, 2022.

Reagan, Timothy G., and Terry A. Osborn. *World Language Education as Critical Pedagogy: The Promise of Social Justice*. Routledge, 2020.

Reece, Bryan. *Social Justice and Community College Education*. Routledge, 2021.

Report of the 100th Arizona Town Hall: "Civic Engagement." 22–25 Apr. 2012, aztownhall.org/resources/Documents/100%20Civic%20Engagement%20Final%20Recommendations.pdf.

Safir, Shane, and Jamila Dugan. *Street Data: A Next-Generation Model for Equity, Pedagogy, and School Transformation*. Corwin, 2021.

shange, ntozake. *for colored girls who have considered suicide/ when the rainbow is enuf*. Bantam Books, 1980.

———. *lost in language and sound; or, how I found my way to the arts*. St. Martin's Press, 2011.

Simon, John. "'Enuf' Is Not Enough." *The New Leader*, vol. 59, no. 14, 5 July 1976, p. 21.

Sims, Jeremiah J. *Revolutionary STEM Education: Critical-Reality Pedagogy and Social Justice in STEM for Black Males*. Peter Lang, 2018.

Smyth, John. *Critical Pedagogy for Social Justice*. Continuum, 2011.

Strunk, Kamden K., and Leslie Anne Locke, editors. *Research Methods for Social Justice and Equity in Education*. Palgrave Macmillan, 2019.

Swalwell, Katy M. *Educating Activist Allies: Social Justice Pedagogy with the Suburban and Urban Elite*. Routledge, 2013.

Thirteenth. Directed by Ava DuVernay, Kandoo Films, 2016.

A Time to Kill. Directed by Joel Schumacher, Warner Bros., 1996.

Trzak, Agnes, editor. *Teaching Liberation: Essays on Social Justice, Animals, Veganism, and Education*. Lantern Books, 2019.

Washington, Booker T. *Up from Slavery: An Autobiography*. 1901. Edited by Natalia Smith, U of North Carolina, Chapel Hill, 1997. *Documenting the American South*, docsouth.unc.edu/fpn/washington/washing.html.

Supporting Marginalized Peoples

The Cost of the System of White Supremacy

Ronald Mason, Jr.

I was one of the first Black students at my Jesuit high school. I had a poor boy's scholarship; otherwise, I would not have been able to attend. One cold Thanksgiving, we collected food to make bags for the poor. I remember one Black family near New Orleans, with little shoeless children, who lived in a wood shack with gaps between the floor planks. They needed the charity of white teenagers on that holiday.

My first job out of law school was with a company that organized poor people's co-ops in the South. The kind of wood shack I had seen in high school was a common sight in the towns we visited, especially in the Mississippi Delta. They were usually near fields of cotton that stretched to the horizon.

My career in higher education started at a predominantly white institution (PWI). As PWIs go, it was somewhere near the bottom of the first tier or the top of the second. It charged high tuition and had a small endowment for a PWI. I was there nearly eighteen years and don't recall ever lacking the resources to buy anything I needed for the job.

I have worked at three historically Black universities (HBCUs). None of their endowments approached even a tenth of that at the PWI where I had worked. Their facilities were not as spacious or shiny. Their students couldn't afford to pay high tuition, but they had at least as much natural talent as the students at the PWI—maybe more, since they had had to overcome more, and sacrifice more, to be in college.

As institutional reflections of Black people, HBCUs have always served America despite America. The four prongs of the system of white supremacy—the fiction of white superiority, the power of wealth, the advantages of whiteness, and the oppression of people of color, especially Black people and institutions—succeeds by suppressing opportunities for Black and Brown children to develop their talent. The competition is rigged for their failure even before they are born, thus stifling and eradicating America's greatest strength, its diverse pool of talent. Overcoming the collateral damage of the system of white supremacy, genocide, slavery, Jim Crow, structural racism, and their ongoing impact on wealth and opportunity will take generations. Healing the fear and guilt may take longer.

If we believe in the idea that we call America—that all have the right to live free and to pursue happiness—then the course is clear. The system of white supremacy in America must be called out, understood, and eliminated.

Our Turn

David Pilgrim

We all die; some of us are murdered.

April 4, 1968, was an awful day in this country's past. Martin Luther King, Jr., was murdered by a coward, safely shooting from a flophouse bathroom across the street from the Lorraine Motel, in Memphis, Tennessee. I was ten years old. Several days later, my fifth-grade teacher at Bessie C. Fonvielle Elementary School brought a small black-and-white television to class. Two dozen students—all Black, most poor—huddled around the television and watched the sad funeral.

I remember the words of my teacher as we watched the horses pull King's corpse from Ebenezer Baptist Church through a large crowd toward the burial ground. It was good, she said, that he had dark skin, like her, and unlike civil rights leaders of the past. With tears in her eyes, she added that King had spent his life fighting racial hatred; he had fought a good fight, and now it was our turn. *To die?* No, God knows there were already too many Black children dying in Alabama. She meant that we must continue the work that King had done, work that might get us killed.

That's a lot of weight for a child to carry.

Long before King was killed, his character was assassinated. Today, we understand that the war in Vietnam was an unholy war, but when King condemned it, he was branded a communist traitor. Insulting descriptions of him in newspapers were many and varied: radical, extremist, criminal, rabble-rouser, troublemonger, charlatan, and so-called preacher. White segregationists sank even lower, labeling him "Martin Lucifer King" and "Martin Luther Coon" ("Historical Parallel"; Bigart). Young Black activists, frustrated with King's strategy of nonviolence, called him "Da Lord" (Edalatpour). King was blamed for race riots, blamed for Black children going to jail, blamed for the bombing that killed the four girls in a Birmingham church, even blamed for his death.

Words hurt; so do fists.

In 1962, during a Southern Christian Leadership Conference meeting, Roy James, a white man, left the audience, leaped onto the stage, and punched King in the face—hit him hard. King dropped his hands and stood there, allowing the assailant to strike him again. When his associates came forward, King said, "Don't touch him. We have to pray for him." King understood that forgiveness is not a weakness.

It is fashionable to criticize King, but those who disparage him have warm breath in their lungs. He, however, is dead, murdered by James Earl Ray, a fugitive from the Missouri State Penitentiary. I am reluctant to use the word *assassinated.* I know that when public figures are killed, it is expected that we say they were assassinated, but that word somehow hides the ugliness of the act. He was murdered—cold-blooded murder. Do not say that he gave his life: his life was taken.

I did not know these things when I was a student at Fonvielle Elementary—did not appreciate the courage shown by King and others. Children think about fairness, not justice. In my brain are images of children marching past police officers during the Children's Crusade in Birmingham. I see a girl, a tiny child wearing a dress and white socks, being put into a police van. I see angry police officers, snarls on their white faces and batons in their white hands, arresting Brown children. These images are real in my mind, but I am not sure if they are memories or images that I encountered later in life.

It has been more than half a century since King's funeral. I remember little, almost nothing, about my five years in elementary school. My teacher was an old woman in 1968; she has gone to her reward. Most of my classmates are likely dead; premature death remains a common occurrence in the African American experience. I have only the vaguest memories of my teachers and schoolwork, but I never shook the words of that one teacher. I am not troubled by her gladness that King had dark skin. For too long, this country has belittled and punished dark-skinned folks. I heard her. And I also remember, as if it were yesterday, her call to embrace King's work, to make it our own, to take our turn.

I grew up in Mobile, Alabama, during the last years of Jim Crow. The governor was George Wallace, a white supremacist during a time when that label was a badge of honor in many places. I once believed those days were spent. I was wrong. Awful days are here again. Politicians with a bloodlust for power feed racial hostilities—and anyone who checks them is called a racist. The racial divide is long, wide, and deep. The rhetoric that I hear from our national leaders is reminiscent of Wallace's rants. Hate and fear, alas, remain primary organizing forces.

Those of us committed to social justice must fight the good fight, expose and combat systems of dominance, run and not get weary, and be people of conscience, social reformers who help the poor and disfavored while also speaking truth to power. We will sometimes be angry, but we must never be dragged so low as to hate others. If this country is to ever become that city upon a hill, that model for the world, that is invoked so often as our purpose and goal, it will be because those of us committed to a just society hate the injustice, not the unjust individual, even when the unjust person does not see their own ignorance, arrogance, and hatred.

WORKS CITED

Bigart, Homer. "St. Augustine Tragedy Lurks." *The Bangor Daily News*, 29 June 1964, p. 3.

Edalatpour, Jeffrey. "New Doc Details the Rise and Fall of the Black Panthers." *KQED*, 2 Oct. 2015, www.kqed.org/arts/10991338/winter-in-america-the-rise-and-fall-of-the-black-panthers.

"Historical Parallel Recalled by Texan." *The Dothan Eagle*, 9 June 1965, p. 4.

Overselling Higher Education to Communities of Color

John Streamas

Here are three anecdotes from recent years of teaching undergraduate ethnic studies and graduate-level American studies:

A brilliant young Black man in a tenure-track position told me that, discouraged by budget cuts and administrators' constant marginalizations of his work, he was seriously considering leaving academia. He is an excellent teacher, loved and respected by students.

A mixed-race female student decided to take time off after graduating, assuming she would pursue graduate education in two or three years. Even after a series of low-paying jobs in retail and "real world" experiences with sexism and racism, she decided that graduate school would not benefit her after all, as it merely looked too much like the world she already inhabited.

An immigrant African student, a gifted queer artist and passionate activist whose work had earned several honors and awards, told me only halfheartedly that she might pursue an advanced degree. She was already tired of being marginalized in settings where, she believed and had come to expect, she should feel welcome.

These are, to be sure, only anecdotes, and though I could easily cite many more such student experiences, still I realize that they may not be typical, representative, or statistically significant. As a teacher of color myself—a tenured immigrant Japanese American in a university where only ten percent of faculty members are people of color—I know these students may more likely confide in me such experiences and feelings. What makes these stories matter to me is that most are so recent: that students of color seem to have become more keenly aware that the campus is not the safe and welcoming space that they had hoped it would be—or that students of color from the 1970s to the early 2000s believed it to be. Surely, some of this reality owes to the bullying ascendancy of the nationalist right, to the rise in confrontational taunting by College Republicans and xenophobic organizations, even to a reaction against the Obama presidency and racists' awareness that in less than a quarter century, white people will become a racial minority in the United States. But these students are smart enough to know the dangers posed by their obvious enemies on campus. What makes them more alert and also, unfortunately, more fearful than their predecessors is their newfound, hard-won knowledge that their universities will not defend, support, or honestly encourage them in ways that are sensitive to their identifying differences. They know that diversity bureaucracies, even when the officers are also people of color, have no real clout or real interest in advancing social justice on campus. Students of color—and faculty members of color too—have become disillusioned with higher education as a sanctuary, a place for learning toward a better world.

I focus here on what I regard as the most important cause of this disillusion: we have oversold higher education to people of color. I advance this claim with a bit of history, the testimony of scholar-activists of color, an analysis of Western education's misguided guiding assumptions, and my own observations and experiences. I recognize that the very act of going to college is, for reasons of cost and culture, increasingly unavailable to many people, and so this may seem insignificant as a social justice issue. Further, I recognize that those already in college have some privileges of status and class, no matter how else they may be marginalized. Still, I counter that the overselling of higher education matters because, for generations and centuries, minoritized peoples have regarded basic education as a goal beyond mere survival, as the best hope for autonomy and self-realization, and higher education has promised to be the pinnacle of that hope.

Two clarifications are in order. First, I do not agree with conservatives' or liberals' most publicized quarrels with universities, especially conservatives' contention that higher education is generally bad for society. In 2017, a Pew Research Center survey showed that "58% of Republicans and Republican-leaning Independents say colleges and universities have a negative effect on the way things are going in the country," even though a similar majority of such conservatives also "said a four-year degree prepares someone very or somewhat well for a well-paying job in today's economy" (Fingerhut). These respondents define higher education as an advanced job training that strains against what they regard as radical social engineering in both admissions policies such as affirmative action and curricular reforms such as multiculturalism. They may seem to clash with conservative elites such as Allan Bloom and E. D. Hirsch for whom "the life of the mind" is a nobler pursuit than "mere" job training, but after all, they agree that "merit" and "tradition" and "legacy" must prevail over social engineering. The quieter liberal movement against higher education worries that universities are failing because they have immersed themselves too much in the outside world, having abandoned the ideal of the "campus on the hill." Such liberals—and even Marxists such as Terry Eagleton—claim to support the goals of a multicultural curriculum but charge postmodernism and deconstruction with a vulgar flattening of values, reducing Shakespeare to the level of greeting cards and commercial jingles. These concerns of conservatives and liberals have more in common with each other than with the needs of students and faculty members of color.

Second, I draw only sparingly on the substantial and rapidly growing literature from the political left on the ills of twenty-first-century universities. Critical University Studies (CUS) has become an urgent and needed field, and already, its concerns are well known. Those concerns often originate in a structural-economic critique, in which the global neoliberalism by which wealthy nations have since the 1970s trapped poor nations in debt bondage has been not only informed but even joined by elite US universities. All complaints of the "corporatizing" of universities partake of this critique.[1] A related critique, slightly narrower in scope but reaching back farther in time, maintains that the curriculum itself originates in a definition of education that normalizes colonizing Western prejudices. Linda Tuhiwai Smith expresses this view as she opens her book *Decolonizing Methodologies*: "From the vantage point of the colonized, a position from which I write, and choose to privilege, the term 'research' is inextricably linked to European imperialism and colonialism. The word itself, 'research,' is probably one of the dirtiest words in the indigenous world's vocabulary" (1). Since this charge targets our ways of schooling, then an obvious solution should be to fix the curriculum and its methodologies. Smith herself has directed the University of Auckland's Institute for Maori and Indigenous Education. The rise and presence of departments in ethnic studies and gender studies, of programs in disability studies, queer studies, animal and species studies, the Anthropocene, and ecocriticism all attest to efforts to reform the curriculum, to subvert the status quo, to queer canons.[2] Yet neither the structural-economic critique of universities nor the curricular critique has solved the problems they have so precisely and passionately named, and so, unsurprisingly, much recent work in CUS has been filled with reports of injustices and disillusion experienced by victims of the system, too often and disproportionately women of color. These reports, like the three stories with which I began, are not supported by massive amounts of quantitative evidence. But then much of the reason for this dearth of data originates in universities' own policy of confidentiality, which they claim protects individual employees. In her collection *Written/Unwritten: Diversity and the Hidden Truths of Tenure*, Patricia A. Matthew recounts her own harrowing experience of tenure denial and gathers testimony from other scholar-activists of color, some of which includes bits of statistical evidence such as Jane Junn's analysis of tenure outcomes at the University of Southern California (USC) (4–5). Summing up Junn's findings, Matthew says that at USC, "the commitment to diversity . . . bumps up against practices of discrimination" (5). Citing Junn's discovering, for example, that, whereas "[n]inety-two percent of white men in the social sciences and humanities were awarded tenure" at USC, only "[f]ifty-five percent of women and faculty of color were awarded tenure," Matthew concludes that such troubling outcomes "hide behind language and processes that seem neutral" (5).

For all the urgency of the critiques and calls for action, however, the disillusion in higher education experienced by students and faculty of color has only worsened. My field, ethnic studies, is now more than a half century old, and still it seems to be no more than an add-on, a disposable option for ignorantly disinterested students and alternately a noisy pest and a prompt to administrators to boast about diversity. At my university, the general "diversity" requirement was slashed by almost one-third when budgets were cut. The diversity bureaucracy exists in a silo that has no contact with ethnic studies and gender studies, and facilitators of university-sanctioned workshops in "cultural competency" never consult with these departments. I have attended two such workshops and could confidently recommend them if all racism were reducible to personal microaggressions and drunken frat-boy pranks. The diversity bureaucracy owes its existence to the institution, and so we cannot expect it even to mention institutional racism, much less offer support and succor to its victims. But while those of us in ethnic studies may easily condemn diversity programs, we must now scrutinize our own field and ask why, in a nation with more college graduates than ever before and with our own five decades of scholarship, so much of the nation and the world are being governed by leaders guilty of flagrantly racist acts. Have we failed?

The structural-economic critique points toward an explanation. Formal schooling in the West has been regarded as so noble, so far above reproach, that its foundational principles of objectivity and disinterestedness have seldom been challenged. They have been a universal yardstick against which all learning is tested. And they persist in standardized tests, admissions policies, grading, funding applications, job searches, and promotion and tenure rulings. Administrators' high-minded defenses of confidentiality in tenure cases depend on an assumption that racial and gender biases could not possibly influence outcomes. At my university in 2015, administrators assured undocumented students that permitting College Republicans to build anti-immigrant "walls" on the campus mall represented only an honoring of the First Amendment and not a support for xenophobia. In this view, disinterestedness is the noblest expression of a truly higher education. Such assumptions were subverted five decades ago, not only, and not even most persuasively, by the new field of ethnic studies but by Paulo Freire's advocacy of bottom-up learning. At the same time, Martin Carnoy attacked the foundations of Western education from a slightly different angle:

> Western formal education came to most countries as part of imperialist domination. It was consistent with the goals of imperialism: the economic and political control of the people in one country by the dominant class in another. The imperial powers attempted, through schooling, to train the colonized for roles that suited the colonizer. Even within the dominant countries themselves, schooling did not offset social inequities. The educational system was no more just or equal than the economy and society itself. . . . (3)

If "within the dominant countries themselves, schooling did not offset social inequities," it trained colonizers' children to fill predetermined dominant roles no less than it trained colonized children to fill predetermined subservient roles. In other words, just like "the economy and society itself," education served to sustain inequalities and injustices. Even if administrative disinterestedness had been a worthy ideal, it was impossible even to imagine in a context of inequality. At all levels, schools merely mirror their social and economic contexts; they cannot rise above them.

To be sure, ethnic studies has extended the civil rights movement and the causes of Black and Brown and Yellow and Red Power into the college classroom. But just as so many civil rights laws and affirmative action policies were eroded, so, too, was ethnic studies circumscribed by schools' colonizing structures. We challenged prevailing methodologies and the Western canon—successfully, to a great extent, as the fierceness of the "culture wars" attests—but finding space to assign Toni Morrison beside Saul Bellow in surveys of contemporary US fiction courses did not and could not change assumptions governing structures of higher education. Even in a field that has concerned itself with curricular reform at the expense of structural revolution, our work has been continually marginalized and its most outspoken faculty members labeled "troublemakers" and denied promotion, sometimes even fired. Steven Salaita is one of many victims of campus racial politics (see Salaita), and below I cite my own experience of the racially motivated censoring of a course syllabus.

Still, since curricular reform has been the best we have achieved, we credit its accomplishments even as we also acknowledge its insufficiency in refuting the claim that we oversell higher education to people of color. I teach courses in Asian Pacific American literature and surveys of multicultural literature, and nowhere else are the hope and promise of education so well defined for people of color as in their literature. I am not referring here to the genre of the bildungsroman, the narrative of a young person's (usually a young, cisgender, heterosexual, able-bodied male's) moral education, for though books such as Ralph Ellison's *Invisible Man* and Leslie Marmon Silko's *Ceremony* might rightly be placed in that category, still the form originates in a Western tradition, and the moral learning of a young white man from a colonizing class differs radically from the moral learning of an impoverished, sex-trafficked Taiwanese woman. In my multicultural literature course, students see by semester's end that most of the fiction and poetry we read concerns the desire and need for learning. In Octavia E. Butler's novel *Kindred*, the twentieth-century protagonist, Dana, travels back in time to the plantation of her enslaved ancestors and risks her life—and violates all rules of time travel—to teach alphabet literacy. She tells her twentieth-century white partner Kevin that back in time she has "started to teach Nigel to read and write. . . . Nothing [is] more subversive than that." When Kevin expresses his hope that Nigel may teach other enslaved persons, Dana worries that in an absence of education "people could be trained to accept slavery" (101).

Another example agrees. Carlos Bulosan, in his memoir *America Is in the Heart*, tells the stories of sacrifices for education—his own, his family's, and his farming community's. When American rule replaced Spanish rule in the Philippines and introduced basic schooling, for a time, "a nation hitherto illiterate and backward was beginning to awaken" (14). After immigrating to the United States, Carlos suffers violence, exploitation, and illness but persists in writing. And when his first book of poems is published, he says, "I had put certain things of myself in it: the days of pain and anguish, of starvation and fear; my hopes, desires, aspirations" (320). He befriends writers and revolutionaries and even comes to regard the two as synonymous. *America Is in the Heart* testifies to the sufferings of working classes and Brown bodies, but it also advances the salvation and hope to be found in writing and learning.

Introductory ethnic studies also narrates the denial of educational opportunity to people of color and our own attempts, often at great risk, to create opportunity. Sometimes those attempts fail, as when Indigenous languages are lost. And often, even when they succeed, their cost is an assimilation that is proportional to a loss of a home cultural identity. By this, I mean that too often, people of color—conditioned to believe that standards of mainstream (which translates to white) education are universal and irrefutable—fail to test those standards against differences in their home cultures and come to assume the rightness of definitions of literacy, time, space, and labor that they might otherwise challenge. Among Asian American writers, Amy Chua, in *Battle Hymn of the Tiger Mother*, and Wesley Yang, in the unfortunately titled *The Souls of Yellow Folk*, surrender Asian Americanness to a Euro-American identity.[3] Still, it is not only white liberals who, asked to name a solution to the nation's racial issues, answer with "education." People of color say this too. And when pressed to elaborate, both white liberals and people of color offer the usual suspects: lessons are needed in white privilege, microaggressions, scientific racism, the prison industrial complex, intersectionality, neoliberalism, the racialized war on drugs, racial capitalism, settler colonialism, "broken windows" policing, racialized border security, dispossession, genocide, exploitation of labor, xenophobia, the "oppression Olympics," resistance, and reparations. Pressed for details, students in 300-level ethnic studies can name and offer textbook definitions of these lessons that beg to be taught, and students of color can cite harrowing personal experiences of profiling and harassment.

For the half century of its existence, ethnic studies has been teaching these lessons. And for most of that time, students have sincerely believed that these lessons were working. Until recent years, most students in my ethnic studies classes and in those I have visited, and most students and colleagues I have met in conferences, have suggested that, though there is still a long way to go, things are getting better. The idea that we are better off than we were before the 1960s movements for civil rights and women's rights has been an assumption of the field. But in recent years—beginning even before the 2016 election—that assumption has been crumbling. In September 2018, when I suggested in a presentation before the Race and Pedagogy National Conference at the University of Puget Sound that people of color are not better positioned in the United States than we were two or three decades ago but are only positioned differently, and possibly worse, many people of color in the audience nodded in agreement (see Streamas, "Overselling"). It is a claim I would not have made fifteen years ago, and the fact that knowledgeable scholar-activists such as those in my audience believe it today, as ethnic studies passes its half-century birthday, suggests that, to some extent at least, we are failing in our mission. I suggest that the failure is not confined to the field but is built into the culture of higher education. I expand upon Freire and Carnoy: American schooling is inherently, unavoidably racist.

In her book *Physics of Blackness: Beyond the Middle Passage Epistemology*, Michelle M. Wright urges readers to challenge assumptions of linear progress narratives (LPNs). In Black history and culture, such assumptions have meant that critics, both by centering slavery as the absolute and exclusive center of African American history, as a "Middle Passage epistemology," and by borrowing from Western history and narrative an assumption that chronology is progress, have come to embrace a belief that Black life is better today than yesterday.[4] This thinking is troubled both in its neglect of important populations—immigrant Africans, for example, comprise a sizable and growing number and proportion of the US population—and in assuming the rightness of a Western way of narrative. In linear narratives, stories resolve in the end, wrongs are righted, and wherever we stand in a story's arc, we may be assured that life is improving. This is, after all, the narrative of Western capitalism: that we grow and accumulate profit, that developing technologies fix problems, that we win.

It is also the narrative of Western education, especially twenty-first-century higher education. University mission statements and fundraising campaign vision statements embrace CEOs' and stockholders' dreams of growth. Bigger is better; biggest is best. Every year for more than a decade, my state university has boasted of a growth it defines in simple terms: bigger state-of-the-art facilities and, especially, burgeoning enrollments. Administrators and regents envision more of this growth in coming years. A bonus prize of this growth is that numbers and percentages of students of color have risen impressively. In this rural southeastern Washington setting, a place that dependably sends conservatives to Congress and the state legislature, people of color are nearly thirty percent of the student population. When I started working here in the early 2000s, they were scarcely more than one-tenth of all students. Even the most cynical faculty members agree that this growth is impressive and necessary, but it means only that the university is eager to extract income from tuition dollars.

Wright draws her warning of linear progress narratives from readings of Black writers such as James Baldwin, but it applies just as urgently to the racial state of higher education today. Three decades have passed since the apex of "visionary" corporate books focused on the theme of excellence, and today, the only institutions that still adhere to themes of excellence are universities. The state university where I work posted its ambitious "Drive to 25" campaign, a plan to make the school one of the twenty-five top public research institutions of its kind in the nation by 2030. Top-level administrators today stay in their jobs for only a few years, and there is no assurance that their successors will adopt such ambitious campaigns. There is likewise no assurance that the "visionaries" who concoct such campaigns will suffer any consequences, even if they remain in their jobs, for failing. Moreover, it is these same people who define "excellence" and "vision," and so they assess themselves by their own standard of objectivity. Of course they do—they are the ruling class on campus. And yet it is these same administrators who also define "diversity" and marginalize ethnic studies, who provide no justice to students of color and almost no support to faculty members of color. The recipe for "growth" and "excellence" does not include racial justice.

Universities are inherently, irredeemably racist because for all their discourse of growth and progress, their real commitment is to preservation of the status quo. This is nowhere else more evident than in the book *Land-Grant Universities for the Future: Higher Education for the Public Good*, a two-hundred-page argument by Stephen M. Gavazzi and E. Gordon Gee that land-grant schools can better serve the world by returning to old verities, taking up again the original meaning and mission of their charter. They apply this idea to other kinds of universities too:

> The Mormon institution of Brigham Young University often gets criticized because it lives by its religious tenets. . . . It is fiercely Mormon. Rather than cast aspersions, we applaud this stance. Similarly, instead of trying to be more like their university brethren, we believe that Catholic institutions should be more fiercely Catholic, Baptist institutions should be more fiercely Baptist, and so on. (31)

How much more widely would they apply this argument? Would they insist that tribal colleges be more fiercely tribal, and that historically Black colleges be more fiercely Black? They do believe that "land-grant universities should become more fiercely land-grant" (Gavazzi and Gee 31). For them, as for administrators deriving their standards for education from the objectivities of the Western tradition, the land-grant mission is a good idea because it brings education to a blank slate of land. Like people and ideas, however, land is never a blank slate, never neutral. The 1862 Morrill Act that enabled land-grant schools could pass only when the South had seceded from the Union, as western lands could then be appropriated for the benefit of Northern industry. Reviel Netz recites the history:

> The Pacific Railroad Act established a northern route for the railroad, offering its developers, as incentive, 6,400 acres of western land (more would be decreed in the future) for each mile constructed. Meanwhile, toward the foundation of state colleges, the Morrill Act gave western land at the rate of 30,000 acres for every senator and congressman each state had. (7)

In other words, the 1860s development of the West was not only or not even primarily a stay against the spread of slavery but was rather a way of making the North a center of trade and profit. The land-grant mission is therefore a capitalist mission. It serves the public good only insofar as capitalism serves the public good—and many people of color argue that capitalism has never served us. Land grants secure a status quo of what has come to be called "racial capitalism." Jodi Melamed traces the evolution of racial capitalism from a start in decolonization to liberal discourses that, while superficially anti-racist, still promoted class and race inequalities (8–9).

Unsurprisingly, Gavazzi and Gee say almost nothing about race. They refer to the 2017 white nationalist march at the University of Virginia in which an anti-racist counterprotester was killed and note what they regard as a knee-jerk reaction by college administrators who barred from campus controversial right-wing speakers: "colleges and universities are doing themselves no favors by taking actions . . . that unwittingly (or otherwise) alienate portions of the US population. . . . [W]e would argue simultaneously that not enough is being done proactively to address the communal need for 'neutral ground' " (19). Only if the "land" in "land grant" is a blank space can any part of a college campus be neutral ground. No schooling in critical and cultural geography should be needed to understand this.[5]

It is a minoritized woman, Toni Jensen, who recognizes that she has worked in a university whose spaces cannot be neutral: "The southern border of this space we call campus, the University of Arkansas campus, is now called Martin Luther King Jr. Boulevard, but was once best known as the Trail of Tears" (37). As of 2018, a new Arkansas law allows licensed owners to bring guns anywhere on campus. Afraid, Jensen recalls her student days spent avoiding a serial rapist: "This story is an ordinary, everyday-violence story from a space considered campus. It is hard to see this space as hallowed when it is filled with so much ordinary, everyday violence. It is hard to see this space, this campus, as mine when it so clearly is not, when it so clearly never was" (41–42). Neutral spaces are a luxury of ruling white men such as Gavazzi and Gee, of administrators who construct diversity programs and who cannot understand our fears.

That this failure—or refusal—to understand our fears drives women and people of color out of academia is underscored in the spring 2019 issue of *Feminist Formations*, devoted to what the editors, Marta Maria Maldonado and Katja M. Guenther, call "critical mobilities," which include feminist scholars' relocations "as a response to discrimination, bullying, harassment, and/or hostile work environments" (vii). Most troublingly, they refer to "critical exits" of feminist scholars who cannot even address their experiences of harassment and bullying, their silence having been secured by nondisclosure agreements that allow "colleges and universities to deny the ongoing presence of problems" (xiv, xv). Unsurprisingly, then, "[a]nother source of quiet in bringing the issue of critical feminist exits into view is trauma" (xv).

Neither students nor faculty members of color are told to expect trauma. We are in fact conditioned to expect the opposite: "a welcoming place," according to Robin D. G. Kelley. Like Maldonado and Guenther, Kelley defines universities as "a cog in the neoliberal order," adding that "as institutions they will never be engines of social transformation." This is why he leans toward the argument by Stefano Harney and Fred Moten for an "undercommons," a "nonplace that must be thought outside to be found inside" (39). The undercommons steers a path around, or under, the binary of reform and revolution that vexes Kelley's subjects. It recognizes and takes advantage of the politicizations of campus spaces:

> It cannot be denied that the university is a place of refuge, and it cannot be accepted that the university is a place of enlightenment. In the face of these conditions, one can only sneak into the university and steal what one can. To abuse its hospitality, to spite its mission, to join its refugee colony . . . to be in but not of—this is the path of the subversive intellectual in the modern university. (Harney and Moten 26)

Kelley rejects popular emphases on affect and trauma; implicitly, Harney and Moten do too, warning that they favor suffering bodies over resisting agents. More than ever before, then, higher education is our own responsibility to define and enact. Wealthy white celebrities may buy their children's way into elite universities, in which case they have bought the education they were sold, but they will never access the spaces of the undercommons. These spaces are priceless because they are free.

My critique of universities has evolved slowly over decades of teaching. As a graduate teaching assistant, I taught for several years in English, American culture studies, and ethnic studies. For more than a decade, I taught English as an adjunct instructor. In all those years, I saw issues in the curriculum and in methodologies, but I never questioned the rightness of university education. Not even when I entered the tenure track in ethnic studies did I realize that, far more than the curriculum or prevailing methodologies, the very nature of higher education was an obstacle to students and faculty of color. In introductory ethnic studies, there were occasional belligerent white students, usually but not always male, who rejected everything in our texts and our class discussions. More often, and more frustratingly, there were white students who seemed to understand some issues and completely misread others, usually those related to immigration, welfare, and affirmative action. I worried more, however, about the occasional student of color who said, "Racism has always existed and will never end." Why would a student who insisted on the certainty of the eternal perpetuation of racism even enroll in ethnic studies? Were nineteen-year-old people of color already so pessimistic? Could a different text or a better lesson plan or a more persuasive teacher change their minds?

In the last several years, however, I have come to see that the major obstacle to racial progress on campus is the very nature of the university itself. If this is so, then we faculty members of color must account for our staying in our jobs. If Kelley believes that the campus has never been and will never be a safe and welcoming space for people of color, why does he continue to work in his university? Obviously, we need jobs and income. But are we being otherwise disingenuous with our students, especially students of color, by continuing to work for institutions that we believe are, by their very nature, irredeemably racist? Are we fooling ourselves into believing that we can slay the beast as we work inside "the belly of the beast"?

I am afraid to walk across the campus where I work. Twice within a decade, members of right-wing groups appeared on *Fox News* to demand my firing. Both times, my voice mail and my email inbox filled with vicious slurs and even threats. The second episode led administrators to censor my syllabus over the innocent word "deferring," which according to *Fox*, our provosts, our dean, and our interim president signified coercion of "certain readers"—not "students." I used the word correctly, and the dictionary supported my usage. This was, after all, a multicultural literature class, and I took pains with language. But administrators accused me of trampling on the speech rights of these "certain readers" and thus justified their trampling on my own speech rights. I became a charter target of the right-wing Professor Watchlist and suffered major depression for more than a year, even needing to take a medical leave (see Streamas, "How We Lost").

Still, though I cannot speak for colleagues, students, and allies, Harney and Moten are largely right in advancing the undercommons as the best site for resistance. The highest concentrations of like-minded thinkers and activists still gather on campus; and even against barriers such as soaring tuition rates and bleak economic prospects, students still want to come. In King County in Washington, the county that includes Seattle, "[m]ore than 96 percent of 7,000 high school students we asked said they want to continue their education beyond high school," Kirsten Avery writes in the *Seattle Times*, but "only 65 percent of our South King County students enroll in postsecondary education, and only 30 percent earn a degree or credential by their mid-twenties." Demographics dictate that universities' goal of enrollment growth will depend increasingly on students of color, and those students will keep demanding more faculty diversity. The result will surely be still greater concentrations of allies.

Working inside the "belly of the beast," or, as Harney and Moten might have it, working under the beast's belly, constantly risks compromise at least, defeat or capitulation at worst. Yet, finally, in an age of environmental degradation, there is no truly safe space. We cannot choose not to engage in the struggle for social justice. We have badly oversold the institution of higher education to people of color, but education itself—defined by our terms, using our methodologies—must remain our goal. Of course, that education must reach beyond classrooms, into public urban and rural spaces where those students in King County who want higher education may get it with or without degrees. We must also improve our education in the classroom, perhaps even inviting our students of color into the "undercommons." May students and faculty members of color alike abuse the university's hospitality, "spite its mission, . . . join its refugee colony, . . . be in but not of" (Harney and Moten 26).

Besides, we have a right to occupy campus spaces. When the Alabama governor George Wallace ran for president in 1968, his slogan, implicitly targeted at Black people, was "America—love it or leave it." Land is never neutral, campus is never neutral, because it serves as a site of racial displacement, exploitation, and violence. As our share of the national population grows, we must insist on occupying our spaces, including campuses. We belong. Until we have social justice, universities will oversell themselves to us. But we can choose not to buy what they sell. We must choose to make campus a truly free and public space to take the kernel of education out of the husk of the university.

NOTES

1. The literature of structural-economic critiques of higher education includes the foundational *The University in Ruins*, by Bill Readings. Three newer important studies include Giroux; Newfield; and Collini; and Childress offers an important new study of adjunctification. Perhaps the foundational structural-economic critique of basic education is Paulo Freire's *Pedagogy of the Oppressed.*

2. Critiques of higher education curriculum and methodology include Chatterjee and Maira; Gordon and Newfield; TuSmith and Reddy; Ferguson; Melamed; and Ahmed; see also Kelley; Harney and Moten.

3. See Chua and Yang for examples of Asian American claims for assimilation. For an insightful critique of Yang's assimilationism, see Nguyen.

4. Arguing against assumptions of "linear progress," Wright would not agree with students of color who insist that racism has always existed and will never end. This is, after all, no less deterministic an argument than LPNs.

5. Still, Gavazzi and Gee would be wise to read Henri Lefebvre's *The Production of Space.*

WORKS CITED

Ahmed, Sara. *On Being Included: Racism and Diversity in Institutional Life.* Duke UP, 2012.

Avery, Kirsten. "Guest Essay: Six Ways We Can Help Students Achieve Their College and Career Goals." *Seattle Times*, 5 May 2019, Education Lab sec., www.seattletimes.com/education-lab/guest-essay-six-ways-we-can-help-students-achieve-their-college-and-career-goals.

Bulosan, Carlos. *America Is in the Heart.* 1946. U of Washington P, 2014.

Butler, Octavia E. *Kindred.* 1979. Beacon, 2003.

Carnoy, Martin. *Education as Cultural Imperialism*. David McKay, 1974.

Chatterjee, Piya, and Sunaina Maira, editors. *The Imperial University: Academic Repression and Scholarly Dissent*. U of Minnesota P, 2014.

Childress, Herb. *The Adjunct Underclass: How America's Colleges Betrayed Their Faculty, Their Students, and Their Mission*. U of Chicago P, 2019.

Chua, Amy. *Battle Hymn of the Tiger Mother*. Penguin Books, 2011.

Collini, Stefan. *Speaking of Universities*. Verso Books, 2017.

Ferguson, Roderick A. *The Reorder of Things: The University and Its Pedagogies of Minority Difference*. U of Minnesota P, 2012.

Fingerhut, Hannah. "Republicans Skeptical of Colleges' Impact on US, but Most See Benefits for Workforce Preparation." *Pew Research Center*, 20 July 2017, www.pewresearch.org/fact-tank/2017/07/20/republicans-skeptical-of-colleges-impact-on-u-s-but-most-see-benefits-for-workforce-preparation/.

Freire, Paulo. *Pedagogy of the Oppressed*. Seabury, 1970.

Gavazzi, Stephen M., and E. Gordon Gee. *Land-Grant Universities for the Future: Higher Education for the Public Good*. Johns Hopkins UP, 2018.

Giroux, Henry A. *The University in Chains: Confronting the Military-Industrial-Academic Complex*. Routledge, 2007.

Gordon, Avery F., and Christopher Newfield, editors. *Mapping Multiculturalism*. U of Minnesota P, 1996.

Harney, Stefano, and Fred Moten. *The Undercommons: Fugitive Planning and Black Study*. Minor Compositions, 2013.

Jensen, Toni. "Carry." *Ecotone*, no. 26, fall-winter 2018, pp. 34–42.

Kelley, Robin D. G. "Black Study, Black Struggle." *Boston Review*, 7 Mar. 2016, www.bostonreview.net/forum/robin-kelley-black-struggle-campus-protest.

Lefebvre, Henri. *The Production of Space*. Blackwell, 1991.

Maldonado, Marta Maria, and Katja M. Guenther. "Introduction: Critical Mobilities in the Neoliberal University." *Feminist Formations*, vol. 31, no. 1, spring 2019, pp. vii–xxiii.

Matthew, Patricia A., editor. *Written/Unwritten: Diversity and the Hidden Truths of Tenure*. U of North Carolina P, 2016.

Melamed, Jodi. *Represent and Destroy: Rationalizing Violence in the New Racial Capitalism*. U of Minnesota P, 2011.

Netz, Reviel. *Barbed Wire: An Ecology of Modernity*. Wesleyan UP, 2004.

Newfield, Christopher. *The Great Mistake: How We Wrecked Public Universities and How We Can Fix Them*. Johns Hopkins UP, 2016.

Nguyen, Viet Thanh. "Wesley Yang and the Search for Asian-American Visibility." *Viet Thanh Nguyen*, 7 Nov. 2018, vietnguyen.info/2018/wesley-yang-and-the-search-for-asian-american-visibility.

Readings, Bill. *The University in Ruins*. Harvard UP, 1996.

Salaita, Steve. "An Honest Living." *Steve Salaita*, 17 Feb. 2019, stevesalaita.com/an-honest-living/.

Smith, Linda Tuhiwai. *Decolonizing Methodologies: Research and Indigenous Peoples.* Zed, 1999.

Streamas, John. "How We Lost Our Academic Freedom." *Teaching with Tension: Race, Resistance, and Reality in the Classroom*, edited by Philathia Bolton et al., Northwestern UP, 2019, pp. 143–62.

———. "The Overselling of Higher Education to People of Color." Race and Pedagogy National Conference, 29 Sept. 2018, U of Puget Sound.

TuSmith, Bonnie, and Maureen T. Reddy, editors. *Race in the College Classroom.* Rutgers UP, 2002.

Wright, Michelle M. *Physics of Blackness: Beyond the Middle Passage Epistemology.* U of Minnesota P, 2015.

Yang, Wesley. *The Souls of Yellow Folk.* W. W. Norton, 2018.

Social Justice Ecologies: Charting Routes for Public Humanities and Postprison Education

Anke Pinkert

"Within these walls," James S. avers, "are people, first and foremost people" (*Education Justice Project*). More than two million people are currently incarcerated behind prison walls in the United States, and James is one of them, serving a lengthy sentence at a Midwestern state prison. James is also a student in the Education Justice Project (EJP), a college-in-prison program affiliated with the University of Illinois at Urbana-Champaign (UIUC).[1] He participates in the advanced college classes and extracurricular programming available to a mere five percent of the population of the prison. I begin by quoting James in order to foreground the power of walls—whether real or symbolic—in effacing people in ways that, as I hope to show, the public humanities must challenge. However, this essay is not about the voices of imprisoned persons; it is neither about speaking in their name nor about drawing on their experiences under the guise of research. Indeed, students in the EJP are themselves published scholars.[2] My point is that academics and society as a whole must examine the unacknowledged role of the humanities in bolstering the conditions of power—between educators, administrators, and the public at large—that prevent these voices from being heard.

In this essay, I chart how the humanities might be used not only to reimagine the possibilities of prison education and higher education after prison release but also, more importantly, to work toward the very obsolescence of prisons as a carceral system. In what follows, I reflect on a meditation group organized since 2011 in conjunction with the EJP by students at Danville Correctional Center and on an initiative to establish a publicly oriented humanities across and beyond campus at UIUC. Despite my reservations about first-person accounts, I draw on my experience as a university humanities scholar and teacher in the field of Holocaust studies and on my involvement from 2010 to 2014 with a collaborative, activist college prison education program. This essay is thus intended both as a provisional reference for other academics, teachers, and administrators in the humanities who want to change the existing carceral educational system but do not know how, and as a plea for participation in this vital project.

The challenges here are multiple even if one sets out with a commitment to college-in-prison programs. To start, education offered in prison, a system constructed to surveil and control, is a complicated if not complicit enterprise. Moreover, there is rarely any robust institutional support for faculty members or graduate instructors, let alone for the incarcerated population and their families, in this type of work. As Christopher Newfield and others have argued, even public universities in the United States function more and more like private businesses and global corporations. Universities are often enclosed by architectural and symbolic walls. In my college town, clear lines are drawn between a highly professionalized campus and the adjacent, segregated, low-income neighborhood. And finally, after decades of highly theorized scholarship and training, the relation between the humanities and public—let alone prison—life remains far from obvious to the academy, as a number of recent conferences and special sessions at MLA conventions have shown (Brooks).

To fight the normalization of massive human warehousing in the United States requires both the interruption of and resistance to systems of inequality, racism, and mass incarceration. Collaborative work involving hundreds of colleagues and students in the EJP convinced me that if the humanities are to participate in this radical project, we must expand the field's repertoire for collective action. Thinking with and from the prison, I explore how the embodied practice of meditation can support humanities work towards educational justice and social transformation. To that end, I describe a meditation program organized at a Midwestern prison as part of the Education Justice Project at UIUC. Meditation is a contemplative or resonant practice where one follows the breath and sits still. It is often associated with relaxation and thus with private modes of passivity, healing, and introspection; these may have been the initial impulses for piloting the mindfulness program. In contrast, I consider how concerted acts of silence—the staging of bodily stillness that mindfulness entails—take on the more overt political meanings commonly associated with forms of critical resistance practiced in prison. And I suggest that the performative display of holding a meditative pose, under the gaze of officers and under conditions of systematic surveillance, disrupts the mechanized rhythm of a carceral institution through a monastic temporality and pace.

The second half of this essay charts possibilities for how a publicly oriented humanities can work toward the obsolescence of the prison, focusing on a multivalent and intersectional "Learning Publics" project at Illinois rather than on what universities often call "outreach efforts."[3] My argument is that when augmented by embodied practices like mindfulness, public humanities initiatives can be a conduit for the deep, granular, slow structural work that enables incarcerated persons, faculty members, students, and communities alike to challenge the carceral system and the structures that support it. I conclude with reflections on the limits and possibilities of cocreating change from within the institutional terrains that often—sometimes unwittingly—support the very systems that they seek to eradicate.

Spacing Silence

Since the 1980s, social, political, and economic forces in the United States have conjoined to produce a prison boom. Despite falling crime rates, the prison industry depends on an endless supply of "criminals." The result is a massively overloaded penal system. The Midwest Correctional Center in East Central Illinois is no exception. Built for only half its current occupancy in 1985, it is a noisy, overcrowded place that houses close to two thousand incarcerated individuals. Quiet is hard to come by there. However, in 2011, the collaborative proposal of six incarcerated men to found a meditation group opened up a space for silence within what Angela Y. Davis and other scholars examine as racialized regimes of mass abandonment and social death (Davis, *Abolition Democracy* and *Are Prisons Obsolete?*; Patterson; see also Gilmore, *Golden Gulag*; Alexander).

Many people at the Midwest Correctional Center issue from those communities of color in Chicago that have been most devastated by economic disparities and gun violence. Others have immigrant backgrounds or come from impoverished rural areas in the Midwest (Kotlowitz). That was also the case for the students in EJP. After attending a pilot session organized by faculty members in the summer of 2011, six students began exploring mindfulness meditation and researched literature on the benefits of contemplative practice. Based on "the transformative nature of that learning experience," they developed a mindfulness program, the Mindfulness Group, as part of EJP. In my capacity as a scholar, a teacher of the Holocaust, and a mindfulness practitioner, I have collaborated since its inception—together with John J., a clinical psychologist with a mindfulness focus and a practice in Champaign, and others—on the development of this important project.

Let me now "take you" to the group. I choose this travel metaphor deliberately, in order to connote the very impossibility of going there, or of the men's arriving here in order to share some semblance of this experience, a semblance that can only be tracked by proxy given the carceral conditions under which it occurs. There are no images of the silent gathering in the cinder-block room.

The campus and community members of EJP from "outside" meet once or twice a week at Common Grounds, the food co-op in town, to carpool to the prison in East Central Illinois, forty-five minutes away. For three years, on Thursday, John and I took I-74, passing by the barren fields as they changed throughout the seasons, until we hit Lynch Road, the highway exit to the prison. Going in, we followed the well-rehearsed procedure; a grinding buzz yanked the steel doors open and then shut. Under the gaze of the watchtowers, we passed into the recesses of the facility and walked up the metal stairs to the education floor. Most nights, Officer S. would greet us with a grin from behind an old wooden desk with a few rookies from the cleaning crew hanging around nearby. He could not wait to blurt out, "I meditate with my guns." My eyes would scan the roster that recorded names and inmate numbers to check whether everyone was still on the sheet (and not transferred out or in segregation). Then, in a drawn-out, ritualized performance, Officer S. would lean back so we could hear the sharp jangling of his key ring and say, "You are wasting your time with those guys; you don't know who they really are." He would then release us into the cinder-block room, and the steel door would clang shut behind us.

Inside the bland, colorless room, chunky, outdated computer monitors lined the empty cinder-block walls, as if to watch. Amidst them, we formed a loose gathering, sitting on an odd assemblage of vinyl, wood, or (for those who got lucky) the rare cushioned chair. Every week, we greeted each other with handshakes—at least when still allowed—and then settled into our circle. A moment of quiet would draw everyone into the room. After talking briefly about the readings for the night, we began our first meditation. In the early days, most students kept their eyes open wide, scanning the room's periphery, as officers looked in from behind the metal-mesh glass panels in the wall. Later, with practice, the men relaxed into a diffuse gaze. Drawing inward, we quieted our minds. And without fail, the metallic taste in the air became just a little lighter. The shouts from the prison yard seemed more distant. On some nights, Luis R. said, even the watchtowers, always present in one's mind, began to fall away.

Silence, whether in or beyond the prison, has often been associated with repression or conformity. Scholars like Hannah Arendt consider silence as the opposite of public action—as in to be silenced, to remain silent, to fail to speak up. But, as Judith Butler argues about a kind of acting in concert that happens wordlessly, collective acts of silence can have a different valence (*Notes*). I argue that the collective embodied practice of silence within the prison can be a public performance of political power. Meditation—showing up, breathing, sitting still, spacing silence—not unlike Butler's examples of groups of protestors lying prone before a tank or going limp when confronted by police—can function as a political stance.

Not everyone, of course, will agree.[4] Maybe because meditation is a practice of "bare attention" or repose, it connotes first and foremost self-possession, intimacy, and acceptance rather than dispossession, struggle, or revolt (Epstein). A recent contributor to *The New York Times* called the current focus on mindfulness a kind of "neoliberalism of emotion"—a pacifying, domesticating strategy, where happiness is seen not as a response to our circumstances but as a result of our own individual mental effort, a reward for the deserving (Whippman). Some meditators in the EJP group have remarked upon these rewards. In fact, Jake W., one of the incarcerated students in the group, observes:

> I've been involved in the Mindfulness Group for three years. It's been one of the most important programs. . . . [W]e talk about meditation and different techniques and how they can be used and applied in education, and in our daily lives . . . and it has helped me so much. . . . It has made me more

> equanimous, more compassionate. You know, I don't get as confrontational about things that I used to nitpick at . . . I am a more easygoing person. I am a happier person. I think this comes through to most people 'cause whenever my family comes to visit me, they always remark on how they are amazed I can be so positive in this environment. And this has mostly been affected by my participation in mindfulness and my practice of meditation.
>
> (*Education Justice Project*)

Mass incarceration in the United States nevertheless regulates human rights and rights of citizenship in irrefutably racist ways while the prison industry works hand in hand with the market to decimate "the right to appear" (Butler, *Notes* 174). Given meditation's reparative and even therapeutic register, in what ways can this interior practice be understood as politically vital for abolitionist prison work? How does the collaborative labor of organizing and sustaining a meditation group within the prison industrial complex help us think through more relational and resilient forms of political social justice work? Mindfulness as an embodied practice cultivates the ability to "observe what is." Sitting together with others in silence can turn into a temporary form of nonengagement, where participants disrupt existing structures and frameworks, be that in the prison context or in public humanities work.

Carceral Disruption

For forty minutes, or more rarely a few hours—the group was eventually permitted to hold a daylong silent retreat twice a year—these incarcerated and nonincarcerated bodies would together suspend the norms on which the prison compound was built: control. Meditation, as a controlled form of breathing, stillness, or monastic temporality, in Roland Barthes's sense, disrupts the mechanized rhythm of institutions (6–9). The members of the group developed a shared breathing practice. At the same time, this meditative space was inseparable from the implacably regular cadence of call passes, permission slips, facility lockdowns, court hearings, and abrupt transfers of men to other institutions or to solitary confinement, as well as arbitrary demands by guards to step outside the steel door of the classroom and face the prison wall.

Eliminating any spaces of privacy and interiority, prisons are designed to manage movement across the carceral space and control contact with nonincarcerated people. However, the meditative practice of collectively focusing on the act of breathing generates a kind of radical receptivity, or *resonance*—understood as a modality that is world-disclosing and opens up new relations—inside the prison's walls, and that despite the ever-present gaze of officers, the shouting in the halls, and the stench of industrial-strength Clorox that permeates the air.[5] Under carceral conditions, the group explored the creative possibilities of rhythmic and synchronic breathing.

I do not wish to idealize the act of breathing. Looking back, there is little doubt that any meditation group in social justice contexts, and especially across carceral spaces, will forever be haunted by the fatal echoes of Eric Garner's rasping whisper—eleven times on a loop—"I can't breathe." Each inhalation and exhalation of Black and Brown bodies, whether inside or outside, is imperceptibly linked to the thousands in Ferguson and Baltimore who shouted, "I can't breathe" to protest racial violence across the country. And no matter how much the meditators, who were Black, Brown, and white, trained to be attentive and to simply observe the passage of time—you breathe, I breathe, even "we" breathe—thoughts about the differential disposability of marginalized lives could not subside on Thursday nights.[6]

Prisons in the United States, as has been argued by Michelle Alexander, are hidden in plain sight. While the media may have given more attention to the issue in recent years, the prisons in our local communities and near our universities often "remain an absent presence, a shame of the nation, a dirty secret" (Berry x). As James S., the meditation participant I cited previously, wrote, "People on the outside have forgotten, within these walls are people, first and foremost people." James's words allow us to understand that, given the spatial regime of surveillance in which these meditation gatherings emerged, there can be a resistant quality in this practice of surrender. As a performance of stillness, or opting out, this exercising of the breath amounts to the refusal to be totalized by the carceral regime or to accept the very terms by which this totalizing is produced.

And what do such exercises mean in practical terms? There is no denying that the meditation practiced in a cinder-block room inside the prison began to engender practices by which bodies, things, and knowledges moved in new and subtly different ways. For instance, some men established individual daily meditation practices on their bunk beds, while walking in the prison yard, or while pacing the small square of concrete in their cell. While such practices required perpetual negotiation in a hypermasculinized prison culture and were not without punitive risks, they were also reported to lead to new interactions on the cellblock (Kupers). Men who were not in the EJP began to inquire about it. Within the prison classroom, while the armed officers patrolled the floor outside the door, the six men who had cofounded the program trained and eventually cofacilitated meetings with additional groups of students from EJP in the semesters that followed. After two years, they led a Mindfulness Group "open house" that was attended by over thirty men from the general prison population.

The EJP meditation group also managed to connect with other public and educational realms. Incarcerated persons are held under the most rigorous conditions of generalized inaccessibility, such that they and their families experience the trauma of being forcibly dislocated from their familiar and familial kinship networks (Rodríguez 97). Despite their ceaseless degradation and displacement, the men talked to family members about their practice, wrote letters to publishers to describe the program, and requested book donations. Some produced op-ed pieces, either as blog posts or in a meditation newsletter facilitated by nonincarcerated teachers or family members, and they found ways to connect with other meditation-in-prison programs by mail. In 2014, the EJP was invited to present on mindfulness and social justice at a conference called Combat to College, organized by the Illinois Board of Higher Education. The men collaborated on the presentation by researching the connections between PTSD and war violence, incarceration and reentry, and the causes for the disproportionate involvement of war veterans in the criminal justice system. Their recorded talk, delivered on a massive stage before hundreds of highly decorated war veterans (many visibly wounded), provoked a stunned silence.

Over three years, some guards—intermittently, and in no recognizable linear fashion—were also affected by the collaborative silent meditation practice. Months into our meetings, Officer S., for example, who had always thrown open the steel door at an arbitrary point during the evening and marched in, shouting everyone to attention, one day instead simply called "Break"—and did so from there on out. A few prisons, such as Rikers Island since 2016, have begun to offer meditation programs for the correctional officers, who are themselves often circulating in conditions of precarity, commuting in some cases from areas where jobs have been decimated by postindustrial and postagrarian shifts (Armstrong).

These transformations may appear minuscule and sometimes imperceptible to others in the prison environment. For some, however, meditation has provided a radical kind of hope under conditions of devastation, where it is often no longer clear what one can hope for (Lear). If every claim we make to the public is also haunted, as Butler suggests, by those who are sequestered, who are missing, then showing up in that cinder-block room—the refusal of the interdiction against appearing—must also be understood as an expressive act, a politically significant event. Let us take note, then, that bodies that assemble in classrooms, under the conditions of imprisonment, are actually redefining public space. It also takes venues such as the academic conferences and journals where students who are incarcerated can place their scholarly work to render this more forcibly true: the men's resistant and creative capacity to say, "We have not become the glaring absence that structures your public life" is a powerful mandate.[7]

Even if what is brought into being here—collaborative meditation and prison education—is not necessarily a function of political action per se, it certainly disrupts the totalizing logic of incarceration. Considering the future of social justice work, closer attention to a wider range of silent enactments of refusal, protest, or resistance would allow larger, more relational networks of solidarities, across discontinuous spaces and distant geographies, to come into view (see Black; see also the *Facebook* group Mindfulness for the People (facebook.com/mindfulnessforthepeople/). Here "ecologies of difference," to draw from Romand Coles (multiple visions and propensities that involve a range of modalities), would be part of a radical political condition with diverse possibilities for collective action (68).

Ecologies of Practice

I argue that ameliorative practices, such as meditation, from within and across prison walls, can contribute both to social justice work and to the larger critical project of taking on mass incarceration. But prison educational work also inevitably engages with a carceral system designed to banish and systematically destroy livelihoods rather than transform them. Bringing meditation practices—or humanities education in its current incarnation—into prisons fails to address this larger issue. In April 2014, I sat across from Rico N. in the resource room on the second floor of the education building in the recesses of the Midwest prison. He had just completed his exit interview with nonincarcerated members of the EJP designed to facilitate pathways for (re)entry, and the purpose of our meeting was to arrange how he would be able to receive college credit and finish the upper-level Holocaust course he took that semester at the prison. Rico, incidentally also a member of the Mindfulness Group, was particularly interested in legal and ethical notions of forgiveness he had encountered in the class in theoretical works by Julia Kristeva and in Ruth Klüger's novel *Still Alive.* A few weeks after his release, I received an email from Rico stating that the impact of the course on him had been profound but that, faced with the challenges of returning to the outside world, he would not be able to finish the class. Any such undertaking must have suddenly appeared frivolous, given the multiple systemic impediments to successful (re)entry and (re)integration—residential segregation, employment discrimination, educational inequality, parole and police surveillance—Rico now faced, especially after a decade and a half of being locked away.[8]

How can work in the humanities actually contribute to easing this process? As many scholars before me have argued, publicly oriented humanities can provide a privileged place from which to rehearse impulses that disrupt the neoliberal carceral order.[9] My point here is not to elaborate the various defenses of the humanities that have emerged in recent years, nor do I have the space to attend to the variegated field of discourse around the public humanities in detail (see Higgins and Pinkert). Suffice it to say that the term itself is contested for good reasons and that advocates have already mobilized a variety of idioms that run the gamut from the engaged to the textual to the civic in order to challenge its limitations. Some call for humanities and arts programs that facilitate collaborations between universities and other civic institutions; others explore how to turn the forms of close reading and cultural critique typically honed in the humanities toward broader public matters, and a few proponents outline pathways linking community-engaged scholarship and practice with long traditions in activism (Sommer 6; Brooks 14; Ellison). Certainly, these articulations move beyond the idea of the public intellectual and toward broader reflections on the humanities in the public sphere; a subfield even appears to be emerging devoted to rigorous collaborative, community-based social justice work that requires critical pedagogies, public-oriented curricula, and attention to the contexts in which knowledge forms. Given the massive institutional pressures on the humanities to scale down, become measurable, and even disappear (while paradoxically also filling large classrooms), humanities cannot afford to ignore larger regimes of systemic inequality and educational injustice. Attention to all these issues is necessary, but it is not enough.

Mass incarceration in the United States is bound up with regulating rights of citizenship, which happens in racialized ways; questions of how the humanities link up with public life also need to contend with racialized and class-based control of the public sphere (Butler, *Notes* 174, 185; "Ordinary" 31). At Illinois in 2016, a group of humanities faculty members and graduate students launched an interdisciplinary research cluster on the public humanities, which led to a three-semester-long Learning Publics Initiative that made it possible to develop a team-taught graduate seminar and undergraduate course and to engage with scholars and practitioners in the emerging field. The initiative culminated in a symposium, The Humanities and Public Life, in the spring of 2018. The shaping of new networks of cross- and intersectional practice was at the very heart of the students' engaged seminar projects, of the conference, and of the campus-wide initiative.

Yet in many ways it was the incarcerated student of color from EJP who presented by proxy as part of a panel on community collaborative work at the symposium who incited the most radical form of praxis. The author's paper was read by an EJP undergraduate student from campus. The incarcerated student's absence in the room alone drew the heterogenous audience members into an unsettled, relational mode of address. In his paper, entitled "Free Thoughts from a Confined Existence," Michael H. implicitly challenged the simple, if not romanticized, assumptions about community engagement, identification, and "outreach" that continue to undergird some of the claims about the public humanities. In particular, his work questioned the implicit and insistent coherence of presumptions about both who is inside and who remains "over there," outside the campus boundaries.

As Michelle Jones and others have shown, incarcerated and postincarcerated scholars today have to contend with exclusion from and disqualification by the very universities that have educated them when they were "inside." Jones writes:

> It is easy to devalue the scholarly work of incarcerated men and women simply because they are incarcerated. It is easy to discount our epistemological standpoint and to fail to see it as valuable assets. Public and private institutions often deny post-incarcerated people's access because their policies are shaped by the prevailing winds of tough-on-crime attitudes. Academia is often complicit in racial criminalization and carceral gatekeeping of all types.
>
> Exclusionary practices destroy our opportunities. (107)

On the surface, the public humanities symposium at Illinois and the panel on collaborative community work seemed poised to examine, if not suspend, these exclusionary regimes. After all, Michael's "voice" reverberated in this bland conference-hotel ballroom and was powerfully delivered by proxy to an attentive audience of about fifty faculty members, graduate and undergraduate students, community members, and administrators. His work was presented alongside other projects developed by undergraduate students working collaboratively with community members or by nontraditional students from Illinois's Odyssey Project who had gained educational access to the university through this alternative program. Yet, just as Jones exposes the "hypocrisy of spirit in the liberal democratic academy" where university elites may want to protect themselves from incarcerated and postincarcerated scholars (108), Michael challenged a number of established presumptions about both "outreach" and prison education. In fact, through his very absence, he questioned "the possibility of liberal education in a carceral setting altogether."[10] Echoing Dylan Rodríguez's notion of radical prison praxis—which the students in EJP studied alongside works by Paulo Freire—this imprisoned student-scholar declared "intellectual resistance" to be the only viable mode of defying the punitive discourses and technologies in which liberal, let alone missionary or perfunctory, prison education is enmeshed (Rodríguez 79, 105).[11] What do I mean by this?

Let us again track what it meant for this counterhegemonic discourse to be delivered by proxy amid a group of collaborative, community-oriented undergraduate projects in a university space. In order to show up in public, this and similar knowledge productions have to move through a variegated matrix of actions. They are forming in and formed by a complex network of materials, things, and labor involving incarcerated and nonincarcerated people (including members of the prison staff)—the issuing of call passes, requesting of resource room time, reading, studying, note taking, deliberating, driving, printing, book deliveries, phone calls, clearance procedures for material, family support, emailing, scanning, handing over of books at the prison's sally port, practicing the proxy speech, all acts and procedures that are embedded within the arbitrary logic and circuits of correctional approval but also exceed them in improvisational ways (see Harlow 10). The result is that the meanings generated by any radical praxis slip from the grasp of more conventional forms of political, academic, even activist—let alone engaged—discourse. Once the presumptive geography of publicly engaged practice deliberately shifts toward an examination of the conditions under which this scholarly work is produced, the epistemological frames undergirding the public humanities cannot help but be unsettled. And this is precisely what happened at our conference.

When the presentation of the student-scholar from EJP ended, there was a palpable silence in the ballroom of the conference hotel, not least because Michael was not physically present to respond to the range of questions posed by members of the audience. That absence, that missing speech act, engendered an important performative gap. Like the silent disruption initiated by meditation inside prison walls, the imposition of the carceral "business as usual" that enforced this silence cut through the academic protocols. Similar to the quietude practiced by meditators "inside," an incisive pause animated the university space. In response, conference participants were forced to face this act of silencing prisoners. This silence was further marked by a performance piece organized by the graduate students from the Learning Publics seminar. One by one, audience members were asked to rise from their seats to weave the enigmatic line "After this, nothing happened"—taken from Jonathan Lear's book *Radical Hope*—into a mournful and disquieting chant. Students showed that critical awareness does not necessarily lead to action. An awkward silence followed. In this moment, students, faculty members, and administrators were inescapably confronted by their own varying implication in the social and educational structures that both dispossess and maintain the carceral world.

This kind of self-reflexive, improvisational practice is what public humanities can be effective at: working to illuminate how bodies, voices, and knowledge are routed and rerouted across the thresholds that separate the carceral world from our own, both inside and outside university walls. College-in-prison programs, no matter how important, can only take us so far. So what are the pedagogies, practices, and communities that need to be mobilized and sustained to create a decidedly *post*prison education? Both prison scholars, Michael H. and Michelle Jones, provide overlapping but particular alternatives. Jones argues, on the one hand, for opening the walls of the university, for access and inclusion. She writes: "There are scholars subject to mass incarceration who are available to interpret the lived experience of incarceration and synthesize its individual impact and societal consequences to academia and the world. Our expertise can contribute to the academy in history, cultural anthropology, psychology, art, literature, and so much more." And on the other, she points to the continued need for a deconstructive critique of systemic barriers and cultural complicity:

> The question is not whether universities should pursue and actively include the (post)incarcerated in their schools or what role probation and parole should play. Rather, we should ask instead, what barriers and structures allow universities to block the (post)incarcerated from degree opportunities, and how can we remove those barriers to allow universities to pursue and actively, even affirmatively, include such scholars? (108)

From this standpoint, the key insight is less that outreach and public engagement (idioms often used by the university administration), or even public humanities or prison education programs, may be dubious enterprises (those risks are always there) but rather that mass incarceration is structurally entwined with the existing, differentially managed educational system. This system continues to rely on dismissive, proprietary, and patriarchal hierarchies and biases. For even after the relatively few prisoners who advance their education in prison are released, as

Jones points out, the structures of parole and (re)entry as well as the politics of admission to universities present severe obstacles to (re)integration.[12] Despite decades of critical reframing, scholars continue to point out that policy and practice on prisoner (re)entry often remain situated within a framework of individual responsibility that fails to acknowledge the structural drivers of criminalization. What is needed, they suggest, are critical and holistic frameworks that attend simultaneously to the physical, mental, and social contexts that shape lived experiences before, during, and after prison (Burch).

However, the incarcerated panelist from EJP whose present absence at the university symposium on the humanities and public life was obdurately felt spoke in an even more agonistic register about the problems of a racialized education system and the need for wide-ranging structural change. As an imprisoned intellectual, Michael H. formulated a systemic critique that challenged audience members to reorient their political and moral imagination toward an education where prisons become obsolete, where the current structures of violence from schools in disinvested communities of color (the so-called school-to-prison pipeline) is exposed and eliminated, and where schools fulfill their promise as the most powerful alternative to jails and prisons. In this light, the public humanities must take on the pivotal role of amplifying the urgent need for postprison education across and beyond university campuses. This public work has to involve goals and aspirations of different scales and be committed to fostering diverse possibilities for collective action. After all, both collaboration and tension are integral to bringing about transformation. Incidentally, aligned with the spatial and spiritual organization of a meditation round, the professor of comparative ethnic studies John Streamas urges that campus power, rather than being structured vertically, as in corporations, be redistributed on the model of the wheel. The spokes of a wheel are equally important, "as answerable to the hub as the hub must be to them." While the wheel is an imperfect alternative model—it may enable false equivalencies—still, he writes, "it holds promise for students and faculty of color" (7). In this domain, modes such as mindfulness meditation or improvisational art would intersect with incisive critical pedagogies or high-intensity political protest. The encounter with silence, both consciously pursued through meditative practices and consciously acknowledged by means of the absent voice, is a central element of this process. Such silences, both chosen and imposed, insist that rather than being separated, education on college campuses and in prisons must interlink visibly and durably with activism for postconviction higher education and anti-racist organizing. Short of such structural transformations, prison education programs and the universities that provide them risk remaining complicit in the prison-industrial complex and in playing a role in building a better prison (instead of redirecting energy and resources toward abolition; see Pinkert). Most importantly, then, a merging of mindfulness practices and postcarceral public humanities activism would create a platform for the abolitionist stance "to imagine a constellation of alternative strategies and institutions, with the ultimate aim of removing the prison from the social and ideological landscape of our society" (Davis, *Are Prisons Obsolete?* 107–08).

To end the biggest prison-building project in the world, all possible forces need to be mobilized. Public uproar has to be turned up and accompanied by the envisioning and creation of new educational infrastructures and embodied practices. Scholars, teachers, and students in the humanities have unknowingly trained for this task. Considering the systemic violence enacted by the prison industrial complex in this country—itself deeply bound up with the differential histories of slavery, the old and new Jim Crow, and intergenerational forms of racial and economic dispossession—it is an ethical and political imperative that we humanists shift beyond a critical framework and into a more radically relational domain of inquiry that pays careful attention to how silence speaks when speech cannot.

A singular focus on the reparative practices of meditative stillness in prison nevertheless risks reinforcing the very mechanisms of repressive tolerance that keep the carceral system alive. And yet, according to its imprisoned practitioners, contemplative self-care can still be an invaluable experience for incarcerated individuals (see Larson 90–109). Survival in such gravely hostile conditions is paramount. In a place designed to deaden the soul, the extraordinary effort of survivors in and of prisons to practice meditation needs to become legible. Indeed, meditation can inform humanities education in ways that augment the acquisition of the experiential and practical strategies necessary for both critical reflection and political action. Mindfulness holds the space of encounter with forms of both aliveness and destruction open in a way that can clarify what we are attempting to—what we must—struggle *for*.[13] We have seen how the staging of bodily stillness in a prison—that is, under the conditions of systemic and bodily violence—can engender confidence, self-authorization, and a stance of resistance, as well as feelings of equanimity, profound kinship, and calm. The meditation circle in the prison also shows that dissenting action does not need to depend solely on street protests or bodies in motion. The purpose of the men gathering in meditation under the gaze of surveillance was to remain still, and yet their resonant breathing practice created polyrhythmic currents that move across and beyond the carceral space, affecting other people, including the officers and the students' families as well as distant professional realms and educational publics.

What are the obligations of universities in the United States, and especially the humanities, to initiate such alternatives? To what extent are faculty members complicit with the current demise of the humanities if we continue to spin in the overworn ruts of our own disciplines, focused on strictly academic genres, inattentive to what is outside the university walls?[14] Has not engagement in the myriad facets of public life been properly bound up from the very start with the fundamentals of humanities education? Surely, the training in free thinking, the aesthetic receptivity, and the development of imagination and judgment that traditionally lie at the heart of humanities pedagogies, while of the utmost importance, are not themselves sufficient to incite structural change. At the same time, I worry that the language of "public engagement" that has recently sprung up in the administrative protocols and strategic plans of campuses around the country masks the ability of the university to absorb dissenting, innovative impulses for community-led collaboration and to control and govern them on its own terms.[15]

What we really need to make a claim for is less a public humanities than (more ambitiously) an alternative (postcarceral) humanities that questions high culture as the sine qua non of humanity and humanistic inquiry and (more radically and acutely) reconceptualizes what counts as human, as viable life. We need to take up the imprisoned scholars' critique of the larger carceral conditions of the education system. Working together, we can reimagine the humanities as social practice to open up the possibilities of prison education and higher education after prison release but also, more importantly, to work toward the very obsolescence of the prison as a carceral system.

This snapshot of the conscious use of silence by imprisoned student-scholars amplifies the structural limits that control whether and how incarcerated people can become audible in the public sphere. It also invites new forms of praxis in which silence joins speech as a tool for the investigation of how systems of oppression and inequality impact access to that vital human arena. And it reminds us that we need to understand ourselves not only as privileged participants licensed to speak in public worlds but also as actors implicated in establishing the very parameters of access to them. Together, insights born of meditation and humanistic inquiry can better equip us humanists to engage consciously in this delicate work.

This essay was conceived before the outbreak of a global pandemic that revealed the racial and economic disparities in the United States even more forcefully, before the murders of Breonna Taylor and George Floyd added to the country's record of countless Black and Brown victims of police brutality, and before the mass protests of the Black Lives Matter movement in the streets here in the US and around the world. This piece was also written before COVID-19 propelled the Midwest Correctional Center—where James S. and 1,763 others are incarcerated in nearly total isolation—to bar entry indefinitely both to university teachers in EJP and, more importantly, to family visitors. As I finish this note in the fall of 2020, the task of organizing a postcarceral public humanities could not have more potent urgency.

NOTES

The names used in this essay are pseudonyms.

1. The college-in-prison program involves about eighty students, who have the equivalent of an associate's degree, and dozens of active members from campus and the community. Along with advanced-level college courses, EJP has offered reading and research groups, for instance on mass incarceration; a theater initiative; and a mindfulness program. EJP has developed an award-winning ESL program where EJP students train as

instructors and teach others. EJP organizes collaborative initiatives with families of the incarcerated, considers the ways in which mass incarceration has impacted communities of color, and has produced a reentry guide.

2. The work of the incarcerated authors Michael Brawn, Daniel E. Graves, Orlando Mayorga, Johnny Page, and Andra Slater is represented in Castro et al. For more on scholarly publication by incarcerated students, see Ginsburg.

3. For a challenge to managerial approaches to public engagement, see Butler, "Ordinary."

4. The ancient form of meditation is after all a compassion-based practice. For a critique of compassion deployed by conservatism, see Berlant 4–5.

5. On radical receptivity, see Coles 68. Resonance is not consonance. See Rosa.

6. On breathing under the conditions of racial and extractive capitalism and imperialism, including Fanon's notion of "combat breathing" (65), see Tremblay 1–32. On decolonization as planetary enterprise, "a deep breathing for the world as opposed to insulation," see Mbembe. On breathing in a shared world, see Butler, *What World Is This?*, especially 6–7.

7. For example, Michael Brawn, Jose Cabrales, and Gregory Donatelli collaborated with this author on a "teacher-student account" published in *Radical Teacher* (Pinkert et al.)

8. Melissa Burch uses the terms *(re)entry* and *(re)integration* to draw attention to the reality that many returning prisoners were not fully integrated members of society prior to their imprisonment.

9. See Ellison; Woodward; Sommer; Hutner and Mohamed; Honig; Smith.

10. Michael posited that "(censored) liberal education within carceral settings is a form of symbolic violence." His paper proceeded to elaborate the complex vectoring of power that occurs when correctional officials approve or condone prison education programs, surveil materials, and arbitrarily decide who is permitted to participate in classes and programming, defining participation as privilege. He argued that incarcerated students—categorically outside the civil domain of social transformation—structurally have no recourse to challenge teachers or curricula, let alone the prison administration.

11. Rodríguez draws on the works of Antonio Gramsci. For a critique of prison education as politically domesticating nomenclatura and, in particular, of the whiteness of prison philanthropy, see Rodríguez 75–112.

12. On the history and failures of the Higher Education Act (HEA), passed by Congress in 1965, and the Pell Grant Programs, see Clear and Frost, especially 102–04 and, on the advancement of education as pathway out of the prison cycle, 178–80. For recent calls to restore Pell Grants, see Oakford et al., according to which only nine percent of prisoners complete some form of postsecondary education behind bars. Most receive a certificate from a college or a trade school, and just two percent of prisoners get an associate's degree. On strategies for navigating the admissions and financial aid process, background checks at universities, and "ex-convict identities," see Ross and Richard. They use the term "invisible minority" to describe "the growing population of former prisoners" on college campuses, point out that "few universities devote resources to recruiting ex-convicts," and state that the formerly incarcerated conceal their criminal record because of the blatant stigmatization (98).

13. Butler makes a similar point when they reflect on the task of the humanities. Rather than refining our skills of dismantling, they propose we link critical practice to ethical considerations, which, in turn, are linked to public questions of what is of value ("Ordinary" 27). In sum, I argue mindfulness can be a vital practice and political tactic in that process.

14. For alternative models, see Stacey and Wolff.

15. For this dynamic and possible strategies to combat it, see the excellent analysis by Randy Martin. For a multipronged approach to address the ameliorative tendency of the corporatized university, see also Gardner et al. For organizing toward radical abolition amid and beyond the embattled academy, see Gilmore, *Abolition Geography* 41–46.

WORKS CITED

Alexander, Michelle. *The New Jim Crow: Mass Incarceration in the Age of Colorblindness*. The New Press, 2010.

Arendt, Hannah. *The Human Condition*. U of Chicago P, 1958.

Armstrong, Jennifer Keishin. "A Buddhist Chaplain Disrupts Suffering in Rikers Island." *Lion's Roar*, 6 June 2018, www.lionsroar.com/disrupting-suffering-in-rikers-island/.

Barthes, Roland. *How to Live Together: Novelistic Simulations of Some Everyday Spaces*. Columbia UP, 2002.

Berlant, Lauren, editor. *Compassion: The Culture and Politics of an Emotion*. Routledge, 2004.

Berry, Patrick. *Doing Time, Writing Lives: Refiguring Literacy and Higher Education in Prison*. Southern Illinois UP, 2018.

Black, Angela Rose. "Disrupting Systemic Whiteness in the Mindfulness Movement." *Mindful*, 12 Dec. 2017, mindful.org/disrupting-systemic-whiteness-mindfulness-movement/.

Brooks, Peter, editor. *The Humanities and Public Life*. With Hilary Jewett, Fordham UP, 2014.

Burch, Melissa. "Approach to Assisting Women Coming Home from Prison." *Critical Criminology*, vol. 25, no. 3, 2017, pp. 357–74.

Butler, Judith. *Notes on a Performative Theory of Assembly*. Harvard UP, 2015.

———. "Ordinary, Incredulous." Brooks, pp. 15–37.

———. *What World Is This? A Pandemic Phenomenology*. Columbia UP, 2022.

Castro, Erin L., et al. "Higher Education in an Era of Mass Incarceration: Possibility under Constraint." *Journal of Critical Scholarship on Higher Education and Student Affairs*, vol. 1, no. 1, 2015, pp. 13–33.

Clear, Todd R., and Natasha A. Frost. *The Punishment Imperative: The Rise and Failure of Mass Incarceration in America*. New York UP, 2014.

Coles, Romand. *Visionary Pragmatism: Radical and Ecological Democracy in Neoliberal Times*. Duke UP, 2016.

Davis, Angela Y. *Abolition Democracy: Beyond Empire, Prisons, and Torture*. Seven Stories Press, 2005.

———. *Are Prisons Obsolete?* Seven Stories Press, 2003.

Education Justice Project: Student Testimonials. EJP, University of Illinois Urbana-Champaign, 2013.

Ellison, Julie. "The Humanities and the Public Soul." *Antipode*, vol. 40, no. 3, 2008, pp. 463–71.

Epstein, Mark. *Thoughts without a Thinker: Psychotherapy from a Buddhist Perspective*. Basic Books, 2004.

Fanon, Frantz. *A Dying Colonialism*. Translated by Haakon Chevalier, Grove, 1967.

Freire, Paulo. *Pedagogy of the Oppressed*. 1968. Translated by Myra Bergman Ramos, Continuum, 2000.

Gardner, Charlie J., et al. "From Publications to Public Actions: The Role of Universities in Facilitating Academic Advocacy and Activism in the Climate and Ecological Emergency." *Repurposing Universities for Sustainable Human Progress*, edited by Iain Stewart et al., Open Access, May 2021, pp. 82–87.

Gilmore, Ruth Wilson. *Abolition Geography: Essays toward Liberation*. Verso Books, 2023.

———. *Golden Gulag: Prisons, Surplus, Crisis, and Opposition in Globalizing California*. U of California P, 2007.

Ginsburg, Rebecca, editor. *Critical Perspectives on Teaching in Prison: Students and Instructors on Pedagogy behind the Wall*. Routledge, 2019.

Harlow, Barbara. *Barred: Women, Writing, and Political Detention*. Wesleyan UP, 1992.

Higgins, Chris, and Anke Pinkert. *Public Humanities at Illinois*. Illinois Program for Research in the Humanities, 2017.

Honig, Bonnie. *Public Things: Democracy in Disrepair*. Fordham UP, 2017.

Hutner, Gordon, and Feisal G. Mohamed, editors. *A New Deal for the Humanities: Liberal Arts and the Future of Public Higher Education*. Rutgers UP, 2015.

Jones, Michelle. "Incarcerated Scholars, Qualitative Inquiry, and Subjugated Knowledge: The Value of Incarcerated and Post-Incarcerated Scholars in the Age of Mass Incarceration." *Journal of Prisoners on Prisons*, vol. 25, no. 2, 2016, pp. 98–111.

Klüger, Ruth. *Still Alive: A Holocaust Girlhood Remembered*. Feminist Press of CUNY, 1992.

Kotlowitz, Alexander. *An American Summer: Love and Death in Chicago*. Knopf Doubleday, 2019.

Kristeva, Julia. "Forgiveness: An Interview." Interview, transcription, and translation by Alison Rice. *PMLA*, vol. 117, no. 2, Mar. 2002, pp. 278–95.

Kupers, Terry A. "Toxic Masculinity as a Barrier to Mental Health Treatment in Prison." *Journal of Clinical Psychology*, vol. 61, no. 6, 2005, pp. 713–24.

Larson, Doran, editor. *Fourth City: Essays from the Prison in America*. Michigan State UP, 2013.

Lear, Jonathan. *Radical Hope: Ethics in the Face of Cultural Devastation*. Harvard UP, 2008.

Martin, Randy. "Taking an Administrative Turn: Derivative Logics for a Recharged Humanities." *Representations*, vol. 116, no. 1, 2011, pp. 156–76.

Mbembe, Achille. "Thoughts on the Planetary." Interview by Tobjørn Tumyr Nilsen, edited by Sindre Bangstad. *New Frame*, 5 Sept. 2019, nettime.org/Lists-Archives/nettime-l-1909/msg00047.html.

Newfield, Christopher. *The Great Mistake: How We Wrecked Public Universities and How We Can Fix Them.* Johns Hopkins UP, 2016.

Oakford, Patrick, et al. *Investing in Futures: Economic and Fiscal Benefits of Postsecondary Education in Prison.* Vera Institute of Justice, 2019, vera.org/downloads/publications/investing-in-futures.pdf.

Patterson, Orlando. *Slavery and Social Death: A Comparative Study.* 1982. Harvard UP, 2018.

Pinkert, Anke. "Unsettled Memory: Learning about the Holocaust at a United States Prison." *Transverse Disciplines: Queer-Feminist, Anti-racist, and Decolonial Approaches to the University*, edited by Simone Pfleger and Carrie Smith, U of Toronto P, 2022, pp. 149–76.

Pinkert, Anke, et al. "The Transformative Power of Holocaust Education in Prison: A Teacher-Student Account." *Radical Teacher*, no. 95, winter 2012, pp. 60–65.

Rodríguez, Dylan. *Forced Passages: Imprisoned Radical Intellectuals and the US Prison Regime.* U of Minnesota P, 2006.

Rosa, Hartmut. *Resonance: A Relationship of Our Relationship to the World.* Translated by James Wagner, Polity, 2019.

Ross, Jeffrey Ian, and Stephen C. Richard. *Beyond Bars: Rejoining Society.* Alpha, 2009.

Smith, Sidonie. *Manifesto for the Humanities: Transforming Doctoral Education in Good Enough Times.* U of Michigan P, 2015.

Sommer, Doris. *The Work of Art in the World: Civic Agency and Public Humanities.* Duke UP, 2014.

Stacey, Jackie, and Janet Wolff, editors. *Writing Otherwise: Experiments in Cultural Criticism.* Manchester UP, 2013.

Streamas, John. "A Vision for Scholar-Activists of Color." *AAUP Journal of Academic Freedom*, vol. 10, 2019, www.aaup.org/sites/default/files/streamas.pdf.

Tremblay, Jean-Thomas. *Breathing Aesthetics.* Duke UP, 2022.

Whippman, Ruth. "Actually, Let's Not Be in the Moment." *The New York Times*, 26 Nov. 2016, www.nytimes.com/2016/11/26/opinion/sunday/actually-lets-not-be-in-the-moment.html.

Woodward, Kathleen. "The Future of the Humanities—in the Present and in the Public." *Daedalus*, vol. 138, no. 1, 2009, pp. 110–23.

Earned Trust and Albion's Big Read

Jess Roberts

The story I could tell here is painfully ordinary, especially for those currently living it. A small postindustrial college town struggles to survive the rising poverty and joblessness that follow a failing local economy, even as it confronts the particular racial tensions so often found between a host community perceived as primarily Black and poor and a liberal arts college perceived as primarily white and wealthy. The plot would be all too familiar. The largest employer in the town, a metal foundry, shuts down. The hospital and grocery store leave. The local school system, after years of bleeding students and funding to surrounding schools, finally shrinks to an unsustainable size and is annexed by its once-rival neighboring school district.

That's the story here in Albion, Michigan.[1] But it's not the only story I could tell about the town I live in and work in and love. There's a far less ordinary and far more inspiring story to be told about Albion, a story about something amazing and beautiful and good, born out of the complicated and troubling situation we face here.

That would be the story of Albion's Big Read, a small public humanities program that I founded and direct at a small liberal arts college (albionbigread.org).[2] Albion's Big Read combats racial inequality by making crucial resources more readily and equitably available to local young people. We do that by teaching middle and high school students how to lead book discussions, creating experiences that make them want to do so, and organizing a month of programming around the discussions they lead. Many participants are Black and Brown. Many of them do not have the luxury of financial security. And all of them went to school in a district that closed while they were students in it. Through Albion's Big Read, those young people gain access to the resources of a local college, including the faculty and the facilities, and the experience of being at a college, which makes going to college feel all the more possible. They gain access to the resources of imaginative literature, a genre that too often is not made relevant to them. They even gain access to the resources that live within them—their own intelligence, courage, creativity, beauty, and love—which they may not always recognize or experience because the world of school and books too often fails to acknowledge and celebrate them. Those young people then go on to do work in their schools and community to address issues of racial and economic inequality.[3]

The story of Albion's Big Read might describe how we recruit, train, and celebrate the eighth to tenth graders who attend our summer college-access and leadership program. It might detail how we distribute a book each fall to our entire town and host a month's worth of speakers and concerts and parades and celebrations, anchored by book discussions that our eighth to tenth graders lead.[4] It might recount the profound positive impact Albion's Big Read has had on participants or the profound positive impact they in turn have had on our community. It might describe how they, book in hand, have managed to do what the adult professors and administrators and politicians in Albion couldn't quite manage, which is nothing less than bringing a fractured community together to talk openly and honestly in ways that we so desperately need.

But that's not the story I need to tell here either. Instead, I need to tell the story of what made this program possible, the story of the foundation upon which every element of Albion's Big Read stands. That is a story about trust. In it, local leaders, town folk, and parents teach me what trust really is, why it matters, how I can earn it, and, above all, why I must. They teach me that earned trust is the essential element of truly effective social justice collaborations between well-meaning academics and allies, supporters, and citizens—and that earned trust matters more than anything else because, without it, collaboration in the context of social justice work will remain only something academics talk and write about but don't actually do.

I am a professor of English at Albion College and the director of Albion's Big Read. Early on in the development of that program, I found myself on the phone with a woman who wasn't sure she wanted to be talking to me. (That was pretty common: lots of folks I talked to in those early months didn't know me and didn't know if they wanted to know me.) Her name was Sherry Grice. Sherry's voice is rough, and she is not interested in people who waste her time or tell her what her business is. At that point, Sherry had worked for Michigan State University, running youth programming throughout Calhoun County, for more than three decades. Under her leadership, the 4H Creative and Expressive Arts Program had allowed some of Albion's most vulnerable kids a space to create something beautiful every year for over twenty years. Running that program is a herculean feat that now, in the tenth year of Albion's Big Read, I am more fully prepared to appreciate. When I asked her what she thought the most important thing was for me to know about working with young people, she said, "If you want them to lead, you have to let them lead." In the context of our conversation, I took her to mean something specific about preparing kids and then giving them the opportunity to succeed or fail on their own: Teach them the work, and then let them do it. Don't do it for them. But I realize now that she was telling me something else as well, something as important as the message specific to kids: Do what you say you are going to do.

If you'd asked me early on what I was going to do in planning Albion's Big Read, I would have told you that I was going to collaborate with community partners and respect their knowledge, resources, and time. Just about any academic interested in the work of social justice and the public humanities would say those things. Yet if my experience is any indication, we don't always know what it looks like to do them or to do them well. Too often when colleges "collaborate" with their host communities, that "collaboration" amounts to asking our communities to get on board with programs they had little role in creating. Too often we, as faculty members, convey implicitly and explicitly that we believe our knowledge, resources, and time to be not only self-evidently important but somehow more important than those of our partners, especially if those partners live outside middle-class structures. Too often, if we are white, as I am, and work in racially diverse communities, as I do, we overvalue our intentions and are too eager to maintain our comfort. Too often, we assume that trust is a thing that we should be given, thanks to our degrees and our institutional affiliations, rather than something that we must earn, often in spite of those things. All of this is particularly true if our efforts at collaboration include not just people outside the academy—by which we tend to mean professionals who don't work at institutions of higher learning but nonetheless have degrees from them—but also people who have neither those degrees nor reason to trust the institutions that grant them.

Among all the many and important ways Sherry helped me on that day and has helped me since, by far the most significant was how she helped me understand the relationship between collaboration and earned trust. Trust is, as I understand it, the confidence that a person will do what they say they are going to do. Earning it is largely a matter of demonstrating that you are good on your word, but that requires understanding what those words mean in the context of your community. If I wanted to earn the trust of people in Albion—white, Black, and Brown people, people with degrees and without, people who already cared about reading and people who didn't—I needed to collaborate with my partners and value what they brought to the table, and I needed to know what those words meant and how to take the actions they signify. That required building structures and timelines that would allow for genuine contribution from all kinds of people and thinking expansively about who my partners were and what their collaboration looked like. It required listening to and learning from my partners, using the information they gave me, and ensuring that the program *we developed* reflected those things. It meant approaching all of these tasks honestly, humbly, and thoughtfully, and with the recognition that the very things that had made so much of my life easier—my whiteness, my class, my degrees—would make what I wanted to accomplish in and through Albion's Big Read harder. Only then would I earn the trust of the people I cared about most. Only then would Albion's Big Read be possible.

Collaboration, Part 1: Albion's Big Read Planning Committee

Albion's Big Read radiates outward from a core group of people: our Big Read Planning Committee.[5] The eleven people in this group were the first people whose trust I earned and whose generosity and credibility granted me access to other people who had been doing social justice work for decades, even though they might not describe their work in that way. Their racial diversity reflected the racial diversity of our community: roughly, one-third of our committee members were Black and two-thirds were white. Most had a history of working with the college, though their primary identities were rooted in the town. The programs and organizations that they had developed or led in our community sought, in different ways, to create opportunity for all Albion kids: the public schools, Kids at Hope, the NAACP, the Albion Community Foundation, the Albion District Library, our local theater, and the Sister City Committee. The Sister City Committee had sent groups of young people from Albion, some of whom had never been outside the state of Michigan, to Noisy-le-Roi and Bailly, France, on programs the community foundation helped fund. Kids at Hope provided mentorship and after-school programming to kids who for various reasons found themselves what is often termed "at risk." The local branch of the NAACP led community efforts to confront issues of prejudice and to increase the likelihood that kids would stay in school. In the context of debates about our schools, particularly those leading up to the closure of Albion High School in 2013, I had witnessed these people say hard, true things about how the educational system, not just the district, was failing our young people and what it might look like to respond meaningfully to that failure. I admired their presence and courage. When they spoke, lots of different people listened. Albion's Big Read needed them.

The Big Read Planning Committee first met as a group in June 2014, a year after our high school closed, two years before we lost our public school district entirely, in the kind of overly large multipurpose room recognizable to people familiar with small-town libraries. It probably fits close to 150 people but more often sees groups of ten to fifteen. I had spent many months recruiting the eleven people who showed up on that day. I called each of them—a process that filled me with something like dread, because I didn't know if they would take my calls, and I did know that the project wouldn't work without them. I didn't think they knew who I was. If the number of times I had seen them in leadership positions in our community was any indication, I had lots of reasons to believe they were very, very busy. Happily, they answered their phones, and when I asked if they would meet with me to talk about the possibility of creating a reading-based community program, they said yes. In those meetings, I asked prospective committee members questions about the community work they had done in the past and about what made collaborations succeed or fail. I wasn't interviewing them for a spot on the committee; I was trying to learn from them things I needed to know in order to do this project well. I realized that if they declined to be on the committee, this might be my only chance. Every single person said the same thing in different ways about collaboration: collaborative projects succeeded or failed based on trust, and trust was something you earned.

I am not entirely sure why the folks who joined the Big Read Planning Committee trusted me enough to meet with me in the first place. I suspect that it had something to do with the fact that my husband and I had lived in Albion for close to nine years before I asked them and that we had been somewhat involved in the community. We owned a home and sent our daughter, Emmylou, to the Albion public schools. We picked Emmylou up from school, volunteered at book fairs and Santa's Secret Shop, and attended school board meetings. I managed a fourth-grade Destination Imagination team. We were a part of the community in identifiable, though limited, ways long before I started asking people to work with me on Albion's Big Read. Though there was a time when I worried that we should have done something like Albion's Big Read sooner, I have come to believe that all those years of being present, of listening without leading, were part of why the folks on the planning committee were willing to work with me. Listening is a critical part of becoming a part of a community, and I had to be a part of the community before I could build something in the community.

That first committee meeting in June 2014 would lay the foundation of Albion's Big Read not only because at it we would choose the book that would guide all our programming but also because it would confirm—or not—that I was willing and able to do what I said I would do: namely, to collaborate. If I understood what collaboration was, I would ensure that the people in that room would select the book together based on information and considerations that we all brought to the table. If I didn't, I would seek their affirmation of a decision that I had basically already made. I don't mean that I would seek that affirmation in some consciously manipulative way. I do mean that my life as a white, middle-class college professor in American literature had likely led me to assume, however unconscious the assumption, that I knew the right book. I needed to work against that.

In preparing for and leading that meeting, what I did do and what I didn't do were equally important. I did select (and read) three books for us to consider and from which to select our Big Read book, but I deliberately didn't develop strong opinions about which book we should pick.[6] I did make soup and bake bread for the committee. I didn't hold the meetings on campus. I didn't talk nearly as much as I listened. I didn't make nearly as many statements as I asked questions. At some point in the discussion, I did believe that every one of the books was going to be *the* book. I didn't expect Ursula K. Le Guin's *A Wizard of Earthsea* to emerge as the favorite, but it did. In the end, we chose and owned that choice together.

For years, I was convinced that the most important thing I did before that meeting was make food—the soup and fresh bread that I prepared in my hot Michigan kitchen in an effort to show the committee that I was thankful for their time and worthy of their trust. That food was important, and it was strange. People didn't tend to prepare homemade food for committee meetings. But I had, and the strangeness of my having made it for that meeting and our subsequent meetings accelerated the creation of our community as a committee. But it wouldn't have mattered how good that food was or how much work it required of me if we hadn't chosen the book together. It was important for me to do the work that was mine to do on my own (such as selecting three appropriate books for us to choose from). It was just as important for me not to do the work that was *ours* to do (such as selecting the book that would be our Big Read book).

Not choosing the book on my own struck me as an easy and obvious choice. But actually choosing the book together required that I believe—I mean *really* believe—that my thoughts about which book might be the one mattered less than anyone else's in that room. That requires a kind of humility that academics don't tend to be rewarded for possessing. Graduate school and the tenure process reward us for being specialists, for knowing things other people don't, including which books are worth reading. We choose books every semester. We choose them for a living. But our expertise is limited to a very specific context: classes on college or university campuses attended by people who have bought into those institutions enough to show up. We aren't actually experts in choosing books for community-based programs in part because we are so rarely experts in our own communities, though that need not be the case. Our perceived expertise may actually work against us in the context of the public humanities: it might encourage us and others to overvalue our opinions, and it might forestall the self-reflection we need to engage in in order to be sure that neither of those things happens.

I don't mean to suggest that we shouldn't have opinions about books in these settings or that our expertise in literature isn't valuable. We should, and it can be. To deny that I had thoughts about the three novels I had asked us to choose from would be absurd. I am suggesting that I needed actively to dispel any notion in others and in myself that I knew which book was the right book—and I needed to be sure that was true. My ability to do so gave the committee reason to believe that I would do what I said I would do. It gave them reason to trust me.

Collaboration, Part 2: Community Elders

The relationships with members of the planning committee were a beginning, not an end. In order to succeed, Albion's Big Read needed to grow outward from that group to include more and more people, but it was particularly important that I not rely on the committee to have relationships with those people for me. That is, rather than farm out the work of recruiting Big Read partners to committee members, I needed to use the information they gave me and the access to people they provided me with to do that work myself. I needed to reach out to the increasing numbers of people in our community who lived and worked at increasing spatial and cultural distances from the college. When committee members told me to call people, I called them. When they told me to meet with people, I met with them. Those people included local leaders, pastors, activists, elected officials, and elders, among others: folks who had lived in and worked in and loved Albion far, far longer than I. In calling those people and meeting with them and meeting the people they, too, told me to meet, I was doing what I had said I would do: I was valuing their knowledge and insights, working to know Albion by meeting the people who had come before me, and demonstrating that I would show up. I was earning their trust.

Those meetings were exercises in listening. I wasn't there so much to tell people about Albion's Big Read as I was to listen to what they had to tell me. At some meetings, I learned about important events of which I should be mindful. At others, I learned the history of programs that had come and gone or come and stayed. I learned the names of elders and what to call them. Most important, I had a chance to ask people who had done the work of living in our community for decades important questions: What did they think was important about working with young people? How do people go wrong when they try to build a community program? What should I know about Albion that I probably didn't? My willingness to ask these questions before and not after we implemented our program mattered. It didn't ensure that I would prove trustworthy, but it suggested that I might. As a result of those meetings, two things happened. First, I showed my committee members that I recognized and was taking advantage of the opportunities they were giving me to learn about who had come before me and what kinds of work they had done and were doing. Second, I expanded the reach and credibility of Albion's Big Read by listening and learning from members of this community.

Creating relationships with the folks my committee sent me to was not always easy. Initial distrust of me wasn't uniform, but it was prevalent. Some people were interested in talking to me, but many were not. Some people returned my calls, but many didn't. Some calls felt more like tests than conversations, probably because they were. For many people, my degrees (BA, MA, PhD), my profession (professor), my class (middle class), and my race (white) suggested that I wouldn't really listen, wouldn't get it, wouldn't stay, didn't really know—and didn't really want to know—what it meant to live in and be from Albion. Community leaders "from Albion" have a healthy distrust of people "from the college" who show up with idealistic plans to "make things better." And for good reason. The leaders "from Albion" have lived their lives in and have given themselves to this place. Their investment in and understanding of this community run deep. The people "from the college" don't often stay long enough to learn what they don't know about this place and the people who make it what it is. What's more, they often talk and act in ways that suggest they think they know what "better" looks like before, it seems, they see clearly what is in front of them.

When I called Sherry Grice, the woman who told me to let the kids lead and who ran the 4H Creative and Expressive Arts program, I felt she was waiting for me to give her a reason to hang up. She may well have been: Sherry is a white woman who has worked with kids of color in Albion for many years. She is deep Albion, invested in Albion's kids, first, foremost, and always, and my interest in working with those kids did not alone constitute a reason to trust me. I needed to show her respect in ways that she felt. How we show respect is, of course, culturally specific, and it is critical that we learn about the cultures and social expectations within our communities so that we can act according to them. Showing Sherry that I respected her in ways that she felt meant I knew enough about the community to know how to do so. If I didn't, what reason would she have to believe that I would respect the Black and Brown young people she had worked with for decades in ways that they would feel?

I realize now that I had plenty of opportunities to give Sherry a reason to put the phone down. I could have asked for "Sherry" rather than "Sherry Grice." When she responded, "This is Ms. Grice," I might not have noticed her correction and still called her by her first name, as I have learned that I and many middle-class white folks do without thinking. I might have told her what I was doing as though she should care. I might have asked her to adjust her program to mine. Luckily, I didn't do those things. I called her Ms. Grice, assumed that she wouldn't care about my program until I gave her a reason to, and explained that I was calling to adjust my program to hers, not the other way around.

But the only reason I got things right that day was that I had gotten them wrong on other days. By that time, I had learned to err on the side of formality until invited to do otherwise—and not to expect that I would ever be invited to do otherwise. I learned to call everyone older than I Mr., Mrs., or Ms. and Black ministers Reverend or Pastor, no matter their age. I learned because people taught me. When I sent an email to the Reverend Donald Phillips, the pastor of the local African Methodist Episcopal church, that began, "Dear Don," he told me what I didn't know: that Black folks in Albion (or anywhere, really) didn't refer to pastors by their first names, and to do so was seen as a sign of disrespect. I was mortified but deeply thankful. Part of earning trust is knowing it when you see it. In that moment, Reverend Phillips trusted me enough to take the time to set me straight. How I responded to that moment of his giving trust would shape how I came to understand how to earn it.

White academics are certainly not above what Robin DiAngelo calls "white fragility," a phrase she uses to encompass various defense mechanisms by which progressive white Americans tend to insulate ourselves from the "racial stress" of reckoning with how we have internalized and perpetuated racism. And by "we," I mean that I, too, have to work against these tendencies. To practice white fragility is to take feedback as attack and to be more interested in declaring that we are not racist than in meaningfully confronting our inevitable racism. Reverend Phillips risked giving me feedback on my cultural misstep—and given the hostility with which white people consistently respond to feedback of that sort, it was a risk. Had he not taken that risk, I would have unwittingly showed signs of disrespect for and to some of the very people with whom I was most interested in working. I needed to be ready to hear when I got things wrong and to figure out how to get them right. I needed to care more about learning from people than about feeling comfortable. I needed to develop a tolerance for various forms of discomfort from which most white Americans shield ourselves.

The folks with whom I met during this stage of developing Albion's Big Read formed the first concentric circle outside the committee. They gave me a different set of coordinates by which to understand where I lived and worked. In order to earn their trust, I had to do what I said I was going to do. I said I wanted to know what they had to say, and that required that I seek them out, come to them, be humble, be open to listening, and often—so often—that I just listen. My husband tells a story about being at an academic conference several years ago and listening to a Native American keynote speaker talk about working with local communities. During the question-and-answer period, a young and, I assume, well-intentioned white academic asked the speaker how she could get started doing social justice work in the host community to which she had recently moved. He replied, "Find the elders, bring them coffee, and listen. Then go back and do that again. After a few years of that, you'll be ready to get started." This may not have been the answer she or many of the other white academics in the room wanted to hear, since it didn't mesh with the tenure-driven timelines of our academic lives. But the speaker's message was clear: If we want to do work in our communities well, that work cannot be governed by timelines that serve our professional interests rather than the community's interests. From where I sit now, I can think of no better advice. Find the elders, bring them coffee (or make them soup or bake them bread), and listen. Listen. Don't just listen for what you think you want to know. Listen expansively. Listen with the belief that what they say and know matters and without the expectation that they will have all the answers.

Listening takes energy, attention, and *time*, so the timelines that we develop must reflect a genuine commitment to listening. By the time I was reaching out to people like Sherry Grice, I had spent six months recruiting the planning committee and another three months meeting with them. The launch of Albion's Big Read was still a year away. Meeting with people on this extended timeline allowed me to see them and hear them, to listen, to process what they were telling me, and to take it into account as we created our program. By listening, I learned about my community and demonstrated my respect for it and the people who made it. By listening, I was doing what I had said I would do. I was earning community elders' trust.

Collaboration, Part 3: Big Read Families

By the early months of 2015, a year after I made my first phone call to a prospective committee member, we had made significant progress. We had secured funds from several local foundations and organizations, submitted our National Endowment for the Arts grant, and gotten approval from the college provost for me to have a reduced teaching load in the fall.[7] We had begun planning for specific events in the fall—speakers, films, art projects, and the like—and we had settled on a way of preparing the young people who would be leading our discussions to do that work: I would run a summer program at Albion College. We would bring rising eighth to tenth graders to Albion College's campus once a week for six weeks in June and July and then for a weeklong camp in August. In that program, we would read that year's Big Read book with our students and college volunteers, blend intellectual work and play, and teach the students how to lead a discussion. The program would increase their academic and social confidence, hone their reading and critical thinking skills, and create intellectually challenging and affirming experiences on a college campus. Things were looking good.

Here's the rub: we were developing a summer program for young people but were missing the young people. Up to that point, none of the work that I had done had included interacting directly with students at the middle or high school or developing relationships with the families of the young people we would ultimately recruit into the program. I had not yet earned the trust of the people who really mattered the most—the young people and their families, many of whom were not inclined to trust me.

The first step was, of course, getting the families to talk to me, which was trickier than I had expected. Calling proved ineffective. Some parents and guardians took my calls, but many didn't. More than one hung up on me. Some of the phone numbers had been disconnected, and the school didn't have updated numbers. So I called in reinforcements. Members of the planning committee looked at the list of young people we were trying to recruit, figured out who their families were—that is, not just their parents but their grandparents, aunts, uncles, cousins, pastors, and former teachers—and started making calls to those people.[8] Desperate, I approached Mike Culliver, the at-risk coordinator at the community school, for help, and he offered to stand beside me in the parking lot and point out the parents whom I had not yet reached. Then he drove me around town, knocked on the doors of students' houses, introduced me to their people, and said, in effect, "This is Jess Roberts. You should listen to what she has to say." These folks had no reason to listen to or trust me yet. But they knew and trusted Mike. They listened to me because they trusted him.

By that time, I knew that nothing I had to say about the program mattered unless these families believed that I would do what I said—unless they could trust me. I said I valued their kids—but would I know their names and say them correctly? I said that I was invested in their kids' being a part of the program—but would I provide transportation and food, without being asked? I said I was willing to do what was necessary to get their kids into the program—but would I listen even if they raised their voices and things got rough on the phone? I said that I respected them and understood where they were coming from—but would I refrain from asking them to be present in ways that their lives just didn't allow?

I didn't know I was answering these questions when I made all those phone calls in the spring of 2015. However, I did know what the Albion community members had taught me, in conversation after conversation: that what we call each other matters; that we need to care about, anticipate, and get rid of practical obstacles; that my good intentions don't mean much; that maintaining my own comfort is not the point; that I needed to listen more than talk; and that the work of earning people's trust is work. I answered those questions by acting according to what I had learned. I gave the students' families reason to believe I would do what I said.

That first year, twelve of the twenty-five families I reached out to allowed thirteen kids to join Albion's Big Read, and they—the families and the kids—became our most important collaborators.[9] I would show them that I was worthy of their trust in part by recognizing their acts of collaboration. They collaborated with us when they let their kids join the program. They collaborated with us when they took my calls and opened their doors, signed the forms I asked them to sign, and came to the meetings I said were required. They collaborated with us when they adjusted their lives in ways I would never see. They went on to become our most powerful spokespeople. They told their friends and family that Albion's Big Read could be trusted.

Verbs of Community

The story I'm telling ends before those thirteen students who signed up for Albion's first Big Read Youth Leadership Program showed up at our first meeting, before they made the first "Big Read Family" (a term the leaders coined to describe themselves), before the first of them led discussions. It ends, that is, before Albion's Big Read officially began. But at that first meeting in an Albion College classroom that veterans of the program still refer to as "the Big Read Room," those of us in that first group stood together on a solid foundation of earned trust, a foundation that the work we did together that summer would strengthen.

Building that foundation taught me about the kind of work required if we want to create humanities-based collaborative programs that advance social justice in our communities. I see that work embodied in verbs: reading books, talking about them, leading discussions, writing grants, making food, designing programs, making phone calls, driving around town, saying names, standing in parking lots, knocking on doors, asking questions, listening, making changes, getting things right, getting things wrong, earning trust, and trusting. In Albion and elsewhere, these verbs constitute the work of living in a community, of being physically, intellectually, and emotionally present in the places where we live. Had I been asked ten years ago to choose which of those verbs were most important to creating a successful public humanities program, I would likely have selected the verbs most closely related to the work I do in the academy: reading, writing, discussing, planning. Today, I know better. Calling, driving, standing, knocking, making, and, of course, earning—these are the verbs that matter most. These must be the verbs of the public humanities because they are the verbs of community.

NOTES

1. Located at the forks of the Kalamazoo River, Albion is a small, racially diverse town that is home to, among other things, Albion College. According to the US census population estimates, 61.4% of our community identifies as white, 32.4% as Black. For reporting about the closure of Albion Public Schools and the changing demographics in the schools, see "Un/Divided." For reporting on the college's broader efforts to reimagine and reconfigure its relationship to the community of Albion, see Belkin.

2. The photos and videos in our website's archive are a useful source of information about the program. Maddie Drury, who served as assistant director of Albion's Big Read for five years, designed the website and produced many of the photographs and videos that fill the archive. Maddie helped me write the first National Endowment for the Arts grant that supported the program in a 300-level writing class and was instrumental in conceiving of, developing, and implementing Albion's Big Read Youth Leadership Program.

3. Graduates of our program founded the youth chapter of the NAACP and a youth Rotary Club at their high school. Some of those students then matriculated at Albion College, where they became charter members of the Albion College chapter of the NAACP. In their capacity as Big Read leaders, they also facilitated some of the most honest and nuanced conversations about race and racism in our community that I have ever been a part of. Graduates have also returned to work with the program. Our current assistant director, Akaiia Ridley, participated in the first Big Read when she was in tenth grade, served as a college volunteer for three summers while she was a student at Albion College, and is currently in her second year as assistant director of the program.

4. In 2020, Albion's Big Read had to adjust to a world in which being together inside was no longer possible. We invited everyone who had ever been in the program to participate that summer, rather than limiting our numbers to students in the eighth to tenth grades, and we moved our meetings outdoors and online. We held our outdoor meetings in a field where the leaders' elementary school had stood before it was razed. For six weeks of the summer, those young people, ranging in age from thirteen to twenty, gathered to read and talk about our 2020 Big Read book: Jason Reynolds's *Long Way Down*. In the fall of 2020, they stood in public parks, wearing their Big Read masks, and read Reynolds's poems aloud with the community members who joined them.

5. The following people served on Albion's Big Read Planning Committee that first summer: Kimberly Frick Arndts, Jamie Bernard, Harry Bonner, Mike Culliver, Mandy Dubiel, Mae Ola Dunklin, Dianne Guenin-Lelle, Joni Parks, Mary Slater, Cindy Stanczak, and Jerri-Lynn Williams-Harper. Since then, Keena Williams, Elijah Armstrong, Nels Christensen, Maddie Drury, Ellen Wilch, Wanda Kemp, Lynette Gumbleton, Rhiki Swinton, and Akaiia Ridley have joined the committee.

6. In the first three years of the program, we applied for NEA Big Read grants, which restricted our choice of books. Applicants for NEA Big Read grants must select their anchor book from the NEA's list (see www.neabigread.org). That first year, we considered Ernest Gaines's *A Lesson before Dying*, Zora Neale Hurston's *Their Eyes Were Watching*

God, and Ursula K. Le Guin's *A Wizard of Earthsea*. Once we stopped applying for the NEA grant in 2018, we were no longer bound by their lists. Beginning in 2015, our Big Read books have included, in the order selected, Le Guin's *A Wizard of Earthsea*, Ray Bradbury's *Fahrenheit 451*, Charles Portis's *True Grit*, Ilyasah Shabazz and Kekla Magoon's *X*, Ibi Zoboi's *Pride*, Jason Reynolds's *Long Way Down*, Renée Watson's *Piecing Me Together*, Lamar Giles's *Fake ID*, and Sundee Frazier's *Mighty Inside*.

7. Albion's Big Read would not be possible without the institutional support of Albion College. I have worked with our grant writers on local, regional, and federal grants that we are eligible for because of the college's 501(c)(3) status. Our business office handles our grant money. When the NEA grant didn't come through in 2017, our office of institutional advancement raised funds for our program. Our graphic designer makes gorgeous logos every year. People in the facilities department reserve the vans that we drive to pick students up and drop them off. We use classrooms and workspaces; we visit the college library, art studios, science labs, and the gym. As important as the college's willingness to support this program is its willingness not to demand recognition of that support.

8. The list was the product of my collaboration with teachers and administrators at our middle and high school. When the program started, we worked with people in Albion Public Schools. In the wake of annexation, we have worked with people in Marshall Public Schools to nominate kids from Albion for the program. Now, with the help of our associate director, I spend the first five months of each year recruiting kids—having monthly meetings with them as a group, calling their parents and guardians, bringing them food, playing games with them, and showing them who and what we are about.

9. The number of students in the program has grown considerably since the first year. Eighteen students participated in the program in our second summer, and every single student who had participated in the first year and was eligible to return for the second did so. Nineteen students completed the program in 2017, twenty-five in 2018, and twenty-two in 2019. During the summer of 2020, we invited all the students who had graduated from the program to join the eighth- to tenth-grade leaders in the summer program. A core group of twenty-five leaders participated that summer, and the total number of leaders sometimes reached as high as thirty-nine. Sixteen students completed the program in 2021, fifteen in 2022, and fourteen in 2023.

WORKS CITED

Belkin, Douglas. "To Save Themselves, Small Colleges Offer Lifeline to Their Hometowns." *The Wall Street Journal*, 21 Dec. 2016, www.wsj.com/articles/to-save-themselves-small-colleges-offer-lifeline-to-their-hometowns-1482316200.

Bradbury, Ray. *Fahrenheit 451*. 1953. Simon and Schuster, 2012.

DiAngelo, Robin. *White Fragility: Why It's So Hard for White People to Talk about Racism*. Beacon Press, 2018.

Frazier, Sundee T. *Mighty Inside*. Levine Querido, 2021.

Gaines, Ernest J. *A Lesson Before Dying*. Knopf, 1993.

Giles, Lamar. *Fake ID*. Amistad Books for Young Readers, 2015.

Hurston, Zora Neale. *Their Eyes Were Watching God*. J. B. Lippincott, 1937.

LeGuin, Ursula K. *A Wizard of Earthsea.* 1968. Clarion Books, 2012.

Portis, Charles. *True Grit.* 1968. Harry N. Abrams, 2010.

Reynolds, Jason. *Long Way Down.* Simon and Schuster, 2017.

Shabazz, Ilyasah, and Kekla Magoon. *X.* Candlewick Press, 2015.

"Un/Divided: The Growing Pains of Annexation in Albion and Marshall." *Michigan Radio*, 2023, www.michiganradio.org/un-divided-the-growing-pains-of-annexation-in-albion-and-marshall.

Watson, Renée. *Piecing Me Together.* Bloomsbury, 2017.

Zoboi, Ibi. *Pride.* Balzer and Bray, 2018.

The Power of Design Justice

Josh Greene

Architecture has always existed as the built manifestation of the social, political, and cultural context of a given time. Each building contributing to a city's urban fabric reflects the explicit goal of an institution and its stakeholders. In concert with one another, these structures form a built environment that exists as a mirror, reflecting power dynamics that govern a society. The design of permanent space through architecture is not spontaneous or ad hoc but rather premeditated. Projects are discussed over various meetings with multiple stakeholders and ultimately approved by consensus. As a result, architecture never lacks intentionality or political influence. As cities grow, they become an outward expression of a society's views and offer insight into the mindset and attitudes of a specific culture. For both private corporations and governments looking to exercise power, architecture becomes a vehicle through which to express influence and concretize the speculative.

In the United States, the significance of architecture as a meter for social change and power throughout the last few years cannot be overstated. In 2020, following the murder of George Floyd, the Minneapolis Third Precinct police headquarters was consumed by fire as protesters demanded the defunding of a systemically racist institution. Furthermore, on 6 January 2021, the world saw American democracy assaulted when rioting US citizens defaced and occupied the United States Capitol, a neoclassical emblem of our nation's democratic principles. Extreme as these cases may be, each instance not only constitutes a protest of perceived injustice in built space but also sheds light on the significance that architecture holds in the social psyche. Through construction, occupation, and destruction, architecture inherently holds power over social thought and thus can be leveraged as a tool to catalyze large-scale social shifts.

On this spectrum of integrity, architects have historically leaned toward injustice, leveraging architecture as a tool for maintaining financial wealth and white supremacy. Since the conception of the United States, architecture and urban planning projects have been leveraged by the white elite to oppress communities of color. The foundation of this country—the US Capitol building included—was built by enslaved African Americans and on Indigenous lands (Wilson 25). Today, the profession of architecture must actively work to dismantle these historic systems of oppression and reclaim Black and Indigenous spaces in order to shift the dynamics of social power.

This essay draws from a concept inherent in the impact-based methodology of MASS Design Group. The Boston-based architecture firm, whose name incorporates an acronym for "model of architecture serving society," believes that architecture is never neutral but rather is capable of both perpetuating systemic injustice and serving as a catalyst for positive social change ("Black Lives Matter"). It is through this lens that I examine the historical injustices associated with Native American boarding schools and the ingrained spatial segregation in African American communities. In contrast, I highlight an array of architectural responses from a social justice perspective that have created positive change. The juxtaposition exposes the agency of the architect and acknowledges the inherent power embedded in the act of creation.

From Master Builders to Gatekeepers

Over the last two hundred years, the practice of architecture has evolved from a trade performed by skilled builders to a profession wielding political status and power. As the profession expanded in Europe and North America, it attracted wealthy white men who could afford the best education, expensive drafting materials, and international travel. The historian John Wilton-Ely claims two major changes in the formation of the architectural profession in England: "the transition from medieval to modern processes of thought and the shift from an agrarian to a capitalism-based society through the industrial revolution" (180). These shifts formalized the architect's relationship to capital, ultimately creating wealth for the industrialized elite through the enclosure of private property. This shift into professionalism by the historic "master builder" perpetuated an exclusive gentlemen's club, gatekeeping the tools and resources for the profession (Woods 34).

As many investors and opportunists from England immigrated to the United States in the nineteenth century, the architects shortly followed. In 1857, the nation's first professional organization, the American Institute of Architects, was created, and in 1868, MIT became the first school of architecture. African Americans were not allowed to practice architecture in the United States until 1892, when Robert Robinson Taylor became the first licensed African American architect upon his graduation from Massachusetts Institute of Technology ("Robert R. Taylor"). Furthermore, women were not admitted into architecture schools until fifty years later, when enrollment dropped as a result of World War II (Rappaport 6).

To this day, architecture continues to be an apprenticeship profession wherein young architects often depend on the mentorship of established designers from within their own communities. As a result, the privilege that architects hold continues to be passed on from generation to generation of elite professionals. Today, systemic injustices limit the number of Black, Indigenous, and People of Color (BIPOC) within the profession, further perpetuating an imbalance of power within the built environment. A lack of exposure to the profession at an early age and bureaucratic licensure requirements make it difficult for those excluded from historic pipelines to pursue a career in architecture. Consequently, only two percent of practicing architects are Black and only eighteen percent are women, as a study from 2015 revealed (*Diversity* 38–39). This nation has created a profession that revolves around whiteness, and the public idolizes white architects as creatives and authorial greats. Indeed, unquestioned trust follows white men who build the spaces that shelter, house, and inspire, and Americans occupy these spaces for approximately eighty-seven percent of our day (Klepeis 239). A preference for whiteness is omnipresent in these built environments, is incorporated into every building, and often goes unchecked. When poorly executed, architecture has the potential to carry unconscious bias and traces of oppression; at its worst, architecture has the power to commit great violence.

Often, the effects of oppressive design go unnoticed or are even written off as normative. However, the effects of design surround us constantly and influence our everyday behaviors. Lighting and acoustics can influence cognitive performance at work (Al Horr), and the inclusion of a patient window can decrease recovery times in hospitals (Ulrich). Although these evidence-based instances have been studied extensively, it is difficult to pinpoint racial injustices in the nuances of a building and call them out as such. However, in historic examples of architectural erasure and oppression, injustices are blatantly obvious and have evolved into large-scale issues of systemic racism. In the United States, for instance, architectural oppression is best framed through the intentional and malicious persecution of Native Americans and African Americans through built spaces. This historic oppression has evolved into everyday injustices that continue to burden this country.

Architecture of Erasure

During westward expansion, European Americans were confronted with the various regional architecture and planning principles of Native Americans across the country. Indigenous peoples exhibited adaptations to regional climates through their vernacular structures and were resourceful in utilizing materials from the earth. However, traditional European methods of teaching and philosophy had not emphasized the importance of the landscape, vernacular building methods, or Indigenous planning. The history that followed is defined by the illusion of white supremacy and ultimately a dominance over Native communities.

Since colonization, buildings—as a concept of permanent rectilinear structures organized on a grid—have been used to commit horrific crimes. The intrusion of industrial built space into an Indigenous society, primarily governed by natural laws, was a deliberate attack on the existing Native architecture and way of life. Black Elk, a medicine man of the Oglala Tribe, speaks as testament: "Our tepees were round like the nests of birds, and these were always set in a circle, the nation's hoop, a nest of many nests, where the Great Spirit meant for us to hatch our children. But the Wasichus [European settlers] have put us in these square boxes" (Black Elk and Neihardt 195). The American historian Carroll Van West comments, "For many Indian reformers, the adoption of new concepts of space, building form, and building arrangement became an important test of the willingness and ability of the Plains Indian to accept the gifts of a 'superior' culture" (91). White settlers believed that forcing an architectural typology within the concept of a civilized educational institution would force Native Americans to live, work, and behave more like them. The forced transition from natural to industrialized space was executed by the United States government, utilizing the architectural profession to justify violence on Indigenous people. Native American boarding schools were then constructed as an instrument of the federal government's mission of Anglo-conformity and followed the mantra of Richard H. Pratt: "Kill the Indian . . . and save the man."

The program, function, and spatial arrangement of the imposed Native American boarding schools was a severe change from traditional Indigenous ways of life. With the introduction of the European-style boarding school came the segregation of the sexes and the establishment of function-specific rooms for eating and sleeping, whereas Indigenous architecture across the country utilized one central space for a myriad of activities. Students were expected to stay on campus throughout the year, speak only in English, and use newly constructed roads to travel between fenced-off buildings (Van West). Through the implementation of weaponized architecture, white settlers were successful in the annihilation and assimilation of Native American culture, using an imposed built environment to enforce behavior and social change that have caused long-lasting generational and cultural trauma.

The Phoenix Indian School serves as an architectural reminder of the history of oppression endured by Native Americans in the Southwest. The campus was positioned on 240 acres of farmland just north of the city, where it could be accessed by multiple tribes and integrated into the economy of Phoenix. In 1896, a *New York Times* article claimed it was the "the largest Indian school in the Southwest and the second largest in the Union." The article emphasizes the school's effectiveness: "It is patronized by the Apaches, the Pimas, and the Maricopahs, who have until the past two years been the most lawless, intractable, and savage tribes Uncle Sam has had to deal with" ("Phoenix Indian School"). The school came to Phoenix through a timely marriage between a small group of investors who wanted to bring development to Arizona's new capital and federal ambitions to expand Pratt's program of industrial schools of Anglo-conformity (Trennert

35–36). In October 1890, Thomas Morgan, the commissioner of Indian affairs, addressed a large crowd of Phoenecians at an opera house downtown. He insisted that it is "cheaper to educate an Indian than to kill him" and that the agro-industrial school would provide cheap labor to a growing economy ("Teaching the Indian").

The school's first few buildings were designed by James Creighton, a Canadian-born immigrant who arrived in Phoenix in the 1880s. Creighton is known to be one of Arizona's first architects and was responsible for a number of prominent institutional buildings in the territory. He was also a founding member of the first Presbyterian Church in Phoenix and was heavily involved in missionary work in the area, teaching at the school for fifty years after its construction ("Pioneer State"). Creighton's design work was heavily influenced by the school's superintendent, Wellington Rich, a respected educator from Omaha who knew little of Native Americans or architecture. Rich, however, claimed to have an eye for design and was instrumental in the school's larger vision and expansion. In 1892, Rich described his planning of various important buildings on campus, including "of what material they would be composed, . . . their form and size, their internal arrangement and style of finish" (Trennert 53).

The decision to federally fund the Phoenix Indian School reflected a shift in American attitudes toward Indigenous people. As Protestant views entered mainstream social thought, Native education reform shifted from a priority of the missionary church to an item in the federal budget. Creighton's main building on the campus legitimizes the insidious intentions of the US government and employs beauty as a method of institutionalized oppression. By many written accounts, the building is well designed, with good ventilation, intricate woodwork, and deep porches to accommodate the heat. Upon first visiting the completed building, the superintendent of Indian affairs, Reverend Daniel Dorchester, exclaimed, "I cannot recall a single building in the Indian School Service, which for excellence of arrangement, quality of lumber, faithful workmanship, and architectural attractiveness, is its equal" (Trennert 53). This reaction epitomizes the architectural profession's betrothal to power. On stolen land, a trained architect utilizes his position as a professional elite to fulfill, legitimize, and beautify systemic injustice enacted by an institution seeking influence and wealth.

While applauded by the media and local residents at the time, the designed buildings were ultimately disconnected from the climate and culture of the Native communities throughout the region. The design and arrangement of Native architecture in the Southwest is typically based on local traditions and reflects shared group ideals transmitted through collective memory. As such, the architecture of a tribe reinforces Indigenous politics, economy, and ways of life. The Phoenix Indian School is the antithesis of this. For the first few buildings, Creighton imported an English Victorian style, constructed out of industrial-sized and mass-produced materials (Tippeconnic Fox and Tippeconnic Fox, "Phoenix Indian School Historic District"). The front doors of the Phoenix Indian School do not face the rising sun in the east, as Pima and Apache dwellings do. The Phoenix

Indian School is not built with earthen walls (which provide a low-tech solution for insulation in an unforgiving desert climate). The school buildings' lack of spiritual and cultural emphasis ultimately isolated students from their culture and from nature. Subsequent buildings constructed after the turn of the century embraced a Mission Revival style, mimicking the Spanish colonial missions that conquered the region and brought disease, displacement, and genocide. The Phoenix Indian School finally closed in 1990, but its architecture played an active and omnipresent role in Anglo-conformity. Furthermore, its culturally irrelevant architectural approach predicated the continuation of state-sponsored architectural atrocities towards Native communities in the Southwest.

Spatial Oppression

Similar to the narrative of Native American displacement, the existence of African Americans in the United States originates in a forced spatial removal of people from their motherland. With the inhumanity of slavery came an architecture to reinforce it. Slave houses quickly became a status symbol for many enslavers who wanted to boast their wealth to their neighbors. These barracks were built to a minimum requirement with poor materials and often led to perilous health conditions. Slave quarters were often segregated from the main house and arranged in a repetitive and utilitarian approach in their connection to the plantation. Offering significantly less space per person than the main house, slave quarters were juxtaposed against the extravagant design of plantation houses and quickly enforced the ideas of white supremacy that laid the foundation for contemporary racism in the United States.

After the abolition of slavery, under Jim Crow laws, the normative views of segregation from the white majority evolved in scale to perpetuate segregation and injustice at the city level. The social, political, and legal institution behind "separate but equal" spaces produced spatial dynamics that reinforced the racism of the era. It was a simple idea: "The architecture of racial segregation represented an effort to design places that shaped the behavior of individuals and, thereby, managed contact between whites and blacks in general" (Weyeneth 13). Two primary tactics were employed to materialize segregation: isolation and partitioning. Isolation of one race from another was achieved through exclusion. Black people were not allowed in specific institutions, and duplicate facilities (like schools) were conceived to ensure races did not cohabitate. When isolation was not an option, partitioning used physical barriers to separate Black and white people, typically including separate entrances and employing separate staff members (Weyeneth 19–25). These constructed barriers, designed by white men, largely influenced the psyche of everyone governed by the same spatial laws and undoubtedly created a lasting impact. Following the success of the 1960s civil rights movement, many of these spaces were architecturally altered to wipe away the memory of spatial segregation. The destruction of these partitions demonstrates the speed with which architecture can be made to adapt to the social and political realities of the time. Yet the intergenerational trauma inflicted by Jim Crow on African Americans, who undoubtedly adapted their spaces and behaviors as a direct result of historical racial injustice and spatial inequity, is not so quickly erased.

Over time, the perception of African American housing as a utilitarian and separate spatial praxis became increasingly institutionalized. In the midst of a housing crisis, and in the name of progress, the city of St. Louis used the 1949 Housing Act to enforce large-scale slum clearance and redevelopment in historically Black neighborhoods. Utilizing federal funds allocated for housing the displaced, the St. Louis Housing Authority in 1956 completed Pruitt-Igoe, a modernist public housing apartment complex designed by the esteemed architect Minoru Yamasaki and inspired by the architectural manifestos of the modernist movement. The project aimed to increase the standard of living for Black residents and to alleviate a pressing housing demand, but poor design and building maintenance instead created concentrated and decrepit areas of state surveillance. As funding from the city ran out, maintenance of the building quickly deteriorated and the project became known as a space for violence and crime. Design features such as the skip-stop elevators made it easy to target residents in muggings and violent crimes in the main lobbies. Many of the gallery windows blew out, and in their absence, multiple residents fell to their deaths. The planned playgrounds, landscaping, and public facilities were deemed too expensive to construct, so open spaces were left barren and overrun by gang members rather than children. Eventually, police officers, firefighters, and social workers learned to avoid the building in fear of its residents. Citing a lack of questioning against the racist planning efforts of the US Department of Housing and Urban Development, Michael Murphy claims that "the complex is a case study for systemic violence where architectural complicity comes into focus" (Murphy 128). On 29 April 1972, spectators watched as the building was decommissioned and demolished on live television in an implosion that brought the modern project tumbling to the ground (Allen and Wendl 103). To this day, the demolition of Pruitt-Igoe is effectively known as the end of the modern architecture movement (Jencks 9).

Spatial segregation has not ended in the United States; it has merely increased in scale. In 2024, swimming pools are not segregated by time, and train stations are no longer divided by partitions. However, an elaborate scheme of redlining tactics, malicious city planning, and racist policies have been responsible for segregating white and Black populations on a neighborhood level. Such segregation has become the basis for large-scale systemic injustices that daily burden African American communities. Black people are more likely to live in high-poverty neighborhoods, which are typically characterized by limited access to quality education, health care, jobs, and transportation, thus creating a cycle of poverty for the communities of color trapped within its borders (Firebaugh and Acciai 1). This widespread inequality seeps into the everyday actions of those affected by poverty and dictates how individuals engage daily in their communities. The inequities of governmental systems in communities of color are felt in infrequent maintenance, a lack of green park space, and limited access to fresh food.

For both Native American and African American communities, the active role architecture has played in their disenfranchisement has evolved in scale. As the spatial laws that govern the US population have become increasingly institutionalized, the people most harmed remain shut out of opportunities to remake them.

Building Empathy

Throughout US history, white male architects have used their privilege to engineer and impose a racialized agenda. When built within an unjust system by the hand of culturally negligent designers, buildings have the power to commit great violence and negatively impact communities. If approached from a perspective of social justice and rigorous contextual research, however, the design of a space can actively protest systemic power structures. Through a rigorous commitment to justice, architects can honor communities through the buildings they design. To promote positive social change, MASS Design Group outlines five principles in their call to action: "find the mission," "immerse in context," "search for proof," "invest upstream," and "justice is beauty" (Murphy and Ricks). Some of these points are explicated in the discussion of innovative architectural methodologies below.

Arguably, the most audacious method whereby an architect can create equitable change in communities of color is that of challenging the status quo. As creatives with the ability to approach a problem holistically, architects often find themselves in a position to ask provocative questions regarding a building's program and purpose. This practice can be helpful in breaking disciplinary rigidity and introducing spatial innovations. The architect acts as a futuristic artist, providing imagery and ideas to help envision an alternative solution that may have been impossible to fathom previously, ultimately pushing the limits of program integration in a way that provides space for dialogue and momentum.

This approach can include reenvisioning the work of historic preservation and reclamation as aspects of social justice design by manipulating the program, or activity, of the building. The proposed transformation of the Phoenix Indian School achieves this by honoring the history of the Native students who attended and celebrating their cultural significance in the valley. Built in 1931, the elementary school building (subsequently the band building) is more modern than Creighton's constructions, showing an Art Deco influence and marking a fundamental transition away from assimilation and toward cultural pluralism (Tippeconnic Fox and Tippeconnic Fox, "Phoenix Indian School Visitors Center"). The building, historically utilized by the US government for Anglo-conformity, has recently been injected with a new architectural program that transforms the space into a community center focused around Native education. The renovation is a collective project of the Phoenix Indian Center, Native American Connections, the city of Phoenix, the Phoenix Local Initiatives Support Coalition, and the Architectural Resource

Team (a local architectural practice). Utilizing community charettes to gather input from various tribal leaders and community members, the building serves as a cultural gathering place where visitors can learn about the school's history and Indigenous people can engage and celebrate their Native practices. The space now hosts multiple community meeting spaces, a commercial kitchen for preparing traditional Native foods, and an exhibit space for sharing visually the school's oppressive history. There is something inherently empowering about reclaiming, whether through language, music, or space, elements originally designed to oppress. Utilizing a property first envisioned as a place of regimented assimilation as now a place for cultural exchange and progress is an example of how society must embrace similar reconstruction internally.

Wanda Dalla Costa, a First Nations licensed architect and professor, claims that "Indigenous people offer a unique way of looking at the world" and identifies four catalysts for Indigenous architecture: place, kinship, transformation, and sovereignty (194). In regard to sovereignty, Dalla Costa proclaims: "While cultural continuity has been interrupted by a number of historical events, namely the reservation system, residential schools and the outlawing of culture traditions, re-operationalizing culture and the resurrection, restoration and revitalisation of traditional methodologies is actively underway" (199). Through the reoperationalization of Indigenous education in a space conceived for Indigenous erasure, the renovation of the Phoenix Indian School can be postulated as a step toward Native sovereignty.

Another example of innovation in spatial programming comes from the Oakland-based firm Designing Justice, Designing Spaces (DJDS), which aims to end mass incarceration through place-based solutions. Founded by Deanna Van Buren, the firm believes that "by transforming the spaces and places where we do justice, we can help our society make the shift from a punitive justice system to a restorative justice system" ("About DJDS"). Throughout their design process, DJDS focuses on community input and collaborates with restorative justice organizations to create human-centered places of healing. In Syracuse, the DJDS team renovated a dilapidated drug house into a peacemaking center by collaborating with the Center for Court Innovation. The building is the first purpose-built space for Native American peacemaking programs outside Native communities and offers a way to reenvision justice. These projects and others in the firm's portfolio demonstrate the role that architects can play in creating transformational social change through the design and construction of purpose-built spaces.

Large architectural projects require immense amounts of capital investment and come with substantial construction timelines. An architect can help direct that investment into communities of color. Prioritizing local materials and collaborating with nontraditional workers allows a project to transcend traditional practice and achieve large-scale sustainable impact. Successful community engagement and cultural proximity of the architect to a community can result in a detailed understanding of the local material palette and craft traditions. The architect can leverage this information by specifying local materials in their drawings. Although typically overlooked, an essential responsibility for an architect is to retain and enhance the local skills of the place and to innovate with materiality. Doing so increases a project's relationship to its surrounding context. A building rooted in the materials of a community leads to a higher likelihood that the public will accept and productively utilize the space. This approach also allows the architect to employ local experts familiar with the material. Retaining project funds within a community proves to the end users that an architect's primary function is to support them and not to ignore or exploit them. Furthermore, utilizing local materials is a logical and environmentally just solution. Importing foreign construction materials requires excessive amounts of embodied carbon in transport and is unnecessary when alternatives are local and abundant. Through innovating with local materials, architects can work with communities in a specific construction method sustainable to the place and familiar to the people. This replicability can create enduring impact through proper training and long-term guidance. Bolstering the design knowledge within a community gives individuals the capacity to implement long-lasting, aesthetically pleasing, and safe structures locally, well after a designer is gone. By specifying regional building methods and mandating the use of local materials, architects can redistribute their power to community members and resources.

Architectural injustices reflect a lack of cultural competence and are supplemented by an idea of cultural neutrality that defines Eurocentric spaces as normative. Intentional cultural proximity requires difficult work and necessitates additional time and resources at the beginning of a project; however, it must be prioritized in order to avoid designing inequitable spaces. The discomfort of cultural immersion and high costs of extensive contextual work factor into a systemic problem of omitting these approaches altogether. However, the history of architectural violence and injustice committed against marginalized communities is evidence that cultural competence must be demanded as architectural common practice. Responsibility for such change must be shared between the architects who design and build spaces and the public, who must demand more of the architectural profession.

The most effective methods of achieving cultural proximity are immersion in context, soliciting community input, and utilizing a diverse team. Immersion in a community requires that the designer spend enough time among its people to understand the larger systems at play. It also demands that the designing architect empathize with and understand the experiences of the local community members. The investment of time and resources needed to effect adequate immersion is substantial, but its yields are invaluable, from the understanding of topography and climatic systems to knowledge of the individual needs and wants of specific community members. Local communities are the experts of their place, and their local knowledge is an absolute strength when making any design decision. For access to local knowledge, the architect must engage with communities, ask the right questions, listen to what is communicated, and simultaneously build consensus.

Intentional community engagement not only brings local expertise to bear on practical issues but also fosters a sense of local ownership and commitment that increases the likelihood that a project will be accepted. Most important, the act of community engagement empowers people from different backgrounds, including people who traditionally do not have the opportunity to be heard in institutional systems (Bassler et al. 4). The act of seeking community input releases the monopoly of power from the architect and the larger systems they represent as it redistributes power back to the affected community. Designing a building is inherently a political act rooted in social contexts. By inviting nontraditional voices to the table and utilizing participatory design methodologies, architects can redistribute both power and resources.

The Italian architect Giancarlo De Carlo was an early advocate for participatory design in the late 1960s, when the modern architecture movement was being widely criticized for its failure to respond to critical social problems. He bluntly asserted that "architecture has become too important to be left to the architects" and that barriers and power dynamics between designers and the end user must be broken down (13). In doing so, De Carlo made an important distinction between planning *for* the end user and planning *with* the end user: "In the case of planning 'for,' the act of planning remains forever authoritarian and repressive, however liberal the initial intentions. In the case of planning 'with,' the act becomes liberating and democratic, stimulating a multiple and continuous participation" (15). De Carlo argued that the act of participation allows the politics of a new architecture to be democratic and that if a public consensus is reached, the project will inherently be used and appreciated long after the designer is absent. As a passionate early advocate for community work, De Carlo may have paved the way for contemporary practices of participatory design.

Architecture firms around the globe have conceptualized unique ways of engaging their communities according to the skill set of their personnel and the context of their environment. A firm that practices some of the most rigorous and effective participatory design methodologies is the Chilean firm Elemental. Elemental has designed social housing in the informal settlements of Chile since 2003, using a participatory and incremental process, including the exhaustive study of communities through immersion, that embeds extensive local knowledge in the architecture. Elemental prioritizes three core objectives during their participatory process. First, they see engagement as an opportunity to inform a community of project constraints. Each project contains inherent economic, environmental, and legal restrictions imposed by various entities. Distilling complex information and educating community members about project limitations is the first step in welcoming those community members as informed codesigners and decision-makers. As such, community members combine their local knowledge with the institutional knowledge of the architect, reducing the power imbalance between builders and a community. This process empowers community members to contribute to Elemental's second objective: communities making informed decisions about their own spaces. In the context of social housing, Elemental argues that "the families should be involved in the decisions—because they are the ones who know better what is more relevant for their everyday lives" (Aravena and Andrés 452). Decision-making by families is what makes a social housing project feel more like a home. The final objective of the Elemental participatory program is to inform a community of the most efficient and suitable methods for home improvement and maintenance (459). The nature of building incrementally means that a community will continue to add to and modify their space well after the architect is gone. Elemental anticipates this eventuality by transferring technical knowledge that renders the architect redundant and empowers the residents of their buildings. Elemental's community engagement process has made their projects successful in their communities, in the public sphere, and in the architectural profession, and their process of addressing social problems directly with a community and utilizing governmental funds is considered to incorporate some of the most effective and comprehensive community engagement methods in architecture today.

Although cultural proximity can be achieved through community engagement and outreach, the most efficient way for an architect to be proximate is to personally identify with the communities with whom they are designing. When the architect is not a community member, it is imperative that a creative community leader be included in the design team. Saving a seat for a respected local leader will give a community voice while allowing the representative to contribute actively to the design of the project. Giving power and income to creative community leaders is an explicit affirmation of the architect's values and commitment and encourages more community context within a project. However, this approach is not a systemic long-term solution to a professional deficit. Architectural firms need to be more diverse and to reach across racial, gender, sexual orientation, and socioeconomic lines. The lack of diversity in the architectural profession is historic and stubborn. The profession must strive to become more diverse and to include more voices at the drafting table. Fortunately, the Floyd protests of 2020 catalyzed some long-overdue change in the profession. In 2021, Chris Cornelius became the first Indigenous chair of an architecture department in the United States. In the following year, Diébédo Francis Kéré was the first person of color, and the first African, to be awarded the Pritzker Prize, architecture's highest achievement. A more diverse profession will allow architecture firms to identify with a multitude of perspectives and experiences that may align with the communities with and for whom they are designing. Architects like Cornelius and Kéré who can draw upon initial proximity to a community are better suited to facilitate community engagement activities and will continue to bring their voice into all stages of design.

Architecture is the built manifestation of power. Those who create space can perpetuate systemic injustice or protest against and resist antiquated power structures. Historically, architecture has been a weapon that oppressed the powerless through segregation of services and access. However, with rigorous applications of socially just design methodologies, equitable spaces can and need to become common practice. Architects must reemerge as thought leaders of the public sphere and innovate through conceptual representation, leverage their designs financially to invest in communities, and be culturally proximate in all stages of the design process. All architecture has inherent social and political impacts, and architects must become educated in the positive and negative implications of the spaces they create. With an increasing body of socially minded work, architects have an opportunity to acknowledge their power and to come to terms with professional and institutional biases and shortcomings. By redistributing their power to the communities within which they work, architects must utilize their platforms to allow individuals to have agency within their spaces and to feel valued within the communities they inhabit. If architects fail to release and distribute their power, they risk continuing to lose political and institutional credibility with the very publics they serve and support. If done with humility, compassion, and respect, architecture can emerge as an advocate and leader for inclusivity and pave the way toward more just and dignified spaces for those who need them.

WORKS CITED

"About DJDS." *Designing Justice + Designing Spaces*, 2021, designingjustice.org/about/#mission.

Al Horr, Yousef, et al. "Occupant Productivity and Office Indoor Environment Quality: A Review of the Literature." *Building and Environment*, vol. 105, 15 Aug. 2016, pp. 369–89. *ScienceDirect*, https://doi.org/10.1016/j.buildenv.2016.06.001.

Allen, Michael R., and Nora Wendl. "After Pruitt-Igoe: An Urban Forest as an Evolving Temporal Landscape." *Studies in the History of Gardens and Designed Landscapes*, vol. 34, no. 1, 2014, pp. 101–12, https://doi.org/10.1080/14601176.2013.850241.

Aravena, Alejandro, and Iacobelli Andrés. *Elemental manual de vivienda incremental y diseño participativo*. Hatje Cantz, 2012.

Bassler, Allan, et al. "Developing Effective Citizen Engagement: A How-To Guide for Community Leaders." *Pennsylvania State University Cooperative Extension*. Center for Rural Pennsylvania, 2008, www.rural.pa.gov/getfile.cfm?file=Resources/PDFs/research-report/archived-report/Effective_Citizen_Engagement.pdf&view=true.

Black Elk and John G. Neihardt. *Black Elk Speaks: Being the Life Story of a Holy Man of the Oglala Sioux*. U of Nebraska P, 1961.

"Black Lives Matter." *MASS Design Group*, 2023, massdesigngroup.org/black-lives-matter.

Dalla Costa, Wanda. "Metrics and Margins: Envisioning Frameworks in Indigenous Architecture in Canada." *The Handbook of Contemporary Indigenous Architecture*, edited by Elizabeth Grant et al., Springer, 2018, pp. 193–221.

De Carlo, Giancarlo. "Architecture's Public." *Architecture and Participation*, edited by Peter Blundell Jones et al., Spon Press, 2007, pp. 3–22.

Diversity in the Profession of Architecture: Key Findings 2015. American Institute of Architects, 2015, www.architecturalrecord.com/ext/resources/news/2016/03-Mar/AIA-Diversity-Survey/AIA-Diversity-Architecture-Survey-02.pdf.

Firebaugh, Glen, and Francisco Acciai. "Black Neighborhood Poverty and Segregation." *Proceedings of the National Academy of Sciences*, Nov. 2016, vol. 113, no. 47, pp. 13372–77, www.pnas.org/content/113/47/13372.

Jencks, Charles. *The Language of Post-modern Architecture*. Rizzoli, 1991.

Klepeis, Neil, et al. "The National Human Activity Pattern Survey (NHAPS): A Resource for Assessing Exposure to Environmental Pollutants." *Journal of Exposure Science and Environmental Epidemiology*, vol. 11, no. 3, 2001, pp. 231–52, https://doi.org/10.1038/sj.jea.7500165.

Murphy, Michael. "The Fall of Postmodernism and the New Empowerment." *Harvard Design Magazine*, no. 42, May 2016, pp. 124–31.

Murphy, Michael, and Alan Ricks. "The New Empowerment." *Architect Magazine*, 16 May 2017, www.architectmagazine.com/design/the-new-empowerment_o.

"Phoenix Indian School; Largest in the Southwest and Second Largest in the Country." *The New York Times*, 5 July 1896, www.nytimes.com/1896/07/05/archives/phoenix-indian-school-largest-in-the-southwest-and-second-largest.html.

"Pioneer State Architect Is Summoned by Death." *The Arizona Republic*, 26 Nov. 1946, p. 7. *Newspapers.com*, www.newspapers.com/article/arizona-republic-james-creighton/53309904/.

Pratt, Richard. "'Kill the Indian, and Save the Man': Capt. Richard H. Pratt on the Education of Native Americans." *History Matters: The U.S. Survey Course on the Web*, historymatters.gmu.edu/d/4929/.

Rappaport, Nina, and Jamie Chan. "Yale Women in Architecture." *Constructs*, fall 2012, pp. 6–7.

"Robert R. Taylor." *MIT Black History*, www.blackhistory.mit.edu/story/robert-r-taylor.

"Teaching the Indian." *The Arizona Republican*, 13 Oct. 1890, p. 1. *Library of Congress*, www.loc.gov/item/sn84020558/1890-10-13/ed-1/.

Tippeconnic Fox, Mary Jo, and Jason Tippeconnic Fox. "Phoenix Indian School Historic District." *SAH Archipedia*, 24 Sept. 2019, sah-archipedia.org/buildings/AZ-01-013-0066.

———. "Phoenix Indian School Visitors Center." *SAH Archipedia*, 24 Sept. 2019, sah-archipedia.org/buildings/AZ-01-013-0066-03.

Trennert, Robert A. "'And the Sword Will Give Way to the Spelling-Book': Establishing the Phoenix Indian School." *The Journal of Arizona History*, vol. 23, no. 1, spring 1982, pp. 35–58. *JSTOR*, www.jstor.org/stable/41695642.

Ulrich, Roger S. "View through a Window May Influence Recovery from Surgery." *Science*, vol. 224, no. 4647, 1984, pp. 420–21, https://doi.org/10.1126/science.6143402.

Van West, Carroll. "Acculturation by Design: Architectural Determinism and the Montana Indian Reservations, 1870–1930." *Great Plains Quarterly*, vol. 7, no. 2, spring 1987, pp. 91–102. *DigitalCommons@University of Nebraska-Lincoln*, digitalcommons.unl.edu/cgi/viewcontent.cgi?referer=&httpsredir=1&article=1324&context=greatplainsquarterly.

Weyeneth, Robert R. "The Architecture of Racial Segregation: The Challenges of Preserving the Problematical Past." *The Public Historian*, vol. 27, no. 4, fall 2005, pp. 11–44. *JSTOR*, www.jstor.org/stable/10.1525/tph.2005.27.4.11.

Wilson, Mabel. "Notes on the Virginia Capitol: Nation, Race, and Slavery in Jefferson's America." *Race and Modern Architecture: A Critical History from the Enlightenment to the Present*, edited by Irene Cheng et al., U of Pittsburgh P, 2020, pp. 23–42.

Wilton-Ely, John. "The Rise of the Professional Architect in England." *The Architect: Chapters in the History of the Profession*, edited by Spiro Kostof and Dana Cuff, U of California P, 2008, pp. 180–208.

Woods, Mary N. *From Craft to Profession: The Practice of Architecture in Nineteenth-Century America*. U of California P, 1999.

After Inclusion: A Trans Relational Meditation on (Un)Belonging

Lore/tta LeMaster

I'm sitting in an onboarding meeting for an academic post. The room is stuffy, sterile, and institutional. The human resources representative, Carol, is nice.[1] Her short blond hair bobs back and forth as she describes our *exciting new role!* Her smile somehow balances the flat affect emanating from the new employees; we are overwhelmed and bored. The mixed crowd of new colleagues comprises staff members and instructors as well as tenure- and non-tenure-track faculty members. While our labors diverge, we are beholden to the same or similar "benefits." And, as Carol reminds us, "These benefits include the *very best* health-care insurance one can buy in the marketplace." What Carol does not disclose is that those benefits are politicized and that the particulars of what is and is not covered are mediated through a governing body of appointed and confirmed state officials and then justified through the so-called "marketplace."

"Are there any questions?" Carol asks the silent room.

My face reddens as I rub my sweating palms between my legs.

Carol scans the silent room. "Yes?"

A white man named Stan prompts Carol, "You mentioned we get discounts at all kinds of places with our ID cards. Can you say more on that?" My colleagues lean in as Carol shares a list of discounts.

"Oh, let me tell you about gym memberships!" The room erupts in laughter.

Somewhere between gym memberships and sporting events, I begin to dissociate and imagine I am elsewhere—anywhere else, but with trans kith and kin. The laughter of the room ebbs and flows with the genre-bending sounds of techno that play in my head. I envision the clashing sounds of ocean waves while waiting for what I consider menial chatter—discounts as corporate moves to innocence and complicity in the perpetuation of oppressive relations—to subside.

"Anyone else? Any other questions on your new benefits before we break for lunch?" Carol's question ruptures my dissociative dream space and prompts me to lean in regardless of my reddening face and sweating palms. "Yes? Do you have a question, sir?"

The "sir" in her voice cuts my breath. I speak nonetheless: "What particular health benefits do we have for transsexual, transgender, and other gender expansive employees?"

Carol's eyes widen as a human resources representative runs to her side from the back of the room. "Hi, I'm Adele and I work with Carol. Can you please repeat your question, sir?"

"It's not sir. My question is: What . . ."

"Oh, my god! I am so, *so* sorry, sir . . . ma'am? I'm sorry, I don't mean to offend you." The room of colleagues has fixed their gaze on my person.

"You can call me Dr. LeMaster, and my pronouns are she/her/hers and they/them/theirs. I asked, 'What particular health benefits do we have for transsexual, transgender, and other gender expansive employees *like myself*?'" My body shivers; sweat drips from my forehead and nestles into my bushy beard. I work hard to suppress the wave of anxiety that threatens to drown out her response.

Adele shuffles frantically through papers before looking back up at me. Carol stands to her side, smiling.

"We don't have that sort of thing here," Adele offers.

I sit silently and stare back into Adele's eyes before responding, "And what is the current status of expanding our health-care plan to include employees who are trans?"

Adele clarifies, "*We do not exclude people from our health-care plan because of their gender.*"

I respond in kind, "I didn't suggest that. What I *am* asserting, *however*, is that we have equal access to trans-exclusionary health-care options. As such, when will our 'inclusive' health care include gender transition support and wellness options particular to trans employees?"

Carol chimes in with confident optimism, "We need more brave people like you to hire here so that we can justify making those important changes!" Carol's smile somehow balances the silent rage boiling under Adele's targeted gaze.

"Thanks, Carol. That was very insightful." *It really wasn't*, I think. I smile, bored and exhausted. My new colleagues gawk in silence.

After Inclusion: Access and Belonging

At the heart of this relational meditation is a simple though complex query: What happens after inclusion? To answer this question, I turn to lived experience as a nonbinary trans femme navigating US academe to interrogate (un)belonging beyond so-called LGBT inclusion. Despite claims that LGBT folks are enjoying greater inclusion, especially since the US federal recognition of marriage equality in 2015, transness reveals the cis-centric limits of such grandiose claims, gestures, and imaginings. As a wing of the settler state, academe was established, in part, to advance and legitimize US empire's enslavement of Black folks, annexation of Indigenous lands, genocide, and eventual colonization of the Pacific—effectively gesturing to the imperial colonization of body-mind-spirit, land, and water (see Grande). In this historic context, questions of inclusion and exclusion are complex at best. As an example, Patricia Hill Collins theorizes Black women as "outsiders within," bearers of "situational identities that are attached to specific histories of social injustice" across intersections of race, gender, and class (86). Theorizing trans and gender expansive faculty as "outsiders within" directs our analytic registers to the situational ways trans and gender expansive faculty members are intersectionally constituted as feeling out of place despite being included.

In this essay, I autoethnographically weave narrative with theory in service of cultural critique. In particular, I use performative writing—including personal narrative, fiction, and poetic forms—to aestheticize lived experience. At the same time, I weave—writing while analyzing—my performative stories through developments in queer and trans relational thought (see LeMaster, "Notes"). To be frank, there aren't many trans and gender expansive faculty members in academe, period. There are many reasons for this: academe has proven hostile to trans and gender expansive folks (see Nicolazzo); Black, Indigenous, and other trans and gender expansive folks of color are pushed out of schooling contexts beginning at a young age (see Rosentel et al.; Snapp et al.); and trans and gender expansive graduate students lack access to trans elders, including faculty mentors, if they do make it to graduate school. In turn, many of us (trans and gender expansive folks) are isolated from one another—forced to fend for ourselves in our respective "inclusive" institutions—while working to cultivate and sustain relating across space and time "together apart." In short, this essay honors trans relational labors and turns to lived experience as communicative media through which to envision relating otherwise and in ways that affirm and enrich trans and gender expansive life.

Four sections constitute the remainder of this essay. First, I trace developments in queer and trans relational thought. In particular, I unpack queer and trans means of relating across space and time and focus on the cultural significance of relating ambivalently as trans and gender expansive folks. Second, I describe critical autoethnography and the particular methodological elements I use in weaving my stories. Third, I perform two critical autoethnographic constellations to reveal trans relational means of relating ambivalently across two dialectics: *feeling excluded—being included* and its dialectic reversal, *feeling included—being excluded.* And, fourth, I close this essay offering trans-affirming modes of relating in political coalition.

Relating Otherwise

Queer and trans artists, scholars, and activists have long troubled normative modes of relating against a backdrop of exclusionary cultural design. At its most fundamental, US empire is sustained through cisheteropatriarchal modes of relating that presume reproductive futurities through which to accumulate wealth on stolen land (see Arvin et al.). Accumulated wealth is then passed on through patriarchal inheritance rights and rituals, which often exclude queer and trans progeny who cannot or will not acquiesce to cisheteronormative relational or corporeal comportment. In addition to familial ostracization, queer and trans workers report high levels of workplace harassment leading to high levels of under- and unemployment—particularly for Black, Indigenous, and other queer and trans folks of color (James et al.). As a result, queer and trans folks are structurally pushed out of—and rendered unimaginable if not unspeakable in—the white cisheteropatriarchal mythos that sustains US empire, beginning at the basic cultural unit of the family of origin. Still, queer and trans folks (re)write their own origin stories, cultivate communal survival, and thrive amidst exclusionary cultural backdrops. As such, queer and trans relational thought decenters hegemonic modes of relating and instead honors and affirms those modes of relating that sustain and ensure queer and trans life at the intersections of difference (see Eguchi and Long).

Gust Yep theorizes queer relational bonds as the constitutive ground out of which queer worlds emerge ("Violence"). In particular, Yep argues that queer relationality facilitates healing from cisheteronormative violence. Through a metareview of the field of communication studies—a discipline that does not take queerness or transness as its proper objects of study and thus provides important insight into similarly normative fields—Yep reveals that heteronormative violences take symbolic, discursive, psychological, and material forms and are constitutive of minoritized sexualities and amplified at the intersections of difference. Moreover, Yep suggests that cisheteronormative violence takes at least four forms: internal, external, discursive, and institutional. In turn, Yep theorizes that healing from these violences requires understanding, critiquing, and demystifying "heteronormativity's invisible power" (26). The effect, Yep posits, is queer worldmaking: "the opening and creation of spaces without a map, the invention and proliferation of ideas without an unchanging and predetermined goal, and the expansion of individual freedom and collective possibilities without the constraints of suffocating identities and restrictive membership" (35). To be certain, queer worlds are "*unrealizable*" in the modern sense of *identification with/as*, and queer worldmaking instead references the relational means by which queer and trans folks cultivate survival and thrive regardless of calls for their demise (Berlant and Warner 558). Queer and trans scholars theorize, affirm, and develop queer relational thought and the constitutive worldmaking potentiality that is affectively rendered therein and beyond (see Byrd; Eguchi; Goltz and Zingsheim; Gutierrez-Perez and Andrade; LeMaster et al., "Unlearning Cisheteronormativity"; Moreman and Briones; Otis and Dunn).

Centering transness in particular, I have developed Yep's queer theorizing to account for relational bonds that are the incommensurable effect of administrative and institutional exclusion and anti-trans oppression ("Notes"; see also LeMaster and Mapes; LeMaster and Toyosaki). While my approach to trans relationality develops the communication discipline's approach to relational thought, there exists a rich history of trans relational thought and worldmaking potential by different names. For example, and particular to this essay, trans materialists conceptualize trans relationality as material grounds through which trans culture is reproduced. Zazanis argues that "trans practices of reproduction generate modes of influence that make possible alternative modes of living. They open new conditions of possibility for trans people's self-realization. This facilitates the process of transgender identity formation, and makes opportunities for transition possible" (43–44; see also Dickinson). In this agential framing, trans folks might seek connection with other trans folks (whether consciously or not) so as to facilitate gender socialization otherwise (e.g., in ways that affirm one's own gender), just as trans folks may serve as communal elders, working to produce and sustain trans-affirming modes of life and living (see Awkward-Rich and Malatino). In both instances, one is caring for one's emerging trans sense of self while caring for trans kin, facilitating relational space through which trans folks might feel a sense of belonging. Care is thus crucially important to trans relational thought and to cultivating worlds worth living (see Hwang; Malatino).

Whereas queer relational scholars focus on nonnormative modes of relating (e.g., queer family vs. family of origin) for their worldmaking potential, trans relational scholars interrogate the ways trans and gender expansive folks cultivate communal worlds as a result of structural exclusions that are the effect of anti-trans cultural design. Taken together, relating otherwise references the spatiotemporal means by which trans and queer folks cultivate and materialize worlds of their/our own unique design (Yep, "Further Notes"). Particular to this project, and in the context of US academe, relating otherwise references the mundane ways in which trans and gender expansive faculty members navigate a relational sense of (un)belonging in the ambivalent space between feeling included or excluded and being excluded or included nonetheless. Placing in dialectic tension the *subjective feeling—structural being* of lived experience, this essay develops "trans relational ambivalences" as an analytic means by which to ascertain cultural meaning about relationally navigating anti-trans contexts, including academe—particularly when one does not have ready access to other trans and gender expansive faculty kin (LeMaster et al., "Trans Relational Ambivalences"). Precisely because I have few trans and gender expansive colleagues, I turn to autoethnography to discern cultural meaning derived from subjective lived experience. As a result, my autoethnographic performance serves as a reflexive blueprint that facilitates relating with and as trans and gender expansive kith and kin navigating academe.

Critical Autoethnography: Lived Experience, Cultural Critique

My use of critical autoethnography as research method in this essay represents a blurred research genre in which cultural meaning is derived from subjective lived experience (see Ellis et al.; Adams et al.; Bochner and Ellis). To be certain, the presumption is not that subjective experience serves onto-epistemic ends in and of itself (though, this is also true) but that lived experience can facilitate nuanced understanding about the structural workings of cultural power so that we might imagine and engage social transformation through agency (see Ellis and Calafell; Johnson and LeMaster). In this regard, a critical autoethnographic project weaves personal narrative with theory and in service of intersectional cultural critique (see Boylorn and Orbe, *Critical Autoethnography*, "Becoming"; Johnson; Parks). Moreover, critical autoethnographic cultural critique is axiologically significant in that the autoethnographer is an agential subject who coconstructs cultural meaning (see Pensoneau-Conway and Toyosaki). As such, the autoethnographer is an active subject engaged in praxis toward cultural maintenance, cultural transformation, or both (see Ellis and Calafell; Toyosaki and Pensoneau-Conway).

While critical autoethnographies take many shapes and forms, I use elements of personal narrative, speculative fiction, and poetry to aestheticize my lived experience. My choice to employ these forms is multiple and particular. I use personal narrative as a means by which to interrogate the interrelations coconstituting lived experience, juxtaposed to hegemonic narratives constraining the same (see Bochner and Ellis). I use speculative fiction to blur and bend the edges of so-called "reality" in service of trans modes of being and becoming that evade the intelligibility of normativity (see Leavy; LeMaster and Johnson). Speculative fiction writing allows trans and gender expansive artists, scholars, and activists to pen radically trans-affirming worlds into existence—worlds in which we are already thriving (Johnson and LeMaster). And, finally, I use poetics to convey the affective ruptures that exceed the confines of typical written prose (see Faulkner). The poetic breaks the reader's flow and gaze, shifting our relational imaginaries toward other ways of reading and thus of being and becoming in relation (see Pelias). In this regard, I use critical autoethnography to weave—writing while analyzing—my experiences navigating trans-exclusionary academe as a nonbinary trans femme.

Trans Relational Ambivalences

In this section, I proffer two critical autoethnographic performances on the page. Each performance is constituted by a constellation of personal narrative, speculative fiction, and poetics that aestheticizes my experience navigating academe as a nonbinary trans femme. As queer and trans relational artists, scholars, and activists have long shown us, questions of inclusion and exclusion are complex at best, particularly at the intersections of difference (see Bey; Cohen). For trans and gender expansive folks, feelings of inclusion are thus constrained by the structural being of exclusion just as feelings of exclusion chafe against the structural being of inclusion. In this regard, the performances explore two dialectic tensions: *feeling excluded—being included* and its dialectic reversal, *feeling included—*

being excluded. These dialectic tensions help to frame trans and gender expansive lived experience navigating the cultural politics of inclusion and exclusion (LeMaster et al., "Trans Relational Ambivalences").

Inclusion Hurts: *Feeling Excluded—Being Included*

"I want you to know that I *am* trying." The tenured professor pleads for my understanding and patience. She could stop there but adds, "It's just hard for me, you know."

I don't know, nor do I care, I think, sitting silently on the phone as my elder colleague details the difficulty in affirming transness. As her words blur, I begin to imagine the trans and gender expansive students who've been subjected to this self-avowed ally's very nice (read: hostile) politic. I wonder how they are doing, what they are doing, and if they arc doing at all.

"Hello? Are you there?"

I am jolted out of my dissociative state. "Yes! I'm here. I think you cut out just a little. What were you just saying?"

"Ah! It's probably my connection. Anyways, I was just saying that it's been hard because when you were hired here, you were using he/him pronouns, you know."

My heart begins to race and my face reddens. This is when my voice shakes the most. I hurl, "I have to stop you there. That is absolutely false. I stopped using masculine pronouns in the early 2000s, when I was an undergraduate student and our paths had not yet crossed." I'm winded and faint.

She is speechless. And means well.

The cost to correct colleagues
who misgender
is . . . not worth it.
There's the emotional cost, like
You know, change is hard and slow, Lore;
You have to be patient with me, I'm trying, Lore;
You don't know how hard this is for me, Lore;
You have to assume best intentions, Lore.
The emotional cost is
having to care for your oppressor
with patience.
Then there's the physical cost, like
collapsing on oneself
imploding into dissociative silence
glazed over, glossy-eyed.

Disembodied.
The physical cost of
painful, deteriorating
self-denial.
But then there's the psychological cost, like
wading through mud
in a fog-filled bog
with no direction.
And then there's the intellectual cost, like
knowing the difference between unwillingness and ignorance
before you realize it's already too late.

Spring 2022

RE: navigating academe when representational optics exceed structural design; field notes and minor reflections

Dear gender expansive comrade,

It's been a tough year. It's becoming even tougher as we exit the academic year and enter the summer flow, making a shift from teaching to writing and reflecting and deeper learning—as the Supreme Court is poised to overturn Roe v. Wade, unfurling an intersectional legal nightmare that touches so fucking many contemporary civil rights, and as state municipalities criminalize trans youth, trans-affirming care for youth, and trans female athletes, while demonizing queer and trans-affirming educators and care providers as sexual predators (see Blum; Romano; Yang and Hastings). I do not know whether I am writing this for you or for me. I do not know whether I've been writing these years of field notes for you or for me. Regardless, I offer three suggestions for navigating academe—reflecting stories and experiences spanning my twelve years moving through these not-so-hallowed halls as a first- *and last*-generation college graduate turned teacher-scholar-artist who experiences "inclusion" with hesitation at best.

Refuse to internalize their refusal as your own. You/we aren't losing y/our minds. By way of example, pronouns provide a perfect distraction for conservative and liberal colleagues alike. The conservative will feign "struggle" while the liberal will feign "mastery" over pronouns; meanwhile, you are lost in their discursive mix. Both responses gesture to an epistemic limit that reveals an ontological problem: both camps privilege *what to say* over *how to perceive and sense* a trans and gender expansive person in relational terms that affirm transness while reflexively implicating dis/comfort with gender multiplicity.

In the historic context of US empire, perceiving transness is less a question of affirming wholeness than it is a question of determining humanness relative to whiteness, effectively revealing the racialized grounds out of which gender difference is rendered knowable if not affirmable in US settler institutions at all (see Detournay; Snorton). To be certain, gender binarism is a colonial technology turned settler refrain in which gender multiplicity is historically binarized in the service of securing imperialist futurities on stolen land—imperialist futurities that are anchored in white supremacist expectancies of and for reproductive manhood and womanhood (see Lugones). Against this historic backdrop, inclusion is and will remain painful for trans and gender expansive folks because the representational optics of inclusion will always exceed the structural capacity for fully affirming the vastness of bodily difference.

Name it for what it is: an exclusionary work environment by design. Trans wellness will most likely be unaccounted for in institutional design. The burden of change will fall on you as human resources representatives "inquire" about the work environment. When they ask to learn from you, be cautious about what and when you share and demand compensation for your pedagogical labor (including the memory work it takes to unlock pedagogical insight derived from structural exclusion).

In the recurring case of having to demand regular access to safe gender-neutral restrooms in the workplace, you will probably hear something about "building codes" or some other discursive trick to distract you from the issue at hand: building codes aren't y/our business—you just need a safe place to piss and shit while trying to complete your work tasks, including teaching and reading and writing and thinking. In most instances, the demand for regular access to safe gender-neutral restrooms in the workplace is discursively framed as a "special request" and placed in a competitive hierarchy of other "needs."

Most common is a trio of features that institutional units use to determine the best spaces for scheduling meetings: (1) access to accessible and gender-neutral restrooms, (2) facilities for catering, and (3) technology suited to the presentation of materials. Of these three "needs," the demand for regular access to safe and accessible gender-neutral restrooms in the workplace directly impacts laboring bodies and yet it is put at par with securing a space in which we can enjoy catered hors d'oeuvres, revealing the classed dimensions sustaining trans-exclusionary organizational design.

Moreover, digital platforms (e.g., *Zoom*) have enabled the discursive framing of physical absence or presence in terms of "choice" and "preference." In this context, y/our physical absence from workplace functions will be understood as a "choice" or as a "preference" rather than as an effect of exclusionary organizational design. This is a crucial distinction to maintain, because y/our valid frustration will be misinterpreted as pointless complaints when "you could just as easily choose to join us via *Zoom*," as a well-meaning colleague reminded me . . . again. The materiality of structural design (e.g., building codes) was and is intended to exclude gender multiplicity through the structural binarizing of gender over time and across various publics, including in the workplace and across university campuses. In short, expect to be disappointed.

Expect disappointment and *honor fleeting moments of affirmation*. Y/our niceness won't rupture institutional complicities. Neither will y/our individuated anger. Know this distinction, because administrators, largely with certificates in critical studies, are eager to jump at any opportunity to warp the materiality of exclusionary organizational design into a "team building opportunity" in which self-avowed "allies" find joy in "taking over" a restroom, as a recurring example. Such sordid attempts at "building community" are nothing more than non-trans moves to innocence such that temporary action is mistaken for sustained social change.

Certainly, I took over restrooms in political coalition . . . as an undergraduate student in the early aughts. In 2022, I'm a forty-one-year-old nonbinary trans femme whose urinary system is fucked from being forced to "hold it" all damn day for years. I'm fucking tired and my disabled body requires accommodations, not attempts to assuage non-trans guilt.

The point is this: Best intentions do not facilitate the change necessary for y/our wellness. The worlds that sustain trans and gender expansive life are constituted in political coalition rather than in institutional gestures that secure the cis status quo. Western academe was designed, in part, to contain and shape gender difference in service of white supremacy. In this historic context, so-called "inclusion" of transness is complex at best.

Today I'm thinking about you, my gender expansive kin, navigating the shit in the thick and *together apart*. I'm angry with you. And I'm filled with joy knowing y'all are doing the thing, staying pissed. Take my words, leave my words—but STAY PISSED.

In solidarity,

LL

A Sense of Hope: *Feeling Included—Being Excluded*

José Esteban Muñoz locates the political thrust of queerness in relational movement toward a horizon (*Cruising Utopia*). In this framing, queerness is best understood as a relational labor, rather than as an identity avowed in modernist terms, fueled by anticipatory affects of *hope*—the hope of eventually traversing the horizon's crest as a liberated, queer collective. While its affective drive is anticipatory, queerness is achieved, though it is not sustained. Rather, queerness as a horizon beckons us to honor the relationally constituted sense of that which is possible (Muñoz, "Race"). For example, while gender expansive folks may experience the materiality of structural exclusion through anti-trans organizational design, they can and do enjoy fleeting senses of joy and affirmation that materialize across relational contexts. Rather than seeking or satiating liberal inclusionary gestures, queerness in this radical Muñozian framing honors the ways in which minoritized kith and kin thrive regardless of oppressive conditions. Together and across our intersectional differences, we imagine and cultivate liberatory futures derived from the worldmaking potential fostered in a relational sense of being and becoming together and across space and time.

Spring 2006

"Whoa! Have you heard of this?" I pick up a heavy paperback book from the shelf and turn it toward Don.

She squints her eyes, leaning in while enunciating the title: "*Transgender Studies Reader,* huh? I have not, but how great!" (Stryker and Whittle). She is quite tall, a large, warm presence. "We did not have those terms where I grew up." Don is an Indigenous elder from the North who "isn't quite man or woman," as she describes herself, though she does "prefer feminine pronouns," she once whispered to me in passing as we walked across our home campus.

I nod, looking into her eyes. "Yeah, it still feels out of reach for me somehow. Even in my women's studies classes, the readings all seem hostile to transgender people." I open the book to the table of contents and run my finger along the chapter titles. "Have you even heard of transgender studies as a field?"

Don pauses to think before shaking her head. "No, I can't say that I've heard of that. Only women's studies, like at our school. Isn't that your major?" She shifts the weight of her body from one foot to the other, an indication that it's time to continue moving.

"You know what? I'm gonna buy this book!" I am eager to return to my hotel room and to begin sifting through the pages.

"That seems like the best choice given that silly smile on your face." Don returns the smile and we laugh as we walk up to the register.

This weekend, Don is my institutional escort, lending both technological and moral support for what will be my first academic presentation of my own original research. But right now, we're just wandering around the city, hopping from craft store to bookstore and stopping to try street foods along the way. Perhaps most importantly, we are connecting as intergenerational gender freaks, away from our home campus and out of the gaze of our (un)knowing peers and colleagues.

Fall 2021

My phone buzzes on the edge of the desk. I pick it up and read the message banner: "We're here!"

I smile, stand, and walk to the door. I glance at myself in the mirror before heading out to greet my guests. *Ugh*, I think, startled by my dilapidated state. It's been six months since a dear queer friend and mentor died by suicide. Together, he and I advised many doctoral students, including tonight's guests. *We will drop this care package off one way or the other*, they insisted.

"Hi, Lore!" they say in unison.

My eyes grow small, suggesting a smile behind my mask.

My words
become tears,
    seeing them.
    And we melt
        into a giant puddle.
    Our hardened edges soften together.

They hand me a basket, filled with goodies: stuffed animals, pencils, precooked meals, candies, toys, and a handwritten card expressing their love and support. They recognize the hurt I struggle to name.

They hold me in my hurt.

As I held them in theirs.

Spring 2013

Graduate school daily schedule (or, I couldn't have done this without you, Crystal)

05:30 Wake, shower, and dress.
06:30 Feed and walk the dogs.
07:00 Head to coffee shop to read, write, and course prep.
11:00 Run back home to walk the dogs.
12:00 Teach undergraduate class 1.
13:30 Teach undergraduate class 2.
15:00 Attend doctoral seminar.
17:45 Run home to feed and walk the dogs.
18:15 Ride two hours with Crystal to see your spouse. Cry with her as she drives.
20:15 Visit with spouse under the nurse's watchful eye (Crystal will stay in the car; the hospital brings up too many hard memories for hir). Hold your spouse in silence while she weeps. Do not say too much because the feelings are too hard to process. Just hold her. Allow her to hold you. Kiss her rope-burned neck. But do not cry.
21:00 Hear the announcement that visiting hours are over.

21:05 Cry with Crystal as she drives you back home. Speak about things and feelings that were designed to be forgotten, sordid attempts at processing unfolding traumas in real time.
22:00 Stop and grab food along the way.
23:00 When you get home, and before Crystal helps you walk the dogs, smoke a bowl of Indica, listen to pop music, and laugh about nothing.
00:00 Stay up to read a bit after Crystal leaves.
01:00 Hope to sleep. Try not to think about the days leading up to this moment: the state of Illinois's kidnapping of your spouse for forty-eight hours "while they find a facility that will take someone like her"; your spouse's latest suicide attempt, of which she has no memory; the abuse your spouse is enduring at the hands of nurses and doctors while "on watch," and the abuse you endure every time you correct the nurses and doctors about your spouse's name and gender—or about your marriage at all. Try to think about laughing with Crystal. Try to think about the classes you're teaching or the papers that are due. Think about anything but what's happening.

Repeat.

Coalitional Subjectivities: A Call for Coconspiratorship

In this essay, I perform trans relational ambivalences across two critical autoethnographic constellations. In the first, I contour the dialectic space between subjective feelings of exclusion and the structural being of inclusion. Common to this trans relational ambivalence (*feeling excluded—being included*) is the tension between representational optics and structural capacity to support changing demographics. A common example in my own experience has included the question of access to safe and accessible gender-neutral restrooms in the workspace. While there is an increase in gender expansive visibility, the lack of access to gender-neutral restrooms intensifies our visibility, forcing gender expansive folks into restrooms designed to assert gender binarism—or forcing us to "hold it in" to our own medical detriment. To feel included against such an exclusionary backdrop requires a relational sense of connection that sustains trans and gender expansive life regardless, bringing us to the second of the trans relational ambivalences in this essay: *feeling included—being excluded.* This relational ambivalence highlights the mundane ways queer communal bonds sustain trans and gender expansive life, being, and becoming. Across the stories, I gesture less to trans and gender expansive kith and kin than I do to the communal bonds that facilitate my intersubjective sense of self as a nonbinary trans femme navigating academe and in relation with non-trans kith and kin who care with and for me as if I were their own.

In the end, this essay works against liberal calls for allies. Rather, it calls for coalitional subjectivities that facilitate intersubjective worldmaking (see Carrillo Rowe). Such worldmaking efforts center political commitment to and with others over institutional gestures that presuppose "community." Indeed, this essay reveals that support of trans and gender expansive folks is found less in memorizing pronouns (though this is also important) than it is in radically reconceptualizing how we relate to and with gender difference, including the ways our intersectional differences exacerbate a sense of connection across difference. In this regard, an ally does not go far enough. Rather, this essay envisions a relational coconspiratorship in which relative privileges are used in the service of facilitating a relational sense of safety, wellness, belonging, and survival for and with others. From this vantage, this essay demands a radical shift in hiring practices such that there are more trans and gender expansive kith and kin in academe. At the same time, this essay demands non-trans coconspirators to use their privileges in the service of enacting changes that a small bloc of gender expansive folks cannot achieve on their own. It is in this radical coalitional sense that I have encountered and felt a relational sense of inclusion despite an exclusionary backdrop that struggles to affirm the vastness of transness. And it is in this radical coalitional sense that we begin to better perceive the double movement required for such change to occur: an end to exclusionary practices and a blossoming of inclusionary measures. Together, we in this movement can help balance the current misalignment between an institutional impulse to increase representational optics and the structural incapacity to support the slow-growing number of gender expansive folks in academe. Life after inclusion is bleak and painful, though it is filled with relational hope.

Suggestions for Coconspirators

Become familiar with (proposed and enacted) legislation targeting trans and gender expansive people in your region; organize to resist the criminalization of transness.

If you have access to health insurance, take the time to learn about the types of trans-affirming care that are and are not covered by your plan. Trans masculine and trans feminine people have different needs, just as nonbinary and other gender expansive folks do. Do not accept surface-level responses from administrative figureheads on the matter of health-care access. Organize to expand your plan to include comprehensive trans and gender expansive health care and wellness needs. This includes access to gender-affirming surgeries regardless of personal beliefs.

Learn where the nearest accessible gender-neutral restrooms are in relation to you at all times and ensure that that information is readily available. Organize to expand access to accessible gender-neutral restrooms in the workplace; strive toward universal design. Remember always that "the restroom debate" is a labor issue and as such impacts all workers differently.

Plan social events at locations with accessible gender-neutral restrooms; *never* plan social events at locations with inaccessible or binary bathrooms.

While using one's name and pronouns is a matter of respect, know that epistemic recognition is never enough. Recognition of transness requires an ontological shift in the intersectional ways we understand, live, and embody gender ourselves. Commit to unlearning and relearning gender and relating otherwise.

Consume more stories by trans and gender expansive creators.

Give your money to Black, Indigenous, and other trans and gender expansive people of color rather than to nonprofit organizations that claim to "offer support." Local trans and gender expansive community organizers of color provide immediate and necessary support that keeps trans and gender expansive folks alive.

Set up a legal fund to protect trans and gender expansive folks in addition to parents of trans and gender expansive youth in your region.

DO NOT LOOK AWAY.

NOTE

1. I draw on fiction writing as research practice to performatively script my critical autoethnographic interrogation of (un)belonging after inclusion in the context of academe. Writing on fiction as research practice, Patricia Leavy argues, "The practice of writing and reading fiction allows us to access imaginary or possible worlds, to reexamine the worlds we live in, and to enter into the psychological processes that motivate people and the social worlds that shape them" (20). Drawing on the social scientific goal of verisimilitude, I seek to craft "realistic, authentic, and life-like portrayal[s]" that "come from real life and genuine human experience" (21). In this regard, all references to people or places are fictionalized and rooted in my own lived experience as a nonbinary trans femme moving through academe.

WORKS CITED

Adams, Tony E., et al., editors. *Handbook of Autoethnography.* 2nd ed., Routledge, 2022.

Arvin, Maile, et al. "Decolonizing Feminism: Challenging Connections between Settler Colonialism and Heteropatriarchy." *Feminist Formations*, vol. 25, no. 1, spring 2013, pp. 8–34. *JSTOR*, www.jstor.org/stable/43860665.

Awkward-Rich, Cameron, and Hil Malatino. "Meanwhile, T4t." *Transgender Studies Quarterly*, vol. 9, no. 1, Feb. 2022, pp. 1–8, https://doi.org/10.1215/23289252-9475467.

Berlant, Lauren, and Michael Warner. "Sex in Public." *Critical Inquiry*, vol. 24, no. 2, winter 1998, pp. 547–66. *JSTOR*, www.jstor.org/stable/1344178.

Bey, Marquis. "Trouble Genders: 'LGBT' Collapse and Trans Fundamentality." *Hypatia*, vol. 36, no. 1, winter 2021, pp. 191–206, http://doi.org/10.1017/hyp.2020.52.

Blum, Steven. "The Alt-Right's Ongoing Obsession with Demonizing Gay People as Predators." *Vice*, 3 Nov. 2017, www.vice.com/en/article/wjgzyq/the-alt-rights-ongoing-obsession-with-demonizing-gay-people-as-predators.

Bochner, Arthur P., and Caroline Ellis. *Evocative Autoethnography: Writing Lives and Telling Stories*. Routledge, 2016.

Boylorn, Robin M., and Mark P. Orbé. "Becoming: A Critical Autoethnography on Critical Autoethnography." *Journal of Autoethnography*, vol. 2, no. 1, winter 2021, pp. 5–12, https://doi.org/10.1525/joae.2021.2.1.5.

———, editors. *Critical Autoethnography: Intersecting Cultural Identities in Everyday Life*. 2nd ed., Routledge, 2021.

Byrd, Jodi A. "What's Normative Got to Do with It?: Toward Indigenous Queer Relationality." *Social Text*, vol. 38, no. 4, Dec. 2020, pp. 105–23, https://doi.org/10.1215/01642472-8680466.

Carrillo Rowe, Aimee. "Subject to Power—Feminism without Victims." *Women's Studies in Communication*, vol. 32, no. 1, 2009, pp. 12–35, https://doi.org/10.1080/07491409.2009.10162379.

Cohen, Cathy J. "Punks, Bulldaggers, and Welfare Queens: The Radical Potential of Queer Politics?" *GLQ: A Journal of Gay and Lesbian Studies*, vol. 3, no. 4, May 1997, pp. 437–65, https://doi.org/10.1215/10642684-3-4-437.

Collins, Patricia Hill. "Reflections on the Outsider Within." *Journal of Career Development*, 26, no. 1, fall 1999, pp. 85–88, https://doi.org/10.1177/089484539902600107.

Detournay, Diane. "The Racial Life of 'Cisgender': Reflections on Sex, Gender and the Body." *Parallax*, vol. 25, no. 1, 2019, pp. 58–74, https://doi.org/10.1080/13534645.2019.1570606.

Dickinson, Nathaniel. "Seizing the Means: Towards a Trans Epistemology." Gleeson and O'Rourke, pp. 204–18.

Eguchi, Shinsuke. "Queer Intercultural Relationality: An Autoethnography of Asian-Black (Dis)Connections in White Gay America." *Journal of International and Intercultural Communication*, vol. 8, no. 1, 2015, pp. 27–43, https://doi.org/10.1080/17513057.2015.991077.

Eguchi, Shinsuke, and Hannah R. Long. "Queer Relationality as Family: Yas Fats! Yas Femmes! Yas Asians!" *Journal of Homosexuality*, vol. 66, no. 11, 2019, pp. 1589–608, https://doi.org/10.1080/00918369.2018.1505756.

Ellis, Carolyn, et al. "Autoethnography: An Overview." *Historical Social Research*, vol. 36, no. 4, 2011, pp. 273–90. *JSTOR*, www.jstor.org/stable/23032294.

Ellis, Cassidy D., and Bernadette Marie Calafell. "Toward Praxis: Interrogating Social Justice within Autoethnography." *Journal of Autoethnography*, vol. 1, no. 2, spring 2020, pp. 203–07, https://doi.org/10.1525/joae.2020.1.2.203.

Faulkner, Sandra L. *Poetic Inquiry: Craft, Method, and Practice*. 2nd ed., Routledge, 2020.

Gleeson, Jules Joanne, and Elle O'Rourke, editors. *Transgender Marxism*. Pluto Press, 2021.

Goltz, Dustin Bradley, and Jason Zingsheim, editors. *Queer Praxis: Questions for LGBTQ Worldmaking.* Peter Lang, 2015.

Grande, Sandy. *Red Pedagogy: Native American Social and Political Thought.* 10th anniversary ed., Rowman and Littlefield, 2015.

Gutierrez-Perez, Robert, and Luis Andrade. "Queer of Color Worldmaking: <Marriage> in the Rhetorical Archive and the Embodied Repertoire." *Text and Performance Quarterly*, vol. 38, nos. 1–2, 2018, pp. 1–18, https://doi.org/10.1080/10462937.2018.1435130.

Hwang, Ren-yo. "Deviant Care for Deviant Futures: QTBIPoC Radical Relationalism as Mutual Aid against Carceral Care." *Transgender Studies Quarterly*, vol. 6, no. 4, Nov. 2019, pp. 559–78, https://doi.org/10.1215/23289252-7771723.

James, Sandy E., et al. *The Report of the 2015 U.S. Transgender Survey.* National Center for Transgender Equality, 2016.

Johnson, Amber. "How Intersectional Autoethnography Saved My Life: A Plea for Intersectional Inquiry." Adams et al., pp. 147–54.

Johnson, Amber, and Lore/tta LeMaster [*published as* B. LeMaster]. *Gender Futurity, Intersectional Autoethnography: Embodied Theorizing from the Margins.* Routledge, 2020.

Leavy, Patricia. *Fiction as Research Practice: Short Stories, Novellas, and Novels.* E-book ed., Routledge, 2016.

LeMaster, Lore/tta [*published as* B. LeMaster]. "Notes on Trans Relationality." *QED: A Journal in GLBTQ Worldmaking*, vol. 4, no. 2, summer 2017, pp. 84–92, https://doi.org/10.14321/qed.4.2.0084.

LeMaster, Lore/tta, and Amber Johnson. "Speculative Fiction, Criticality, and Futurity: An Introduction." *Communication and Critical/Cultural Studies*, vol. 18, no. 3, 2021, pp. 280–82, https://doi.org/10.1080/14791420.2021.1953699.

LeMaster, Lore/tta [*published as* B. LeMaster], and Meggie Mapes. "Embracing the Criminal: Queer and Trans Relational Liberatory Pedagogies." *Queer Intercultural Communication: The Intersectional Politics of Belonging in and across Differences*, edited by Shinsuke Eguchi and Bernadette Marie Calafell, Rowman and Littlefield, 2019, pp. 63–78.

LeMaster, Lore/tta, and Satoshi Toyosaki. "Ally as an Emerging Critical Orientation: Performing Praxis-Oriented Ally Subjectivity." *Journal of Homosexuality*, vol. 70, no. 1, 2023, pp. 88–110.

LeMaster, Lore/tta, et al. "Trans Relational Ambivalences: A Critical Analysis of Trans and Gender Non-conforming Relational (Un)belonging in Sport Contexts." *Women's Studies in Communication*, vol. 6, no. 1, 2023, pp. 42–64, https://doi.org/10.1080/07491409.2022.2156418.

LeMaster, Lore/tta [*published as* B. LeMaster], et al. "Unlearning Cisheteronormativity at the Intersections of Difference: Performing Queer Worldmaking through Collaged Relational Autoethnography." *Text and Performance Quarterly*, vol. 39, no. 4, 2019, pp. 341–70, https://doi.org/10.1080/10462937.2019.1672885.

Lugones, María. "Gender and Universality in Colonial Methodology." *Critical Philosophy of Race*, vol. 8, nos. 1–2, Jan. 2020, pp. 25–47, https://doi.org/10.5325/critphilrace.8.1-2.0025.

Malatino, Hil. *Trans Care*. U of Minnesota P, 2020.

Moreman, Shane T., and Stephanie R. Briones. "Deaf Queer World-Making: A Thick Intersectional Analysis of the Mediated Cultural Body." *Journal of International and Intercultural Communication*, vol. 11, no. 3, 2018, pp. 216–32, https://doi.org/10.1080/17513057.2018.1456557.

Muñoz, José Esteban. *Cruising Utopia: The Then and There of Queer Futurity*. New York UP. 2009.

———. "Race, Sex, and the Incommensurate." *Queer Futures*, edited by Elahe Haschemi Yekani et al., Ashgate, 2013, pp. 103–16.

Nicolazzo, Z. *Trans* in College: Transgender Students' Strategies for Navigating Campus Life and the Institutional Politics of Inclusion*. Routledge, 2016.

Otis, Hailey N., and Thomas R. Dunn. "Queer Worldmaking." *Oxford Research Encyclopedia of Communication*, edited by Isaac N. West et al., 2022, oxfordre.com/communication/view/10.1093/acrefore/9780190228613.001.0001/acrefore-9780190228613-e-1235.

Parks, Elizabeth S. "The Hybrid I/Eye: A Critical Autoethnography of Intersecting Race and Disability Identities." *Journal of Autoethnography*, vol. 2, no. 1, winter 2021, pp. 26–38, https://doi.org/10.1525/joae.2021.2.1.26.

Pelias, Ronald J. "Writing Autoethnography: The Personal, Poetic, and Performative as Compositional Strategies." Adams et al., pp. 121–32.

Pensoneau-Conway, Sandra L., and Satoshi Toyosaki. "Automethodology: Tracing a Home for Praxis-Oriented Ethnography." *International Journal of Qualitative Methods*, vol. 10, no. 4, 2011, 378–99, https://doi.org/10.1177/160940691101000406.

Romano, Aja. "The Right's Moral Panic over 'Grooming' Invokes Age-Old Homophobia." *Vox*, 21 Apr. 2022, www.vox.com/culture/23025505/leftist-groomers-homophobia-satanic-panic-explained.

Rosentel, Kris, et al. "Black Transgender Women and the School-to-Prison Pipeline: Exploring the Relationship between Anti-Trans Experiences in School and Adverse Criminal-Legal System Outcomes." *Sexuality Research and Social Policy*, vol. 18, 2021, pp. 481–94, https://doi.org/10.1007/s13178-020-00473-7.

Snapp, Shannon D., et al. "Messy, Butch, and Queer: LGBTQ Youth and the School-to-Prison Pipeline." *Journal of Adolescent Research*, vol. 30, no. 1, 2015, pp. 57–82, https://doi.org/10.1177/0743558414557625.

Snorton, C. Riley. *Black on Both Sides: A Racial History of Trans Identity*. U of Minnesota P, 2017.

Stryker, Susan, and Stephen Whittle, editors. *The Transgender Studies Reader*. Routledge, 2006.

Toyosaki, Satoshi, and Sandra L. Pensoneau-Conway. "Autoethnography as a Praxis of Social Justice: Three Ontological Contexts." Adams et al., pp. 557–75.

Yang, John, and Dorothy Hastings. "Michigan Sen. Mallory McMorrow Explains Why She Stood Up to a Culture War Attack." *PBS*, 22 Apr. 2022, www.pbs.org/newshour/show/michigan-sen-mallory-mcmorrow-explains-why-stood-up-to-a-culture-war-attack.

Yep, Gust A. "Further Notes on Healing from 'The Violence of Heteronormativity in Communication Studies.'" *QED: A Journal in GLBTQ Worldmaking*, vol. 4, no. 2, summer 2017, pp. 115–22, https://doi.org/10.14321/qed.4.2.0115.

———. "The Violence of Heteronormativity in Communication Studies." *Journal of Homosexuality*, vol. 45, nos. 2–4, 2003, pp. 11–59, https://doi.org/10.1300/J082v45n02_02.

Zazanis, Noah. "Social Reproduction and Social Cognition: Theorizing (Trans)Gender Identity Development in Community Context." Gleeson and O'Rourke, pp. 33–46.

Confronting Privilege

Into the Fray: Let's Go Forward into Justice and Topics Far-Reaching

Simon J. Ortiz

Justice? What justice? What is justice, anyway? Are you talking to me and about me as an Indigenous person?

Yes, those feel like questions I've felt quivering inside of me since I was very young. I've mentally and bodily experienced these sorts of questions since I was a little boy at home in Deetseyaamah (McCartys on the state road map), on the Acoma Indian reservation in New Mexico, in the United States of America, where I grew up with my family. That's where, when, and how I became conscious of the world and life around me. And it is the locale and context in which I became aware I was an Acoma boy who lived in an Acoma world.

I think perhaps even before I had fully learned to express myself—before I realized I had to express myself in order to understand and cope with the world around me, and before I realized it was necessary to express myself as an "Indian kid" who already had come to know it felt wrong to be Indian—yes, back then, when I felt belittled, degraded, demeaned, and restricted because I didn't understand much English, I began to realize I had to learn English in order to survive. Is that when I began to think, What is justice, anyhow? Yes, of course, needless to say, as a little boy I did not yet know and understand the concept of justice either.

Meh'rii-gaano dzeh-nee: American speech. American white people—Meh'rii-gaano neeyah gah-dzeeya—spoke that language. I learned that fact before I went to school, actually. I overheard a conversation between my parents and other Acoma relatives. They were talking about an Indigenous man from a tribe in Washington state, a teacher at McCartys Day School, the Acoma reservation school. That is when I learned from my Acoma Pueblo parents and other Acoma relatives that it was wrong to speak our Indigenous Acoma language at school. Because school was for the purpose of learning the Meh'rii-gaano dzeh-nee neeyah, speaking our Aacqumeh dzeh-nee was not permitted there. Students were punished harshly when they spoke their tribal language to each other in school.

Overhearing that conversation made me wary of going to school. Although I was perhaps only four years of age then, I began to feel nervous and uneasy about school. When I asked my parents about school and why we had to go, they told me school was important because it was helpful to learn the ways and customs of American life, since we had become American citizens. And we might even come to live amongst Meh'rii-gaano teetra in the future. I admit I did not like the idea of living with them much. It made me nervous and anxious to think about that. That meant change, including the use of the Meh'rii-gaano dzeh-nee.

I didn't fully understand what I'd been told, so later I asked my mother, "Kqow Meh'rii-cano meh neewowtra tudruu'mah?" ("The American way—is it going to be like that for us?") Years later, I became concerned and worried about Americanism that is founded and based largely upon the conquest and acquisition of Indigenous lands and resources (generally called colonial settlement by force). Will we become like that too if we're not already? Will we become like them? Will our Indigenous human sense of things and our Indigenous—by the late 1990s I had pretty much stopped using the word or term "Indian"—culture, identity, language, feelings, and our way of life be no longer possible?

And then what?

I'm now almost in my mid-eighties. I'm a parent of three grown children, all with college degrees, and a grandparent to a number of growing grandchildren and great-grandchildren. I'm pretty near the eldest of the Dyaamee Hanoh (Eagle Clan) at Aacqu, my original cultural life source. I'm a relatively educated person, a retired university regents professor, and an internationally known poet, writer, and Indigenous elder.

"And then what?" is not a resolution. I'm still somewhat stuck behind the barriers of what I began this brief essay with: Justice? What justice? What is justice, anyway? Are you talking to me and about me as an Indigenous person?

For now, that is my situation. And it's the situation that all the millions of Indigenous Peoples of the North, Central, and South Americas are in too.

Phoenix

Austin Davis

1.

This red and orange
bird rising from its ashes
is my home.
In its belly, our coldest days
are a summer night to most.
Our language is water,
ice,
gathering inside a Circle K
for air conditioning.
Two bodies dance in the canal,
a shot of Tito's chills the bone,
so much skin is washed
in the gutters and lakes
once we're all asleep.

2.

Phoenix,
where our rooftops
are slanted like wings,
but the adobe tile
is too smooth to lie on
and watch the stars from.

Phoenix,
where we shake hands,
laugh about our shared sweat,
admire the shapes of cacti,
but never look each other in the eye.
Phoenix,
where the state capitol
is two blocks from the tent city
and wealth and poverty
are two sides of the same street.

3.

A mother waters
the tumbleweeds
with dark brown urine.
Two lovers spoon on the sidewalk.
A child thinner
than the sycamore branches
stares at the sun
but doesn't blink,
cry, or look away.
We've been caught in the flames
for so long, I can only hope
we'll still be reborn.

You Do . . . and So Do We

Nikki Giovanni

Who needs to understand a Billionaire is the most unnecessary thing on Earth? *You Do.*

Who needs to know there can be no joy nor pleasure just because there is power and money? *You Do.*

Who needs to know Health is the one personal thing that doesn't belong to you? *You Do.*

Who needs to insist Water should be pure, Air should be clean, and Animals should have parks to live and breed in? *You Do.*

Who needs to vote that senators and representatives can only serve as long as the president? *You Do.*

Who needs to quit being afraid of folk who have different-colored skin, who worship God differently, who speak another language, who love another or the same person? *You Do.*

Who needs to think why Edward VII couldn't marry a white American divorcée; Margaret couldn't marry Peter Townsend; but Prince Harry could marry a Black woman? What did the Queen have in mind? Maybe that Rule Britannia should be more than a song so the fifth in line marries a Black American divorcée and everyone is happy. Who needs to think how long it will be before the Crown reaches out to the Gay community? *You Do.*

I remember when irons got hot enough to scorch clothes, telephones were on something called a party line, and there were signs that said Colored and White. *Do You?*

But mostly, who needs to be ready to concede when another life form visits us that we are not from the United States in North America or France in Europe or China in Asia or Ghana in Africa or any country or continent but Earth? *You Do.*

There is some joy and reason in the meeting of Europe and Africa that we have not explored.

Who needs to pay our teachers and graduate students so that we can explore that relationship? *You Do.*

It is time to move to the Twenty-First Century. Who is brave enough to go forward and save our Democracy? *We Are. Maybe.*

The Uses and Abuses of Privilege

Maureen T. Reddy

The idea that people can use their privilege for good has gained considerable popular currency in recent years. How-to articles, blogs, and social media posts offer tips on ways that white allies of people of color, male allies of women, straight allies of 2SLGBTQIA+ people, or cis allies of trans people might employ their own socially privileged positions to further the cause of social justice. A *Google* search in mid-September 2020 returned 329,000 results for the phrase "use your privilege," an increase of 242,400 from the same search in May 2019. Few of those results are from earlier than 2016. Although I would like to find unalloyed hope in such efforts, Audre Lorde's warning about the master's tools echoes in my head. Isn't *any* use of privilege by definition employing the master's tools? Was Lorde wrong—can those tools actually dismantle the master's house? Can using privilege eventually lead to ending privilege? Or is this notion of using white privilege, to focus on the most frequently cited type of privilege in these contexts, just another way of placing white people at the center once again and making them (us, in my case) feel okay about their (our) status in the world in the absence of meaningful change? Many suggestions for using privilege initially seem relatively unproblematic, such as the idea that those of us who are not under direct attack should speak up *every time* we see or hear something bigoted or the assertion that those with privilege should use not only our voices but also our votes and any other tools available, including our bodies (at marches and rallies, for example), in the service of social justice.

At the same time that the concept of using one's privilege has become familiar, organizations explicitly dedicated to allyship of various kinds have proliferated, and some older ally organizations have gained new life by greatly increasing their membership. Two of the oldest such groups, Parents and Friends of Lesbians and Gays (PFLAG, founded in 1972) and Showing Up for Racial Justice (SURJ, founded as Community Change Inc. in 1968), are also perhaps the best known. Both offer extensive resources and support for allies, and PFLAG established a related organization, Straight for Equality, in 2007 to share resources online with those who have straight privilege. The trenchant critiques of these organizations by people from the groups they were supposedly founded to support illustrate precisely the difficulty with attempting to use one's privilege. As the activist DiDi Delgado wrote in 2017, "White people have a sense of entitlement that POC rarely develop, and they bring that entitlement with them everywhere." Describing the results of her attempts to discover the relationship between SURJ and the Black people to whom they claimed to be accountable, Delgado sums up her views:

> If there's one thing white people DON'T need, it's more spaces reserved for their comfort at the expense and exclusion of people of color. I understand there are white folks eager to openly dismantle racism and flex their social justice vocabulary without burdening POC. To those people, I'd suggest focusing on pre-existing white spaces: their homes, their office buildings, their college campuses, their financial institutions, their health care facilities, their shopping centers, and every other space designed exclusively with them in mind.

Delgado jokes that SURJ looks a lot like the Klan in its whiteness. Using privilege often looks a lot like enjoying privilege.

Using privilege can be identical to enjoying privilege in fact as well as in appearance. Two recent examples illustrate that unfortunate truth. The Wall of Moms, a group invented to put white bodies between Black protesters and the Portland, Oregon, police at demonstrations in the wake of the murder of George Floyd by Minneapolis police officers in May 2020, quickly devolved into a space that centered white experiences and white authority. The group imploded around accusations that its founder, who describes herself as a white-appearing Mexican American woman, had not been truthful about the relationship between Wall of Moms and the Black-led Don't Shoot Portland. That founder's filing to incorporate the group as a 501(c)(3)—without the knowledge or participation of any Black people—exacerbated the tensions within and surrounding the group.[1] Those same demonstrations led to calls on institutions of all kinds to join efforts to dismantle white supremacy and bring about social justice. Those calls, in turn, led to a flood of often empty pledges and statements of support, many of which stand as performances of privilege disguised as performances of allyship; arguably, "performative allyship" is a distinct form of performing privilege. In one egregious example, Harvard University's president, Lawrence Bacow, issued a statement billed as "a message to the Harvard community on the killing of George Floyd." Bacow's statement included just one sentence on the murder and otherwise focused on Bacow's personal memories of 1968 and vague hopes that "we" will do better. This statement performs privilege by centering white experiences and by taking for granted that his readers will care about one white man's experiences more than they care about the murder of George Floyd or the experiences of *any* Black people. A Harvard PhD candidate, Nadirah Farah Foley, told a reporter, "As I read his message, with its affirmation of his belief in the American Dream, constitutionally-guaranteed civil rights, and American exceptionalism/imperialism, I couldn't stop thinking about how privileged one must be to write those words while Black people's reality consistently shows many of President Bacow's beliefs to be mere myths" (McKenzie). While almost certainly imagining himself to be *using* his privilege to advocate for social justice, Bacow in actuality *performed* his privilege. The uselessness of performative allyship seems obvious to BIPOC, whereas many white people seem not to realize that it exists even as we engage in it. That obliviousness is not unique to white people at colleges and universities, but it may be more pervasive on campuses than elsewhere, because college and university faculties have a preponderance of white people who see ourselves as progressive or liberal and who also are used to being seen by others as authorities. Both the founder of the Wall of Moms and Bacow abused their white privilege by using it to reinforce that privilege.

This essay interrogates the use of privilege—regarding race, gender, and sexuality—in the service of social justice, with a particular focus on the college classroom, where privilege usually masquerades as authority. I consider whether there is a meaningful difference between using privilege for good and simply accepting unearned privilege and, if so, whether that difference is visible to others, which I believe matters. That is, to offer one example, can students tell the difference between my using white privilege to advance racial justice and my accepting unearned authority as my due? If so, how? The former action supposedly undermines white privilege whereas the latter reinforces it, yet the distinction only holds if it is obvious to observers. My motives don't matter; the effects of my actions do.

Let me offer an anecdote that illustrates part of the problem with conferred authority on college campuses. In 2018, I was one of three speakers at a panel discussion on activism sponsored by a Black student organization at Rhode Island College (my home institution). At the end, a Black student asked the panel for advice on hanging onto hope for anti-racist activism in the face of what felt like increasingly horrible national news. I turned to another panelist, a Black man who is well known locally because he is often at the forefront of actions for social justice, but he nodded at me and then toward the audience, which made me realize that many audience members were looking at me and seemed to be waiting for my answer. I said that it wasn't for me—a white person, a faculty member—to tell her, or any Black student, what they should do; they needed to make that decision themselves, but I could tell her what helped me when I felt hope and energy flagging, which I did. Once the event ended, the student who had asked the question sought me out and thanked me, saying that I had made her feel hopeful and more determined than ever to keep fighting for racial justice. I was glad I had been helpful but left the event puzzled and concerned. Why had people turned to me to respond? As I drove home, I went back over the remarks I had made and those made by the other two speakers (both Black men) but didn't recall anything that would explain why I had seemed to many of the students (and to the other two speakers) to be the person who should answer that particular question. Of the sixty people at the event, only four had been white-appearing. In a room full of people of color, I would never have looked to a white woman to answer this question posed by a student of color, and I was taken aback that others had. What was that about, I wondered. Was there something in the way I presented myself that made me seem especially hopeful or authoritative? Or was it my whiteness? Did I project an air of entitlement? Did my whiteness signify "authority" even to students of color and even on the subject of race and anti-racist work? Or had the listeners and panelists turned to me because in that specific place in that moment, I was an obvious representative of the people who *should* work against white supremacy and racism? That is, white supremacy and racism belong to white people. We created them and we maintain them; we therefore should be the ones working most assiduously to dismantle them. I hoped that was the reason, but I did not know and had no way to find out without making the student questioner feel uncomfortable. How do white people effectively work against racism in racially mixed spaces when even as we do that work, racism is being reinforced by our very presence, our assumed right to speak, our assumed authority? One option might be to restrict ourselves to all-white groups, but that option has its own major problems, as I note above. Similarly, how do straight, cis, and straight-cis people work against gender and sexuality biases when 2SLGBTQIA+ authority with straight, cis, and straight-cis people derives partly from conformity to privileged social positions?

When Bonnie TuSmith and I were working on our collection of essays, *Race in the College Classroom: Pedagogy and Politics*, in the early 2000s, more white people were in denial about the continuing significance of racism in all our lives than are now as I write this essay in 2020. I believe there is still today more awareness of how racism negatively affects BIPOC than of how white supremacy positively affects white people, despite increased lip service given to white privilege. It would be hard to cling to the view that racism is an artifact of the past in the face of the constant barrage of news reports of overt racism, from police murders of Black people to white supremacist gatherings and marches to casual remarks by the forty-fifth president of the United States. Nonetheless, I suspect that some of what Bonnie and I found in 2002 continues to be the case almost two decades later, perhaps especially in the ways that white people benefit from white supremacy. For instance, quite a few of the college and university professors with whom we spoke then, including several who contributed to our collection, described experiences of being punished for teaching about race, including in student evaluations and in peer evaluations for tenure or promotion. Unsurprisingly, perhaps, faculty members of color were far more likely to report such an experience than were white faculty members, at least some of whom acknowledged that they had been rewarded for teaching exactly the literature and history that faculty members of color had been criticized for discussing. I am certain that this gap—a clear example of white supremacy positively affecting whites, not just of racism negatively affecting BIPOC—persists.

As another example of what endures, my own essay in that collection—"Smashing the Rules of Racial Standing"—focused on my still-ongoing attempts in my classes to undermine what Derrick Bell lays out as the structure of the authority to speak about race. According to the second "rule of racial standing" posited by Bell, "Not only are blacks' complaints discounted, but black victims of racism are less effective witnesses than are whites, who are members of the oppressor class. This phenomenon reflects a widespread assumption that blacks, unlike whites, cannot be objective on racial issues and will favor their own no matter what" (113). Although Bell focuses on the Black/white divide, what he has to say about standing—that is, the right to speak and to be heard—works across most privileged / not privileged divides and is not limited to Black-white interactions. In that essay, I argue that when white-conferred authority (as opposed to earned authority) is not openly examined in the classroom, it insidiously retakes its powerful position, regardless of the professor's intentions. I was confident in 2002 that no white person could use conferred authority—the most pervasive variety of white privilege in predominantly white academic institutions—to fight against racism, in part because few students understand what legitimate academic authority should rest upon and how narrow its limits are. The default position of most students seems to be that the person at the front of the classroom deserves to be there, but that default is only certain when the professor is a white, straight-appearing man.[2] Anyone else can expect at least occasional doubts about their professional authority. Trying to use one's white, straight, and/or male privilege to bolster student confidence in professors who lack that privilege is a doomed and contradictory effort. Instead, such a use of privilege simply reinforces and extends privilege so that the white, straight, and/or male professor presents as an authority not only on one subject or in one classroom but also on the very composition of all of academe, with the right to determine who belongs there. Conferred authority—privilege—is one of the master's tools that those of us whom it benefits must discard; indeed, we have to discard it over and over again, all the while knowing it will keep coming back.

One reason that conferred authority has such staying power in classrooms is that the academy remains a white, straight, cis place with some 2SLGBTQIA+ people and people of color in it. Academe is sometimes called an ivory tower, a phrase I quite dislike and seldom use because it is often meant disparagingly, intending to suggest that we who work in higher education are out of touch with the "real world" and that while our scholarship may sometimes be interesting, it is certainly useless—more a decorative object than a tool for living. Although this perception of academics surely applies to some professors, for the most part, it is a mistaken or at least largely outmoded one. Our campuses reflect the larger society in a variety of ways; we live not apart from society but in a kind of compressed and therefore especially intense version of it. However, the ivory tower deserves that name in one obvious way, and that is when we consider that ivory is a color. Academe is largely ivory (white), both in its populations and in its values and ways of operating, including its underlying assumptions. Further, towers were in the past often built as fortresses to defend against invaders. Academe functions as a tower in this way: as a kind of stronghold protecting traditional (that is, white-authorized) ways of knowing and objects of knowledge, including even what counts as "knowledge." Surveys tend to show that academics are generally more liberal or progressive than conservative in their views, which loosely corresponds with conservative nonacademics' stereotypes of the academy (Jaschek). However, the views that people espouse and their self-conceptions may be very far indeed from how they actually behave. Even liberal and progressive white people participate in reproducing the structure of white supremacy in myriad ways every day. One fairly objective way to examine academe's behavior is to look at some numbers.

In 2022, according to a census update, the population of the United States was 58.9% "white alone" (separating out respondents who selected "white" as a subcategory of "Hispanic or Latino"), 19.1% "Hispanic or Latino," 13.6% "Black or African American alone," and 6.3% "Asian alone." Other groups, including those listed in the census as "two or more races," each accounted for less than 3% of the population ("QuickFacts"). Of the only two gender identity options offered, 49.5% of respondents identified in the census as male and 50.4% as female ("Table B01001"). In the fall of 2016—the most recent report available and close enough to the date of the census report that the numbers are broadly comparable—of all full-time professors at postsecondary degree-granting institutions,

> 41 percent were White males; 35 percent were White females; 6 percent were Asian/Pacific Islander males; 4 percent were Asian/Pacific Islander females; 3 percent each were Black males, Black females, and Hispanic males; and 2 percent were Hispanic females. Those who were American Indian/Alaska Native and those who were of Two or more races each made up 1 percent or less of full-time faculty in these institutions. (McFarland et al. 185)[3]

In other words, every group other than white males and females and Asian or Pacific Islander males and females is underrepresented in the professoriate, particularly Hispanic or Latino males and females (18.1% vs. 6%) and Black males and females (13.4% vs. 6%). Leadership roles in postsecondary education are unrepresentative not only of the general population but also of the already unrepresentative professoriate. According to the American Council on Education's college president survey of 2017, 70% of college presidents are men; 83% are white; and so-called minority presidents are more likely to lead public institutions than private ones and far more likely to lead associate-granting institutions than any other Carnegie category (that is, they are clustered in the less prestigious and less well-paid places). The least represented group across all institutions, according to the survey, is Black women (*American College President Study*). A report in *Inside Higher Ed* in February 2022 noted a surge in the hiring of college presidents in the eighteen months following the murder of George Floyd and the ensuing protests. During that period—June 2020 through November 2021—35.4% "of presidents and chancellors that American colleges and universities hired were members of racial minority groups," 25% of them Black, although only 13% were women of color (Lederman). Yet the vast majority of the top jobs remain in the hands of white people, especially white men. In sum, the racial makeup both of the professoriate and of presidencies suggests that postsecondary education *belongs to* white people; the overrepresentation of whites in higher education reinforces white authority as a norm in postsecondary institutions.

And what about the students? The good news—or what at first seems to be good news—is that the college enrollment gap between white people and people of color has narrowed across time. Recent high school graduates enroll in two-year or four-year colleges at similar rates across racial lines: in the 60%–70% range for Black, white, and Latino students and somewhat higher for Asian students (Casselman). But there is "a big gap in the number that ultimately matters most: 'educational attainment,' or the amount of school a person completes. In 2013, about 40 percent of whites between the ages of 25 and 29 had a bachelor's degree or more, as compared to about 20 percent of Blacks, 15 percent of Hispanics and 58 percent of Asians, according to data from the Current Population Survey" (Casselman). The seventh annual college completion report by the National Student Clearinghouse Research Center shows that, despite increases of more than 1% between 2017 and 2018 in the six-year completion rates of Black and Hispanic students, "Asian and white students continue to have much higher completion rates than black and Hispanic students, regardless of the level or sector of the starting institution. . . . Asian students showed the highest completion rate at 70.3%, followed by white students at 67.1%. Black and Hispanic students had much lower completion rates (41.0% and 49.6%, respectively)" (Shapiro et al.). Other racial groups attend and complete college in such small numbers that they are not tracked in these reports or are lumped together as "Other."[4]

Anyone who wants to use their white privilege to combat racism needs to understand the reality in which we are actually operating. That is, in terms of race, academe as a whole continues to be an ivory tower, where the whiteness of the academy reproduces itself. People of color run up against myriad discriminatory attitudes and practices within that ivory tower, some of which are subtle enough not to occur to most white professors right away. For example, Stanford University's Center for Education Policy Analysis released a study in 2018 that demonstrates strong racial and gender bias in online education, an area that has often been touted by its proponents as more equitable than in-person education (Baker et al.). That bias became especially troubling in 2020 as postsecondary institutions across the US moved their classes online in response to the COVID-19 pandemic. A collection of essays about the emphasis on "accountability" in recent educational policies stresses how accountability systems across the US postsecondary landscape have overlooked and therefore undermined issues of racial and economic injustice (Orfield and Hillman). Considering the gap between completion rates for white and Asian students on the one hand and Black and Latinx students on the other, it is indisputable that there are persistent barriers to true racial equality in academe. This is concerning not only for its own sake but also because of the outsized role of postsecondary education in determining other life chances. Without social justice in academe, the chances for justice in the wider society are diminished, especially that important component of social justice, economic justice.

College and university presidents are well positioned to use their power—and, as is often the case, their white privilege—to take bold steps in the service of social justice. Although official statements by presidents in response to the unrest sparked by the murder of George Floyd tended to be akin to Bacow's in their emptiness, several presidents and other administrators seized the moment to do more. The president of the University of Minnesota, Joan Gabel, for example, ended the school's contract with the Minneapolis police department, which the university had used for security at big events (Adams). Some decisive actions have been taken by individual departments as well; the University of Chicago's English Department drew predictable criticisms after announcing it would admit only graduate students interested in pursuing Black studies in the 2020–21 admissions cycle (Flaherty). That decision—to admit only five students total—has proved to be far more controversial than the decisions of many humanities departments around the US to suspend PhD admissions entirely for the 2020–21 academic year.

In addition to broad political action at both the local and national levels to advocate for policies and practices that increase the participation and achievement of people of color at all levels of the postsecondary system, on our own campuses and on others, there are things professors with privilege can do individually that may make a difference in the lives of our students and our colleagues who lack that privilege, but they do not involve "using" our privilege except to undermine that privilege. We who have privilege can legitimately use it in our classrooms and on our campuses to remind others with privilege about that shared advantage and to fight against continuing inequities. Any other use is an abuse. We can leverage our privilege to pressure our institutions to behave in a more equitable way, whether that is through changing hiring practices, removing police from campus, or similar efforts. We can push the administrations of our institutions to act boldly in the manner of the University of Minnesota and the University of Chicago's English Department.

One of the simplest direct actions faculty members can take individually involves examining the content of our courses to be sure they are as broadly representative as possible instead of narrowly traditional. To do so, we can draw on decades of scholarship about creating more inclusive courses in virtually all periods and genres of literature in English. It is especially easy to include issues of race, gender, and sexuality in one's courses when one remembers that race, gender, and sexuality are always relevant in studying all literature because they are always in play in our society. For instance, some years ago, I shifted the focus in a course from the novel *Dracula* to the *Dracula* culture text. My students and I spend quite a bit of time analyzing Bram Stoker's portrayal of Count Dracula as a racial Other as well as the ways in which the novel works as a disquisition on the dangers of "foreigners" and women to the hegemony of white, British men. I also include elements of the *Dracula* culture text that come from cultural backgrounds different from Stoker's, such as Jewelle Gomez's *The Gilda Stories*, about a Black lesbian vampire and US history.

We in English departments also need to remember that committing to teaching a breadth of literatures from multiple cultures and perspectives is only a small albeit helpful gesture toward social justice. What we teach is inextricably intertwined with how we teach; ignoring one while attending to the other is guaranteed to undermine any attempts to support inclusion and diversity in our classrooms and our institutions. Trying to adopt elements of a social justice pedagogy while teaching only canonical texts from canonical perspectives serves to reinforce the ivoriness of the ivory tower by suggesting that only white-, male-, straight-authored texts and white-, male-, straight-authorized perspectives are worthy of scholarly attention. Similarly, although perhaps not as obviously, teaching a breadth of literatures and perspectives is close to useless if it is done in a way that reinforces conferred authority and therefore, ultimately, heteronormativity, sexism, and white supremacy. We need to think about every element of our teaching if we are committed to reducing the effects of privilege in our classrooms.

Some of those elements have little to do with the content or the pedagogy of our courses and more to do with the general atmosphere we establish in those classes. If one has cis privilege, for example, calling the roll at the start of a semester may seem uncomplicated. It will never feel threatening to me for the person at the front of a roomful of strangers to call out, "Maureen Reddy." If I presented as male but had that name and had not been able to change it legally to reflect my actual gender identity—because I lived in a state in which that was difficult or even impossible, because I was under eighteen and therefore without the rights of an adult, or for many other reasons—it might well feel terrifying, because it would be an outing of me without my permission or choice. I stopped calling the roll a long time ago for exactly that reason and instead begin each new class by handing out a brief questionnaire and asking students to complete it. The first three questions are "What do you want me to call you?" "What is your name in the RIC system?" and "What pronouns do you use (she/her, his/him, they/their)? Unless you say otherwise, I will refer to everyone as 'them.'" I then call the roll from the questionnaires, using the answers to that first question, and later sort out in private who is actually registered by comparing the students' answers to the second question to the official course roster. This is a tiny, easy thing to do that makes a material difference in the lives of trans and gender nonconforming students by not taking for granted that all people are cisgender and either male or female. It is not *using* privilege but trying to diminish some of the consequences of privilege, including my own.

The student body at my college is about 40% students of color, with a large number of students (both BIPOC and white) from immigrant families whose home language is not English. Students' names reflect that diversity. When I call the roll from the students' questionnaires, I ask them to correct me if I mispronounce their names, and I pause after every name, including those that seem simple in an English-language-dominant context, such as Lindsay Smith. I write down on the questionnaire the phonetic pronunciation if I am unfamiliar with a particular name so that I don't mangle it in the future. Again, a small thing, surely, but one that helps students understand that every one of us has the right to be treated respectfully, which includes being addressed as we choose and having people pronounce our names correctly. A West African student once wrote on the questionnaire that he used the name Ken, which seemed to have no relationship either to the name on the class roster or to the name he used on his papers and exams in class. In conversation in my office about halfway through the term, I asked how he had happened to come by that nickname and why he had chosen to use a different name for his classwork. Ken was not his nickname, he explained, but he had learned from experience that the name his family and friends called him, which was his second name, was hard for Americans to pronounce. He had started using Ken in high school because one of his teachers who had struggled to pronounce his name correctly had suggested it. In short, this young man had accepted that his teachers' comfort outweighed his right to be called by his own name; a clearer illustration of privilege and the lack thereof in action in the field of education is hard to imagine.

Helping students better understand the legitimacy and the limits of earned authority and the illegitimacy of conferred authority in the classroom is another small but useful step each of us can take toward social justice in every class we teach. Knowing that most students assume that the white man in the front of the classroom knows what they are talking about and are less likely to make that assumption when there is a white woman or a person of color at the front of the room, for many years now I have been addressing the issue of authority directly in my classes. On the first day, when we go over the syllabus and introduce ourselves to each other, I always briefly describe my own background in whatever the subject is and how I came to choose a particular course topic. This is not very elaborate, and I do not label it as being about authority. I simply say something like—in the case of my "Women, Crime, and Representation" course—"I have been researching gender and race in crime fiction for about thirty years and have published a couple of books and a number of scholarly articles on those topics. I'm currently most interested in how race and gender work in Irish crime fiction." I have sometimes suggested to white colleagues, especially men, that they do this kind of thing, and several of them have. It is small, but it does put the focus on academic preparation as the ground for classroom authority, which our colleagues of color also possess, although they do not have white (or, sometimes, male) privilege and therefore miss out on conferred authority, while white women enjoy some portion of that same conferred authority. All of us taking on that task of explaining academic authority to our students seems to me a better, more equitable option than allowing white male privilege to protect some of us while requiring the rest of us to justify ourselves over and over again. This strategy also suggests to students that they have the right to know how professors come to occupy their positions, which helps demystify academe. Why should they listen to me? I don't at all mind explaining, nor do I mind limiting the scope of what they should listen to me about: just because I know a lot about crime fiction does not mean I know a lot about anything else. None of this is directly about undermining white supremacy, but every intervention that challenges the assumed authority of white people is a move in the direction of dismantling that structure.

I have come to understand that this approach is especially useful for helping undergraduates from non-elite backgrounds acclimate to college and to feel like they belong there, which is a key element in persistence and attainment. Many of the students at Rhode Island College are first-generation college attenders. Much of what we who work in academe take for granted is mysterious and confusing to them, including basic vocabulary (e.g., What is a bursar, and why do I have to contact the bursar about my student loans? What is an "academic advisor" for?), as indeed it once was to me, a first-generation college attender from an immigrant, working-class background. When my college instituted a first-year seminar program, I decided to incorporate a "welcome to college" element into my course. It had been a long time since I had taught first-year students, and I figured that both they and I would benefit from a shared understanding of the parameters of professor-student relationships and classroom etiquette. I explain, for example, that refraining from comment when someone is studying their phone instead of our shared text during class does not mean I have not noticed. It means that in this college environment I am counting them absent without calling them out in front of their peers. At first, I thought of this approach as communicating basic information that could help students negotiate my first-year seminar and, not incidentally, minimize my annoyance at predictable blunders stemming from unawareness of what office hours are for, how to address professors, how to write an email to a professor, and so on—but my understanding of its function greatly expanded across time, and I came to think of it as "how to do college." In the first few weeks, I covered the basic information students would need to acclimate to campus. Starting in the fourth week, I set aside five or ten minutes at the start of each class meeting to address student concerns that fall under the "doing college" rubric. Students could ask questions or email them to me in advance if they preferred anonymity. I thought of that time not as "wasted" or as "irrelevant" to our course materials but as a concrete, useful contribution to social justice through supplying key information to which students had not had equal access before joining my class. This practice helped reduce the advantage that more privileged students might possess from growing up in a family where the adults have college degrees, for instance, or from attending a wealthy high school with a strong college preparatory curriculum. My students expressed such appreciation for this element of our course—both directly to me and also in course evaluations—that I started incorporating a bit of the "doing college" material into some of my upper-division courses as well. In addition, on the *Blackboard* site for each of my courses, I posted a folder labeled "Success in College," into which I occasionally put articles about research on that subject.

Several years ago, reflecting on my position as a senior professor who had recently won my college's faculty leadership award, I realized that although I had no official position that would allow me to create new courses outside my own department, I had the power to ensure that every student had access to the information that I had been providing to students in my classes. I proposed a one-credit course for incoming first-year students that would focus entirely on "introduction to college" information. A collaboration between the academic affairs and the student success divisions at my institution, the course for the past several years has been a requirement for all students. It is too early to know how much (if any) effect the course has had on student persistence and attainment, but the course evaluations thus far show that students who took it believed they learned a lot and felt more confident about their ability to succeed in college by the end of the course than they had at the start. This intervention is far smaller than what college presidents can do to use their positions and privilege to advance social justice, but it is not merely performative allyship and is a good use of my own privilege.

None of what I suggest here has the potential to destroy privilege based on race, gender, or sexuality or even to make a huge difference in the countless inequities between those of us who have privilege of various kinds and those who do not. It does, however, have the potential to make some small but meaningful differences in the lives of both students and colleagues who lack privilege, and to repeatedly remind those of us with privilege of various kinds about that privilege. The greatest privilege of all is being able to get through every day without having to think about one's specific privilege. Doing whatever we can both to keep ourselves conscious of that privilege and to try to reduce some of its effects is quite literally the least we can do if we care at all about social justice.

NOTES

1. The Wall of Moms' brief history and the controversies surrounding it attracted much media attention. For more detailed accounts, see Blaec; Piñon.

2. My points about race in this paragraph apply only to predominantly white institutions.

3. McFarland provides a list of the ethnic categories used in the report and explains that "some of the category labels have been shortened in the text, tables, and figures for ease of reference. American Indian or Alaska Native is denoted as American Indian/Alaska Native (except when separate estimates are available for American Indians alone or Alaska Natives alone); Black or African American is shortened to Black; and Hispanic or Latino is shortened to Hispanic. Native Hawaiian or Other Pacific Islander is shortened to Pacific Islander" (vii).

4. So far as I have been able to determine, there are no studies comparing straight and 2SLGBTQIA+ or cis and trans college attendance and completion rates, which is why my focus here is on race alone.

WORKS CITED

Adams, Susan. "Harvard's President's Statement on Protests Invites Criticism as College Leaders Speak Out." *Forbes*, 1 June 2020, www.forbes.com/sites/susanadams/2020/06/01/harvard-presidents-statement-on-protests-invites-criticism-as-college-leaders-speak-out/?sh=5f38ddf310ab.

American College President Study. American Council on Education, 2017, www.acenet.edu/Research-Insights/Pages/American-College-President-Study-Past.aspx.

Baker, Rachel, et al. "Bias in Online Classes: Evidence from a Field Experiment." CEPA Working Paper No. 18-03. *Stanford Center for Education Policy Analysis*, 2018, cepa.stanford.edu/content/bias-online-classes-evidence-field-experiment.

Bell, Derrick. *Faces at the Bottom of the Well: The Permanence of Racism*. Basic Books, 1992.

Blaec, Jagger. "The Complicated Rise and Swift Fall of Portland's Wall of Moms Protest Group." *PDX Monthly*, Aug. 2020, www.pdxmonthly.com/news-and-city-life/2020/08/the-complicated-rise-and-swift-fall-of-portland-s-wall-of-moms-protest-group.

Casselman, Ben. "Race Gap Narrows in College Enrollment, but Not in Graduation." *FiveThirtyEight*, 30 Apr. 2014, fivethirtyeight.com/features/race-gap-narrows-in-college-enrollment-but-not-in-graduation/.

Delgado, DiDi. "Whites Only: SURJ and the Caucasian Invasion of Racial Justice Spaces." *Medium*, 1 Apr. 2017, medium.com/the-establishment/whites-only-the-caucasian-invasion-of-racial-justice-spaces-7e2529ec8314.

Flaherty, Colleen. "Wanted: Black Studies Scholars (Only)." *Inside Higher Ed*, 16 Sept. 2020, www.insidehighered.com/news/2020/09/16/university-chicago-english-faculty-prioritizes-black-studies-graduate-students-2021.

Gomez, Jewelle. *The Gilda Stories*. Firebrand Books, 1991.

Jaschek, Scott. "Professors and Politics: What the Research Says." *Inside Higher Ed*, 27 Feb. 2017, www.insidehighered.com/news/2017/02/27/research-confirms-professors-lean-left-questions-assumptions-about-what-means.

Lederman, Doug. "Diversity on the Rise among College Presidents." *Inside Higher Ed*, 14 Feb. 2022, www.insidehighered.com/news/2022/02/14/colleges-have-hired-more-minority-presidents-amid-racial-reckoning.

Lorde, Audre. "The Master's Tools Will Never Dismantle the Master's House." 1979. *Sister Outsider*, by Lorde, Penguin Books, 2020, pp. 100–03.

McFarland, Joel, et al. *The Condition of Education 2018*. U.S. Department of Education, 2018, nces.ed.gov/pubs2018/2018144.pdf.

McKenzie, Lindsay. "Words Matter for College Presidents, but So Will Actions." *Inside Higher Ed*, 8 June 2020, www.insidehighered.com/news/2020/06/08/searching-meaningful-response-college-leaders-killing-george-floyd.

Orfield, Gary, and Nichols Hillman, editors. *Accountability and Opportunity in Higher Education: The Civil Rights Dimension*. Harvard Education Press, 2018.

Piñon, Natasha. "Wall of Moms Faces Allegations of 'Anti-Blackness' from Portland Community Group." *Mashable*, 3 Aug. 2020, mashable.com/article/wall-of-moms-breakdown-portland/.

"QuickFacts." *United States Census Bureau*, 2023, www.census.gov/quickfacts/fact/table/US/PST045218.

Reddy, Maureen T. "Smashing the Rules of Racial Standing." TuSmith and Reddy, pp. 51–61.

Shapiro, D., et al. *Completing College: A National View of Student Completion Rates—Fall 2012 Cohort (Signature Report No. 16)*. National Student Clearinghouse Research Center, 2018, nscresearchcenter.org/signaturereport16/.

Stoker, Bram. *Dracula*. London, 1897.

"Table B01001: Sex by Age." *American Community Survey*, United States Census Bureau, 2018, data.census.gov/table/ACSDT1Y2018.B01001.

TuSmith, Bonnie, and Maureen T. Reddy, editors. *Race in the College Classroom: Pedagogy and Politics*. Rutgers UP, 2002.

Teaching Whiteness Studies in the Twenty-First Century

Anthony Q. Hazard, Jr.

On 27 April 2019, at Politics and Prose, a bookstore in northwest Washington, DC, a group of white supremacists interrupted a book talk being given by Jonathan Metzl, a professor of sociology and of medicine, health, and society at Vanderbilt University. Metzl's recently published book, *Dying of Whiteness: How the Politics of Racial Resentment Are Killing America's Heartland*, had apparently raised the ire of members of the American Identity Movement (AIM), also known as Identity Evropa. The protesters reportedly chanted, "This is our land" and "AIM," ensuring the author and audience members would identify the group. According to Metzl, who was interviewed within days of the interruption, the nine men and one woman of AIM marched to the front of the room and began giving prepared remarks on "their homeland" and "the white working class" (Mangan; Dvorak). This moment of protest—directed against Metzl rather than against the billionaire reality TV and real estate mogul who from the White House proffered policies (in line with those of past Republican presidents) that actually damage the white working class—provides a glimpse into the current controversies surrounding whiteness in both scholarly and public spaces (Lombardo). As Petula Dvorak of the *Washington Post* reported, the AIM members sought to create spectacle in defense of their identitarian politics rather than actually engage the larger claim in Metzl's book that the white working class is suffering not because of "illegal immigration" or "liberal" policies but rather because of the Republican Party policies they embrace that cause them harm. This politics of resentment, Metzl argues, shines a spotlight on one particular way whiteness functions in the United States of America in this historical moment. The AIM members didn't interrupt Metzl's talk to debate policy or to explore historical fact; they sought to publicly proclaim their whiteness.

This was the very politics of the forty-fifth US president. His public claims to whiteness, his othering of the first African American president of the United States through the birther conspiracy, and his criminalization of immigrant communities from the Global South helped open up political space for vitriolic expressions of whiteness (Serwer; Arce; Kaplan and Lipstadt). Of course, Trump's emergence as a viable presidential candidate occurred in the midst of other racialized political energies that followed Barack Obama's unlikely victory in 2008. Yet the election of the first Black president in US history followed by the election of what Ta-Nehisi Coates calls "the first white president" together delineate an undeniable historical moment. Between these two elections, I completed my PhD and two postdoctoral fellowships, then became one of the handful of Black professors to receive tenure in the College of Arts and Sciences at Santa Clara University. As a historian, I am admittedly taken by moments, epochs, changes over time, and continuities. I cannot help but think back to the 2008 election, in the second year of my postdoctoral fellowship at Northwestern University, and the electric energy of my students of various backgrounds, who had spent the evening in Grant Park celebrating history. I'm equally riveted by the memory of the palpable despair that emanated from students and colleagues in the days following the November 2016 election. The beginning and subsequent development of my academic career occurred within this historical moment, directly impacting both my teaching and research.

When I first designed the course Whiteness and Immigration in the US at the beginning of my career, I focused on the existing literature produced in the 1990s, which took as its main theme the ways that notions of whiteness shaped and were shaped by the waves of European immigration in the eighteenth, nineteenth, and early twentieth centuries. In 2017, I redesigned the course in order to engage the manifestations of whiteness seen across the country in response to President Barack Obama's eminence and subsequent rejection by the politics of the candidate Donald Trump and of his many followers. The contemporaneity of the central questions of my redesign was both intellectual and cultural. In this new course, Whiteness Studies in the Twenty-First Century, I focused on two questions: What does whiteness look like in the second decade of the twenty-first century? How is whiteness functioning in institutions, electoral politics, on campuses, and in cultural spaces?

This essay offers an experiential and pedagogical examination of how to incorporate both scholarly and popular media sources in the teaching of whiteness studies in the post-Obama era. The rise of Trumpian white nationalism offers new challenges to the teaching of whiteness studies in the twenty-first century. Teaching whiteness studies as a Black, heterosexual, cisgender male at Santa Clara University, the predominantly white Jesuit university of Silicon Valley, complicates the layers of campus politics that I engage as the designer and instructor of this course. As a small, private university with a faculty that is approximately 70% white and male, and a student body that is just 2% Black, I enter the pedagogical fray of whiteness studies carrying potential triggers for white students and faculty members alike, by virtue of my Black body and the subject matter itself (see DiAngelo, "White Fragility" 57). The pedagogical practice of whiteness studies, which involves the critical interrogation of the social, political, and economic power of white bodies, relationships to the state, and shifting boundaries of who is counted as "white" over time, has remained controversial. Whereas I have established myself on campus as an "expert" in ethnic studies courses in which I center the history, everyday practices, politics, and subjectivities of Black people, my teaching whiteness studies potentially presents a unique challenge, particularly in the current historical moment and political milieu.

While the field of whiteness studies was originally driven by historical, literary, and anthropological scholarship in the early 1990s, those disciplinary contributions remain foundational and resonant in this new century (see Brodkin; Morrison; Roediger, *Wages*). By incorporating recent theoretical insights by white anti-racism educators and activists such as DiAngelo and Tim Wise, I argue for the use of DiAngelo's term "white fragility," the basic lack of experience and strategies of white-identifying people to deal with the stressors of engaging issues of race, as a tool to challenge white folks to examine their positionalities across the current political spectrum while providing nonwhite people additional theoretical resources to interrogate circulations of whiteness within predominantly white spaces and institutions (see *White Fragility*).

A Brief Genealogy of Whiteness Studies

Writing in 2017, the historian David Roediger offered the following revelation concerning his own groundbreaking work in whiteness studies: "While it is most often pointed out that Du Bois's *Black Reconstruction* (1935) inspired the title of *Wages of Whiteness*, it structured the book multiply and even entirely" (*Class* 63). The readily made observation that W. E. B. Du Bois's discussion of the psychological value or "wage" of whiteness to white workers and citizens following the end of chattel slavery in the United States provided Roediger with the title of his 1991 publication was not the whole story. For Roediger, it was Du Bois's ability in *Black Reconstruction* "to place the self-activity of the Black worker and the whiteness of the white worker at the very center of US history . . . that made Du Bois so indispensable" (63). Other whiteness studies scholars have recognized the inspirational role of Du Bois's work on their own, including Noel Ignatiev, whose *How the Irish Became White* is counted among the initial wave of the field (Roediger, *Class* 62). In the first iteration of my undergraduate course at Northwestern University, I taught both Roediger and Ignatiev in addition to other standards, including the anthropologist Karen Brodkin's *How Jews Became White Folks and What That Says about Race in America*, the historian Matthew Frye Jacobson's *Whiteness of a Different Color: European Immigration and the Fabrication of Race*, Theodore Allen's *The Invention of the White Race*, and Toni Morrison's *Playing in the Dark: Whiteness and the Literary Imagination*.

The intellectual line from Du Bois to Roediger, however, involves other historians who, as early as the 1960s, offered investigations of constructions of race. As the historian Peter Kolchin has pointed out, the work of whiteness studies scholars in the 1990s built upon previous work that had "long been preoccupied with the changing ways of making race." Included in this historiography are Thomas Gossett's *Race: The History of an Idea in America*, Winthrop Jordan's *White over Black: American Attitudes toward the Negro, 1550–1812*, Barbara J. Fields's "Ideology and Race in American History," and Joel Williamson's *The Crucible of Race: Black-White Relations in the American South since Emancipation*. For Kolchin, whiteness studies scholarship was "less a radical departure than an evolution" of historical scholarship (172). But Kolchin rightly points out that scholars outside the historical discipline contributed to the emerging field in the 1990s, particularly in cultural studies, sociology, education, and law (154).

In the two decades following Kolchin's assessment of the field, the range of works produced across disciplines proved to be the standard rather than a trend. The public scholar and activist Tim Wise's *White like Me: Reflections on Race from a Privileged Son* marked an autobiographical intervention from an author connected to but not firmly embedded in academe—and directly informed his hourlong documentary of the same title. The literary scholar Veronica T. Watson's examination of the longer history of Black scholars' examinations of whiteness appeared as *The Souls of White Folk: African American Writers Theorize Whiteness*. The white educator and activist Robin DiAngelo's contemporary assessment of the phenomenon of "white fragility" was published as a journal article and was followed up in a best-selling book-length examination of the same topic, and the esteemed historian Nell Irvin Painter provided readers with a magisterial treatment in *The History of White People*.

Most recently, Samuel Jaye Tanner's study of a yearlong teaching and learning project with white high school students, *Whiteness, Pedagogy, and Youth in America: Critical Whiteness Studies in the Classroom*, offered a penetrating analysis of whiteness beyond the framework of white privilege. In *Digital Whiteness and Medieval Studies*, the literary scholar Dorothy Kim has contributed a stirring examination of the uses of medieval studies by white supremacists in digital spaces. Metzl's sociopolitical study of medicine, *Dying of Whiteness*, is, as we have seen, already impacting the public discourse on whiteness in the Trump era. The American Identity Movement's interruption of Metzl's book talk, however, is far from an origin moment of controversy over whiteness studies within and beyond the academy. In fact, as Kolchin was making his extensive review of the field in the leading historical journal in the United States, established scholars, graduate students, and activists directly engaged the controversies, animating whiteness studies at the turn of the twenty-first century.

In November 2001, the New York University History Department, the Committee on Historical Studies at the New School, and the journal *International Labor and Working-Class History* sponsored a forum to discuss the shortcomings and controversies of whiteness studies, mainly from the perspective of US labor history. Seven well-established historians provided remarks on the field, illuminating existing debates. A few scholars posited that whiteness studies had to that point deployed an unwieldy definition of whiteness that presupposed a working-class unity amongst the presumably not-quite-white immigrant populations and Black people. Critics also problematized what they perceived as a tendency of scholars to reduce racism to racial identity, privileging the significance of individual attitudes on race over that of structural racism. In terms of methodology, some questioned the veracity of scholarship on whiteness produced without conducting archival research on primary materials. Those responding to these critiques argued that whiteness studies had indeed produced historical works that deepen understandings of the structural and interpersonal dynamics of European immigration. In particular, one respondent argued that the historicizing of racial classifications and categories by scholars in the field was a central contribution. By moving race to the center of the study of US history, whiteness studies scholarship had raised new and important questions about nationhood and national identity, certainly a timely observation in the shadow of the 9/11 attacks and the racialized rhetoric and violence that ensued (see Haake and Aziz). The forum, the speakers, and the audience by no means arrived at consensus on the methodological and political tensions within whiteness studies, but the extant controversies were certainly identified (Spear). As Kolchin concluded his essay in 2002, looking ahead to a potential "coming of age" for whiteness studies over the next decade or so, those of us entering the ranks of the professoriate during that very period would contend with unforeseen historical moments, particularly the election of the first Black president of the United States and the political and cultural backlash that followed, that reshaped the political and intellectual arena around whiteness and race (see Anderson 138–60). It is to that moment I now turn.

Reshaping the Course in the Age of Trump

When Donald Trump descended the escalator of his gilded midtown high-rise to officially launch his 2016 presidential bid, he made clear his racist strategy of stoking fears of a violent invasion across the southern border: "When Mexico sends its people, they're not sending their best. . . . They're bringing drugs. They're bringing crime. They're rapists. And some, I assume, are good people" (Phillips). This, of course, followed years of demanding to see Barack Obama's birth certificate, as if the Columbia University– and Harvard Law–educated Obama had worked his entire life to carry out the largest political con in United States history. Between the "Don't Re-Nig" bumper stickers (Keyes), the posters of Obama's face with bones through his nose (Fantz), and the late Arizona senator John McCain's having to correct a white woman at a town hall who stated plainly that Obama was "an Arab" (Martin and Parnes), Ta-Nehisi Coates's argument that Trump's presidential victory was the manifestation of a wave of discrediting, racializing, and negating the presidency of Barack Obama seems on firm ground. Coates argues further that Trump "is a white man who would not be president were it not for this fact." And more damaging, for Coates, is that Trump's basic "ideology is white supremacy."

The Coates essay appeared in a timely fashion, as I was in the midst of redesigning the Whiteness Studies and Immigration in the US course. In my reading, Coates brings into stark relief the regressive cultural politics of the anti-Obama coalition, whose mélange of nationalism, resentment, and outright racism seemed anachronistic yet very contemporary. Whereas in 1981, Lee Atwater, an aide to Ronald Reagan and former aide to Richard Nixon, had warned his Republican colleagues, "You start out in 1954 by saying, 'N—, n—, n—.' By 1968 you can't say 'n—'—that hurts you, backfires," Trump's politics and the accompanying anti-Obama energies emanating across the country for eight years plowed through the pretenses of the Southern Strategy (Perlstein). Coded language remained in the political discourse, but it was now accompanied by outright racist proclamations about Black, Indigenous, and People of Color, citizens and noncitizens alike. Upon Trump's victory, I felt the pain and fear of my students of color. Trump's anti-immigrant politics and birtherism amounted to a nullification of their humanity and my own. Black studies and ethnic studies call upon their professors to embrace scholarly activism, to work for our communities, and to educate young people to become educators. With fast-approaching deadlines for submitting my tenure packet, I took a calculated risk: I would teach this potentially controversial, even explosive, course as an assistant professor without tenure.

Adding the Coates essay was the first change I made from the previous syllabus, not only because I find the essay powerful but also because I knew students were familiar with Coates's body of work and his propensity to explore the underbelly of American history through powerful and accessible prose. In seeking to find a balance of contemporary commentary and the whiteness studies canon, I assigned Brodkin's *How Jews Became White Folks* and Stefano Luconi's *From Paesani to White Ethnics*. In addition to these case studies, I included Kolchin's sympathetic yet critical historiographical essay and the introductory chapters of Matthew Frye Jacobson's *Whiteness of a Different Color* (1–12) and Nell Irvin Painter's *The History of White People* (ix–xii). My goal there was to embed the students in the historiographical debates within whiteness studies while also providing a historical foundation on European immigration and the development of concepts of race in North America. We completed this grounding work over the first half of the quarter-long course and then transitioned into a contemporary exploration of whiteness through media and theory.

On theory, I chose DiAngelo's paradigmatic "White Fragility" and Andrew Pierce's "The Myth of the White Minority." In the Pierce essay, I recognized a challenge to continue to think through the ever-changing boundaries around categories of race, including whiteness, the government-created "Hispanic" identity, and the bourgeoning "whites will soon become a minority" discourse in the US. I found Pierce's larger claim that white supremacy was actually being buttressed by the notion that white people were becoming an aggrieved minority to be trenchant and timely. The Pierce essay would push the class to make connections between what "taking back" the country and making "American great again" mean for whiteness in the twenty-first century. DiAngelo's succinct prose and direct challenge to her fellow white-identifying folks resonated in personal as well as intellectual ways. Upon reading the essay, I immediately connected her focus on the role of "racial stress" to the experiences of my students of color and white students. I recalled the many instances of heartfelt tears in my Introduction to African American Studies class when exploring chattel slavery, showing depictions of children being sold away from parents and sexual violence against enslaved women. More than a few times have my white students revealed that they had no idea "how bad" slavery was or that state violence levied at Black people was the status quo. I recalled private conversations with my students of color about the burdens of being at a predominantly white institution of higher learning; for me, that "racial stress" accompanies my professional experiences as one of the very few Black faculty members at my institution. What I also find so powerful about DiAngelo's essay is her ability to articulate how people of color in this country are forced to carry the weight of history while the very structure of white supremacy insulates most white people from such exposure. Those stressors of our memories of the Middle Passage, seasoning, colonial violence, genocide, slavery, and our existence in predominantly white spaces are ours, and when white people are challenged to know and feel that, their fragility emerges. Tears, "defensive moves" (54, 57), and a refusal to engage facts demonstrate that fragility. In retrospect, the additional power of DiAngelo's theorization is that we see it in the Trumpian sphere: the scoffing at factual information, the moral indignation at accusations of racism, and the sheer anger at being challenged to think about the connections between America's racial past and present.

I also elected to screen Wise's documentary *White like Me* and the first episode of W. Kamau Bell's CNN show *United Shades of America*. In this episode, which aired in April 2016, Bell visits several members of the Ku Klux Klan throughout the southern United States ("New KKK"). His first episode was a timely venture for him in the Trump era and, according to him, an exploration necessary for his survival as a Black man.[1] Bell's comedic and analytical skills allow him to navigate explosive topics and moments with humor, wit, and historical knowledge. I anticipated our screening of the Klan episode accomplishing those elusive outcomes. Wise's documentary, of course, grew out of the memoir through which he explicates his own whiteness and the notion of white privilege writ large. The style and tenor of Wise's book and documentary are more an appeal to white folks to consider the basic elements and ramifications of their privilege. In making these two choices, I, of course, had in mind the "audience," or the students that I anticipated enrolling in the class in the winter quarter of 2018.

Of the twenty-seven students enrolled (in a class limited to thirty), eleven were majoring in ethnic studies and two in history, both departments with which

I have long-standing campus relationships (eleven of the students in the course had no prior relationship with me as an instructor). The course was cross-listed in the two departments, and nineteen students enrolled through ethnic studies while eight enrolled through history. The class was diverse in terms of majors, class standing (five first-year, five second-year, six third-year, and eleven fourth-year students), and ethnic or racial identification (eleven white students and sixteen students of color). Students entered the course with varying levels of knowledge of US history, divergent experiences in studying race and ethnicity at the college level, and certainly different lived experiences according to race, class, gender, and geography. All the assigned readings and media were discussed in class, and students led the discussions of the Luconi and Brodkin chapters in the first half of the class. For the midterm project, students worked in groups to research and deliver an audiovisual presentation that reflected on the history of whiteness in the United States, inclusive of the colonial period, through the twentieth century. In this project, I sought to push the students to talk through potential topics, deciding on those they could agree were important and interesting, and to uncover a particular aspect of the history of whiteness to share with the class. The final project was similar but focused on whiteness in the twenty-first century. I envisioned the final project as an opportunity for the students to apply the theory that we had read and discussed in the second half of the course.

The majority of the students found the historical and historiographical readings useful but felt particularly inspired and energized by the DiAngelo essay on white fragility. Ethnic studies majors of numerous ethnic or racial backgrounds, white nonmajors, first-year students, and seniors connected to the essay and engaged in lengthy debates about its merits and applicability. In subsequent conversations inside and outside my classes, students continue to utilize DiAngelo's concepts to understand how whiteness is functioning in and around them. The Coates essay on Trump's presidency was also a lightning rod, resulting in a scintillating class discussion. I do recall a bit of discomfort among a few of the students and an effort to push back on aspects of Coates's analysis, particularly Trump's blatant racism. This was unsurprising, and in fact, I was impressed by the level of cordiality of our discussion despite the intensity and immediacy of the material.

Several students seconded my assessment of the classroom environment in their anonymous evaluations. One student felt it was a "great course" with an "excellent learning environment." Others said I had created a comfortable and welcoming environment in the "controversial but necessary course." As in my other classes, I spoke openly and honestly about why I teach the course and how my personal and scholarly background inform my teaching goals. Students appreciated that candor. A few students remarked upon the effective organization of the course and commented that I was "respectful and really enhanced the learning that occurred." However, one student wished I had "set some guidelines for class discussions" to ensure respectful dialogue since discussion sometimes became "very tense." Nevertheless, this student concurred with others that "this is an important class . . . excellent." Another student stated simply, "wouldn't recommend this class." Some students thought more broadly about the course's potential, one remarking that "all students and faculty should be required to take this course." Another had an "incredibly eye-opening" experience and was moved to engage in "hours of healthy discussion." Still others were grateful for "the opportunity to critically think and learn on a deeper level." One student reflected on consistently talking "about issues of race and its construction but never directly within the context of whiteness." For this student, "it was really great" to have the "opportunity to understand whiteness and discuss it in more specific terms."

The students' anonymous assessments of the course reveal the importance of the way I went about organizing the material and engaging the students in earnest yet respectful and supportive ways. For the vast majority of the students in the class, the larger takeaway has been the application of both history and theory to their daily lives within and beyond the university. To varying degrees, the work of Wise, DiAngelo, Bell, and Coates challenged the class to think beyond the white working class or southern US as loci of racism (Beech 173). In fact, the readings and media opened up intellectual space for us to speak frankly about circulations of whiteness in the cultural fabric, pedagogical practices, and leadership structure at our prestigious, social-justice-oriented Jesuit university. Critiques of the course materials added an important layer to those discussions. Students were keenly aware, echoing more recent critics of anti-racism scholarship, of the potential privileged position white scholars hold in the booming and lucrative industry of anti-racism workshops, speaking engagements, and best-selling publications (Bergner; McEvoy). Even within the ostensibly progressive spaces of anti-racism work, the students realized, the politics of the production of knowledge still mattered. What was also brought into striking relief over the course was the students' awareness that, unlike San Francisco State, where the historian Amy Sueyoshi has described teaching whiteness studies, Santa Clara University is not "a largely immigrant, working-class, student of color university in the queer capital of America" (374). The work the students did in my class allowed them to embrace their lived experiences in a predominantly white, class-stratified space. That confirmation is powerful and for an instructor by far outweighs the controversial or difficult moments in the classroom. But since some students experienced a less fulfilling outcome and seemingly would not be as keen as others to recommend the class to their friends, or to carry on conversations about the course material with loved ones, a challenge remains. I am reminded of a recent conversation I had with a student writer who has experience covering the whiteness studies debates on our campus for the university newspaper, which I detail below. While interviewing me for her senior journalism thesis on free speech and whiteness, Kimi Andrew asked me how I might approach encouraging students to take whiteness studies who have expressed little to no enthusiasm for the material, methodology, and theoretical interventions. In the spring of 2018, just weeks after the conclusion of the new iteration of my whiteness studies course, that opportunity presented itself in the midst of a campus controversy.

Campus Whiteness Controversy

During the first week of the spring quarter in 2018, the community facilitator of the Unity residence hall at Santa Clara created a bulletin board examining whiteness and white privilege.[2] Since the community facilitators had been encouraged to use a Disney-related theme for their bulletin boards, Unity's facilitator created a board titled "S-Know Your Whiteness," adorned with images of Snow White and other recognizable characters from *Snow White and the Seven Dwarfs* (fig. 1). The board included notes and images conveying that race is socially constructed and relational and that whiteness functions within the realm of power while working as a baseline or unconscious identity. A second-year student denounced the board on *Facebook*, posting, "Shame on Santa Clara University for allowing this in their dorm halls" (Andrew). Clearly upset by the board, the student tagged in the post the controversial conservative political commentator Ben Shapiro and Charlie Kirk, founder of Turning Point USA. The Washington-based website *The Daily Caller* picked up the story and offered a succinct description of the board, accompanied by two images, submitted by an anonymous student. According to

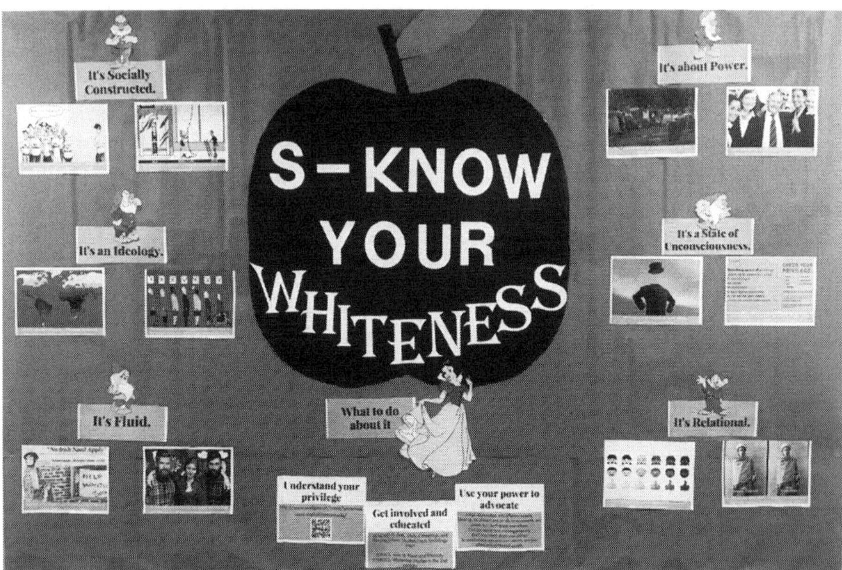

Figure 1. J. J. Burwell. "S-Know Your Whiteness" bulletin board. Santa Clara University, 2018. Photograph by Alex Stewart.

The Daily Caller, that anonymous student described the board as "located in a county in which 73 percent of the vote went to Hillary Clinton in 2016." For the anonymous student, Santa Clara was an "echo chamber," where "what is considered undeniable fact can venture into the realm of extremism," suggesting that merely engaging whiteness studies was not valid academic work (Shimshock).

Kimi Andrew reported in *The Santa Clara* that the Unity residence hall staff, along with its community facilitator, invited residents to "explore the bulletin board" and to "reflect further on where" any personal discomfort might be coming from. I was soon contacted by the community facilitator to discuss potential changes to the board, and I did provide additional conceptual clarifications regarding whiteness. The board was then revamped as "What Is Whiteness?," featuring what the article describes as "less accusatory" subheadings. The student who had authored the critical *Facebook* post and alerted members of the right-wing media claimed, however, that in reinstating the board, "the University is discriminating against people with white skin" (Andrew).

As the Unity community facilitator then went about organizing a panel on whiteness to include me and two of my colleagues from women's and gender studies and sociology, the Santa Clara University College Republicans released a statement condemning the original board. The group described the board as "a blatant display of racism" that failed "to unify the student body" because "it perpetuates the racial tensions that are already prevailing on campus." For the College Republicans, it was "truly disappointing that Santa Clara University resorts to dividing and categorizing students based on their racial identity instead of promoting collaboration in order to obtain a common goal of unity." For me, looking back on this attempt of the College Republicans to deploy an ahistorical political discourse of "colorblindness" and on the second-year student's objections reveals crucial elements of the remaining challenge of teaching whiteness studies at Santa Clara. In the assessment of the student, recognizing that whiteness is a real thing that has existed in this country for centuries constituted discrimination. For the College Republicans, the university was somehow to blame for the community facilitator's attempt to engage a timely and relevant topic that spoke to the realities of race in the United States and at Santa Clara. The College Republicans, it seems, preferred to embrace the postracial discourse that emerged after the 2008 presidential election, all the while supporting a political party headed up by an openly xenophobic, racist commander in chief who himself had demonstrated very little historical acumen. Such efforts to make whiteness invisible hark back to Atwater's warnings about openly racialized politics, but today, a denial of the existence of systemic racism is buttressed by "alternative facts" and utter lack of interest in historical fact. The intellectual disingenuousness of the College Republicans' statement is symptomatic of these larger energies circulating in the public political discourse, where President Barack Obama was allegedly dividing the country when he recognized the fact of his Blackness following the murder of Trayvon Martin, and Unity was therefore dividing the university by recognizing the fact of whiteness (Martin).

At the panel on whiteness organized by the Unity RLC and the coordinating facilitator who had constructed the board, I was asked what might be done in the face of this ongoing challenge to anti-racism. I recommended that white people join Showing Up for Racial Justice, an organization for and by white people to mobilize against racism. I also stated that at Santa Clara, the single core course requirement in "diversity" was not enough. The very presentation of one diversity course ghettoizes the study of race and ethnicity at the university. The single diversity requirement does a disservice to the students, particularly in the light of the university's alleged social justice, Jesuit mission. The question-and-answer period following the panel's comments is revelatory on that point.

Among the anonymous questions were, "Are all white people racist?" "Why isn't there a white male on the panel?" and "What about Asian privilege?" I found myself throughout the question-and-answer session stating that those issuing such questions should have familiarized themselves with the whiteness studies field and literature prior to attempting to engage in a discussion on the subject and should have taken the opportunity to engage the "S-Know Your Whiteness" board rather than outright rejecting it (Martinez). The anonymity of the questions created a buffer between the questioner and the very potential of discomforting responses, eliminating the possibility of direct conversation in an effort to maintain a safe space for the discussion. Upon completion of the session, many audience members continued the conversation in smaller groups, and I was invited by the community facilitator to join him in speaking with students who I later learned were members of Santa Clara's politically conservative Turning Point group. The conversation was interesting, at times tense. The group seemed amenable to the idea that race was socially constructed—that genetically, we're all pretty much the same. I recall one of the members eagerly repeating that critiques of racism were "groupthink." I pointed out that whiteness studies has a long and storied history, from Du Bois to the 1990s cohort of highly respected scholars at Ivy League institutions. I vividly remember inviting the predominantly white, male Turning Point students to email me, or stop by my office, to engage with me in an exploration of whiteness studies. We did shake hands at the conclusion of our chat, but to this day, I have never heard from any of them. In those audience members posing ill-informed questions, and in the Turning Point students, there was, as DiAngelo describes racial arrogance, "no compunction about debating the knowledge of people who have thought complexly about race." Symptomatic of a Trumpian intellectual engagement, these audience members and students felt "free to dismiss these informed perspectives rather than have the humility to acknowledge that they are unfamiliar, reflect on them further, or seek more information" (DiAngelo, "White Fragility" 61). These are the folks who call to mind Kimi's question about engaging students who resist learning about whiteness studies. A few days after the event, I ran into a senior colleague, someone I consider a dear friend and a mentor, who had been in the audience. He shared with me that "I had convinced a lot of people" during the panel of the historical fact of whiteness in the US. The conversation was brief, but I suppose my takeaway from it provides one answer to Kimi's question: speaking the truth in these overwhelmingly white educational spaces can be effective enough. Verifiable historical facts about the centrality of race and exclusionary whiteness to the foundation of US society can, in some instances, be meaningful. It does not seem, however, that members of an organization whose national leadership has exuberantly expressed racist beliefs, and whose members of the University of Nevada, Las Vegas, chapter have been captured on film shouting "white power," and "fuck n—s" (Campbell), have any real interest in learning about whiteness studies. The unwillingness of this group at large to articulate their actual beliefs about how they view connections between anti-racism and American economic exceptionalism is again telling of the intellectual dishonesty we have to traverse in order to have useful conversations with some members of the Santa Clara community.

Equally troubling in terms of the challenges anti-racism educators now face, as reported by Celia Martinez in *The Santa Clara*, a first-year student who was in the audience stated, "I really enjoyed the event, but I wish they would have looked at things more from the other side." How does one define this other side? Is it a negation of history? Not just a devaluing of the expertise of scholars of race but a dismissal of the experiences of people of color? Does this "other side" care more about scoring rhetorical political victories than the humanity of Black and Brown people? Is this other side comfortable with or complicit in upholding white supremacy? What role do university administrators play in this dynamic?

"Onward into the discomfort," writes the white literary scholar Lee Bebout of Arizona State University (175). Chronicling the media storm and threats of violence that encircled his spring 2015 course US Race Theory and the Problem of Whiteness, Bebout recalls being accused of harassing white students, receiving hate mail and death threats, and being the subject of conversation with Elizabeth Hasselbeck on *Fox and Friends* (163–65). My teaching whiteness studies at Santa Clara has not resulted in threats to my life, but Bebout's experiences bring me back to my beloved alma mater, where I was challenged to embrace the discomfort of race by educators like Nettie Obleton, Joseph Graves, Mike Mitchell, Diana Ramey Berry, and Neal A. Lester. I am not quite sure if the stakes of my intellectual work back then are similar to those I encounter today, on the other side of the lectern. What I am sure of is that those of us who are anti-racism educators have a responsibility and duty to push our students the way my undergraduate professors pushed me. Some of these students may not be particularly comfortable with the truth of race and the facts about racism.

We must challenge our students, colleagues, and administrators to stop protecting white fragility. At our home institutions, we must call out the cover given to racism vis-à-vis "free speech" rhetoric, and we must create spaces in our classrooms and around our campuses in which people actually put their names on their ideas about race, because anonymity does not breed genuine intellectual work or growth. We must work within our academic departments and on the core curriculum to create more classes on whiteness studies and the historical realities of race in the United States. Indeed, the weight of the neoliberal university is upon us, but so is the weight of history. We must challenge trustees and university presidents to put as much consideration into hiring and paying experts on race as they do into endowments and new buildings. Our white allies within the professoriate must challenge themselves to become coconspirators and actively use their privilege to push for and contribute to these changes while being honest about their own potential fragility and racial arrogance. We must also create and maintain supportive spaces for untenured professors of color that allow folks to work through pedagogical challenges of race and whiteness. And, as anti-racism educators of color, we must invest in and foster the mental, physical, and spiritual health of one another while doing this work, particularly in environments that are overwhelmingly white, reactionary, or only passively anti-racist.

NOTES

1. For the school year 2017–18, Kamau was the Frank Sinatra Artist in Residence at Santa Clara's Center for the Arts and Humanities. My dear friend and colleague Christina Zanfagna was codirector of the Center and reached out to Kamau, who kindly agreed to comment, by email to Zanfagna in March 2018, concerning the pilot episode of *United Shades of America*.

2. Residence halls at Santa Clara University are themed. According to the university website, "Unity Residential Learning Community (RL) is a traditional-style, co-ed community of first and second-year students, focused on the themes of diversity and civic engagement" ("Unity RLC").

WORKS CITED

Allen, Theodore. *The Invention of the White Race*. Verso Books, 1994.

Anderson, Carol. *White Rage: The Unspoken Truth of Our Racial Divide*. Bloomsbury, 2016.

Andrew, Kimi. "White Privilege Is No Fairytale." *The Santa Clara*, 19 Apr. 2018, scholarcommons.scu.edu/cgi/viewcontent.cgi?article=1067&context=tsc.

Arce, Julissa. "Trump's Anti-Immigrant Rhetoric Was Never about Legality, It Was about Our Brown Skin." *Time*, 6 Aug. 2019, time.com/5645501/trump-anti-immigration-rhetoric-racism/.

Bebout, Lee. "Onward into the Discomfort: Teaching for Racial Justice in an Era of Media Outrage, the Alt-Right, and the Neoliberal University." *Teaching with Tension: Race, Resistance, and Reality in the Classroom*, edited by Philathia Bolton et al., Northwestern UP, 2019, pp. 163–78.

Beech, Jennifer. "Redneck and Hillbilly Discourse in the Writing Classroom: Classifying Critical Pedagogies of Whiteness." *College English*, vol. 67, no. 2, Nov. 2004, pp. 172–86.

Bell, W. Kamau. Email to Christina Zanfagna. 1 Mar. 2018.

Bergner, Daniel. "'White Fragility' Is Everywhere. But Does Antiracism Training Work?" *The New York Times*, 15 July 2020, www.nytimes.com/2020/07/15/magazine/white-fragility-robin-diangelo.html.

Brodkin, Karen. *How Jews Became White Folks and What That Says about Race in America.* Rutgers UP, 1995.

Campbell, Andy. "College Republican Group Turning Point Has a White Supremacy Problem." *HuffPost*, 10 May 2019, www.huffpost.com/entry/tpusa-college-republican-group-turning-point-has-a-white-supremacy-problem_n_5cd58fdbe4b0796a95dac4f6.

Coates, Ta-Nehisi. "The First White President." *The Atlantic*, Oct. 2017, www.theatlantic.com/magazine/archive/2017/10/the-first-white-president-ta-nehisi-coates/537909/.

DiAngelo, Robin. "White Fragility." *International Journal of Critical Pedagogy*, vol. 3, no. 3, 2011, pp. 54–70.

———. *White Fragility: Why It's So Hard for White People to Talk about Racism.* Beacon Press, 2018.

Du Bois, W. E. B. *Black Reconstruction in America: An Essay toward a History of the Part Which Black Folk Played in the Attempt to Reconstruct Democracy in America, 1860–1880.* Harcourt, Brace, 1935.

Dvorak, Petula. "It's Scary': Why We Flinch When White Nationalists Stage a Protest at a Bookstore." *The Washington Post*, 29 Apr. 2019, www.washingtonpost.com/local/its-scary-why-we-flinch-when-white-nationalists-stage-a-protest-at-a-bookstore/2019/04/29/ac2c70a4-6a80-11e9-a66d-a82d3f3d96d5_story.html.

Fantz, Ashley. "Obama as Witch Doctor: Racist or Satirical?" *CNN*, 17 Sept. 2009, www.cnn.com/2009/POLITICS/09/17/obama.witchdoctor.teaparty/index.html.

Fields, Barbara J. "Ideology and Race in American History." *Region, Race, and Reconstruction*, edited by J. Morgan Kousser and James M. McPherson, Oxford UP, 1982, pp. 143–77.

Gossett, Thomas. *Race: The History of an Idea in America.* Southern Methodist UP, 1963.

Haake, Braxton, and Sahar Aziz. "No Justice for Post 9/11 Discrimination." *Al Jazeera*, 11 Sept. 2020, www.aljazeera.com/opinions/2020/9/11/no-justice-for-post-9-11.

Ignatiev, Noel. *How the Irish Became White.* Routledge, 1995.

Jacobson, Matthew Frye. *Whiteness of a Different Color: European Immigrants and the Alchemy of Race.* Harvard UP, 1998.

Jordan, Winthrop. *White over Black: American Attitudes toward the Negro, 1550–1812.* U of North Carolina P, 1968.

Kaplan, Roberta, and Deborah Lipstadt. "Three Years Later, Charlottesville's Legacy of Neo-Nazi Hate Still Festers." *CNN*, 12 Aug. 2020, www.cnn.com/2020/08/11/opinions/charlottesville-three-years-later-hate-festers-lipstadt-kaplan/index.html.

Keyes, Alexa. "Don't Re-Nig in 2012: Maker of Racist Anti-Obama Sticker Shuts Down Site." *ABC News*, 16 Mar. 2012, abcnews.go.com/blogs/politics/2012/03/dont-re-nig-in-2012-maker-of-racist-anti-obama-sticker-shuts-down-site/.

Kim, Dorothy. *Digital Whiteness and Medieval Studies*. ARC Humanities Press, 2019.

Kolchin, Peter. "The New History of Race in America." *The Journal of American History*, vol. 89, no. 1, June 2002, pp. 154–73.

Lombardo, Timothy. "Why White Blue-Collar Voters Love President Trump." *The Washington Post*, 16 Sept. 2018, www.washingtonpost.com/outlook/2018/09/17/why-white-blue-collar-voters-love-president-trump/.

Luconi, Stefano. *From Paesani to White Ethnics: The Italian Experience in Philadelphia*. State U of New York P, 2001.

Mangan, Katherine. "He Wrote about Racial Resentment in the White Working Class, Then They Proved His Point." *The Chronicle of Higher Education*, 29 Apr. 2019, www.chronicle.com/article/he-wrote-about-racial-resentment-in-the-white-working-class-then-white-nationalists-proved-his-point/.

Martin, Adam. "Obama: 'If I Had a Son, He'd Look like Trayvon.'" *The Atlantic*, 23 Mar. 2012, www.theatlantic.com/national/archive/2012/03/obama-if-i-had-son-hed-look-trayvon/330207/.

Martin, Jonathan, and Amie Parnes. "McCain: Obama Not an Arab, Crowd Boos." *Politico*, 10 Oct. 2008, www.politico.com/story/2008/10/mccain-obama-not-an-arab-crowd-boos-014479.

Martinez, Celia. "What Is Whiteness?" *The Santa Clara*, 25 May 2018, the-santa-clara.squarespace.com/blog/what-is-whiteness.

McEvoy, Jemima. "Sales of 'White Fragility' and Other Anti-Racism Books Jumped over 2000% after Protests Began." *Forbes*, 22 July 2020, www.forbes.com/sites/jemimamcevoy/2020/07/22/sales-of-white-fragility-and-other-anti-racism-books-jumped-over-2000-after-protests-began/.

Metzl, Jonathan M. *Dying of Whiteness: How the Politics of Racial Resentment Is Killing America's Heartland*. Basic Books, 2019.

Morrison, Toni. *Playing in the Dark: Whiteness in the Literary Imagination*. Harvard UP, 1992.

"The New KKK." *United Shades of America*, created by W. Kamau Bell, season 1, episode 1, CNN, 24 Apr. 2016.

Painter, Nell Irvin. *The History of White People*. W. W. Norton, 2010.

Perlstein, Rick. "Exclusive: Lee Atwater's Infamous 1981 Interview on the Southern Strategy." *The Nation*, 13 Nov. 2012, www.thenation.com/article/archive/exclusive-lee-atwaters-infamous-1981-interview-southern-strategy/.

Phillips, Amber. "'They're Rapists.' President Trump's Campaign Launch Speech Two Years Later, Annotated." *The Washington Post*, 16 June 2017, www.washingtonpost.com/news/the-fix/wp/2017/06/16/theyre-rapists-presidents-trump-campaign-launch-speech-two-years-later-annotated/.

Pierce, Andrew. "The Myth of the White Minority." *Critical Philosophy of Race*, vol. 3, no. 2, 2015, pp. 305–23.

Roediger, David. *Class, Race, and Marxism.* Verso Books, 2017.

———. *The Wages of Whiteness: Race and the Making of the American Working Class.* Verso Books, 1991.

Santa Clara University College Republicans. Email to Santa Clara U Listserv with subject line "SCU College Republicans' Response to the 'S-Know Your Whiteness' Bulletin Board." 7 May 2018.

Serwer, Adam. "Birtherism of a Nation." *The Atlantic*, 13 May 2020, www.theatlantic .com/ideas/archive/2020/05/birtherism-and-trump/610978/.

Shimshock, Rob. "'S-Know Your Whiteness' Bulletin Board Hits Cali School." *The Daily Caller*, 4 Apr. 2018, dailycaller.com/2018/04/04/santa-clara-university-s -know-your-whiteness/.

Snow White and the Seven Dwarfs. Walt Disney Productions, 1937.

Spear, Michael. "A Public Forum: Scholarly Controversy: Whiteness and the Historians' Imagination." *International Labor and Working-Class History*, no. 62, fall 2002, pp. 189–93.

Sueyoshi, Amy. "Making Whites from the Dark Side: Teaching Whiteness Studies at San Francisco State University." *The History Teacher*, vol. 46, no. 3, May 2013, pp. 373–96.

Tanner, Samuel J. *Whiteness, Pedagogy, and Youth in America: Critical Whiteness Studies in the Classroom.* Routledge, 2018.

"Unity RLC." *Santa Clara University*, 2023, www.scu.edu/living/residential-living -options/rlc-undergraduate-housing/unity---mclaughlin-walsh-hall/.

Watson, Veronica T. *The Souls of White Folk: African American Writers Theorize Whiteness.* UP of Mississippi, 2013.

White like Me: Race, Racism, and White Privilege in America. Written by Tim Wise et al., Media Education Foundation, 2013.

Williamson, Joel. *The Crucible of Race: Black-White Relations in the American South Since Emancipation.* Oxford UP, 1984.

Wise, Tim. *White like Me: Reflections on Race from a Privileged Son.* Soft Skull Press, 2004.

Dwelling in the Borders: Scoring Fairly in Advanced Placement Writing

Leslie Anne Singel and Ash Evans

Many instructors of writing agree that assessing writing is subjective because readers value various elements of composition differently, even after rubrics. Valerie Balester explains: "In teaching, writing rubrics share the spotlight with textbooks as a means to train novice teachers and to express and enforce common standards. Because of their powerful influence in instruction, rubrics announce forcefully how we define 'good' writing" (63). In this essay, we take up the conflict between two definitions of subjectivity in scoring the Advanced Placement (AP) English Language and Composition exam: scorers' personal subjectivity—their sociocultural and political identities—and the subjectivity of assessment—how the identities of scorers can undermine the AP rubrics' reliability.

Mass-market standardized tests with significant consequences (college admission, credit, or placement) like the AP exam are held to the highest standards and expectations. Our essay focuses directly on the scorers of one particular standardized test. Because the AP English Language and Composition exam has educational and economic consequences for students, this study analyzes scorers' subjectivity and identifies the student populations who are most affected by that subjectivity. Our study of the 2017 exam reading highlights groups of students who are potentially overlooked because of scorers' personal subjectivities and lack of effective training.

This study arises from our own experiences at the reading for the AP English Language and Composition exam.[1] Even with the calibration process meant to train the hundreds of readers to the same rubric interpretation, we could not avoid observing scorers' personal subjectivities during assessment. During the AP reading in 2015, one author, Leslie Singel, occasionally overheard high school teachers criticizing scorers who taught at the college level, implying that they were reading too fast, not considering all the elements of the essay, and as a result were scoring essays too low. Both authors witnessed similar comments at the AP readings in 2016 and 2017. Yet we, as college instructors, were impressed by the quality of essays that had been produced in only forty minutes of writing and felt that we might be scoring leniently as a result. One experienced AP scorer and college instructor whom Ash Evans interviewed admitted, "I tend to score high because I want to give students the benefit of the doubt and encourage their development, even if it's not really fair." Both Singel and Evans heard scorers say something to the effect of "My students write much better than this" or "Remember: these could be our kids" while scoring essays. Similarly, the majority of teachers interviewed in this study reported thinking about "the student behind the essay," especially when students mention their personal lives explicitly in their writing. These varying personal subjectivities are issues of assessment.

The AP assessment process for the English Language and Composition exam appears to be a well-honed operation, but Educational Testing Service (ETS) and the hundreds of scorers involved must continue to ensure that each student is provided a reliable reading. With our study, we add to the growing body of work that examines how the AP scoring process fails to reliably assess all exams. The scope of this study extends the work of previous assessment scholarship devoted to ensuring that the subjectivity of scorers does not hinder writing assessment (see, for example, Inoue, *Antiracist Writing Assessment Ecologies* and "Theorizing Failure"; Breland). In joining this scholarship, we agree that the layers of training, scoring, backreading, and digital auditing of the AP reading theoretically produce a finely tuned rating process. But scorers' subjectivities guarantee that perfect calibration can never be achieved, thereby contributing to a possible erosion of validity.

Norming for the AP Reading for English Language and Composition

The AP reading annually assesses thousands of high school students' exams—including more than 1.74 million essays in 2018 and 1.71 million in 2019 for the English Language and Composition exam alone—and scorers implement the *AP English Language and Composition Scoring Guidelines* as a control function to manage the varying subjectivities that can infiltrate reliable writing assessment. Scorers must either teach AP Language and Composition or be college composition instructors; as long as they score within an acceptable range, they are invited back to score the following June. The first session of the weeklong reading focuses entirely on learning about, applying, and working toward what AP leaders commonly refer to as "internalizing" the scoring guide, a rubric based on descriptive features of thinking and writing. For example, essays that are "sophisticated in their argument" and "impressive in their control of language" merit the highest score, while students who fail to develop an argument or control diction and syntax, or who use evidence "inappropriately" or "unconvincingly," receive lower scores. For eight hours a day, scorers read in large rooms or exhibit halls, divided in small groups and placed at folding tables. Each essay question has a question leader who guides the training of four hundred to five hundred scorers and manages time, and each scorer has a table leader who provides individual feedback, guidance, and occasional backreading (systematic checking of scores to ensure reliability). Throughout the week, scorers have multiple chances to discuss the writing criteria found in the scoring guide through the guidance of a question leader or individually with a table leader; the scoring guide is thoroughly dissected, followed by application and examination in sample essays every day.

While subjectivity cannot be entirely removed from any writing assessment, this training is designed to calibrate scorers and to keep them normed for the entire week according to the agreed-upon interpretations of the scoring guide by the AP development team. Holistically, the scoring process operates effectively for the AP reading. After all, as Hunter Breland points out, the Educational Testing Service (ETS) has made great strides in establishing reliability since its inception. For example, in 1961, ETS distributed three hundred essays by first-year students to fifty-three professional scorers from different fields. On a nine-point scale, thirty-seven percent of essays received eight different ratings, twenty-three percent received seven different ratings, and thirty-four percent received *all possible ratings* (Breland 1). The present-day calibration system ensures a much more uniform scoring process and, it is hoped, a more reliable one.[2]

It would seem that a comprehensive rating process should produce reliable scores. According to ETS's identified standards of reliability (Baldwin et al.), the AP reading is reliable. Doug Baldwin defines reliability as "the consistency of measurement" (328), and Baldwin, Mary Fowles, and Skip Livingston describe a holistic process of scoring that requires independent assessment tasks evaluated by multiple scorers, a process tailored to account for potential misreadings of tests. For example, "If the scorer reacts in an atypical way to the response (e.g., the response may have an unusual approach to the task), the test taker's score for the entire assessment will be inaccurate. . . . The safest way to minimize this effect is to provide thorough training and to increase the number of different scorers whose ratings determine an individual test taker's score" (Baldwin et al. 11). Yet the present-day scoring process focuses almost entirely on addressing subjectivity of assessment or the scorers' interpretation of rubrics. Training is not tailored toward addressing personal subjectivities of assessment, such as how scorers' sociocultural and political beliefs affect scoring. If we interrogate ETS's requirements for reliability, we find that the "anomalous ratings" are affecting students (11).

Methodology

In order to examine the training and holistic scoring of the AP English Language and Composition exam, we considered the following questions:

> Why might scorers rate essays more rigorously or generously, especially when considering their own personal subjectivities?

How might gaps in scorer training lead to unreliable readings for some students?

Who is in danger of being overlooked or disregarded due to such training gaps and/or rubric application?

With these questions in mind, we analyzed the exam scoring process at the 2016, 2017, and 2018 AP readings, including accompanying materials, training sessions, and individuals involved with the scoring and development of the exam. We chose to perform interviews at the 2017 reading in order to examine materials and individuals most pertinent to our research questions, including individuals immediately associated with the AP exam, such as ETS associates who develop the AP exam.

During the 2017 reading, Evans estimates that she read more than twelve hundred student essays over seven days. Singel estimates that she read more than a thousand student essays over seven days. The AP development team meets one week prior to the scoring each year to establish scoring parameters, to develop best training practices, and to select several student essays to function as norming essays during training sessions the morning of the first day of the reading and throughout the week. For example, Evans received a packet of eighty sample student essays, ranging in length from one word to five pages. To ensure student anonymity in the following pages, we have invented writing examples that contain similar sentiments as the essays we encountered. The objectives and quality of the responses, however, remain the same.

Over seven days, we orally interviewed fifteen scorers at the AP reading about personal subjectivities in scoring. Three scorers were interviewed with the same questions by email in order to obtain textual transcriptions of interview answers. The scorers interviewed included two first-time scorers, seven experienced scorers, two table leaders, one question leader, and one chief reader; these interviewees are provided pseudonyms to preserve their anonymity. Interviewing those directly involved with the organization of the AP exam (scorers, table leaders, question leaders) informed many of the observations we gathered about student essays. Our own observations are included; the articulation and recording of personal experiences provided relevant insight to help us explore the complexities of our research questions. Interview questions are listed in the appendixes.

The only documents examined in this study are those made publicly available by the College Board or ETS; we do not directly reference or include classified or private documents provided to us during the AP reading. We accessed the documents available online at *AP Central* (apcentral.collegeboard.org), including "AP English Language and Composition" (apcentral.collegeboard.org/courses/ap-english-language-and-composition/exam), and *College Board* (www.collegeboard.org), all of which AP scorers were given the option to access for supplementary materials. We also assess materials created by ETS, as ETS is the company that develops the AP reading exam for the College Board. All AP reading materials are copyrighted property of the College Board or ETS.

Scorers' Responses to Personal Writing

All AP English Language and Composition scorers at one point or another come across test booklets that are considered "off-topic" (*AP English*) and therefore do not merit a score above a zero or one. These essays are entirely blank, include doodles or song lyrics, or become a canvas for a bored, unprepared, or disengaged student. Many off-topic essays are entertaining to read; some provide a quick glimpse into the psyche of an anonymous teenage student. As we demonstrate in this section, the influence of scorers' personal subjectivity becomes more complex when the self-disclosure becomes more complex.

Scorers are advised to score essays that stray from the prompt as "off-topic," as prescribed in the scoring guide, and move on to the next essay, but we argue that purposeful personal writing, from private information to attempts at directly communicating with the assessor, should not be discounted altogether. Indeed, the stakes for personal writing on the exam are much higher than those for everyday classroom writing, and the willingness to throw away opportunities for college credit deserves attention as evidence of a student's state of mind. The most benign forms of personal writing are submitted by student writers who may want their reader to know something particular about their lives that may influence the way the prompt is scored. This personal writing in the exam can often include an aside from the student directed at the reader. We have both seen comments at the end of essays in the same spirit as "I'm sorry this is so short. I'm having a bad day" or "Please go easy on me!" Obvious instances like these suggest that students might assume scorers will rate them differently if they reveal personal information.

More specific forms of personal writing—like references to students' socioeconomic, religious, or cultural backgrounds—seem to be included for various rhetorical (or less purposeful) reasons. Some scorers consider personal disclosures as part of the student's argument, but that does not always make such content easy to score. For example, in the question Singel rated in 2016, one student included an emotional personal narrative that sparked an impassioned conversation throughout the entire room: some scorers suggested that the personal disclosure potentially overrode the quality of that student's writing, while other scorers argued that the personal disclosure contributed to the student's purpose. A score of six for the synthesis essay, or an "adequate" score, requires that the student use "evidence and explanations" that "appropriately and sufficiently support the writer's position" (*AP English*). The scoring guide does not clarify whether the evidence students must include should come primarily from those six sources students are provided as AP exam materials, however. D. W. Brown and Laura Aull's corpus-based study of the grammar and linguistic phrasing utilized in AP English exams revealed that "many lower-scoring writers commonly use a more involved, interactional style, expressing their literary judgments in ways that appear less formal" (405). Yet Brown and Aull suggest that "source-focused arguments" receive higher scores (412). Scorers who believe that the holistic scoring process is effective do not see such disclosures as problematic because they do not take them into account at all. An interview with a table leader, Samuel, who has attended the AP reading for thirteen years, revealed that such disclosures would not be registered in his reading:

> Other than the anchor essays and the scoring guide, nothing influences my assessment of the student essays. While I may get momentarily disappointed by an essay that doesn't quite reach the adequate range on the scoring guide (disappointed because I am rooting for the student and trying to reward her for what she does well), I never let my heart play into my assessment.

While Samuel reported that he would not react to a student's personal disclosure, he still admitted that there is an emotional connection to the anonymous student's essay and that he tries to read generously.

Yet the prompt for the argument essay in 2017 (see appendix C), which included a quotation about the role of artifice in politics and consumer culture, would have challenged even the most objective scorer because of the number of politically charged responses. Numerous students responded to the prompt by writing about the 2016 presidential election; their responses laid bare their own political affiliations and opinions. Scorers were reminded to discard their own personal subjectivities (political biases) when scoring, but there was no training in how to do so.

One scorer we interviewed, an experienced high school AP teacher and scorer, explained how he approached essays with personal content: "I remember kids writing about families that had different linguistic environments and what that meant for their own facility with language. I think I rewarded them if the example worked well to prove what they were trying to prove (but I think that is what we are supposed to do)." This scorer was quick to reflect on his own subjectivity when scoring this way. He added, "I wonder if I overvalue essays that make personal connections." Such admission and reflection seem crucial to acknowledging subjectivity in scoring.

Consensus on key terms given in the scoring guide remains elusive. What constitutes an "adequate" use of personal writing or personal disclosure; what is "off-topic," what is "effective," and what is information that hinders reliability of a scorer's reading? Some scorers treat personal disclosure in responses to certain essay prompts, like the source-based synthesis essay, as "inappropriate" or "off-topic," while others regard it as a rhetorical move. Other scorers insist that their personal subjectivities do not influence their scores.

Scorers' Responses to "Disturbing Content"

Providing scores for students' personal writing becomes more complicated when essays contain potentially harmful self-disclosures. Because some students use the anonymity of the AP exam to self-disclose, scorers need training to understand when "off-topic" responses have veered from the personal and have entered the realm of the problematic. These essays might include content that is illegal or harmful in some way (e.g., violence or abuse, depression or suicide, rape, self-harm, or cheating on the test). Our interviews with scorers, table leaders, and question leaders reveal a lack of general knowledge surrounding the process of identifying and scoring essays that contain problematic content.

During the 2017 reading, question leaders instructed synthesis essay scorers to mark any essays that contained "disturbing content" (a term not used in the scoring guide) with a Post-it note, to continue scoring the other essays, and then to pass the folder on to the table leader. They explained that scorers were expected to discuss the flagged essays with their table leader. If the table leader agreed that an essay should be flagged, they would pass the essay booklet to the question leader. The question leader was then in charge of deciding whether further action was needed, and the essay might be passed on to another employee at ETS for handling. Yet many such essays may not even make it to the table leader in the first place. After all, as mentioned above, scorers are trained to assign a score of zero to the essay if it "indicates an off-topic response" (*AP English*).

The lack of culturally responsive training and lack of language in the scoring guide about what constitutes "disturbing content" exacerbates the hazy line between an "off-topic" personal disclosure and a signal that a student requires intervention of some sort. For example, Singel encountered an essay in which the student spent their entire allotted time for all three responses writing about their state of mind. In this short memoir, the student recounted many personal experiences and choices that had contributed to self-destructive behaviors and made several confessions about their emotional state, including an indication of possible self-harm. Having submitted the necessary paperwork that accompanies a "disturbing content" essay, Singel received this booklet back from the question leader. She was told it did not "meet the qualifications" for a crisis essay. Thus, Singel's question leader did not judge the student's essay to be "disturbing content," despite Singel's assessment that the writing suggested its author might be suicidal.

The line between receiving a zero and receiving help is fraught. In another instance, one student spent their allotted time writing an apology note to the scorer; the student admitted that a health problem was preventing their completion of the essay. However, rather than stopping there, the student continued writing, sharing detailed descriptions of their home life and health situation that seemed to be a call for help. This student's disclosure did not pose a clear and present threat, yet Singel had the impression that the student's suffering needed to be addressed by an adult in authority. However, she was instructed to score this essay as "off-topic."

Part of the inconsistency in determining what is "disturbing content" surely results from the lack of culturally responsive training, but another part may result from a specific scoring protocol orally communicated to individual scorers: as explained to Singel during the 2016 reading, an essay is only deemed disturbing if the student writes about an impending danger in the present tense. Examples might include "I am suicidal," "I am being abused," or "I am bringing a gun to school." In another essay Singel encountered, a student appeared to misunderstand the writing prompt, which asked students to make an argument for or against the concept of disobedience. In what was either a poorly chosen example or an actual threat, the student said something to the effect of "You have to get what you want. You have to take a gun and shoot it. If there are bullies, you have to take care of it." This essay was not even passed up to the question leader, because it was not a direct, present-tense threat. In the first example above, a student neglected their chance to earn college credit in order to write for help for two hours. The latter example was in definite need of further examination, especially when considering the potential threat of violence to others; there would have been very little harm in making sure this student was simply attempting to supply the prompt with an example rather than suggesting a violent act or thinking about a school shooting. Yet no action was taken to follow up with either student, and the strict parameters defining "disturbing content" most likely meant these students received "off-topic" scores of zero. As Lauren, an AP teacher of ten years' standing, remarked about a "disturbing content" essay with a suicide note that she had encountered, "This happened a month ago, that's the only thing. Hopefully someone caught up with this kid between then and now."

Part of building a culture of scorers who are aware of how to handle "disturbing content" essays is creating awareness that these kinds of essays are not necessarily uncommon. There is no accessible data regarding how many essays of this nature are read every year. We have not encountered disturbing content in any sample essays during our years of training at the AP reading, yet we both have come across disturbing content and have had multiple scorers at our tables (in each year we have attended the reading) who have also encountered such content.[3] Scorers we interviewed are aware of this inconsistency. When asked about the process for handling disturbing content at the reading, one experienced scorer noted, "[M]y impression is that they don't want to be too explicit about it." He continued, "Everyone wants to pass the buck a little bit when that comes up. There's always this hesitancy about going on record and saying 'this kid is at risk for some reason' because then they would feel implicated."

What also became clear through our interviews is that many scorers and table leaders reported a different process for disturbing content, all the way down to training. One table leader reported that she did not receive any training in identifying disturbing content but "absolutely" thought table leaders should be receiving such training. One interviewee on the AP development team reported that "disturbing content" essays are "discussed at various levels of leadership." That was the most information they would share with us. This interviewee believed these discussions were "very useful" because chief readers were able to join "with ETS personnel to discuss periodically what does or does not qualify as 'disturbing.'"

Similar discussions would benefit the rest of the scorers at the AP reading as well: the scorers and table leaders we interviewed did not know what happened to these essays once they left their tables and scoring rooms. The three question leaders we interviewed said they were unsure about what happened to the essays after they were given to ETS, other than that someone there determined how to handle them. One former chief reader was not even sure what happened to the flagged essays. From what we gathered during the recent AP reading, the next step was assumed to involve contacting the student's parents, law enforcement, or DCFS, depending on the content. The number of scorers flagging essays with disturbing content suggests that scorers think ignoring these students at their most vulnerable is vastly irresponsible. These students can be found and contacted; their test booklets identify their schools and initials. Such examples lead us to believe that these students' voices are being largely ignored.

Scorers' Responses to Variations on Standard Written English

Scorers are not properly prepared to address self-disclosed content, and many are also improperly trained to score the variety of student voices they encounter. The scoring guide instructs scorers to rate based on Standard Written English (SWE), and while essays on the high end of the rubric are allowed some leeway—scorers are reminded that these essays can be flawed—essays that have grammar or mechanics issues are destined to receive very low scores despite whatever content students might include. The scoring guide instructions state that scorers should never "give a score higher than 2 to a paper with errors in grammar and mechanics that persistently interfere with your understanding of meaning." This wording reflects a 2017 change by the AP Language and Composition leadership from "distracting errors in grammar in mechanics" to "errors in grammar and mechanics that persistently interfere." According to an interview with a question leader, the term "distracting" was believed to be more likely to result in inconsistent scoring. As the question leader described it, an individual scorer might be "distracted" by comma splices, for example, and have difficulty scoring holistically, while another might discount grammatical errors altogether. In other words, one reader's interpretation of grammar rules could determine a student's ability to earn college credit.

Focusing on lapses in argument, style, or mechanics allows scorers a broad range of reasons to lower a score for an essay with an atypical writing style. But one AP scorer, Jason, who teaches at a large high school that he describes as ethnically and racially diverse, complicates this idea by challenging what the SWE policy means:

> That still begs questions about what Standard Written English is and how we discern that. And fine if that's what it is [the requirement to write with SWE], but we don't receive any training about what constitutes that. That means it's all going to be based on the racial status quo that is going to privilege one thing and not another.

If scorers follow the scoring guide and abide by the SWE policy, it would seem that there is no reason to question the reliability of scoring: the test is reliable because it scores what it is designed to test. However, without clear acknowledgment in sample essays, training discussions, and the scoring guide of what SWE stands for (including what specifically comprises "elements of effective writing" or "lack of control"), the risk of unaddressed personal subjectivity and personal biases remains.

Our interviews revealed a discrepancy between scorers' training experiences and what College Board representatives report occurring in regard to non-SWE essays. A former chief leader insisted that samples are provided that address non-SWE essays and that these essays are discussed at the table level. The authors have never had discussions about a non-SWE essay during their time at the AP reading; some interviewees reported scoring at the reading for several years and could not remember having these conversations either. Jason's account above mirrors several other scorer interviews regarding non-SWE, English as a Second Language (ESL), or English Language Learner (ELL) writing. The policy to adhere to SWE in the classroom and on the exam calls attention to the scoring problems that arise when SWE is not the writer's writing style or when English is not the writer's first language. In his interview, Jason wondered what kinds of judgments are made about his students and what perceptions surround his African American students' writing at the AP reading. He reflected,

> I've been thinking a lot about what it means when the rubric says "control of language" and what people in this room may or may not decide is or is not "control of language," such as if a verb is inflected the way that Black English might have inflected it. Does that get read as "not controlled" in an otherwise good essay? I wonder how many people in this room are like, "Oh, this person probably is a little less intelligent," even though they're not less intelligent.

Jason thought the same subjectivity might affect ELL students, whereas students who write with SWE could receive a "bump" in their score. A debate overheard by Evans between a scorer and a table leader involved a student who either did not "have a sense of sentence structure" or who "was writing so quickly [they] didn't bother to put periods." When scorers make assumptions about students' gender, race, or ability to compose with SWE, it is unclear if the student is actually receiving a score based on a holistic read.

The transparency about SWE and the treatment of all non-SWE essays is left open to interpretation for individual scorers, which raises questions about the integrity of training and norming. In an interview, Lauren explained that the scoring guide is "somewhat helpful" when she comes across ESL and ELL essays, including essays wherein students self-identify as speaking a first language other than English. But because an essay may not make clear whether its author is an ESL or ELL student, Lauren uses the scoring guide to guide her reading:

> I go back to the rubric: "control of language." Can I understand it without the articles? Yes. Can I understand it when the verb tense agreements are off? Sort of. But for the most part if I can understand it and the control of language isn't too off the charts confusing, I have been putting it as "adequate" if I get the gist of it depending on the rest of the essay.

We are particularly concerned about scorers who might encounter non-SWE for the first time and who lack training that asks them to address their potential biases or prejudices before providing a score. From our observation of these essay examples and discussions about essays with interviewees, our sense is that scorers do not receive enough training for scoring non-SWE essays.

Implications for the AP Composition and Language Exam

As demonstrated in the study recounted above, the personal subjectivities of AP scorers are complicated by factors such as a student's personal writing, "disturbing content," and non-SWE writing; we conclude by offering recommendations for addressing each of these complications below.

Personal Writing

There are immediate improvements the College Board can implement so that students' personal writing is no longer ignored during the training and scoring process. It is unclear how scorers can understand what is considered "acceptable" personal writing if they do not encounter examples in their training. Indeed, scorers who are under the impression that personal writing constitutes an "off-topic" response may feel obliged simply to assign a score of zero.

Perhaps even more important for the College Board to consider during training is scorers' need for practice in addressing their own subjectivities toward personal disclosures. To the instances we mention above, readers bring their own subjectivities, whether consciously or not. Even with redundancies in place to verify scores, some students' scores might be the result of one person's subjectivities.

Discussing essays during training that include personal disclosures would allow scorers to address, articulate, and adjust their own personal subjectivities in their readings of student essays that address emotional states of mind, socioeconomic status, religious affiliations, or cultural background.

Because the AP reading offers an opportunity for instructors to discuss pedagogical approaches, the treatment of personal content also provides productive material for scorers to review before returning to the classroom. To further progress such a discussion, AP course resources could include relevant scholarship and pedagogical guidelines for responding to such writing during the school year. Dan Morgan, author of "Ethical Issues Raised by Students' Personal Writing," proposes that instructors actively work with students who self-disclose in the classroom by aligning teaching pedagogies with their needs; he argues, for instance, that teaching rhetorical theory in the high school classroom could help students gauge appropriate times and settings for self-disclosure. Merely having these conversations in the classroom is a first step that AP instructors can take to help students who may feel that their only option is to self-disclose to anonymous audiences during the AP exam.

"Disturbing Content"

The issue of personal disclosure is further complicated by the lack of language in the scoring guide about "disturbing content." This is why training must occur before scoring begins. Without training, scorers may pass over students' self-disclosures or treat them as "off-topic" or "inappropriate" evidence. Scorers must operate with a more comprehensive definition of what constitutes "disturbing content" and thorough instructions about how to handle it. Training conversations guided by question leaders and open questioning by scorers at individual tables would allow scorers to discuss the complicated interpretation of such essays and help scorers who may not have encountered "disturbing content" become familiar with such themes. Likewise, a comprehensive guide about the characteristics of distressed or disturbed students could help scorers so that they know how to handle such essays. If time is an issue at the AP reading, scorers can be given detailed instructions in instructional packets about such essays or can be required to complete online training modules before attending the reading. These materials might also be made available to students on the AP reading website as part of the transparency policies of the test. Our hope is that future training will encourage scorers to err on the side of caution, reminding them that students have much at stake when making the decision to self-disclose on this test.

To continue improving transparency, the AP reading leaders can consider developing a more systematic and open approach for reporting disturbing content. The process of reporting disturbing content is currently laborious and unclear. When asked in June 2017 about what happens to these essays after they leave the AP reading, ETS was unable to comment, citing confidentiality reasons. While we respect and understand the legal privacy that students are granted regarding these matters, the process of what happens to essays can still be visible to scorers; it is unclear why ETS is unable or unwilling to reveal the process without revealing specifics about students' identities or their situations.

The College Board can also revise its policy for the treatment of disturbing content. Phrasing threats in the present tense is illogical in some contexts. Few students will say, "I'm going to end my life today" or "I am shooting someone later." If students are writing about any sort of personal or traumatic experience, past or present, we must listen attentively. Joanne Drechsel argues that while theory and practice must inform writing assessment, our humanity must inform it as well; students write honestly and with emotion, she argues, and so their risk-taking deserves human attention. Drechsel makes a case for listening to students in all writing contexts, including standardized assessment: "A placement procedure that ignores the social dynamics of writer, text, and reader marginalizes the very students we profess to help. By disregarding what students have to say, we silence their voices" (382).

We take the same stance with AP reading students: they must be identified and contacted when they demonstrate distressed or disturbed states of mind, no matter how minor the incident might seem. Scoring policies that neglect the very human aspect of writing fail to align with classroom practices that allow teachers to address students' personal, emotional, and mental stability, whether by talking to parents, guardians, or counselors at the high school level or by referring students to the varied services on campus at the college level. We must make sure that these same students receive attention at the AP exam and that this awareness influences the pedagogies that AP promotes. Maybe these students are bored or simply exercising creative writing skills. Maybe these students are truly hurting or thinking about committing some sort of violent act, as in the essays Singel came across.[4] If AP leaders and ETS, whether through policies that are too stringent or too vague, are in effect asking scorers to ignore these students, then they risk silencing students while asking teachers to neglect a major responsibility assigned them to support all students' learning.

Non-SWE Writing

Finally, SWE and non-SWE essays must be assessed using the same scoring guide and the same scorers, but both the scoring guide and scorer training must directly address how to score non-SWE essays. Bypassing training and discussion of non-SWE writing is not serving all students taking the AP exam. Writing studies frequently appears to champion students' identities, but policies—like those found on the scoring guide of the AP exam—still privilege the language of the dominant class. We are not the first to recognize this disparity, of course. Previous scholarship examines the intersection of writing and identity politics through the lens of rubrics, test assessment, and pedagogy. The National Council of Teachers of

English—an association for English teachers of all grade levels, kindergarten through college—has a position statement titled "Resolution on the Students' Right to Their Own Language," available since the mid-1970s. This statement affirms the diverse range of languages and dialects that students bring into the classroom. However, ETS policy and practice—at least in terms of the AP Language and Composition exam—demonstrate how harmful standardized writing exams can be for students if policy is not translated into action. Balester argues that many forms of rubrics "oversimplify and standardize writing, thus failing a significant segment of our student population, namely, students of color or students whose first language is not always Edited American English" (63). A majority of students who are ESL or ELL, or who might choose to write in non-SWE—such as African American students or students who speak a language other than English at home—fall into these categories and are profoundly and unfairly disadvantaged by this cultural bias. Recent scholarship quantifies this disadvantage. For example, Eugene Judson and Angela Hobson reveal that passing scores for Hispanic students decreased by 4.2% between 2001 and 2012 and that African American students had the lowest passing rate between 1997 and 2012. Asao Inoue questions similar results on university tests at Fresno State University, noting that even if teachers are racially unbiased, the low test scores for students of color or multilingual students cannot be ignored (*Antiracist Writing Assessment Ecologies* 7).

The scoring guide states that any deviation from proper SWE analysis style, writing style, grammar, and mechanics is unacceptable, but there is no training to help scorers read essays from diverse writers, which can take a variety of forms and require different kinds of holistic approaches. Inoue importantly asks, "How many prototypes or exemplars of good writing for any given assignment does a white, middle-class teacher have for, say, a local Black English Vernacular or Spanish?" ("Theorizing Failure" 344). In other words, if the assessor does not have an example of what "good" non-SWE writing looks like, then the baseline might be failure. Instead of docking students for not conforming to a privileged form of writing, rubrics reward diverse-language writers for what they do well. This is similar to what Jason suggested for his own students: he would like to teach his students about "negotiating" their Englishes rather than having to "punish them" or "correct them." The more variables there are to work with during the reading week—having more student essays but the same amount of time to read them, for example—the less time there is to devote to every issue that could arise when scorers are reading. Less training might suffice for experienced scorers, but that still results in new scorers every year asked to read without the proper training and guidance to score all voices effectively and fairly. Ellen Cushman has stated, "When dwelling in the borders, all possible knowledges, languages, ways, and values become apparent, each with their own unique means for judging the veracity of statements." We argue that "dwelling in the borders" is not something to be dispelled in composition assessment but something to be better understood and more successfully navigated to ensure the future success of all students.

NOTES

1. We received Institutional Review Board approval for the study, titled "Scoring Fairly in Advanced Placement Writing."

2. Breland's conclusions, drawn from his own research and many past studies, also reflect what ETS is doing right when it comes to AP assessment: reliability of direct writing assessment increases if there is a large number of scorers, scorers are assessing together in a controlled environment, there are multiple samples for each student scored independently, the scoring model is on the larger side, and holistic scoring is emphasized.

3. The 2018 essay prompt used a quotation by Anne Morrow Lindbergh: "We tend not to choose the unknown which might be a shock or a disappointment or simply a little difficult to cope with. And yet it is the unknown with all its disappointments and surprises that is the most enriching" (Lindbergh 113). When asked to write about "the value of exploring the unknown," students related a surprising quantity of disturbing thoughts and events, resulting in many stacks of flagged essays on the question leader's table.

4. Perhaps this is a question of labor: if more disturbing content is submitted than there is capacity to address by, at a minimum, contacting a teacher, then it is certainly time for the College Board to consider why students might be using this test to write personal disclosures in these essays at such a substantial rate.

WORKS CITED

AP English Language and Composition Scoring Guidelines. College Board, 2018, secure-media.collegeboard.org/ap/pdf/ap17-sg-english-language.pdf.

Baldwin, Doug. "Fundamental Challenges in Developing and Scoring Constructed-Response Assessments." *Writing Assessment in the 21st Century: Essays in Honor of Edward M. White*, edited by Norbert Elliot and Les Perelman, Hampton Press, 2012, pp. 327–41.

Baldwin, Doug, et al. *Guidelines for Constructed-Response and Other Performance Assessments.* Educational Testing Service, 2008, www.ets.org/pdfs/about/constructed-response-guidelines.pdf.

Balester, Valerie. "How Writing Rubrics Fail: Toward a Multicultural Model." *Race and Writing Assessment*, edited by Asao B. Inoue and Mya Poe, Peter Lang Publishing, 2012, pp. 63–77.

Breland, Hunter M. *The Direct Assessment of Writing Skill: A Measurement Review.* College Entrance Examination Board, 1983, pp. 1–27. College Board Report No. 83-6.

Brown, D. W., and Laura Aull. "Elaborated Specificity versus Emphatic Generality: A Corpus-Based Comparison of Higher- and Lower-Scoring Advanced Placement Exams in English." *Research in the Teaching of English*, vol. 51, no. 4, 2017, pp. 394–417.

Cushman, Ellen. "Decolonizing Validity." *The Journal of Writing Assessment*, vol. 9, no. 1, 2016, journalofwritingassessment.org/article.php?article=92.

Drechsel, Joanne. "Writing into Silence: Losing Voice with Writing Assessment Technology." *Teaching English in the Two-Year College*, vol. 26, no. 4, 1999, pp. 380–87.

Inoue, Asao. *Antiracist Writing Assessment Ecologies: Teaching and Assessing Writing for a Socially Just Future*. WAC Clearinghouse, 2015.

———. "Theorizing Failure in US Writing Assessment." *Research in the Teaching of English*, vol. 48, 2014, pp. 330–52.

Judson, Eugene, and Angela Hobson. "Growth and Achievement Trends of Advanced Placement (AP) Exams in American High Schools." *American Secondary Education*, vol. 43, no. 2, 2015, pp. 59–76.

Lindbergh, Anne Morrow. *Gift from the Sea*. Pantheon, 1955.

Morgan, Dan. "Ethical Issues Raised by Students' Personal Writing." *College English*, vol. 60, no. 3, 1999, pp. 318–25.

"Resolution on the Students' Right to Their Own Language." National Council of Teachers of English, 1974, www.ncte.org/positions/statements/righttoownlanguage.

Appendix A: Scorer, Table Leader, and Question Leader Interview Questions

1. Do you think you score high or score low? Why is that?
2. Do you compare the essay you're reading to your own students' writing? Does that influence your decision?
3. Do you tend to read objectively, or do you think about "the student behind the essay" as you read?
4. Do you see any other potential problems with the overall scoring system? Do you see it as a problem that subjective teachers score all the essays?
5. What do you do when you encounter disturbing content during the reading (for example, a student essay that includes self-harm)?
6. What happens to the booklet containing disturbing content after it is taken to the question leader?

Appendix B: ETS Interview Questions

Questions have been lightly edited for inclusion in the present volume.

1. What constitutes "disturbing content" in an essay? The AP scoring protocol deems an essay "disturbing" only if the student writes about an impending danger in the present tense; is this correct?
2. How do you think the scoring guide helps raters score essays that include personal and reflective writing, including essays that touch on disturbing content?
3. What happens to these essays after the AP reading?

4. What language from the scoring guide should scorers use to calibrate and train for nonstandard English writers or linguistically diverse writers? How might a reader use the scoring guide to perform a holistic reading for an essay with nonstandard English (for example, African American English)?

Appendix C: 2017 AP English Language and Composition Argument Prompt

The passage below is an excerpt from *Empire of Illusion* by Chris Hedges. Read the passage carefully. Then write an essay in which you develop a position on Hedges' argument that "the most essential skill . . . is artifice." Use appropriate, specific evidence to illustrate and develop your position.

> The most essential skill in political theater and a consumer culture is artifice. Political leaders, who use the tools of mass propaganda to create a sense of faux intimacy with citizens, no longer need to be competent, sincere, or honest. They need only to appear to have these qualities. Most of all they need a story, a personal narrative. The reality of the narrative is irrelevant. It can be completely at odds with the facts. The consistency and emotional appeal of the story are paramount. Those who are best at deception succeed. Those who have not mastered the art of entertainment, who fail to create a narrative or do not have one fashioned for them by their handlers, are ignored. They become "unreal." An image-based culture communicates through narratives, pictures, and pseudo-drama.

Building Connections

Listening to and Hearing Others

Jami Proctor Xu

Growing up as a girl in Tucson, Arizona, near the border with Mexico, I first became aware of social justice as an embodied reaction against the kinds of inequality I witnessed and experienced—seeing teachers treat Spanish-speaking students as unintelligent, the passage of an English-only law, and experiencing sexual harassment in class. In high school, I began to understand that these were part of the systematic inequality that exists here and around the world in terms of race, class, and gender. Working at a family-owned Chinese restaurant in Tucson led me to study Chinese, and I pursued graduate work in Chinese literature and women's studies at the University of California. In response to various injustices I witnessed and encountered, I left academia, decided to carve my own path as a poet and translator, and began participating in poetry events around the world.

Later, I became an organizer of international poetry events in China and South Africa, bringing poets from several countries together for readings, discussions, translation workshops, writing workshops, and local community events. I edit anthologies for these events, and for other projects, with the aim of making the works of more poets from all over the world available in translation. As a writer, I bear witness to injustices I see around me, both in the United States and as I travel, weaving in historical violence and its impact and continuation in the present while highlighting our connection to the earth and to all living beings. As a writer translating the work of other poets—primarily Chinese poets into English, but also poets from the US, India, and other countries into Chinese—I see translation as a way of using my platform to share and amplify Others' voices. As an organizer, I insist on inviting poets from diverse linguistic and cultural backgrounds, and I've fought hard for gender equality at poetry events, more than once refusing to attend an event unless they invited several more women poets (which they did). Much of my work as a writer, poet, teacher, and organizer involves trying to listen to and hear others and trying to create space for their voices to be heard.

Starting with the Children

Nathan McCullough-Haddix

In 2017, the city of Evansville, Indiana, was rocked by a viral social media photo depicting a group of white elementary school students, wearing towels and hooded sweatshirts reminiscent of Klan hoods over their heads, holding a Black baby doll by a noose around its neck, accompanied by the caption "Slaughter Gang" (Fater and Erbacher). The city's primary school corporation addressed the photo through a written statement that, while arguably well-intentioned, presented an incomplete understanding of diversity, limiting its definition to race and religion (Erbacher). In response to this incident, the Louis J. Koch Family Children's Museum of Evansville immediately found itself uniquely positioned to embrace fully its role as a leader in actively building an inclusive community in a more tangible way.

The museum created the Children's March on Evansville as a platform to amplify the voices of local young people relative to social justice issues that our city's students were facing in their schools, homes, and communities. Nearly three hundred children and parents came together for a rally featuring student speakers from local elementary, junior high, and high schools before being led by a student drumline to Evansville's city hall. In partnership with our local library system, displays were created within each of Evansville's library branches featuring children's books chosen to prompt children and their families to engage and discuss race, diversity, and inclusion in a direct and meaningful way in the comfort of their own homes. Additionally, our museum worked with the Arts Council of Southwestern Indiana to create a call for student art that expressed the march's themes through an array of media, such as painting, poetry, and sculpture, to be displayed in the museum's *Love, Not Hate Expressions* art exhibit ("Children's March"). This annual event continues to attract intergenerational audiences to emphasize the need for social justice at every level.

WORKS CITED

"Children's March on Evansville." *Artswin: Arts Council of Southwestern Indiana*, www.artswin.org/childrens-march-on-evansville/.

Erbacher, Megan. "EVSC Superintendent Reacts to Viral Racist Photo." *Courier and Press*, 26 Sept. 2017, www.courierpress.com/story/news/education/making-the-grade/2017/09/26/evsc-superintendent-reacts-viral-racist-photo/705013001/.

Fater, Tori, and Megan Erbacher. "Sheriff Investigating Photo That Shows Boy Mimicking Lynching Doll." *Courier and Press*, 25 Sept. 2017, www.courierpress.com/story/news/local/2017/09/25/vcso-investigating-photo-shows-boy-mimicking-lynching-doll/700488001/.

Social Justice of the Heart

Dianne McIntyre

When I was four years old my grandfather was pointing out different countries to me on the globe. He said, "McIntyre is not your real name. It is the slave master's name. Slavery was the worst atrocity in the history of the world. Do not ever forget that."

In the 1950s, at age nine, I was in an after-school dance program. We danced to freedom songs of Odetta. We meant everything we danced.

In 1970, I choreographed for the director and professor Chestyn Everett, who instilled in us that our primary duty as artists is to elevate Black consciousness in everything we do.

These memories stuck with me as I forged a path in dance and theater.

In dance we can paint a picture of atrocities, protest through our moves, or call for action through our choreography.

My avenue has been to speak to the heart. Once in a diversity workshop a white woman shared with me that she was afraid of Black men. I asked her why. She said, "Aren't all Black men violent?" I thought, "She is talking about my father." Soon I created a work about my father, *I Could Stop on a Dime and Get Ten Cents Change*—his stories. White audience members would say, "Oh, that sounds like my father." Once after I did a solo dance performance, an older white woman told me, "I never understood the blues until I saw you dancing it. And it's me!"

Sometimes the energy in my work emboldens audiences to go out and fight injustice or go out and take care of the family with more nurturing. Social justice in dance and performance can carry any audience straight to their heart so they are rejuvenated with vitality, understanding, and even love.

Engaging Social Justice Transculturally in a Team-Taught Language Course

Gabriele Maier and Sébastien Dubreil

Being a faculty member in a modern languages department is not an easy task given the dire situation in foreign language education nationwide. According to the *Chronicle of Higher Education*, more than 650 language programs were closed down recently over a three-year period (2013–16), and the latest report from the Modern Language Association confirmed this downward trend in enrollments (Lusin et al.). This decline in modern languages programs apparently coincides with a decline in students' interest in foreign language courses due to a strong prioritization of STEM programs (Johnson).

Yet not all language departments face low enrollment. The executive director of the Modern Language Association, Paula Krebs, maintaining that "when institutions support language instruction, students take language courses," declares, "Many institutions have had increases in enrollment" (Flaherty). And while more research needs to be done on the reasons that certain departments display higher success rates than do others, many authors point to pairing language learning with other subject areas as an important factor. "Languages are not a side dish that's extra, but it's a side dish that complements other skills," says Rachel Hanson, currently a research analyst with the American Institutes for Research, continuing, "You can use it to augment and fortify other skills that you have, and expand the application of these skills" (Friedman). Such an approach is thought to make the benefits of language studies more concrete for students who may not readily identify the pursuit of foreign languages as affording them necessary or even desirable skills on the job market.

Terry A. Osborn shares this sentiment when he laments the disconnect of language teaching to "the real world." Osborn criticizes language curricula for their folkloric view of the world and even compares current language curricula to a ride at Walt Disney World that features "automated puppet-type characters singing the theme song in various languages" (133–34). Instead of outdated foci on, for example, traditional family constellations or stereotypical food preferences, Osborn suggests a strong emphasis on social issues with the intention to "affect language and language forms, values and evaluative frameworks, political relationships and cause-and-effect relationships in our social world" (134). Language teaching must not happen in a vacuum but must be intimately connected to societal developments, challenges, and possible opportunities. Teaching for social justice, according to Christine Sleeter, needs "to challenge oppression, and to use schooling as much as possible to help shape a future America that is more equal, democratic, and just, and that does not demand conformity to one cultural norm" (qtd. in Hobbel and Chapman 237).

In foreign language teaching, issues of social justice have been gaining more traction and interest over the past years. Two reference books, *Words and Actions: Teaching Languages through the Lens of Social Justice* (Glynn et al.) and *Teaching World Languages for Social Justice* (Osborn), have been published, and conference panels are becoming more ubiquitous. For example, our careful perusal of convention programs revealed that in 2017 and 2018, the American Council on the Teaching of Foreign Languages (ACTFL) convention respectively featured twenty-one and twenty-five presentations that focused on or at least mentioned social justice.[1] Yet we find few language courses that deal explicitly with issues of social justice or place them at the core of their educational enterprise. The course presented in this essay fills that gap in the general language curriculum, and a collaborative class on the very topic seemed a particularly timely undertaking at Carnegie Mellon University (CMU).

Teaching for Social Justice at Carnegie Mellon University

Teaching for social justice at a university such as CMU, known for its high tuition fees (implying a student body composed of wealthy individuals), seems to be an important feat in and of itself. Yet the *Needs Assessment of Collegiate Food Insecurity in SW Pennsylvania: The Campus Cupboard Study*, commissioned in 2017 by the Greater Pittsburgh Community Food Bank, brought to light unexpected results: nineteen percent of all CMU students fall into the category of moderate to high food insecurity, and another nineteen percent of students are at risk of becoming food insecure (see Laughton; Semple). Those numbers reveal a very different side of a school that is commonly known for its state-of-the-art technology—namely that within the cohorts of high-performing students that help give CMU its reputation, some achieve in spite of difficult or adverse conditions. Therefore, in order to counteract a problem that touched nearly four out of ten students, CMU's first food pantry was scheduled to open its doors in November 2018, a date that coincided nicely with our plans to teach for social justice in the same semester.

From a demographic standpoint, the CMU undergraduate population presents an interesting profile: almost thirty percent of the student body identifies as Asian, twenty-five percent as white, four percent as Black, two percent as Hispanic, and a little over ten percent as multiracial ("Diversity"). In the light of these student demographics, we decided that teaching a course focused expressly on social justice at CMU was not only timely but critical to addressing social issues such as access to food, health care, education, and housing as well as the stigmas associated with lacking any of the above. We followed the advice of Jessica Papa and Rosemary Papa, who charge that "[i]t is the mission of all college/university instructors to become social justice instructors across the disciplines at the college/university level and encourage their adult learners to grow in their understanding of others, in this diverse world" (28). In doing so, we conceptualized a course that not only provided students with a thorough overview of the French and German welfare state but also covered social justice issues in the US through comparisons with US social institutions. We endeavored to alert students to challenges in their own communities that were closely linked to similar problems in France and Germany and often defied an easy fix.

This decision to design this course also stemmed from our own positionality vis-à-vis questions of social justice and our personal questioning about the role of educators in the twenty-first century, particularly at an institution that seeks to position itself as a leader in innovation and excellence in the face of the mounting challenges of our time. In our view, innovation and excellence do not simply equate to academic achievement and job placement. They also mean being able to engage critically with the various social, cultural, economic, and political issues; how those issues interact with one another; and what can be done to sort them out and propose interventions. As private citizens, we can take action at our own individual levels. As foreign language educators, by couching our teaching in transnational contexts, we can invite and guide students to consider various perspectives on what it means to build a society, to examine the influence of cultural systems on the ways in which issues are envisioned and solved (or not), and to engage with their own cultural assumptions and perspectives. As Anthony Liddicoat writes,

> The learning of culture cannot be isolated from the symbolic and interactional practices that constitute the learners' existing cultural repertoires. For this reason, language education has come to emphasize processes of decentering—stepping outside existing cultural assumptions to view the world from different perspectives—and mediation—interpreting cultural realities across cultural boundaries. (xi)

Using the approach Liddicoat describes, we can guide students to see the world and their own lifeworld differently and to ask critical questions of it. We can also link foreign language education with the proverbial real world in a social pedagogy (Dubreil and Thorne) through which students can envision a pathway to praxis—that is, to consider how education is linked to the communities around them and how they might transition from awareness to action.

Theoretical Foundations and Course Design

Conceived as a joint course, our class was taught in the Department of Modern Languages, where team teaching is not a common occurrence. Because we wanted to maintain a robust target language dimension, we offered our class under separate upper-division course numbers in French and German respectively so that it could be counted as part of students' major or minor requirements. Over the course of the semester, students used the target language during the portion of the course taught separately in French and German respectively but also collaborated across languages and cultures through seven "joint sessions," in which they conversed in English and participated in class projects.

While the improvement of French and German skills was an essential goal, our primary emphasis was on social justice issues in Germany, France, and the US and the knowledge and practical tools our students needed to become social advocates. We wanted our students to achieve the following learning objectives: to critically engage with social justice issues in France vis-à-vis Germany and the United States and compare these nations' different societal concepts and ideologies, to learn firsthand from practitioners in the field and from people in the respective countries, and to understand social justice activism and explore possible opportunities for future student involvements. We heeded the call by Nikola Hobbel and Thandeka K. Chapman to "explore social issues of social justice for the individual, community, and world" (236), which meant that through our classes, students came in contact with a variety of social justice issues and learned about individual advocacy projects. We wanted to engage our students in the spirit of Sonia Nieto's definition of social justice as "a philosophy, an approach, and actions that embody treating all people with fairness, respect, dignity, and generosity" (46).

Overall, we used a student-centered teaching approach wherein students chose their own articles for in-class presentations, led class discussions, and created their own websites that showcased their interest in social justice advocacy projects. Before we introduced students to the terrain of social justice in three different cultural contexts, we explicitly prompted students to voice their awareness of their own culture (Kramsch 25–26) and how it informed their views on social justice. Claire Kramsch argues that this introspective gesture of understanding oneself and explicitly articulating one's beliefs and values as a cultural being is a sine qua non condition for learning about another culture. We reassured our students that their perspectives mattered and were valued as part of the classroom discourse and experience (see Gay; Ladson-Billings on culturally responsive pedagogy).

In order to support students in their explorations of social justice issues, it was important to strive toward "cultivating a safe and inclusive classroom environment, where students' world views [could] be thoughtfully explored with a critical lens" (Harven and Soodjinda 3). We made sure that all opinions were equally discussed and became "*active* and *open-minded* listeners" (5) who encouraged everyone else to do the same. We often sat in circles to create a "sense of community among students" (6) and emphasized collaborative group work throughout the semester. Above all, our goal was to foster "an atmosphere of respect and acceptance of difference" (Harris 19) and to emphasize values that we wanted our students to carry outside of the classroom (e.g., when they embarked on their respective interviews with community partners).

To help us achieve these objectives and frame the course pedagogy, we turned to a rather small corpus of scholars who use social justice pedagogy in the foreign language classroom and amplified it with additional references. Indeed, social justice pedagogy is closely related to critical pedagogy and multicultural education and is anchored in the work of the Brazilian scholar Paulo Freire. Freire imagines a shift in the students' role from "docile listeners" to "critical co-investigators in dialogue with the teacher" (61–62), which can lead to "education as the practice of freedom—as opposed to education as the practice of domination" (62). Unsurprisingly, social justice education, according to Maurianne Adams, is rooted in the work of "generations of anti-racist educators, grassroots educators in the Civil Rights Movements, intercultural and MCE educators, feminists in the Women's Movement, experiential educators and T-group facilitators, educators working with social identity and cognitive development approaches" (74–75). It is supposed to "serve a curriculum whose goals include personal awareness of social justice issues, openness to different perspectives on complex social questions, . . . and motivation to take action to create social change" (62–63).

Whereas a wealth of books and articles on social justice instruction in the classroom (be it in social studies, English, arts, or even in mathematics) have been published, surprisingly few specifically deal with teaching for social justice in the world language classroom. To date, the two primary references are *Teaching World Languages for Social Justice* (Osborn) and *Words and Actions: Teaching Languages through the Lens of Social Justice* (Glynn et al.), the latter aimed primarily at the K–12 context. Still, these authors offer an impressive array of resources, including lesson plans, websites, rubrics, and more. Using both texts as our starting point to structure our course in general and our learning activities in particular, we also turned to sources outside world language instruction to inform the philosophy of our joint educational enterprise. Specifically, we drew inspiration from Chapman and Hobbel's edited volume *Social Justice Pedagogy across the Curriculum*, which offers both a historical and theoretical foundation of social justice and relates it to a number of educational contexts, as well as Özlem Sensoy and Robin DiAngelo's *Is Everyone Really Equal?* for the way in which it clearly explains various facets, some tacit, of discriminatory practices and discourses.

Themes and Learning Activities

The overarching theme in both courses was social justice in Germany, France, and, to a lesser degree, the United States, which meant that there was too much material to explore with any modicum of depth. After much deliberation, we chose as topics the welfare state (including its history, unemployment benefits, health care, and childcare), which afforded us the ability to address the foundations of social justice in each national context; the educational system (K–12 and higher education); and migration (with a specific emphasis on the European refugee "crisis" and the rise of right-wing movements in Germany and France). We supplemented these three main topics with shorter units on poverty (food insecurity and homelessness), environmentalism, and the relationship between the digital divide and precarity.

Our courses met twice a week for eighty consecutive minutes and for fifteen weeks. Each topic was covered over a three-week period (except for poverty and the environment, which formed one unit and were followed by only one joint session due to time constraints). Classes met separately to explore each topic in their respective target language and then came together for a week of two joint sessions with the goal of learning from one another and engaging in various projects.

As Glynn, Wesely, and Wassell state, world language teachers are uniquely positioned to "encourage direct comparisons among the target cultures and the students' first cultures, as well as question stereotypes and myths that students have about people living in other cultures" (190). Our goal was to emphasize the comparison between multiple countries and teach students how to "think critically about power structures in another culture . . . as a rehearsal for then focusing their analysis on their own communities" (Glynn et al. 223). To achieve these goals, we followed Glynn and colleagues' suggestions (310–24) and incorporated the following student activities and assignments into our syllabi.

Students were asked to submit a reflection journal every week in their target language (French or German) that focused on class content and feedback for us instructors. As Raquel Oxford states, "[S]tudents documenting their learning in journals . . . can be meaningful assessment of progress" (305). Students summarized and commented on key concepts discussed in class and assessed their progress regarding reading, listening, writing, and speaking in the target language. They also addressed collaborative activities with the other "half" of the course and were free to suggest different topics, genres, or a change in the methodology we used to facilitate learning.

Students were matched with informants from their target cultures in order to gain a deeper understanding of the issues from an insider's perspective. We chose the term *informant* because it is used in social science research to designate an individual who, often as a group insider or member of an organization, is able to provide specialized knowledge or expertise about a particular culture or community (Allen). In this course, informants were either students who are native speakers of the cultures taught or subject matter experts (or both), whether in the US or abroad. Students of German partnered with university students in Germany, whereas students in the French class met virtually with a graphic novel illustrator and a social worker who directs an NGO that facilitates refugee relocation. Both groups conducted interviews about the influx of refugees into the European Union. Interviews were transcribed and added to our class website. In addition, all students participated in a *Skype* interview with a German lawyer from the Federal Office for Migration and Refugees to learn about refugee camps and the process of seeking asylum. Finally, we invited guest speakers from the Pittsburgh area who discussed community social justice issues and described how our students might get involved.

For every class session, we assigned texts about French and German social justice issues that students summarized and commented on. Texts—in the form of newspaper articles, documentaries, infographics, comics, and academic journals or book chapters—provided the basis for group discussions and served as a springboard for a comparison with the US.

Our classes were student-centered and focused heavily on discussions. Students worked in groups, led discussions, and devised critical questions that delved deeper into the laws and regulations of the respective country, its historical developments, and current statistics regarding social justice. Students were asked to engage with the class materials and to repurpose them in the form of various deliverables (see description of joint sessions below).

Since, according to Sensoy and DiAngelo, critical thinking skills are "often underdeveloped in college students" (2), it was important to us to cultivate critical thinking—to make our students "think with complexity, to go below the surface when considering an issue and explore its multiple dimensions and nuances" (23). We wanted students to compare course readings with their own research and to arrive at a picture of French and German societies that differed from the ones portrayed in mainstream media. Our emphasis was on "the historical and cultural context in which knowledge is produced, validated, and circulated" and how it affects all of us through socialization processes that can often promote unconscious discrimination (42). We placed strong emphasis on textual analysis and open class discussions, where traditional values and dominant power structures became subject to intense scrutiny and, at times, heated debates.

Course Structure and Materials

Since the welfare state is a topic in constant flux, and every new government changes existing laws and passes new regulations, we needed to be as current as possible to teach our students accurate information. We relied on newspaper articles, recent documentaries, academic journals and book chapters, and interviews with experts in the field. In order to cover more material, we split our respective classes into groups and assigned different readings to each team. Each student group received ten minutes at the beginning of each class session to prepare short summaries for their classmates and to delineate the arguments found in their texts, followed by a brief Q and A session. Often, students drew parallels to situations and phenomena in the United States analogous to the ones described in the readings, which allowed them to see differences in power structures across countries and cultural systems. In addition, one student per class session researched latest developments of the topic at hand and provided a brief summary of the current topic or situation.

Our joint sessions were conceptualized to build on the readings and discussions in our respective classrooms and explicitly incorporated the US perspective into our teaching. Emphasizing student-centered learning meant our students educated themselves and each other about culture-specific perspectives on the topics we discussed in our separate courses. Apart from giving brief instructions about class activities, we held back and let our students take over.

Our first set of joint sessions began with two slideshows about the German and French welfare systems, including unemployment, health care, and childcare, that students had prepared in advance. After a brief discussion about the content, a guest speaker covered the US context. Students asked questions about state subsidies for child-rearing, unemployment benefits, and health insurance policies and compared the answers to what they had learned about their respective countries. At the end, students created three posters, each featuring one of the above topics, that were displayed in the Askwith Kenner Global Languages and Cultures Room, a designated multimedia room for the Department of Modern Languages at CMU.

Our second set of joint sessions focused on the different educational systems in all three countries. Students played a game in mixed-language teams that featured facts, data, and statistics on flash cards that had to be matched with the appropriate countries. The objective was for students to inform each other of what they had learned previously and come up with valid arguments as to why a particular fact would represent a certain country. After fifteen minutes, we revealed the correct answers and gave students another five minutes to discuss their two most surprising discoveries. The rest of the class was spent preparing for a debate for our following session, on the question "Should education be free and open to all?" Our debate model was based on Edward de Bono's six thinking hats—six colored hats that represent different perspectives and personalities we adopt when thinking about or debating issues. Red is emotional, yellow is optimistic, white is factual, green is utopian, black is pessimistic, and blue is the executive function or moderator. Students in mixed-language pairs were assigned one hat color per group and instructed to prepare their arguments accordingly. One of the pairs acted as moderators who initiated the debate by framing the issue, led the discussion, and intervened when students veered off topic or held the floor too long. The debate allowed students to explore different points of view and to research valid arguments to support their positions. They had to think creatively about an issue and respond to arguments that were not rational (red hat) or were overly pessimistic (black hat). The last twenty minutes of the session were spent debriefing and reflecting on the debate, both in terms of content and form.

Our third set of joint sessions featured plenary talks with guest speakers. Andrew van Treeck, a refugee and immigrant volunteer coordinator with the Jewish Family and Community Services of Pittsburgh, and Estelle Tian, a former ESL and citizenship instructor with Compass AmeriCorps, discussed the situation of refugees and immigrants in the Greater Pittsburgh area; explained the process of obtaining asylum and, eventually, US citizenship; and alerted students to the many volunteer opportunities that existed around them.

Another guest speaker, Zurie Choi, spoke by *Skype* from Germany. Serving as a lawyer in the Federal Office for Migration and Refugees, Choi reported on the refugee situation in Europe and explained her work in Germany and at the border between Greece and Turkey. Furthermore, she addressed the rise of the right-wing party Alternative für Deutschland (Alternative for Germany) and the general attitude toward refugees in different regions in Germany.

Our final joint session brought together all social justice issues discussed over the semester. Students worked in three mixed-language teams that created *Google* slides of students' outstanding questions and, after slides had been exchanged among groups, responded in writing to their classmates' questions. Our student-centered approach encouraged students to reflect on what they had learned, to demonstrate, beyond fact gathering, an understanding of issues, to examine critically what they still did not know, and to turn these gaps into cogent questions.

An essential component of the success of the course was our ability as instructors to reflect, communicate, and adjust as needed. This happened both between class meetings and during our joint sessions. Whereas most classes were taught separately, our joint sessions provided an opportunity for us as instructors to observe firsthand how the materials had been received, reconsider our respective teaching methodologies, share ideas and suggestions, and assess how the group was collaborating. Team teaching facilitated our self-development as instructors because it allowed us, as Marilyn Cochran-Smith and Susan Lytle write, to "collaboratively theorize, study and act on those problems in the best interests of the learning and life chances of students and their communities" (123). Planning sessions together, sharing previous experiences, and debriefing after each session helped us check our own prejudices before class, discuss our impressions of student reactions, and devise strategies to move the class in a different direction. Overall, team teaching became an indispensable asset and created an environment in which we could grow and self-reflect as teachers and social justice advocates.

Participants and Assessment

Our courses consisted of seventeen students—four men and thirteen women—with advanced-low language skills on average. Nine of those students (four men and five women) were enrolled in the German course, and eight students (all women) were part of the French course. Most students knew each other from previous classes and had taken courses with us before.

Our evaluation of coursework and students' learning was based on weekly reflection journals students submitted that featured comments and suggestions on the course. We also included class assignments (article presentations in groups, a midterm, and a final project) and exit interviews conducted anonymously and in writing.

The final projects, though connected, differed slightly in each course. The German students researched a nongovernmental organization (NGO) and explained in detail their personal interest in the NGO, the goals and successes of the NGO, the relationship of their chosen organization to similar NGOs in Germany, and suggested improvements to the NGO. Students presented their work to their classmates in the form of a website. The French students identified a social justice issue they wanted to support and a place in France where this issue was particularly felt. They then created a (fictitious) NGO to address this issue, which involved research on existing organizations (e.g., public authorities, other NGOs), on the gap their own NGO would fill, and on the logistics of their action plan.

Learning Outcomes and Discussion

The discussion of learning outcomes is based on evidence of learning we were able to gather from student projects and reflective journals, classroom observations, and final surveys.

Students critically engage with issues of social justice in France vis-à-vis Germany and the United States and compare their different societal concepts and ideologies.

"Learning not only language but culture and societal conditions of other peoples can build bridges and new relationships," Oxford argues (300). This statement precisely reflects our goals for the semester: to focus on a comparison between the French and German welfare states and to highlight their different ramifications for their respective populations. According to comments in the reflection journals, students enjoyed the opportunity to study more than one country in class. Many commented that learning about European countries had informed their understanding of social justice issues in the United States—testament to the importance of studying other cultures for better understanding of one's own. One student stated, "I really liked collaborating with [the students from the German class] for a lot of reasons. It was good to have a debrief at the end of each section by meeting with them." Students felt that having this multiplicity of perspectives allowed them deeper understanding of social justice and the national context they had set out to study. One reflected, "I don't think I always give social justice much thought because I am entrenched in my own life and getting good grades but I think this course really broadened my horizon. . . . I definitely learned a lot, not only about the French but also the American side."

Since the aim of the course was cultural exploration through the lens of social justice, the course structure made salient the necessity of acknowledging one's own cultural norms and values for the success of the enterprise: "I like the small-group work, especially with the Germans because we had time to talk to them. I like the projects that we did. . . . We had the French perspective and they had the German perspective but all of us live in the US so we all have—or should have—a perspective on the American context. So, we were able to share." Students witnessed and understood the importance of the US perspective, but they also realized that it was in the interaction between the three contexts where learning occurred. This awareness dovetails meaningfully with two of ACTFL's world-readiness standards for learning languages: comparisons and communities (*World-Readiness Standards*; "Standards Summary"). Students reported that the nature of the class allowed them to reflect on and recontextualize their own communities as well as broaden their perspectives on the issues we studied. One student characterized the collaborative sessions as "really valuable. We could have done it all in the French context, but having this other point of view made the class different and unique and a more meaningful experience."

Students' engagement with and critical reflection on issues of social justice was showcased in their work. In one activity, a group of students chose to examine critically the challenges of childcare from the perspective of a single mother (a character they created) and how these challenges manifested differently in the three national contexts. Their poster went beyond the exposition of information and demonstrated not only a deep understanding of each context but also an ability to package information in a manner that triggered reflection and empathy. More importantly, it demonstrated students' ability to understand how societal values and public policy support or constrain people's choices and lived experiences.

In addition, students showed signs of autonomous learning and the ability to extend their thinking beyond the context of the course, in particular in our last joint session, when students created questions for one another. One student found that session "really interesting because we ended up talking about all sorts of in-depth things; we ended up looking up things we hadn't even learned." This sentiment was echoed by most students, who felt that they had benefited from the interaction and that it had expanded both the scope of the class and their understanding of the complexity of the issues examined.

Even though most students enjoyed the focus and collaborative aspect of the course, we received some critical feedback as well. Some students in the German class felt that they "didn't learn much about the French context," which they attributed to the short period of time we spent with one another: "the depth of content was not really there; a lot of surface-level information." Some students criticized our joint class projects which "felt rushed . . . and I didn't think I got much from them." Overall, students preferred class discussions to teamwork in smaller groups, where not everyone contributed and conversations easily veered off topic. Yet students praised the opportunity to express complex ideas in their mother tongue, since it gave them a chance to clarify difficult concepts and "allowed [them] to be more articulate and put together." All students felt that the ability to speak English sporadically not only did not take away from learning French or German but rather enhanced the quality of their classroom experience.

Students learn firsthand from practitioners in the field and from people in the respective countries.

A significant part of our course involved meeting informants in person or virtually in Pittsburgh or abroad—university students, artists, professionals, and community members who had been selected for their expertise in the field of social justice. Students listened to presentations, interviewed informants, and overwhelmingly reported that our invited guest speakers afforded them firsthand perspectives on major issues related to social justice and validated the information they had gleaned from articles: "The guest speakers were really interesting because they each had their own expertise and it added a lot to the class." Another student described the conversation as "hard evidence" that supported the data and statistics in class: "Having guest speakers makes things more tangible and offered new perspectives." What became particularly visible for students was how complex and current these issues were: "Being able to ask questions of people who have information firsthand was really amazing, especially since we are studying issues that are changing still, and there are new developments all the time." Becoming aware of this ever-changing context and the need to be informed acquired a new importance for students. In sum, as one student phrased it, the guest speakers were "one of the highlights of the course."

Yet students clearly differentiated between guest speakers from the Pittsburgh communities they could talk to in person and the *Skype* interviews we conducted with speakers from Europe. In particular, the *Skype* interview with the German lawyer was met with mixed reactions. Whereas some of the German students felt overwhelmed by the plethora of details shared, several French students, conversely, remarked enthusiastically on the newly gained knowledge regarding the intricacies of the asylum process, both in Europe and the United States: "The lawyer was the most interesting speaker because I had no idea how the asylum process worked and speaking to someone who knew it so well was like a breath of fresh air."

In contrast to the *Skype* interviews, all students appreciated having speakers from Pittsburgh "because we are so much stuck in the CMU bubble that you don't really think about the outside Pittsburgh community that much, so I really enjoyed learning that we have much more than 'Hey, this is Pittsburgh; you go to school here.'" The general consensus was that careful preparation was instrumental in being better able to ask informed questions. One student stated, "For the speakers, I feel as though if you prepare more, you get more out of it." One major contribution of the speakers was that students felt inspired by their actions and got a sense of where to start to be part of a solution.

Students get a taste of what social justice activism can be and explore possible opportunities for future involvements.

Even though students did not actively go out into communities to volunteer as part of our course, class discussions revealed that many students were already involved in various social justice activities: they either volunteered on campus or with nonprofit organizations in the Pittsburgh area. Students eagerly shared their experiences with minoritized community members and even tried to recruit their classmates to join them. In particular, the interviews with refugee activists instilled an urgency in our students, who suddenly realized that refugees resided right in our backyards. "Social justice isn't just something that you hear about but something that is going on around you," one student remarked, echoing the feeling of many of their classmates.

The French students enjoyed their final project, which was the creation of a new NGO, and particularly appreciated the idea of starting from what they called a "gap," meaning a social need they wanted to address. After they had done their research, they identified where their fictitious organization could operate to add value to their target context. As one student commented, "I really like the final project. I thought it was fun and good to find a gap rather than just write about something that already exists." Another student stated, "I had a lot of fun with the final project. I really liked the challenge of having to research an area you want to improve, then research what is out there, and then create something of your own to fix a gap in what is already being done." Their organizations ranged from democratizing access to computer science education to alleviating the issue of medical deserts in France. While working on their projects, students began to envision feasible ways to address a social justice problem and gained an awareness of the logistics of implementation. Students commented that their nascent understanding of social justice, combined with their relative inexperience, was actually an asset in their ability to envision new practical solutions. In the words of one student,

> Even though there is a lot to consider in creating a new program, it may not be as easy as other more established ones, but I think that the fact that we are

> relatively inexperienced gives credit to the simplicity of certain solutions, and even though there may be resistance from some politicians and from the context, some of these solutions are easy to find and, with some refinement, could be adjusted, seriously thought about, and implemented.

She proposed an organization to help schools start community gardens to teach children about the environment and to provide access to fresh, organic food. She hoped that "[her] project could be implemented in some of the local Pittsburgh schools."

The German students created a website about a nonprofit organization they had determined they wished to support. Students researched the efficacy of the organization, compared it with similar organizations nationwide, and decided whether they wanted to contribute time or money to that organization in the future. During the presentations of their final projects, personal stories came to light. In creating a space where students shared their interests and experiences and received compassion and understanding from their classmates, our final presentations affirmed the value of empathy when teaching for social justice (see Jocson 257). Most students voiced their strong willingness to get more involved in social justice work—both during their final presentations and in their exit interviews. One student concluded, "This course gives me hope in the future, hope that there will always be people invested in the future of the planet, in the future of mankind, and in more equity."

Overall, our collaborative project on issues of social justice was successful. Despite sharing some critical feedback, students reacted positively to the course content and format. Additionally, we understood from the very beginning that "social justice is a journey of process and inquiry: Not a destination" (Oxford 301), and we were prepared to rethink our initial course methodology after every class session. What really stood out to us was the value of team teaching in the classroom. As stated above, sharing pedagogical approaches was invaluable and helped us both grow as instructors. We can only second Therese Quinn, who charges that "it is important for educators interested in developing an arts-based (or any) social justice curriculum to make it a priority to build connections with others who will support their efforts, including colleague educators in their own and other subject areas" (228). The course design supported our multiple focus by presenting regular opportunities for comparative study. Without the joint sessions, it would have been more difficult to justify assigning a selection of articles that specifically addressed comparisons between France and Germany.

In the future, our class will focus on direct advocacy in Pittsburgh communities and on campus. We know that the world language classroom does not have to be insular and limited to the target language. As instructors, we can and should branch out and seek collaborations with different communities, since "students and community members win when language study becomes a real-world experience" (Oxford 306). Judging from our students' comments, student-centered projects can indeed inspire students to become future social justice advocates, but actual community projects could be even more effective. In the words of the social justice advocate Ira Shor, social justice education "invites students and teachers to develop as citizen-activists, as critical readers of their world and its words, as community change-agents, as equality-advocates, as earth-stewards, as peacemakers, as constructive skeptics enabling group action, and as democratic partisans" (311–12).

NOTE

1. In the absence of available digital editions, personal copies of print programs from 2017 and 2018 are cited.

WORKS CITED

Adams, Maurianne. "Roots of Social Justice Pedagogies in Social Movements." Chapman and Hobbel, pp. 59–85.

Allen, Mike. *The SAGE Encyclopedia of Communication Research Methods.* SAGE Publications, 2017. 4 vols. *SAGE Research Methods*, https://doi.org/10.4135/9781483381411.

Chapman, Thandeka K., and Nikola Hobbel, editors. *Social Justice Pedagogy across the Curriculum: The Practice of Freedom.* Routledge, 2010.

Cochran-Smith, Marilyn, and Susan L. Lytle. *Inquiry as Stance: Practitioner Research for the Next Generation.* Teachers College Press, 2009.

de Bono, Edward. *Six Thinking Hats.* Penguin Books, 1985.

"Diversity, Equity, Inclusion, and Belonging." *Carnegie Mellon University*, cmu.edu/diversity/tartans/index.html. Accessed 17 Dec. 2023.

Dubreil, Sébastien, and Steven L. Thorne, editors. *Engaging the World: Social Pedagogies, Language Learning, and Language Programs in the Twenty-First Century.* Cengage Publishing, 2017.

Flaherty, Colleen. "L'Œuf ou la Poule." *Inside Higher Ed*, 19 Mar. 2018, www.insidehighered.com/news/2018/03/19/mla-data-enrollments-show-foreign-language-study-decline.

Freire, Paulo. *Pedagogy of the Oppressed.* Translated by Myra Bergman Ramos, Continuum, 1970.

Friedman, Amelia. "America's Lacking Language Skills." *The Atlantic*, 10 May 2015, www.theatlantic.com/education/archive/2015/05/filling-americas-language-education-potholes/392876/.

Gay, Geneva G. *Culturally Responsive Teaching: Theory, Research, and Practice.* Teachers College Press, 2010.

Glynn, Cassandra, et al., editors. *Words and Actions: Teaching Languages through the Lens of Social Justice.* ACTFL, 2014.

Harris, Michelle. "The Politics of 'Being': Faculty of Color Teaching to Social Justice in the College Classroom." Papa et al., pp. 15–22.

Harven, Aletha M., and Daniel Soodjinda. "Pedagogical Strategies for Challenging Students' World Views." Papa et al., pp. 3–14.

Hobbel, Nikola, and Thandeka K. Chapman. "Writing in Academic Genres: Is Social Justice a Learning Outcome?" *Social Justice Pedagogy across the Curriculum.* Chapman and Hobbel, pp. 236–49.

Jocson, Korina M. "Writing, Pedagogy, and Social Justice." Chapman and Hobbel, pp. 250–61.

Johnson, Steven. "Colleges Lose a 'Stunning' 651 Foreign-Language Programs in Three Years." *The Chronicle of Higher Education*, 22 Jan. 2019, www.chronicle.com/article/Colleges-Lose-a-Stunning-/245526.

Kramsch, Claire. "Teaching Language along the Cultural Faultline." *Culture as the Core: Interdisciplinary Perspectives on Culture Learning in the Language Curriculum*, edited by Dale L. Lange et al., Center for Advanced Research on Language Acquisition, 2000, pp. 15–31.

Ladson-Billings, Gloria. *The Dreamkeepers: Successful Teachers of American Children.* Jossey-Bass, 2009.

Laughton, Stephanie. "On Food Insecurity: Why It Is an Issue We Care About." *Student Government*, 8 Nov. 2018, www.cmu.edu/stugov/gsa/Blog/CMU-Pantry.html.

Liddicoat, Anthony. Foreword. *Developing Critical Languaculture Pedagogies in Higher Education: Theory and Practice*, by Adriana Raquel Díaz, Multilingual Matters, 2013.

Lusin, Natalia, et al. *Enrollments in Languages Other Than English in United States Institutions of Higher Education, Fall 2021.* Modern Language Association of America, 2023, www.mla.org/content/download/191324/file/Enrollments-in-Languages-Other-Than-English-in-US-Institutions-of-Higher-Education-Fall-2021.pdf.

Nieto, Sonia. *Language, Culture and Teaching: Critical Perspectives.* Routledge, 2010.

Osborn, Terry A. *Teaching World Languages for Social Justice: A Sourcebook of Principles and Practices.* Routledge, 2005.

Oxford, Raquel. "Second Language Education: With Liberty and Languages for All." Chapman and Hobbel, pp. 299–308.

Papa, Jessica, and Rosemary Papa. "Social Justice: Reframing Social Justice for the Adult Learner." Papa et al., pp. 23–31.

Papa, Rosemary, et al., editors. *Social Justice Instruction: Empowerment on the Chalkboard.* Springer, 2016.

Quinn, Therese. "Social Justice and Arts Education. Spheres of Freedom." Chapman and Hobbel, pp. 225–35.

Semple, Mandi. "CMU Food Pantry Opens Nov. 9." *The Piper: CMU Community News*, 16 Oct. 2018, www.cmu.edu/piper/news/archives/2018/october/cmu-food-pantry.html.

Sensoy, Özlem, and Robin DiAngelo. *Is Everyone Really Equal? An Introduction to Key Concepts in Social Justice Education.* 2nd ed., Teachers College Press, 2017.

Shor, Ira. "The Power of Not Yet in Power." Chapman and Hobbel, pp. 309–12.

"Standards Summary: Summary of World-Readiness Standards for Learning Languages." *ACTFL*, 2024, www.actfl.org/educator-resources/world-readiness-standards-for-learning-languages/standards-summary.

World-Readiness Standards for Learning Languages. 4th ed., National Standards Collaborative Board, 2015.

Social Justice Pedagogy and Collaborative Counterstorytelling: *We Are Reading*

Laurie Grobman, Heidi Mau, and Cheryl L. Nicholas

The dancers slide, thrust, wiggle, and pop as one. The power and forceful grace they portray can be described in no other way than mesmerizing. If you look closely, though, each dancer brings his or her own story and energy. The individuality that fuses together in their choreography can be better understood after learning more about each dancer because, like any art form, the mediums and juxtaposing elements create the beauty, depth, and catches the interest.

—Rachel Hayes, in *We Are Reading*

Theresa Gonzalez, Ashanique Monlyn, Liyanah Mann, Stephanie Seda, Caliph Shabazz, and Jaymes Williams performed in Lynn Nottage's multimedia storytelling project, *This Is Reading*, over three consecutive weekends in July 2017 in downtown Reading, Pennsylvania. Nottage created *This Is Reading* from the same materials and stories that led her to write *Sweat*, recipient of the 2017 Pulitzer Prize for Drama. *Sweat* exposes economic and racial fractures by following a group of steelworkers whose lives unravel when the company they and their families have worked for threatens to move the local factory overseas. Nottage developed *This Is Reading* as community-based public art with a social change mission. As she states in an interview, "We did the play [*Sweat*], but it felt like our artistic engagement was not complete. We didn't want to feel like carpetbaggers: people that sort of go in, take stories and then leave" (Collins-Hughes). Combining storytelling, acting, dancing, video, audience participation, and digital media, *This Is Reading*, showcased at the once-abandoned Franklin Street Railroad Station, aimed "to capture the voice of a city that is grappling with how to reclaim a narrative that has been fractured along racial and economic lines" ("This Is Reading").

Five months later, *We Are Reading*, a counterstorytelling collaboration, began with the six dancers from the production, five student writers at Penn State University, Berks (in a class cotaught by Laurie Grobman and Cheryl Nicholas), and seventeen students in a digital design class at Albright College (taught by Heidi Mau). This collaboration extended and expanded the story that Nottage had started in *This Is Reading* and *Sweat*. *We Are Reading*—the name the dancers chose for their dance group as a deliberate turn away from "This Is Reading"—endeavored to reshape and represent narratives about Reading, this time in the voices of Reading's young artists. *We Are Reading* is also the name chosen for the book and website emerging from the collaborative storytelling project. The book and website include the dancers' stories and images and are based on social justice principles embedded in the course design and pedagogies, from learning theoretical and conceptual perspectives on storytelling to conducting and transcribing in-depth interviews and doing collaborative counterstory-making. It was clear to us from the start that the circumstances and limited scope of this single project would not create significant material changes for the dancers or the residents of Reading. With this understanding, we turned to aspects of Iris Marion Young and Jacques Rancière's philosophies of nondistributive justice, recognizing the particular power of collaborative counterstorytelling and performance to achieve nondistributive outcomes.

This essay illuminates our path to achieving nondistributive forms of social justice. First, we discuss social justice principles of self-determination and self-development within our process and efforts toward making collaborative counterstory. Young argues that theories of justice must likewise concern themselves with social structures and patterns underlying distribution (*Justice* 15). For that reason, we did not focus solely on what people have or do not have, are given or are not given by dominant institutions. Interpreting Rancière, Thomas May argues that "[d]istributions happen to people; people do not make them happen. Or, if people make them happen, it is only indirectly, by making others make them happen" (47). To Rancíére, politics is equality, and politics "happens very little or rarely" (*Disagreement* 17). *We Are Reading* made politics happen. We aimed to empower the dancers as makers of their lives by considering concepts of domination and oppression as they impact "procedural issues of participation in deliberation and decision making" (Young, *Justice* 34); that is, the institutional rules, policies, and actions that determine both material and social goods (16). As Young argues, norms are just only if not coerced, and social conditions are just only if they permit all people to satisfy their needs and act freely (34). People must have the freedom and opportunity to make choices, to communicate with one another, and to develop and exercise their faculties (38).

To pursue these principles, we first focused on the process of incorporating critical pedagogical methods such as building a lateral learning community, finding and questioning "voice," and developing self-awareness into the overall strategy. Moreover, project meetings and participant interactions became sites for negotiating participants' understanding of their roles in developing and perpetuating self-development and self-determination. As we shaped the project around these nondistributive social justice goals, we also shaped the pedagogy so that our diverse student writers and designers would learn about Young's social justice principles (see also Young, *Inclusion and Democracy*) by participating in and being self-reflective about ethical and perspectival considerations when writing about marginalized individuals and groups.

By promoting self-determination and self-development, we sought to create a space for counterstory, a method of critical race theory. Daniel G. Solórzano and Tara J. Yosso define counterstory as "telling the stories of those people whose experiences are not often told (i.e., those on the margins of society)" both by responding directly to the dominant discourse and by revealing and sharing the "numerous unheard counter-stories" within minority communities (32). Thus, counterstories have the potential to awaken racial reform efforts as well as "help strengthen traditions of social, political, and cultural survival and resistance" (32).

Through counterstory, the dancers (as tellers and learners), the students (as writers, designers, and learners), and the instructors (as mentors and learners) cultivated what Jared Colton and Steve Holmes, citing Rancière, describe as "active equality"—"an ongoing process of self- and collective verifications of equality" by individuals and groups, independent of "permission" from dominant institutional structures and from redistribution of resources (6). In addition, we hoped students would understand and build on their potential change agency as "active" cocreators of social justice (11), individuals who attempt to persuade another person to understand, perhaps for the first time, another's "human equality" (13).

Setting the Stage: *This Is Reading*

When Nottage first arrived in Reading in 2011, she encountered one of the many postindustrial cities struggling to "identify new economic drivers to replace their lost manufacturing base and to address changing social and demographic conditions" (Mallach 125). In many of these cities, the more affluent Black and white people who leave the city for the suburbs as Latinx populations increase "leav[e] behind an increasingly marginalized and impoverished community" (145). After interviewing hundreds of diverse residents and workers in Reading, Nottage realized that Reading's fractures are racial and economic. As in many other cities in the United States, minority scapegoating for current conditions in Reading is common. As Nottage discusses in various media interviews, when her interviewees would describe Reading, "they inevitably began with the phrase, 'Reading was' . . . This is a city that no longer can imagine itself in the present tense. It has lost its narrative" (Hatza). *This Is Reading* was Nottage's attempt to offer a more nuanced narrative about Reading, juxtaposing memories with current images of the city.

From our first meetings, the dancers expressed their appreciation for the experience of taking part in the event but were not satisfied with what they understood as the performance's main narrative. They felt that *This Is Reading* successfully portrayed the "voices" of Reading's past but fell short of equally representing Reading's present. In our conversations with the dancers, we learned that they and their peers felt strongly that the performance neglected to delve into their stories—the stories of Reading's present-day population, neighborhoods, and in particular, young people of color—the city's future.

Collectively, these six dancers described themselves as people of color and identified closely with hip-hop culture. Theresa is Latina and of Puerto Rican descent; Stephanie was born to an African American parent and a white parent but was raised from infancy by her Puerto Rican adopted parents. Jaymes, Asha, and Liyanah are African American, preferring this identity label over Black. Caliph, also African American, emphasized his mixed-race Puerto Rican, Cuban, and West Indian heritage. They claimed that richer white communities in the Reading suburbs avoided the city and looked down on its inhabitants. Stephanie told us several times that she is frequently asked, "You live in *Reading*?" at her job in the suburbs and that her colleagues won't "cross over the bridge" into the city. Moreover, the group said that jobs were scarce and opportunities limited, but they still saw their city as a place with much to offer; after all, this was their home, where their friends and family lived and where they found their stories. Caliph and Jaymes, who identify as gay/queer, discussed their sexuality as an integral part of their dance identity. For these young gay men of color, the dance community was a place of refuge and liberation. This is where they were free to be themselves, to act and behave in ways that validated their queer identities, and to be with others like them. From our earliest engagements with Jaymes, Asha, Caliph, Liyanah, Stephanie, and Theresa, they had a lot to say about themselves, their communities, and their limited opportunities as artists and individuals in Reading. They saw this storytelling project as a way to be heard.

Finally, the dancers hoped the project would give them some professional traction for career advancement. Working in various full- and part-time jobs, each aspired to be a professional dancer while recognizing that options were limited in Reading. Although the *We Are Reading* book and website would offer some visibility and promotion, we explained that should they partner with us, the focus of the project would be on telling their stories and addressing their lack of representation in larger narratives about the city. We emphasized that none of us were business professionals who could strategically advance their careers beyond exposing their work to different audiences. Yet, given their career hopes, we brought on a local dance professional (now teaching dance at a college after dancing for several years while living in Philadelphia and obtaining an MFA) who agreed to mentor the dancers. We also secured funding for a three-year subscription for their web domain and offered training in maintenance of the site. It would be the only professional website they had, and they seemed eager about its possibilities for promoting themselves and as a mechanism for potential booking. Still, the main aim of the project was on building self-determination and self-development toward creating a space for counterstory. We explained to the dancers, in practical terms, the realities of what counterstory could and could not accomplish.

Counterstories challenge majoritarian stories by bringing other stories to the fore. Rancière posits that "the call for equality never makes itself heard without defining its own space" (*On the Shores* 50). Counterstory, as it is produced and in its publicly shared form, defines such a space as an act of "active equality," one that "verifies a person's equality without waiting for permissive social and political structures" and thus enacts social justice through the person's creative expressions (Colton and Holmes 12). Rancière further suggests that "emancipation" happens through "the verification of the equality of any speaking being with any other speaking being" ("Politics" 65). The *We Are Reading* book and website, arguably itself a counterstory (Grobman), empowers the tellers by providing an avenue for the dancers to speak, to tell their stories unbounded by Nottage's *This Is Reading* or by the university structure that was being employed to facilitate the counterstorytelling.

The analyses here are based on information collected from a variety of sources that highlight the dancers' and students' voices and perspectives. We looked closely at the unedited transcripts of the dancers' interviews along with the stories written by the student writers. We conducted group interviews and discussions with the dancers and writers during formal project meetings and informal interviews in dyadic or smaller groupings. We observed verbal and nonverbal behaviors, often asking questions to clarify the meanings and purposes behind those behaviors. Throughout the process, we performed what ethnographers call "member-checking," where we checked our perception or interpretation of what was expressed with the person expressing it. The stories themselves involved many layers of participant-checking, working closely with the writers and dancers, going back and forth, making sure that both parties felt the stories accurately represented their perspectives.

Process: Equal Participation and Negotiating Positionalities

Remaining focused on nondistributive social justice principles, we designed the project's process such that the dancers would be heard and seen. Through manipulation of interactional and relational spaces in the story-making process, we wanted to inspire and to witness stronger self-determination and self-development for the group generally and for the dancers specifically. Along with these efforts, we incorporated teaching strategies to meet the pedagogic outcomes for the student writers and designers. From the start, the students and we consulted with the dancers in every step, including pairing them with writers, developing the interview questions, the design selection, and the conceptualization and organization of the book. We wanted to create a space where the dancers and students were equally involved, given their different roles, and where their critical engagement with each other—given equal participation and their unique positionalities (differing perspectives and cultural locations)—would nurture self-awareness and authentic voice.

Equal Participation

Our project meetings took place in the city, not on our suburban campus; it was important that we meet in the city about which we were writing and that the dancers not feel like outsiders on our campus. During one of our early group planning meetings, we took time to get to know all participants and explored collectively the goals for the project, emphasizing equal participation in the process as a fundamental goal. We asked the dancers what specific topics they wanted written about and emphasized. They discussed their time at Reading High School, the people who mentored and supported them, family life, the role of dance in their lives and their futures, and their vision for the city, among other subjects. Jaymes noted that it was crucial that people outside of Reading get to see "all the positive things" that Reading offered, such as its diversity and arts communities.

We then asked the dancers to pick the themes that were most meaningful for them, as we would fashion the interview questions from their choices. The dancers and writers took turns writing on a whiteboard as different topics were introduced, from artistic and family influences to their minoritized identities. They explained that Reading was perceived by outsiders as a "bad" place, imbued with urban decay and fraught with hopelessness and loss. The dancers told us that they felt the stories should have a good balance of "keeping it real" while also breaking through these problematic perceptions about Reading and its communities. They wanted the stories to inspire other youths in Reading.

In these initial sessions, the group worked to come up with open-ended questions for the storytelling interviews. We worked separately with the writers to meet the course's learning objectives. As the students created the stories, they retained close communication with the dancers. The writing time was constrained by the parameters of an academic semester and the dancers' schedules, but it was critical to the principle of self-determination that the dancers help shape their own stories.

Each writer was paired with a dancer for their interview. Over a two-week period, writers and dancers met at least twice to complete audiotaped interviews. The interview method was taught to the students as part of the course, and the interview questions were generated in one of the group's early meetings with the dancers. The writers transcribed the interviews verbatim and shared the transcripts with the dancers, other writers, and faculty members, who together edited the transcripts for clarity and accuracy. The writers then crafted the dancers' stories

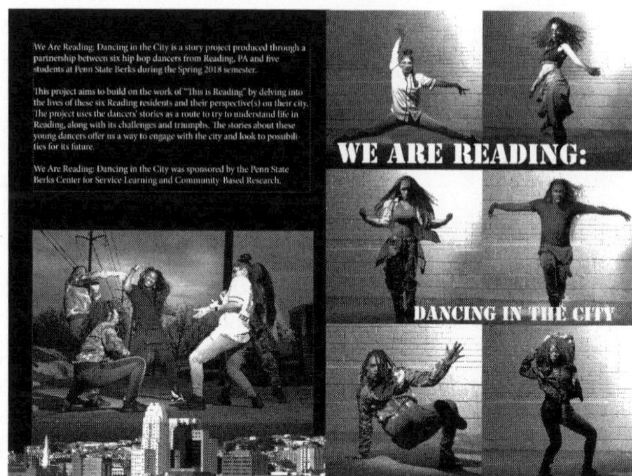

Figure 1. Cover design for *We Are Reading: Dancing in the City*, Penn State University, Berks / Albright College, 2018. Photography by Regina May Bross, Willow Street Pictures. Cityscape image courtesy of the Greater Reading Chamber Alliance.

while still in consultation with their dancer-partners. The completed stories were shared with the dancers for feedback and further editing before publication.

As importantly, and despite some challenges, Mau ensured that the dancers were involved in decisions about the visual aspects of storytelling in the book. Mau integrated the project within a digital design course and fostered students' affinity with the project through conversations about design and representation alongside ongoing discussions about centering the dancers' voices. A local photo studio provided professional photo shoots for the dancers to use in the project, and other images were taken by amateur photographers in the group. The dancers and writers selected photos from these sources, which the student designers reviewed along with the dancers' stories. The designers worked individually to produce seventeen separate book cover designs but worked in two teams to design the overall book layouts.

Voted on by the writers and dancers, the winning cover design (fig. 1) used stenciled typography for titling, incorporated a panorama of downtown Reading, and featured photographs of the individual dancers in action provided by a local photography studio. The dancers and writers picked the design that appeared more assertive and edgy than the option that incorporated static portrait images and allowed the dancers to be clearly identified in contrast to the option that depicted more abstract representations of dance (fig. 2). Caliph and Liyanah told Nicholas that the design made them seem "fierce" and ready for any challenge. The dancers' acknowledgement of this visually induced agency, working in concert with their choice for the book design, was a negotiation of equal participation as a core course goal.

Figure 2. Second-ranking (top) and third-ranking (bottom) cover design choices for *We Are Reading*. Photography by Regina May Bross, Willow Street Pictures.

Negotiating Positionalities

In the classroom, we focused on complexities of positionalities, interpretation, collaborative storytelling, and the practicalities of what can and cannot be expected in any interview setting. The writers were asked to be mindful of how their interpretations would be affected by their cultural location and positionalities. Among the student writers, Symone is Black and from Philadelphia; Imane is of African–Middle Eastern descent and from the suburbs of Reading; Megan and Rachel are white, also from the local suburbs; and Chelsea is white and from rural Berks County. These students were selectively invited to participate in this project by virtue of their social justice spirit and writing acumen. As part of their coursework, the writers learned about interviewing as a method of community-engaged inquiry. We spent time explaining to the writers the need to balance their voices as interviewers and writers with the lived stories and authentic voices of the dancers. Four of the students had read and studied most of the chapters in *Telling Stories to Change the World* (Solinger et al.) in an earlier course and were able to share these insights with the other students. The students were reminded to be conscious of issues of power and reciprocity in their engagements with others. While they shared many similarities with the dancers, such as age and interests, they came from different socioeconomic or cultural backgrounds. Symone, for example, who hailed from Philadelphia, was curious about whether her own experiences would align her with the dancer she interviewed even if they shared a racial identity.

Moreover, the writers had to navigate their role in writing others' stories. Students read Rebecca Jones's reasoning for her decision to do "extensive condensing and manipulation of the text" in an oral history project (27). However, after careful consideration of Jones's rationale and the changes to the transcripts, students determined that Jones had gone too far in erasing her narrators' voices. Jones's article ignited several ways of thinking about shared voice and authorship in telling other people's stories. Megan and Chelsea were concerned that their positionalities as suburban white women would influence the story-gathering process: Would the dancers be comfortable enough with them as white women? Would the dancers trust them enough to be vulnerable with them? Would they, as suburban white women, be able to hear the dancers' stories in the way they were meant and needed to be heard?

Symone challenged the idea of voice and authority, registering concern that the retelling of the dancers' stories by the writers would dilute the dancers' voices. Thinking back on issues raised in *Telling Stories to Change the World*, "Whose story is it anyway?" she asked, "If we took their words and retold [their stories] in our own, how will each writer find the right balance with their dancer-partners?" Symone, Rachel, and Imane wondered if there was even such a thing as "authenticity" in the storytelling endeavor, given its collaborative ethos. All students, as artists themselves (writers), were nevertheless asked to put their artistic choices in the back seat, behind the dancers'. We were impressed with the thoughtful questions and concerns that students raised, further solidifying their commitment to the social justice principles we collectively pursued.

The collaborations between writers and dancers were fruitful even though the length and depth of the final stories varied. We attributed these discrepancies to the dancers' and writers' identities within the interview-writing relationships. The writer-dancer relationships were fostered intentionally through planning meetings, lunches, and interviews, but several relationships grew deeper organically as the weight of the project along with concomitant time together allowed writers and dancers to gain insight into one another's lives. Symone discusses this development in the book's "Meet the Writers" section:

> The TIR story project challenged me as a writer and as a communicator. The process of getting to know my dancer was rewarding as I found that she and I were not so different even though we come from two different places. Her background was compelling and gave me an understanding of who she [is] behind the dance scene. She trusted me, a complete stranger, to turn her story into a narrative she could be proud of. (Antosy et al. 50)

In an end-of-semester debriefing, writers considered how the interactions with the dancers and the process of writing these stories had made them more mindful of their own identities and cultural locations. In nascent threads of trust and awareness, they had encountered new ways to understand others and themselves. Megan and Rachel stated that their awareness of their whiteness and their "outsider" status had contributed to feelings of discomfort. We discussed the privilege involved in feeling comfortable and the possibility that the students' discomfort had allowed them a glimpse into similar types of dissonance felt by minoritized individuals and communities. Imane stated that the interactions had helped her better understand intersectional identities within communities of color; feeling connected to the dancers as a person of color, she had nevertheless experienced "distance" from them because of her socioeconomic background and religion. The group discussed the difficulties in striving toward equal participation, noting that idea as something that had to be continually reinforced throughout the storytelling project because it was so easy to take liberties in the story-making process.

The student designers did not share these learning outcomes with the same intensity. The designers, overall, were diverse—over half identified as nonwhite—with an even split between male and female. Based on our conversations with the designers, many connected with the dancers through race, social class, or first-generation college student status. Designers with aspirations in the arts found communion in the dancers' struggle to work in their hometown within their chosen art form, a struggle some of the designers felt they would share after graduation. We noted, however, that the designers spoke about their affiliation to the dancers' stories in more general terms, some even seeing the project as a business transaction where the dancers were "clients." The course size of seventeen students made it difficult to schedule the designers' participation in group project meetings. This part of the collaboration taught the organizers the importance of integrating social justice thinking as a core learning objective from the outset. When it came to the designers, we realize that we were not as successful in our goal of equal participation.

Counterstory: Making the Invisible Visible

Promoting justice principles of self-development and self-determination through a process of equal participation and conscious attention to power and privilege enabled the dancers, with other project participants, to coconstruct the platform for their counterstory, allowing them a stake in their own story-making. Counterstory "serves to expose, analyze, and challenge stock stories of racial privilege and can help to strengthen traditions of social, political, and cultural survival and resistance" (Martinez 38). As a tenet of critical race theory, counterstory draws attention to the stories by and of people often silenced by those who have power in a society, embracing the practice of storytelling in African American, Latinx, and Native American communities as historically linked to survival and resistance. Critical race theory commits to social justice through an agenda that "eliminates racism, sexism, and poverty and empowers subordinated minority groups" (Yosso 7). We argue that the dancers' and student writers' and designers' publicly shared counterstories realized Rancière's notion that "an act of social justice is any act that makes visible the equality of even one person whose voice has been suppressed and whose equality has been erased or ignored" (Colton and Holmes 13).

The dancers' stories collectively and individually gave "voice" to life in Reading, expressing frustrations with systemic barriers that thwart opportunity while celebrating the places and people that support and offer hope. The dancers wrote themselves into Reading's grand narratives as people and artists, challenging majoritarian stories. Their stories are empowering, urging us to see them and their city differently, as Stephanie says in the book and on the website: "Don't listen to the negativity that you hear about Reading. Go out and experience the city for yourself. Experience it, meet its people, and get to know them. Don't listen, but watch" (Antosy et al. 31). Liyanah, too, expressed her empowerment as she connected her own success to that of her city: "When I make it, my city makes it, too" (38). Symone, writing Liyanah's story, offered that, "[g]rowing up in Reading, Liyanah had a lot of stereotypes that she had to break through and ultimately, dance through. . . . Liyanah is truly a successful product of her environment, having made over a 4.0 grade point average by the time she graduated Reading High" (38).

Moreover, several of the dancers used counterstory to challenge the disadvantages and oppressions related to their race and ethnicity, gender identity, and sexuality. Critical race theory puts race and racism at the center of analysis but also positions it intersectionally with other systemic oppressions. With great confidence and pride, Liyanah told the story of being an African American woman in hip-hop dance and culture. Although "there are a bunch of stereotypes . . . , I've been shutting them down. I don't take offense to it if I don't fit it. Even if I do fit it, I don't take offense because I know who I am." She looked back with pride at one of her first dance battles: "I was in there beating dudes. Once I got to the final four, I lost to a B-boy but he didn't underestimate me" (38).

Stephanie and Theresa, both Latinx/mixed-race, female, and lesbian, and Caliph and Jaymes, both Black and gay/queer, related how they contended with these identities while often being viewed as "Other." Caliph offered these words about identity negotiations as he worked to challenge negative perceptions and make possible his agency as a young queer African American dancer in Reading: "I feel like people should be comfortable in their own skin. Everybody deserves a chance. . . .

That's what I feel I need to put out there, too. I know I deserve a chance. . . . When we were offered to perform places, I know people would have their prejudice, that . . . being dark skinned, we would be more 'thuggish'" (34). Jaymes, ten years older than Caliph, felt more comfortable with his various group identities. Imane explained in Jaymes's story: "Ranging from the LGBTQ to Hispanic and Black and the arts communities, Jaymes is able to connect with and relate to different groups of people. . . . He has found a vibe, one that helps inspire and create the community around him. He likes to get the party going, get the work started, and bring people together" (24). Moreover, dance empowers Jaymes's self-acceptance: "If he wants to be rough, soft, masculine, feminine, he can do it. . . . Dance allows him to express himself however he wants. . . . It is a sense of power, a feeling"; according to Jaymes, "just the *feeling* of dance is so good" (25).

Counterstory also enabled the dancers to express the importance of dance as a space for refuge and catharsis, away from the sources of the oppression that permeated many areas of their lives. For Asha, dance was a space for liberation and self-care: "God gave me the wiggles and I have to release them. I've always danced. I just dance because it feels good. A lot of times, when I'm going through whatever I'm going through, I sit with my headphones in my ears and try to make up dances and I just go from there. [There has] always been something in me that wants to dance" (47).

Jaymes, on the other hand, explained dance as a place for communal healing and empowerment. Jaymes hoped to own dance studios in different locations that would offer a safe haven for young people: "Once you walk through the door you can let everything go and just dance" (27). Both Asha and Jaymes stressed needing "safe spaces" that can offer refuge and transformation and viewed dance and hip-hop as a space where that could happen. The dancers currently teach hip-hop classes to young children as part of RIZE, a youth arts nonprofit organization committed to sharing the passion for hip-hop with a younger generation.

A year after *This Is Reading*, the dancers discussed feeling as though their careers as dancers had not advanced as they had hoped. They had experienced fleeting moments as local celebrities during the three weeks of *This Is Reading* in 2017. Liyanah explains, "*This Is Reading* was dope. It got us a lot of exposure, the pay [from Lynn Nottage and her team] was great, as well as the outfits. It felt like we were really up there. We felt like we were famous" (40). But now the dancers talked about the limited career options available in Reading as well as in the practical barriers to leaving. Caliph describes:

> Just having an ultimatum in your head. . . . Do you want to work, or do you want to dance? Do you want to follow your dreams, or do you want money to get out? You know? And it's just hard to try and combine those things 'cause it's always separate. . . . It just seems like there's no way to get out [of Reading], but you have to just keep digging. Keep digging. People just give up. You just won't get nowhere giving up. (36)

Liyanah explained that "there's a lot of talent in the city that's so small that it gets unnoticed because of our reputation, and I want it to be seen. Part of my dream is to make the unnoticed, noticed" (39). Here, Liyanah suggests a need to be both visible and valued—a sentiment her fellow dancers expressed again and again.

This desire to advance their careers as unique dancers and as a troupe manifests in the name the dancers chose for their group and this project: *We Are Reading*. As noted earlier, Jaymes, Asha, Caliph, Liyanah, Stephanie, and Theresa expressed appreciation for their experiences as performers in *This Is Reading*. Yet they also expressed a lingering feeling that they, who represent Reading's present and future, had gone unheard as real people with real stories that would shed light on Reading in the present, not only in the past. Liyanah adds, "You would think that the spotlight would have been on us as dancers from Reading, but it was more so on other dancers that weren't from here." Moreover, they were determined to break away from the theatrical hip-hop dance they had performed in *This Is Reading* under the direction of choreographer Lorenzo "Rennie" Harris, eager to perform and show their own dance styles.

The dancers named themselves We Are Reading, or WAR, a deliberate narrative shift away from *This Is Reading*, not only to put themselves into Reading's present and future narratives but also to take on a more deliberately political stance than the hip-hop they had performed under Harris's direction. Counterstories "tear down at the same time as they create" (Lovvorn 101). In this instance, it was important for the dancers to "tear down" their association with *This Is Reading* and to recreate themselves as WAR as they looked toward their futures as dancers with pride in representing their city.

The book design also strategically synced with WAR and operated as counterstory. The design students worked in two teams to produce two options. The first team used the winning cover design as a guide and made each individual story a two-page spread that prominently features the dancer photograph and story (fig. 3). The second team used the photographs to create a silhouette of each dancer, focusing on a more conceptual approach (fig. 4). In making the final choice, the whole group discussed the transmission of "voice" through visuals and design, and the dancers and writers agreed upon the selected design because they interpreted it as providing the agency and voice they sought and felt they had achieved. The selected design is engaging, energetic, and unapologetic. The design relies strongly on the emotions and impressions conveyed in the photography, including lines and colors that move the eye across the page. One of the dancers says that the font, a bold stencil, gives the typography "street credibility" because of its popularity with graffiti and street artists.

Design and imagery also operate as counterstory by offering a distinct visual perspective. We used images that were compelling and insightful, telling the dancers' stories through mise-en-scène, and one of Nicholas's former students, a photographer at a local studio, donated her time to the project. The dancers were ecstatic; it would be their first time doing a professional photo shoot in a "high-class

Figure 3. Sample layout for *We Are Reading.* Photography by Regina May Bross, Willow Street Pictures. Cityscape image courtesy of the Greater Reading Chamber Alliance.

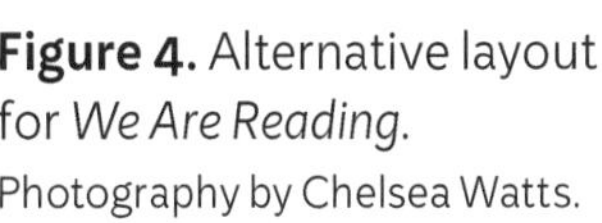

Figure 4. Alternative layout for *We Are Reading.* Photography by Chelsea Watts.

Figure 5.
Action shots and headshot of dancers participating in *We Are Reading.*
Photography by Regina May Bross, Willow Street Pictures.

photo studio," as Jaymes noted. The photographs captured the dancers in three ways (fig. 5): an individual dance pose, a headshot, and a group photo.

In the top left image in figure 5, Liyanah portrays strength and power through her choice of posture and backdrop. Stephanie stated that her choice of headshot (top right) exudes the simple joy she finds through her edgy dance style. Her emotion is foregrounded by soft lighting and simple framing in contrast to the shiny yet harsh steel background. In the group photo (bottom), the colors, lighting, and clothing, along with the dancers' facial expressions and individual movement within a collective circle, tell a counterstory of talented and passionate young people who share a love for each other and for dance. The images capture both the dancers' unique individual positionalities and group cohesiveness.

This project also included candid and posed photographs taken at project meetings and of the dancers in various locations in Reading. These images document the dancers' lives in Reading as well as the project process. These images, included in the book and on the website, show hardworking young people trying to make a future for themselves (fig. 6). The images also highlight the dancers' fortitude as individuals and as a collective. Together, these images are a counternarrative to the existing problematic narratives about Reading and its inhabitants.

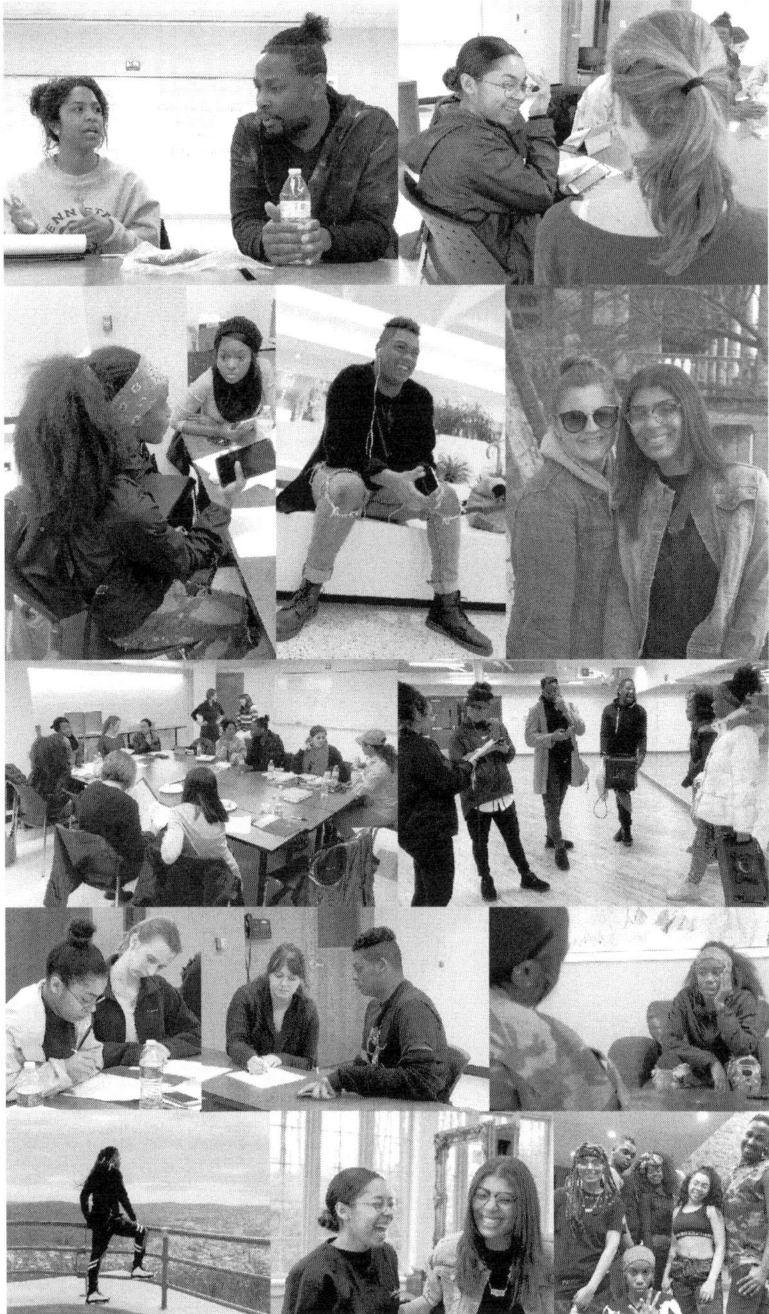

Figure 6. Behind-the-scenes montage of creative collaboration during *We Are Reading*. Photography by Luis Borrero, Cheryl L. Nicholas, and Chelsea Watts.

Reflecting (on) Social Justice Pedagogy Outcomes

The atmosphere was festive, with loud music, incessant chatter, and platters of warm food and sweet desserts. About one hundred people gathered in the local dance studio where the dancers taught their classes and where we held the book launch party. In the crowd were family members, children from the hip-hop classes, local activists and artists, and groups of people from the city and county who had seen the news report about the collaborative story project in the local paper and decided to wander in. A long line of attendees waited their turn for book signings by the dancers. The event culminated with the WAR dancers performing.

As we celebrated the *We Are Reading* book launch, we also thought about what would come next for the dancers. In this setting, Jaymes, Asha, Caliph, Liyanah, Stephanie, and Theresa were telling their and their city's stories through words, images, and dance. Yet now, as we end this essay, Theresa and Stephanie have left Reading for New York City, Liyanah is a new mother, Caliph is finding success as a *YouTube* influencer, Asha has a steady job and cares for her children, and Jaymes has a new job in a local hospital. Asha, Caliph, Liyanah, and Jaymes are still involved with RIZE, the after-school hip-hop program.

At the launch party, we reflected on the challenges that still faced the dancers, the city, and the types of relationships that still needed to be built. We questioned in that moment, as we do now, the value of social justice pedagogies that cannot be expected to enact material change, considering that what we, as pedagogues and scholars, see as benefits of a project may not translate in the same way to community and lay audiences, who may see and experience progress very differently. This discrepancy certainly reveals the different worldviews, expectations, and privileges inherent in academic and community groups, implicating social justice pedagogy. Moreover, we also recognize the limits of working with younger populations that are continually changing and shifting, trying to find footholds in their own sense-making in terms of their place and identity.

Still, there is much value in what we were able to achieve. The dancers may no longer be pursuing dance in the same way, but the project offered the dancers another platform for their stories as young artists in Reading. Their stories endure in the *We Are Reading* project and in the many ways project participants—dancers, writers, designers, and teachers—learned about and from each other and from our process. As humanists, we are very aware of the potency of ideological and symbolic agency in shaping and reshaping conditions that can bring about various types of progress, including material gain. This is not easily achievable, however, in a single initiative. Rather, through collective and sustained effort, as this volume attests, such strides can be actualized and this justice work can continue. Yet, as Yosso suggests, "counterstories teach us that construction of another world—a socially and racially just world—is possible" (15). Through projects such as this one, traditionally silenced communities may continue and extend their stories in the hope that, as Liyanah says, "the unnoticed gets a little more noticed," and that the project's voice, in unison with similarly disadvantaged voices, makes change possible.

WORKS CITED

Antosy, Megan, et al. *We Are Reading: Dancing in the City.* Penn State U, Berks / Albright College, 2018, bpb-us-e1.wpmucdn.com/sites.psu.edu/dist/0/167747/files/2023/09/We-Are-Reading.pdf.

Collins-Hughes, Laura. "A Look at Lynn Nottage's Next Act." *The Village Voice*, 22 May 2017, www.villagevoice.com/2017/05/22/lynn-nottages-next-act/.

Colton, Jared, and Steve Holmes. "A Social Justice Theory of Active Equality for Technical Communication." *Journal of Technical Writing and Communication*, vol. 48, no. 1, 2018, pp. 4–30.

Grobman, Laurie. "Lynn Nottage's *This Is Reading*: (Re)Identifying a City in Story." *Storytelling, Self, Society*, vol. 15, no. 2, 2019, pp. 166–90.

Hatza, George. "Lynn Nottage Panel Reveals Art's Palliative Power." *Reading Eagle*, 11 Nov. 2015, www.readingeagle.com/2015/11/15/lynn-nottage-panel-reveals-arts-palliative-power/.

Jones, Rebecca. "Blended Voices: Crafting a Narrative from Oral History Interviews." *The Oral History Review*, vol. 31, no. 1, winter 2004, pp. 23–42.

Lovvorn, Jason F. "Theorizing Digital Storytelling: From Narrative Practice to Racial Counterstory." *Narrative Acts: Rhetoric, Race, Identity, and Knowledge*, edited by Debra Journet et al., pp. 97–112, Hampton Press, 2011.

Mallach, Alan. "Parallel Histories, Diverging Trajectories: Resilience in Small Industrial Cities." *Revitalizing American Cities*, edited by Susan M. Wachter and Kimberly A. Zeuli, U of Pennsylvania P, 2013, pp. 126–45.

Martinez, Aja Y. "A Plea for Critical Race Theory Counterstory: Stock Story versus Counterstory Dialogues Concerning Alejandra's 'Fit' in the Academy." *Composition Studies*, vol. 42, no. 2, 2014, pp. 33–55.

May, Thomas. *The Political Thought of Jacques Rancière: Creating Equality.* Edinburgh UP, 2008.

Nottage, Lynn. *Sweat.* Theatre Communications Group, 2017.

Rancière, Jacques. *Disagreement: Politics and Philosophy.* Translated by Julie Rose, Minneapolis UP, 1999.

———. *On the Shores of Politics.* Translated by Liz Heron, Verso Books, 1995.

———. "Politics, Identification, and Subjectivization." *The Identity in Question*, edited by John Rajchman, Routledge, 1995, pp. 63–70.

Solinger, Rickie, et al., editors. *Telling Stories to Change the World: Global Voices on the Power of Narrative to Build Community and Make Social Justice Claims.* Routledge, 2008.

Solórzano, Daniel G., and Tara J. Yosso. "Critical Race Methodology: Counter-storytelling as an Analytical Framework for Education Research." *Qualitative Inquiry*, vol. 8, no. 1, 2002, pp. 23–44.

"This Is Reading." *Project&*, projectand.org/project/this-is-reading/#/project/this-is-reading/.

Yosso, Tara. *Critical Race Counterstories along the Chicana/Chicano Educational Pipeline*. Routledge, 2006.

Young, Iris Marion. *Inclusion and Democracy.* Oxford UP, 2000.

———. *Justice and the Politics of Difference*. Oxford UP, 1990.

Incorporating Anti-Speciesism in Social Justice Praxis

Tara Roeder

At a faculty meeting with a flyer about a "food justice" event on the overhead projector and a platter of sandwiches filled with the body parts and secretions of nonhuman animals in the center of the table, I found myself thinking of how many classes, events, and meetings I've attended where conversations about imperative issues such as social equality, educational access, and economic justice took place around such platters. I can recall a number of conversations with scholars and teachers who engage in serious work around issues of human inequity and also engage in practices such as equating veganism with eating disorders or sexual frustration, taking selfies with captive non-Indigenous species, and making jokes about how they couldn't survive without bacon. As someone who is committed to liberation for human and nonhuman animals, I see my goal in this essay as highlighting some of the ways that anti-speciesist and vegan theory can widen and contribute to conversations about social justice without derailing indispensable discussions about human oppression.

Many years ago, while cofacilitating a writing workshop for parents experiencing homelessness, as part of a partnership between the Department of Homeless Services (DHS) in my city and my university, I began thinking more critically about some of the connections among food justice, human dignity, and the rights of nonhuman animals. The first day of the program, the "lunch" provided by DHS was soggy bologna sandwiches and child-sized juice drinks, which prompted a conversation about one participant's increasing struggle with diabetes and the difficulty of living as a vegetarian in a shelter that provided few plant-based options. My cofacilitator and I thereafter brought varied, tasty, nutritious, and age-appropriate food to our meetings, but the conversations about the ways many workshop participants felt infantilized and denied meaningful sustenance (both literally and metaphorically) by the shelter system continued. I began to become more attuned to the food practices of institutions, including but not limited to city shelters, public schools, and prisons, that raise serious ethical questions about not only the human right to access healthy—including plant-based—food but also serve as an example of one of the many ways that government-subsidized "big agriculture" encourages institutional food practices that devalue the autonomy and lives of both humans and nonhuman animals. President Trump's 2018 proposal to cut Supplemental Nutrition Assistance Program (SNAP) benefits in half by replacing funds available to program participants with boxes of government-chosen "nonperishable" food items, including animal products, simultaneously diminishing recipients' agency and their health—a practice that has long been in effect on reservations for Indigenous people in the US—is but one of many examples (Godoy).

Our institutional education about the "otherness" of nonhuman animals begins early—in classrooms where living nonhuman animals, often separated from others of their kind, may be passed around from child to child to take home for the weekend; in cafeterias where children are exhorted to drink the milk cows produce to feed their calves and eat the flesh of nonhuman animals who have been imprisoned and slaughtered on federally subsidized factory farms; on school trips to zoos, aquariums, and circuses where nonhuman animals are held captive and prone to psychological and physical abuse; in science labs where students are asked to cut into the corpses of frogs and fetal pigs; and in an anthropocentric curriculum that often ignores our historical, biological, and philosophical interconnectedness with other species.

I remember visiting a local elementary school to attend an evening performance. While searching for a classroom afterward, I accidentally opened the door to a dark room filled with caged rabbits, guinea pigs, turtles, snakes, and other animals. I would later hear this disturbing place referred to as "the science room." I wondered not only about how the nonhuman animals themselves felt spending their lives in a dark room for human children to handle occasionally in the name of "science," but also about what kind of message it sends to young humans when we allow them to believe early on that the purpose of other creatures is to edify humans or aid us in developing "responsibility."

Implicit instruction in speciesism—which not only involves an assumption of human superiority but also treats members of some nonhuman species, such as those designated "pets" or "endangered animals," as morally more important than members of other nonhuman species, such as "livestock" or "pests"—is reinforced through educational institutions at every level. Despite long-standing objections to the efficacy and ethics of animal experimentation, for example, millions of captive nonhuman animals are experimented on and killed each year in the United States, often in university laboratories. In 2018, "University of Michigan animal testing laboratories accidentally lost a mutant rabbit, poisoned nearly 11,500 zebra fish with bleach, caused 53 mice to die of thirst and gave an unknown number of mice terminal gastrointestinal cancer" (Burns). And land-grant institutions in states such as North Carolina and Iowa are especially beholden to "big agriculture," leading to conflicts over academic freedom between funding organizations, such as state pork councils, and academics who produce research on issues likc the environmental impact of industrial hog farming (Cox and Brown).

We can also see the results of institutionalized speciesism in the food options available at many US colleges and universities. Every semester, students in my courses express frustration with the lack of inclusive, plant-based food options on campus.[1] And while some colleges and universities (e.g., Appalachian State University, Brock University, and New York University, among others) offer concentrations in animal studies, much academic discourse often seems to de facto take for granted the inferior status of nonhuman animals. The privileging of "rationality" (often constructed as white, western, male, able-bodied, and heterosexual) that has long been contested by many feminist, anti-racist, queer, anti-ableist, and decolonialist theorists, is also contested by those invested in anti-speciesism. As the disability theorist-activist and nonhuman animal advocate Sunaura Taylor writes in *Beasts of Burden: Animal and Disability Liberation*, "The problem is not reason itself but rather the ways in which reason has been held up as separate from and more valuable than emotion, feeling, and other ways of knowing and being. This definition of reason stems from a history of patriarchy, imperialism, racism, classism, ableism, and anthropocentrism, and too often carries these oppressions within it" (71). Using "rationality" as a ground for establishing worth has long been a way of denying the inherent value of not only nonhuman animals but also large segments of the human species.

This essay explores what an intersectional anti-speciesist framework and pedagogy looks like on a variety of levels: how we can underscore the connections among capitalism, speciesism, sexism, environmental racism, and the degradation of the natural world in our scholarship and activism; how we might challenge the neoliberal commodification of sentient beings; how we might rethink our assumptions about nonhuman animals and teach every subject from history and science to rhetoric and art in ways that value their experiences; and ultimately how we might, as educators, reinforce an ethics of empathy, equity, and dignity with respect to individuals both human and nonhuman.

Veganism

Established in 1944, the Vegan Society defines veganism as "a way of living which seeks to exclude, as far as is possible and practicable, all forms of exploitation of, and cruelty to, animals for food, clothing or any other purpose" ("Definition"). While the term *vegan* was created to establish a difference between vegetarians who consumed the ovulations and milk of other species and those who did not, the practice of abstaining from animal products for ethical and spiritual reasons has of course been around for centuries. Buddhism and Jainism, for example, have long traditions of vegetarianism and nonviolence. I refer here specifically to the Vegan Society's definition because the phrase "as far as possible and practicable" concisely voices a significant precept for many in the contemporary vegan and animal rights community who take an intersectional approach to issues of oppression and injustice. The reality is that food apartheid largely affects low-income Americans of color, limiting access to affordable plant-based foods; many low-income families rely on donated clothes and have little choice or purchasing power should they wish to avoid animal products; and a multitude of lifesaving medications are tested on animals, leaving those in need with little choice about supporting an industry they might prefer to resist. Both humans and nonhuman animals are routinely harmed in the harvesting of the food crops that make plant-based diets possible but also are used to feed farmed animals who will be slaughtered for human consumption. Within this context, "veganism" is not and can never be about individual humans being "perfect" or "pure." For many who seek to dismantle the foundations of both human and nonhuman oppression, veganism is instead about a larger commitment to anti-oppressive praxis within a capitalist and structurally unjust culture. Taylor has described it as "an embodied act of resistance to objectification and exploitation across difference—a corporeal way of enacting one's political and ethical beliefs daily" (202).

In an era of celebrity-endorsed food fads, some nonvegans may conflate veganism with restrictive diets; however, while plant-based eating does have demonstrated health benefits for humans, veganism is neither a health fad nor a "diet."[2] Instead, veganism calls us to recognize the existence of other animals not as tools for us to use but as individuals with their own relationships, unique personalities, desires, fears, joys, and sufferings.

For many activists whose liberatory projects include both humans and nonhuman animals, this recognition sometimes begins with a relationship to an individual nonhuman animal. The labor activist and United Farm Workers cofounder Cesar Chavez, for example, said, "I became a vegetarian after realizing that animals feel afraid, cold, hungry and unhappy like we do. . . . It was my dog Boycott who led me to question the right of humans to eat other sentient beings" (qtd. in Brook). In their book *Esther the Wonder Pig*, the Canadian couple Steve Jenkins and Derek Walter chronicle their adoption of and life with Esther, a pig whom they later found out was born on a factory farm. One morning while they are cooking bacon, they make a connection between the "food" on their stove and the living companion in their kitchen. However, they note, "[W]e weren't instant vegans. For the moment, at least, it was just: 'We can't eat Esther.' . . . When we looked at bacon, we saw Esther. But when we looked at a burger, we still saw a burger. . . . It's a prime example of the disconnect and walls we had built up" (Jenkins et al., *Esther* 49).

The longtime feminist and animal rights activist Carol J. Adams recollects a similar kind of cognitive dissonance that she experienced after her beloved pony passed away: "That evening, still distraught about my pony's death, I bit into a hamburger and stopped in midbite. I was thinking about one dead animal yet eating another dead animal. What was the difference between this dead cow and the dead pony whom I would be burying the next day? I could summon no ethical defense for a favoritism that would exclude the cow because I had not known her" (xxii). Such realizations highlight some of the ways that making connections with individual others can facilitate making larger connections among our ethical and activist commitments and practices. As Taylor writes, "The feeling that first led me to hold my breath when seeing the hens caged on trucks eventually led me to understand animal issues as profoundly relevant and even essential to other social justice issues, including disability" (xv). By putting individual narratives in dialogue with the larger sociopolitical contexts in which these narratives take place, we begin to ask important questions about empathy, personhood, and who is included in our social justice praxis.

Intersecting Oppressions

In 2018, millions of farmed animals died horrific deaths in Hurricane Florence. Legally constructed as property, chickens, pigs, and turkeys were left behind—sometimes locked in structures with no means of escape—as other inhabitants across North and South Carolina were evacuated. Tellingly, incarcerated human beings in some of South Carolina's evacuation zones were also left behind—despite protests from the ACLU and the fact that past hurricanes such as Katrina, in which "people were trapped in flooded cells with nothing to eat or drink" (Gross), had a devastating effect on prison inmates.

In white capitalist heteropatriarchy, we receive clear messages every day about whose lives are valued and whose are not. The nonhuman animals we objectify, commodify, destroy, and consume are not the only victims of institutionalized speciesism. The harmful effects of animal agriculture on what are disproportionally low-income communities of color was also magnified in the aftermath of Florence, when the environmental and public health risks of manure lagoons (long a concern for those who reside near industrial hog farms and those invested in dismantling environmental racism) became a topic of national conversation. As the scholar A. Breeze Harper points out,

> [T]he movement in the black community for racial and class liberation is not disconnected from the environmental sustainability movement, which is not disconnected from ending exploitation of animals. Think of all the toxic waste coming out of the agribusiness industry. Where does it end up? It doesn't end up in the backyard of Beverly Hills, but where there are working class people of color. If we dig to make those connections, we realize eating animals does affect me as a poor person of color. A lot of waste is going in my backyard and causing my community lots of health disparities and suffering.
>
> ("Sistah Vegans")

Unsurprisingly then, the systems and institutions that exploit and abuse nonhuman animals also exploit and abuse human beings. Taylor writes,

> Why, one might ask, are we focusing on animal objectification and not human objectification? I think the question misses the fact that oppressions are not mutually exclusive: they are entangled and interlocking, as is so clear when we look at slaughterhouses themselves, where . . . animal and environmental destruction are wrought on the backs of largely low-income people, who are funneled into such undesirable jobs due to class, disability, and immigration status. (201)

Slaughterhouse workers—the majority of whom are low-income people of color and many of whom are immigrants—face dangerous working conditions, high rates of injury, and high rates of PTSD in addition to the long hours, low pay, and on-the-job abuse experienced by many food industry workers ("Slaughterhouse Workers"). There are also a number of studies on the effect that the violence against nonhuman animals that is socially sanctioned in slaughterhouses may have on violence in surrounding human communities. In the words of a former poultry plant worker, "[T]he more I [killed chickens], the less it bothered me. I became desensitized. The killing room really does something to your mind—all that blood, killing so many times, over and over again" (Taylor 187). According to a 2009 study by Amy J. Fitzgerald, Linda Kalof, and Thomas Dietz, "[S]laughterhouse employment increases total arrest rates, arrests for violent crimes, arrests for rape, and arrests for other sex offenses in comparison with other industries." Fitzgerald and colleagues propose the "existence of a 'Sinclair effect' unique to the violent workplace of the slaughterhouse" (1).

In *Beyond Words: What Animals Think and Feel*, Carl Safina reminds us that in the 1500s, "[b]ringing ivory to ladies in parlors were traders trafficking in both tusks and humans" (116). The systemic violence perpetuated under capitalism and colonialism has long relied on the dehumanization of human beings and the objectification of nonhuman animals. In the context of the contemporary US foodscape, the activist Angela Y. Davis notes, "[S]entient beings . . . endure pain and torture as they are transformed into food for profit, food that generates disease in humans whose poverty compels them to rely on McDonald's and KFC for nourishment" (qtd. in Loria). Discussing the commodification of nonhuman animals in the agricultural industry, Adams writes:

> [W]e are told in effect to "Forget the pig [or a cow, a chicken, etc.] is an animal." Instead, call her and view her as a "machine in a factory." She becomes a food-producing unit, a protein harvester, an object, product, computerized unit in a factory environment, egg-producing machine, converting machine, a biomachine, a crop. A recent example of erasure of animals can be found

> in the United States Department of Agriculture's description of cows, pigs, and chickens as "grain-consuming animal units." (50)

It's no coincidence that the same factory farms and slaughterhouses that transform terrified nonhuman animals into dismembered pieces of "meat" for human consumption also employ marginalized human workers who are often viewed as cogs in a machine. Their value is reliant on their ability to increase production at any cost to their physical and emotional health or to the nonhuman animals they are "processing," who are sometimes boiled, skinned, or dismembered alive in the rush for profit (Warrick).

A rich body of scholarship now analyzes the intersections of human and nonhuman oppression and liberation. Centering the voices of vegans of color, vegans with disabilities, feminist vegans, and vegans involved in other radical movements is crucial in challenging the whitewashing of veganism and the ableism, misogyny, racism, and fatphobia in which many mainstream animal rights figures and organizations (including PETA) have engaged. *The Sexual Politics of Meat*, by Adams, analyzes the sexualized discourse and imagery that surrounds meat consumption and challenges readers to make critical connections between institutionalized misogyny and speciesism. Taylor's *Beasts of Burden* explores the complex connections between ableism and speciesism and links animal and disability liberation. Harper founded the *Sistah Vegan* project, which focused on issues such as diversity and the ethical dimensions of our food systems (Harper, "Home"). Her collection *Sistah Vegan: Black Female Vegans Speak on Food, Identity, Health, and Society* explores the multifaceted experiences of Black vegan women navigating the terrains of racism, health, and veganism. Harper is one of a number of contemporary vegan theorists and activists whose work decenters whiteness and highlights the voices of vegans of color, who are often marginalized within the mainstream vegan movement. Another is the critic Aph Ko, who founded the website *Black Vegans Rock* to "highlight influential Black vegans who were doing incredible work to dismantle the stereotype that veganism was a 'white person's thing'" ("About"). She and Syl Ko are the authors of the collection *Aphro-ism: Essays on Pop Culture, Feminism, and Black Veganism from Two Sisters*, and her recent book *Racism as Zoological Witchcraft: A Guide to Getting Out* explores connections between white supremacy and the consumption of flesh. The researcher and lecturer Christopher Sebastian McJetters's work "focuses on animal violence and how it influences anti-black racism, queer antagonism and class discrimination throughout the global west" (McJetters). Organizations such as the Food Empowerment Project, founded by Lauren Ornelas, are also a powerful example of the kind of intersectional activism that benefits humans and nonhuman animals alike. The organization promotes veganism, access to healthy food, awareness of the child labor involved in the chocolate industry, and farm workers' rights ("Mission and Values").

As the devastating global environmental impact of meat production can no longer be ignored, an understanding of veganism as a politicized, liberatory movement that resists neoliberalist, consumerist, or individualist approaches is more important than ever. Cultivating a systematic, inclusive, and interdisciplinary approach to issues of environmental, food, and social justice can benefit human and nonhuman animal communities (including those being increasingly displaced from wild areas by animal agriculture and capitalist development) as well as the planet as a whole.[3]

Towards a Nonspeciesist Pedagogy

Scholars and educators who wish to research and teach from an anti-speciesist position may take a wide variety of approaches. In my own field of composition and rhetoric, where questions of voice and audience structure many conversations, the act of listening can be a powerful way of challenging our assumptions about alterity. The feminist rhetorician Krista Ratcliffe defines rhetorical listening as a "stance of openness that a person may choose to assume in relation to any person, text, or culture" (17). By adopting such a stance, we can begin to engage with both the voices and the silences of those whose experiences or expressions may be unfamiliar to us—including nonhuman individuals. Despite the perceived "voicelessness" of nonhuman animals, Taylor points out that

> [a]nimals consistently voice preferences and ask for freedom. They speak to us every day when they cry out in pain or try to move away from our prods, electrodes, knives, and stun guns. Animals tell us constantly that they want to be out of their cages, that they want to be reunited with their families, or that they don't want to walk down the kill chute. Animals express themselves all the time, and many of us know it. If we didn't, factory farms and slaughterhouses would not be designed to constrain any choices an animal might have. We deliberately have to choose not to hear when the lobster bangs on the walls from inside a pot of boiling water or when the hen who is past her egg-laying prime struggles against the human hands that enclose her legs and neck. We have to choose not to recognize the preference expressed when the fish spasms and gasps for oxygen in her last few minutes alive. Considering animals voiceless betrays an ableist assumption of what counts as having a voice. (63)

Listening to and amplifying the voices of those who have historically been denied agency is a crucial step in developing inclusive analysis and praxis. As Josephine Donovan and Adams point out in *The Feminist Care Tradition in Animal Ethics*, doing so allows us to situate individual experiences in a wider cultural context:

> The feminist ethic of care regards animals as individuals who do have feelings, who can communicate those feelings, and to whom therefore humans have moral obligations. An ethic of care also recognizes the diversity of animals—one size doesn't fit all; each has a particular history. . . . [T]he feminist care approach recognizes the importance of each individual animal while developing a more comprehensive analysis of her situation. Unlike "welfare" approaches, therefore, the feminist care tradition in animal ethics includes a political analysis of the reasons why animals are abused in the first place. (3)

Across the humanities, disciplines as varied as philosophy, sociology, comparative literature, and English studies have created tools and language to theorize human violence and strategize ways of connecting with others. The work of scholars like Taylor and Donovan and Adams reminds us that nonhuman animals are also meaningful participants in our social, cultural, and economic systems. Some of the models we have developed to theorize relationality in human communities may, as evidenced above, be constructive when considering our relationships with nonhuman animals.

Those who employ deconstructionist and posthumanist theories, for example, provide us with tools to undo problematic binaries in anthropocentric thinking. Critically considering the Western "human"/"animal" binary (and the fact that such a binary is far from universal) can continue to illuminate our analyses of other discursive binaries around gender, race, and disability. Decolonialized approaches to history can help us better theorize the devastating effects of Europe's imposition of wide-scale animal agriculture on a variety of Indigenous peoples' food cultures and ecological networks.[4] Studying the portrayal of nonhuman animals in art history, as well as the creations of nonhuman animals—whether nests in the wild or paintings in a rescue environment—can widen important conversations about what constitutes art itself. And fields from philosophy to ecology can help us develop nonanthropocentric models that can enrich our understanding of the interconnectedness of species.

We can also pay attention to the ways in which the language we use shapes our relationality to nonhuman animals. Common idioms such as "like shooting fish in a barrel" and "killing two birds with one stone," for example, implicitly reinforce the normalization of violence against nonhuman animals. Words such as *bacon*, *pork*, and *beef* also render the individuals whose bodies we consume (as well as those who must kill and package them) invisible. By paying attention to the linguistic choices we employ with regard to nonhuman animals, we can push back against rhetoric that reduces sentient beings to "parts" for our consumption. One way in which we might build connections and coalitions among those invested in dismantling systems that devalue the lives of the marginalized human beings and nonhuman animals who bear the disproportionate brunt of capitalist violence might be using the term *depersonification* (defined by the *APA*

Dictionary of Psychology as "treatment of another person as something other than the unique individual that [they] really [are]"), rather than *dehumanization* (an anthropocentric term that relies on historically white male constructions of human superiority), to widen who is included in our quest for justice in the face of structural inequity.

In thinking back to my own education, one particular incident of speciesism stands out. In my first semester of high school biology, the teacher explained that we would be dissecting worms. She asked whether anyone had a moral objection to dissection, and I raised my hand. Evidently exasperated, she asked if I would trust a doctor who had not dissected a human cadaver to operate on me. As I had zero interest in becoming a worm surgeon, I was confused by the analogy, but I lacked the language to articulate why I found this logic to be faulty and was told I could be given a failing grade if I was not compliant—a practice that is no longer legal in a number of US states ("Student Choice Laws"). In an advanced biology class I took as a senior, I was given the opportunity to write anti-vivisection papers in lieu of dissecting frogs and fetal pigs. That began my formal research into the ethical debates surrounding the use of nonhuman animals in the sciences. The understanding and assignment adaptation that my senior biology teacher offered is something I've often remembered throughout my own teaching career.

Like many vegans who operate within an intersectional framework, challenging the oppression of humans is an inextricable part of my vegan praxis. Creating a classroom environment in which students feel empowered to discuss the issues that affect their daily lives is a crucial element of my pedagogical approach. Because I'm aware that our classrooms are politicized spaces and that teachers hold a position of power, I use a participation-based contract model for grading, and students collaboratively design their own rubrics to mitigate my own ideologies affecting the topics students are comfortable (or uncomfortable) writing about as well as my assessment of their work.

Because it is a core part of my identity, the fact that I'm a vegan is something I generally share with my writing students. Nonvegan students often have interesting and thought-provoking questions for me, and vegan students may be pleased to find a faculty member who shares their values on a campus where the rights of nonhuman animals are not an institutional priority. During our discussions of structural oppressions such as institutionalized racism, homophobia, misogyny, ableism, and linguistic chauvinism, students in my writing courses make connections between their lived experiences and the larger contexts in which these experiences take place. Because students design their own multimodal research projects in my course, many students choose to research issues that affect their daily lives. Some recent projects have examined NCAA restrictions that harm low-income athletes, the diverse experiences of college students who wear hijab, the process of dealing with diagnoses of mental illness while in college, ways students have challenged homophobia in their families and religions, and the #MeToo movement's effect (or lack thereof) on campus.

Students who have engaged in projects about speciesism, animal rights, food justice, and plant-based diets bring these issues into our larger conversations in productive ways. One student wrote about the link between Hinduism and vegetarianism and created a guide to plant-based eating on campus for her Hindu student peers (as well as for others who practice vegetarianism and veganism). Another student did a series of projects on speciesism: a memoir describing her experiences with animals and veganism growing up in South America and later Israel, a website for college students offering a guide to healthful plant-based eating, and a children's book on veganism.[5] Being engaged in dialogue around such issues also invites students who are not vegan to incorporate new perspectives on nonhuman animals and food. Several students who were researching various food options in the boroughs of New York City or creating cultural recipe books, for example, included vegan dishes they said they would not otherwise have considered after listening to the experiences of their vegetarian and vegan peers and teacher.

There is no one-size-fits-all approach to developing anti-speciesist teaching practices and curricula, but educators from preschool through graduate school can aid students in cultivating respectful and empathetic attitudes toward others. The elementary school I attended in Queens, New York, sometimes took students on day trips to sites where nonhuman animals were exploited, such as zoos and circuses. Schools that engage in such practices might instead arrange trips to sanctuaries for farmed animals or screen documentaries that better capture the lives of "wild" animals. Children's books such as *The True Adventures of Esther the Wonder Pig* provide young students with nonheteronormative and anti-speciesist ways of thinking about families and nonhuman animals (Jenkins et al.). TeachKind offers free dissection software and models to schools wishing to create more inclusive and humane science classrooms ("Humane Dissection"). Simply introducing the perspectives of nonhuman animals in history and art classes can facilitate engagement with nonhuman animals as persons worthy of consideration. And several school districts "from Maine to California" (Povich) are recognizing the health benefits of serving plant-based options in cafeterias—a step that is also more inclusive of an increasingly diverse student population.

I'm mindful of the approach adopted by vegans like the Indigenous activist Margaret Robinson, who draws on the Mi'kmaw tradition of noninterference and says, "You model behaviour that you want to see other people adopt, rather than telling people when they're doing something wrong. . . . I do tend to bring vegan food to events but I don't tend to tell people it's vegan food. . . . You can definitely sway stomachs before you can sway minds." Jenkins and Walter express a related sentiment when they write in *Happily Ever Esther: Two Men, a Wonder Pig, and Their Life-Changing Mission to Give Animals a Home*, "You can't demand that people do something that goes against what they've been taught their entire lives.

You need to teach by example. You need to open up your life to how beneficial [veganism] is for humans and animals alike" (195). This includes human health benefits, as Harper points out in her *Satya* interview:

> In my experience, the majority of Sistah Vegans first approached veganism from a health perspective. They realized if they didn't, they would lose their breasts, their uterus, or die from diabetes like many people in their families. For many of them the catalyst didn't come from being aware of animal rights, it was understanding that we are basically dying and had to combat and resist that. Many of us first saw our health has been compromised because of racism and classism, and then started connecting that with the mistreatment of nonhuman animals. . . . This is something mainstream animal groups that are largely white and middle-class should take note of if they want to enter communities of color. They should make the health aspect links first. ("Sistah Vegans")

In a society of tremendous human inequity, and one in which the consumption of nonhuman animals and their secretions is normalized through the work of powerful lobbies, government funding, and media saturation, beginning dialogue around food can be a productive starting point. I bring plant-based food to class celebrations, meetings, and events, for example, where people are often surprised by how good it is, as well as how many food items that are already part of their diet are vegan. Several of my students have also done work on the health benefits of plant-based eating.

Whatever our starting points, more humans are beginning to realize the toll that speciesist ideology takes on our planet. The suffering and injustice caused by supremacist models is borne on the backs of the most vulnerable among us, both human and nonhuman. By centering these voices and working to disrupt the systems and institutions that facilitate the objectification of sentient beings, we can work together to eschew the hierarchies that value some lives at the expense of others to create a more just and sustainable future for all earthlings.

NOTES

1. It's not just students who are vegan, vegetarian, or plant-based for ethical, health, or religious reasons who are disserved by almost exclusively animal-based fare. Many non-vegan Muslim students, some Jewish students, and lactose-intolerant students, some of whom come from cultures where the European tradition of consuming the lactations of other species is uncommon, for example, also find themselves with limited options.

2. The title of a recent book by Carol J. Adams, Patti Breitman, and Virginia Messina is significantly called *Even Vegans Die*.

3. The animal agriculture industry is "the second largest contributor to human-made greenhouse gas (GHG) emissions after fossil fuels and is a leading cause of deforestation, water and air pollution and biodiversity loss" ("Animal Agriculture's Impact").

4. As a non-Indigenous person, I'm mindful of the words of Indigenous vegans like Sarambi, who writes, "[W]e are not a monolithic peoples [sic] as the colonizers want us to believe we are" and points out that it is "in many cultures and structures . . . meat eating was a rare thing saved for the elite primarily on special occasions." While media coverage often focuses on conflicts between predominantly white vegan organizations protesting traditional events like Inuit seal hunts (Randhawa), the Mi'kmaw scholar Margaret Robinson writes, "I sort of feel like sometimes people have presented Indigenous folks and vegans as if they're like this natural set of enemies, when in reality I think we have a lot of values in common, even if we're not expressing them in the same practices." Western constructs that automatically link indigeneity with hunting elide the fact that there are hundreds of tribes in the US alone, each with their own cultural food practices. The Cherokee and Choctaw vegan scholar Rita Laws points out that many Indigenous peoples relied mainly on vegetables: "How well we know the stereotype of the rugged Plains Indian: killer of buffalo, dressed in quill-decorated buckskin, elaborately feathered headdress, and leather moccasins, living in an animal skin teepee, master of the dog and horse, and stranger to vegetables. But this lifestyle, once limited almost exclusively to the Apaches, flourished no more than a couple hundred years. It is not representative of most Native Americans of today or yesterday. Indeed, the 'buffalo-as-lifestyle' phenomenon is a direct result of European influence." The relationships among Indigenous hunting and food practices, colonialism, and veganism are complex and deserve their own conversation space.

5. There are a number of vegan children's books available; see, in addition to Jenkins et al. (*True Adventures*), Crawford; Cole.

WORKS CITED

"About." *Black Vegans Rock*, 2019, www.blackvegansrock.com/about.

Adams, Carol J. *The Sexual Politics of Meat: A Feminist-Vegetarian Critical Theory*. 1990. Bloomsbury, 2015.

Adams, Carol J., et al. *Even Vegans Die: A Practical Guide to Caregiving, Acceptance, and Protecting Your Legacy of Compassion*. Lantern Books, 2018.

"Animal Agriculture's Impact on Climate Change." *Climate Nexus*, climatenexus.org/climate-issues/food/animal-agricultures-impact-on-climate-change/. Accessed 10 May 2016.

Brook, Dan. "Cesar Chávez and Comprehensive Rights." *United Farm Workers*, 30 May 2007, ufw.org/ZNET-Cesar-Ch-vez-and-Comprehensive-Rights/.

Burns, Gus. "University of Michigan Lab Lost Mutant Rabbit, Poisoned Fish, Gave Mice Cancer, Reports Show." *Mlive*, 22 Mar. 2019, www.mlive.com/news/2019/03/university-of-michigan-lab-lost-mutant-rabbit-poisoned-fish-gave-mice-cancer-reports-show.html.

Cole, Abioseh. *I Am Not Food*. Illustrated by Kayleigh Castle, Vegan Publishers, 2019.

Cox, Kate, and H. Claire Brown. "Academics across the Country Say Agribusiness Has Outsize Influence on Their Research." *New Food Economy*, 31 Jan. 2019, newfoodeconomy.org/agriculture-industry-influence-money-academic-research/.

Crawford, Leslie. *Sprig the Rescue Pig*. Illustrated by Sonja Stangl, Stone Pier Press, 2018.

"Definition of Veganism." *The Vegan Society*, www.vegansociety.com/go-vegan/definition-veganism.

"Depersonification." *APA Dictionary of Psychology*, 2018, dictionary.apa.org/depersonification.

Donovan, Josephine, and Carol J. Adams. *The Feminist Care Tradition in Animal Ethics: A Reader*. Columbia UP, 2007.

Fitzgerald, Amy J., et al. "Slaughterhouses and Increased Crime Rates." *Organization and Environment*, vol. 22, no. 2, June 2009, pp. 158–85. *Sage Journals*, https://doi.org/10.1177/1086026609338164.

Godoy, Maria. "How Might Trump's Food Box Plan Affect Health? Native Americans Know All Too Well." *NPR*, 25 Feb. 2018, www.npr.org/sections/thesalt/2018/02/25/588098959/how-might-trump-plan-for-food-boxes-affect-health-native-americans-know-all-too.

Gross, Daniel A. "South Carolina Did Not Evacuate Its Prisons for Hurricane Florence, and Those Inside Are Bracing for the Worst." *The New Yorker*, 14 Sept. 2018, www.newyorker.com/news/news-desk/south-carolina-did-not-evacuate-its-prisons-for-hurricane-florence-and-inmates-are-bracing-for-the-worst.

Harper, A. Breeze. "Home." *The Sistah Vegan Project: A Critical Race Feminist's Journey through the 'Ethical Foodscape' . . . and Beyond*, sistahvegan.com. Accessed 27 Oct. 2023.

———. *Sistah Vegan: Black Female Vegans Speak on Food, Identity, Health, and Society*. Lantern Books, 2010.

———. "Sistah Vegans: The *Satya* Interview with Amie Breeze Harper." *Satya*, Mar. 2007, www.satyamag.com/mar07/harper.html.

"Humane Dissection for Your School." *PETA*, 2023, www.peta.org/teachkind/humane-classroom/dissection/free-virtual-dissection/.

Jenkins, Steve, and Derek Walter. *Esther the Wonder Pig: Changing the World One Heart at a Time*. With Caprice Crane, Little, Brown, 2016.

Jenkins, Steve, et al. *Happily Ever Esther: Two Men, a Wonder Pig, and Their Life-Changing Mission to Give Animals a Home*. Grand Central Publishing, 2018.

Jenkins, Steve, et al. *The True Adventures of Esther the Wonder Pig*. Little, Brown, 2018.

Ko, Aph. *Racism as Zoological Witchcraft: A Guide to Getting Out*. Lantern Books, 2019.

Ko, Aph, and Syl Ko. *Aphro-ism: Essays on Pop Culture, Feminism, and Black Veganism from Two Sisters*. Lantern Books, 2017.

Laws, Rita. "Native Americans and Vegetarianism." *VRG Journal*, Sept. 1994, www.vrg.org/journal/94sep.htm#native.

Loria, Joe. "Angela Davis: Feminist, Civil Rights Activist, and Vegan." *Mercy for Animals*, 22 Sept. 2016, mercyforanimals.org/angela-davis-feminist-civil-rights-activist.

McJetters, Christopher Sebastian. "Christopher Sebastian." *Christopher Sebastian*, 2018, www.christophersebastian.info/.

"Mission and Values." *Food Empowerment Project*, 2019, foodispower.org/mission-and-values/.

Povich, Elaine. "Vegan School Lunches Expand despite Opposition from Meat Industry." *Stateline*, 2019, www.pewtrusts.org/en/research-and-analysis/blogs/stateline/2019/09/30/vegan-school-lunches-expand-despite-opposition-from-meat-industry.

Randhawa, Selina. "Animal Rights Activists and Inuit Clash over Canada's Indigenous Food Traditions." *The Guardian*, 1 Nov. 2017, www.theguardian.com/inequality/2017/nov/01/animal-rights-activists-inuit-clash-canada-indigenous-food-traditions.

Ratcliffe, Krista. *Rhetorical Listening: Identification, Gender, Whiteness*. Southern Illinois UP, 2005.

Robinson, Margaret. "This Indigenous Scholar Says Veganism Is More Than a Lifestyle for White People." Interview by April Johnson. *Vice*, 27 Mar. 2018, www.vice.com/en_ca/article/7xd8ex/this-indigenous-scholar-says-veganism-is-more-than-a-lifestyle-for-white-people.

Safina, Carl. *Beyond Words: What Animals Think and Feel*. Henry Holt, 2015.

Sarambi. "Deconstructing Myths Surrounding Veganism and People of Color." *The Anarchist Library*, theanarchistlibrary.org/library/sarambi-deconstructing-myths-surrounding-veganism-people-of-color. Accessed 27 Oct. 2023.

"Slaughterhouse Workers." *Food Empowerment Project*, 2019, foodispower.org/human-labor-slavery/slaughterhouse-workers/.

"Student Choice Laws." *American Anti-Vivisection Society*, 2019, aavs.org/animals-science/laws/student-choice-laws/.

Taylor, Sunaura. *Beasts of Burden: Animal and Disability Liberation*. New Press, 2017.

Warrick, Jo. "They Die Piece by Piece." *The Washington Post*, 10 Apr. 2001, www.washingtonpost.com/archive/politics/2001/04/10/they-die-piece-by-piece/f172dd3c-0383–49f8-b6d8–347e04b68da1/?noredirect=on&utm_term=.a1482215ea22.

Reimagining Social Justice in Public Libraries: A Conversation

Cynthia M. Landrum and Nicole A. Cooke

For half a century or more, equal access and social responsibility have been core values of library and information science (LIS). These tenets emerged as the profession reckoned with its complicity in upholding systems of oppression, like Jim Crow laws, or de facto segregation, in ways that excluded and marginalized library workers and library users. Over the last half century, the profession has taken positions on social concerns as varied as wars, organized labor, systemic racism, mass surveillance, whistleblowing, and outdated and derogatory Library of Congress subject headings. Thus, particularly in the past decade, social justice has become core to LIS scholarship, research, and praxis. LIS has centered social justice in conferences, scholarly literature, graduate education, and other professional development activities. Associations like the Urban Libraries Council have adopted equity, diversity, and inclusion statements that embed social justice principles and concepts. In 2017, the Public Library Association (PLA) formed an equity, diversity, inclusion, and social justice task force (EDISJ). A key outcome of the inaugural task force was the integration of EDISJ as a strategic goal in 2018–22 PLA strategic plan. Substantive and influential social justice research and its pedagogical implications are being published in LIS peer-reviewed and trade publications. Libraries of all types are reimagining policy, programs, and libraries as place through an equitable, diverse, inclusive, and socially just lens. Considering the past decade and looking ahead to the next, Nicole A. Cooke, Augusta Baker Endowed Chair, University of South Carolina, and a former practicing librarian, and Cynthia M. Landrum, a former public library administrator and current doctoral student, explore the state of social justice and library and information science (LIS) in a candid discussion from their unique autoethnographic experiences as practitioner-scholars.

The Conversation

Cooke: To preface our discussion of social justice, what is our working definition of social justice and library and information science?

Landrum: Since I live in a space between practice and scholarship in the academy, I have adopted a hybrid definition of social justice because definitions of social justice are varied. In practice, social justice is viewed along the lines of creating equity in the library and in terms of what the library does to create greater equity within communities. Of course, this is not the only way to think about social justice. There are a variety of ways of defining social justice inside and outside of the discipline, but LIS practitioners tend to focus their energies on social justice in primary services, such as collection development and programming.

Cooke: I would definitely agree with that. I would add to that the idea of advocacy and action. When I talk with students about cultural competence, I tell them, "You're getting everything that you need to be aware of, you're extending your own education, you're reflecting, but now you actually have to do something." That's where the social justice piece comes in, and it's also part of being proactive as opposed to being reactive. I don't think the reactive part is social justice; rather, social justice requires asking, "I'm aware of what the library does, I'm aware of what's happening in the community, but what can I actually do that isn't Band-Aiding, or fixing a problem for the short term, but rather addresses problems in a substantive and systematic way?" The thought process should not be simplistic or reactionary. It needs to go beyond "Oh, we screwed up. We need to fix this" or "Oh, we don't have any Black Lives Matter books. Let's put up a quick display for the month of February."

To your point, there are so many definitions of social justice, yet there is not one cohesive definition. I do think that is a problem for the field; it hinders how we talk about it, and it keeps us from doing as much as we can. There are many other reasons that we don't do what we're supposed to do, but I think it becomes this very nebulous "Oh, well, I can't save the world" perception that leads to not doing anything.

Landrum: Recently, I had this conversation with a colleague who was stressing over the future of public libraries—libraries in general, but public libraries specifically. Since libraries have situated themselves for so long as community gathering places, what does that mean in the age of COVID-19? I said to this individual, "I've always worked under the premise that *library* is an action word." When we center only the building, it is a worry in times like these. When we think about what it means to gather people, do I need to have that building? Or do I need to be gathering people where they are and where their needs are, even if that's in a digital space? So I am less concerned about that aspect of our work. Obviously, we spent millions of dollars on these physical library spaces, but the physical spaces are less of a concern for me in relation to the work that is possible or that we could be doing if we're talking about creating equity.

Cooke: What are your thoughts on the idea of "mission creep"? We're talking about social justice and how we meet our communities where they are, whether it's in physical or virtual spaces.

For example, COVID-19. We've heard reports out of Arizona and San Francisco from librarians who have said they're essentially doing the work of social workers, doing contact tracing and working at testing centers because the library's buildings are closed and they work for the city, which has the right to redeploy them as they see fit. We've seen this before with librarians administering Narcan and doing other things that are perhaps out of our scope. Is there a fine line we're crossing, is it something that we just need to deal with, or are we devaluing our base by indulging the additional tasks as assigned? Are there particular roles that we shouldn't be taking up in terms of social justice and LIS?

Landrum: During a job interview, I was asked if there were things I thought the library shouldn't do. Clearly, there are many things libraries can't do. If we embrace community engagement as the idea of doing with our communities as opposed to doing to and for the communities, then "shouldn't do" is not so absolute. My answer to that question when it was asked of me was "I think it depends on what communities need."

I started my library director position almost one hundred years to the day since the library hired Lilian Childress Hall, the first professionally trained African American librarian in the entire state of Indiana. She integrated a lot of what would have been described as public aid into her practice. Someone would definitely say that raising money to provide Christmas gifts and food for needy children is mission creep. I know that there are many individuals who believe that today's library Feed and Read programs, for example, are mission creep. We can also say that these programs meet needs. In 1916, Ms. Hall recognized that nobody else was trying to meet those children's needs. She saw a space and a place to do that work that made sense. The library was her tool. The library is often a microcosm of communities. It becomes problematic when we are not trained to do this work. Social workers are trained to be social workers. Hire one at your library. Collaborate with your local human and social services organizations to be part of a collective effort addressing the needs.

Another aspect of mission creep is the defining mission. If the mission doesn't center community, a genuine understanding of its needs and expectations, then anything community-focused will feel like mission creep. That gets us back to this whole idea of community engagement. Library employees have embraced community engagement because we need to be out talking to people or sharing our wares. The idea of the staff and the community working with each other, as opposed to an institution doing something to or for the community, looks different. It helps us understand local needs and inequities and the library's role in solving and perpetuating inequities.

Cooke: As a scholar thinking about the definition of social justice, teaching people who go out into the world, and looking at what is happening in practice, what do you think about the disconnect between the academy and practice, and how might practitioners and scholars come together to bridge that gap when it comes to social justice?

Landrum: This is an age-old question that is not just limited to social justice and equity work. For those of us whose experiences balance theory and practice, it's actually relatively easy to have conversations with colleagues across the spectrum of the field. LIS professionals who occupy the space between theory and practice can facilitate understanding across the theory-practice continuum. If we are educating librarians to be social-justice-oriented, we must be aware of what they will encounter in practice. We must prepare them for those experiences. We also must look at our library organizations and talk about what it means to hire a librarian with a social justice orientation. If we fail to create some shared understanding and definition around social justice in the profession, the gap will persist and widen.

Cooke: When I complete annual reviews or when I have to justify myself to higher ed administration, it's not uncommon for me to be asked why all my presentations are at practitioner conferences. I have to tell them that's where my people are. Not only am I talking to them about what we're doing on campuses and what we're doing in the LIS classroom, but that is my opportunity to find out what they're dealing with on the ground, at the service points, because I haven't worked a service point in almost ten years. It goes back to your earlier point about having these conversations, and we have to have that realization and be cognizant that scholars and practitioners need each other. We're talking about a whole field, and there's a lot of disconnect, just like there's a disconnect in the library between the "real librarians," or the degreed librarians, and the staff. Aside from needing more people in that middle area, we must strive to be more intentional and more proactive as part of social justice work to have those conversations. So maybe it's not at a conference. Maybe it's not in a classroom, but maybe it's you and me writing a chapter together. Or maybe it's having a panel where there's a representation of different ideas and different work priorities to facilitate these conversations. We need to have them consistently, because, as I say in the classroom when I'm talking to the students about how they need to be thinking about their communities, "Your community could turn over in a year; there's a lot of the literature that describes the community analysis process and suggests surveying the community every five to ten years. No! This work should be done every year, if not continually." More practitioners and scholars must be more intentional and deliberate about having these conversations and taking action as a result of having them.

Landrum: To your point about LIS scholars and practitioners working with each other, it is such an interesting divide. As a practitioner who is also a doctoral student, I have been told that I am "too academic." It was meant as an insult. I came to realize that my inquiry needed to be part of my social justice practice. In practice, we make lots of assumptions and tend to react to those assumptions. I recall when I was working in Illinois, there was this persistent and ever-increasing achievement gap between Black, Latinx, and white students in this very progressive community. The question was "What can we, the library, do?" The immediate response was "Oh, we'll do a tutoring program." There were ten of those all over the community. My question was "Do we even understand the achievement gap?" There are the technical definitions of the achievement gap, and we may have a semblance of understanding the concept, but do we understand the achievement gap in this community? What is the context? What assumptions are being made about this issue across different constituents in this community? We learned a lot just by taking the time to bring a variety of people to the table to get their understanding of the issue. The business community's perspective was that the achievement gap exists across the board because high school students weren't able to perform in local internships. Parents, social service professionals, and teachers all had their own lens through which they experienced the achievement gap. It's very problematic to rush to solutions, especially when navigating social justice and equity concerns. A working knowledge of theoretical frames gives you a lens to move toward a nuanced understanding of these issues.

Cooke: When I went into my PhD program, I was still working full-time, and one of the professors attempted to insult me by saying, "You're too practical. You have to think more deeply about these things." And I said to him, "Yes, but at some point, we actually have to make a decision and get work done." I set him back on his heels. There was a distinct lack of middle ground between this practitioner and a career academic. So you're "too academic," and I'm "too practical." At what point do we take that information we gleaned from the community and apply some theory to it and think about what we can do and just try it out? Just because you try something doesn't mean you are wedded to it forever; you try it, you see what happens, you assess it, you regroup, and then you try it again. There's a process to that, and all of that process is in that middle ground. That's what we're missing because practitioners like you are told that you're "too academic," and I'm told that I can't be "practical" because we have to talk things to death. And we can't actually implement anything because it will never be perfect. The point is not for it to be perfect. The point is to be proactive. The point is to have that inclination and that desire to improve things and your communities. The current anti-racism discourse is directing some of those efforts by challenging ideas that we have upheld as part of civil rights and liberation work, namely the notion of who can be a racist and how we define power. How should libraries and librarians, especially nonwhite librarians, consider these ideas in their work? Add to that what you were saying about critical race theory (CRT), intersectionality, and cultural competence. I always say that LIS seems to be a good ten years behind every curve. Once education, law, and applied health sciences have been talking about these theories for decades, we "discover" them and cherry-pick the pieces that are most useful. I remember that a colleague incorporated critical race theory into her dissertation and one of her committee members criticized her because she only wanted her to focus on counterstorytelling. Counterstorytelling is but one part of critical race theory; it is not critical race theory in its entirety. For every person in LIS that you ask to define intersectionality, CRT, diversity, or social justice, you're going to get a different answer, and they're applying it in different and curious ways.

Landrum: I think about power in relation to this discourse and how libraries and librarians, especially nonwhite librarians, should consider these ideas in their work, or should begin to consider them. For quite some time now, probably a decade, I have said that this notion that the library is the great equalizer doesn't have any historical footing. We look at narratives, some of which we are just now embracing, around the library as an instrument of disenfranchisement at various points in its history. Moving past that history, if libraries are the great equalizer, what are we equalizing? We need to have that critical conversation. That conversation needs to start with an understanding of where libraries are situated in power structures and systems—understanding that even though we may not be able to change an entire system, we can begin by looking at why we do what we do and how we do it.

Take this emerging conversation about police and the library. Should police be in the library? Shouldn't they be in the library? That's the wrong place to start the conversation, because if you're going to say, "Well, we're not going to have officers or our duty officers in the library," then what else are you saying? Often, those decisions don't come with critical thought about the policies that necessitated an administrator's bringing officers into the library or the way you think about what it is you want that library experience to be. So, if officers are not in the library, are you bringing in social workers? Are you implementing restorative justice in the library? What is the library experience you're trying to create? I would contend that prioritizing social justice doesn't necessarily mean that officers are not the right people to be in the library. I've worked with officers who are former social workers, those who have been victims' advocates. They had a very different approach to working in the library, not because the library told them to have a different approach, but that's just how they approached their work in general. If the library has a punitive perspective, then this will be reflected in its policies. I say policy is proxy for the relationship the library wants to have with users. Whoever is enforcing library policies, if the policies themselves disenfranchise people and don't empower them or engender mutual trust, then that is how they will be enforced. That's problematic. The library needs to start internally, looking at library histories, and have a come-to-whoever moment. There are many librarians sitting in libraries right now who have absolutely no clue that their library had some policy that was essentially either overtly or covertly excluding groups of people.

Cooke: Absolutely. And to piggyback on what you were saying about having come-to-Jesus moments or reflections, in many institutional attempts at cultural competence, intersectionality, anti-racism, or whatever the theory du jour is, the motivation is not correct. The discussion that you brought up about police and libraries goes along with the idea of defunding the police. Why are people interested in that now? Is it because that's what the field is talking about or because that's what they see on television? Libraries tend to have this thing about keeping up with the Joneses, and you know when it's anything related to diversity and equity, it becomes the hot topic, because there's grant money, conferences, and writing opportunities attached to these topics people really don't fully understand or truly embrace.

I remember presenting at the 2014 American Library Association conference, discussing diversity and other core issues, and someone in the Q and A said, "Well, what happens when this is no longer trendy?" and I said, "I've been doing this work for almost twenty years. It's not trendy to me." It may be trendy to people now, and when they decide that this five-year trend is over and they move on to something else, I'll still be doing this work. It's like jumping on the bandwagon but not digging deep enough, and when that funding opportunity is done, or when that conference is over, or when it gets too hard because people are trying to do work that they haven't properly prepared for, then they just abandon it for the next biggest and greatest thing. That lends itself to not understanding the theories as a whole. It lends itself to not applying the theories correctly, and it goes back to what you were saying about community engagement. If you don't know your community the way you should, maybe intersectionality is not the right theory for you to be using. There are many different levels here, but to your point, it all starts with knowing yourself and knowing the community.

Landrum: Even with all our discussions about staff diversity and inclusion in the profession, recruitment is not the only way to create a culturally competent library staff. You can be in a community that is fairly homogeneous, and having a librarian who is not of that community or maybe doesn't share any identities with people in that community isn't necessarily a demonstration of your commitment to equity, diversity, and inclusion. I would much prefer that you actually invest in training the people in the library community to think about equity, diversity, inclusion, and social justice every day when they are doing their jobs and when engaging with people. A purely quantitative approach doesn't advance EDI and social justice. You may get one, two, or whatever number of "diverse" librarians only for them to turn around and leave in five years.

Cooke: Right, the tokenizing never works, whether you're doing it with the staff or with the community. In addition to knowing your community and doing your own self-reflection, I remind my students that I can't teach them everything they think they're supposed to know. So, when the next theory becomes popular, they get on social media or jump into a Q and A and say, "I never learned that in library school." Well, you weren't supposed to, because just as the world and society evolve, so should you. We need to know what's happening and should have a healthy level of cultural and intellectual humility. A lot of people don't. There's always going to be a new theory, there's always going to be a new technique, and there's always going to be a new cause that you didn't know about. Library school is a professional program that's supposed to teach you how to think and learn, and it gives you a foundation. The rest is up to you to be curious and seek some enlightenment for yourself.

Landrum: I don't expect my attorney to know every law, but I expect them, when they come across a situation that doesn't fall neatly into a specific statute, or there is no precedent, to seek out new knowledge and information. It's up to that individual to think and use what they have in the foundation of their education and to be curious. That's not just in our profession; I find people are less curious.

Cooke: Yes, and it's interesting or ironic for our profession in particular because we espouse lifelong learning. The different ways hypocrisy shows up in the profession. . . . We have librarians promoting anti-racism workshops who have actively and knowingly abused students and colleagues of color, and we have librarians and other library professionals promoting diverse books who will routinely call the police on their rowdy, probably Black and Brown, teenagers. We have a profession that is still over eighty percent white and female, but we're always talking about we need to diversify the profession. We talk about recruiting diverse students, but we don't talk about retaining those students. We also have librarians who maintain and or double down on policies and practices that exclude or create barriers for the least of those in their communities. These are internal issues that require reflection and accountability. We need to know ourselves before we can even get to the community. Do we have an internal social justice issue? Is there an external social justice issue, or is it all one *big* social justice issue? What are your thoughts on this kind of internal hypocrisy?

Landrum: It's like an inside-out thing. How are we going to project outward to the community if we are not doing the work inside the library? This is not just in terms of this social justice work. We talk about collaboration with communities. We don't even collaborate with our colleagues. How we are going to collaborate with people down the street? There is lots of internal work that needs to be done. I wonder if shining an external light can help us see our internal challenges. I'm also realistic. The person giving out the diverse book list is also throwing the Black and Brown teenagers out of the library. Some EDISJ activities can be performative. They can be done in a way to allay one's guilt. The performative act is not necessarily wrong if it causes one to examine and change behaviors. Do I see that happening? I'm farther away from practice than I was a few years ago. I see some people being intentional in their LIS social justice work. To your point about trends, yes, it's the trendy thing to do a reading or watch list or a solidarity statement on the website. If we take a deep dive, how do library missions, strategic plans, policies, budgets, organization structure, staffing, and on and on square up with the reading list and the statement? When we look, the incongruences are stark. Yes, we have an internal problem. How great is our desire to actually address that problem in a real way?

Cooke: That reminds me of ongoing conversations that you and I have about whether people are in LIS because they want a job or because they want a career. Another conversation we frequently have is the distinction between performative action and substantive or systemic change. Both of those can exist on a spectrum, and neither of these things is binary. And part of the challenge of social justice work, internally and externally, is trying to get people to move further along on the spectrum towards career and systemic change as opposed to "This is just a job, and I need to check off the trendy boxes." We don't have many in the middle; we have some of the big talkers in the middle, not big doers.

We've talked about hashtag activism and those people who are so loud and profound online but don't actually do anything, or who think they have a lock on a particular subject or a particular activity, but that's only in the online space. In the middle there are people for whom this is just a job and they're just going to check the box and put this diverse books list out so they can go on their way. And then there are the ones that are perhaps on the other end of the spectrum who are working on systemic change. Maybe they're not hooked into the conference circuit, or maybe they don't have time to write the book or write all the articles. Sometimes those are the folks that tend to have a different motivation. They're not doing it so everyone knows about it; they're doing it to actually make the change. It's hard to move people out of their respective spaces on said spectrums.

Landrum: There are library administrators who are not the best when it comes to creating systemic change around equity and social justice. Some may not have an interest in the work. That's fine as long as they don't create obstacles for others who do. There are other library administrators whose work on the surface may not seem to be impactful. In reality, it doesn't look a certain way. If you drill down to the administrator's decision-making, you see where resources are going, policies, or how they are shaping the work, and the impact of those decisions in their communities is really significant. As for the career librarian versus the job librarian, there is nothing wrong with being a job librarian. Libraries need staff members who come in, do their work, and go home. Where it becomes challenging is, as you said, when the individual becomes a barrier to others. The library is trying to become more equitable and social-justice-oriented. That shift will mean my job will change and the expectations will change. I don't want my job and the expectations to change. Part of the job narrative is that if you want to do the job, and the job has changed, then you need to adjust if you want to continue to work at the institution. Again, there is nothing wrong with approaching LIS work as a job. Everybody is needed. Then there are the folks in the middle. The people in the middle between the job and career librarians may be very loud. They may have all the language of equity and social justice, but then when the tide actually turns in the organization towards social justice, they haven't built a social justice practice.

Cooke: Exactly, because now the organization says, "You know what? You're right, we were wrong," and if they haven't built a foundation of practice where their work actually matches the rhetoric, then they're screwed too.

Landrum: Absolutely. In this situation, there are the staff members on the other side of the spectrum. They have been quietly working away. They've been doing the social justice work, and they can become jaded and miffed if folks in the middle are being centered, pushed forward, and given resources to do work for which they haven't built a practice. Staff members who have been committed to the work for years on end, have been out in the community, are champions, and are overlooked. It feels like a losing battle.

Cooke: We started by defining social justice for the purposes of our conversation, and you touched on it in your last response. What are your thoughts about what social justice leadership looks like, and how do we prepare for it? We're still dealing with a very homogeneous student body, which is part of the reason we have a very homogeneous workforce. And when we talk a lot about empathy, cultural competence, reflection, and flexibility, I refer to those as the precursors to social justice, because social justice is action. What are students going to be *doing* after they leave my classroom? I tend to focus a little bit more on the attributes of a social justice leader, and I don't necessarily think that's something you can call yourself; it's something that you have to earn, because it's what you're doing from the practice side. From the perspective of someone who studies leadership and from someone who's been in LIS administration, what does social justice leadership look like to you?

Landrum: I participated in a leadership workshop with some well-regarded leaders of color in our profession. They were speaking specifically about leaders of color, but this doesn't just apply to leaders of color. The leader comes into that work with an equity agenda, especially if they've been someone whose library career has revolved around equity. Similarly, the social justice leader often comes to their work with a social justice agenda or an understanding of social justice. It's possible to evolve and adopt a social justice lens as a leader. I know that some leaders understand the power of the library and understand how even in some small way they can ensure that the library lives up to the ideal that it is "the great equalizer."

Library leaders have to embrace the idea that social justice work is not easy. It is difficult work. Social justice practice in real time in the library challenges the library status quo. You will face internal and external resistance. When you are the leader, everything begins and ends with you. It has been said that the leader gets all the blame and very little of the credit. As the leader, you will have your values tested, especially as the internal culture changes. I can remember being in a staff day session. I was not presenting. The library equity and well-being officer was presenting on the issue of diversity in the profession. The library equity and well-being officer showed a chart of what the field would look like if it matched the demographics of this country. A member of the staff asked, "What if *those* people don't want to work in libraries?" The tension in the room was palpable. As the director, I had to make a decision to address it in the moment or later. I scanned the room and observed people's body language. I could hear moans and gasps. I had to address this comment. My approach was to lay out the historical, economic, and social circumstances that have created perpetual barriers to entry into the profession for underserved, underresourced, and underrepresented groups. It's not merely lack of desire; it is lack of opportunity. The library can do all the outward-facing social justice work, but if it is not doing the internal work, it won't take root.

Social justice and equity practice in the library has to be internal and external. It is an imperfect practice that can take years to build. The practitioner may not always enjoy the fruit of their labor. I can still see the foundation that I laid in many libraries, even if I'm not seeing the exact work I was doing and the particular way I did it. I can look at what is being done, knowing that wouldn't be possible if boundaries hadn't been pushed and policies and thinking hadn't been changed. For me, the essence of social justice and equity practice in the library is not just changing what the library does but how it thinks about what it does. Are you seeing this in the academy?

Cooke: Indeed, although I don't see it as much in LIS. LIS leadership is often very flat (i.e., not a lot of middle management) and is a function of library professionals "waiting their turn" for a position to open up. As LIS professionals, we have been taught an emphasis on management and not leadership, and we know those are two very different things. There are several professional development leadership institutes, usually for academic librarians, but that cannot take the place of the substantive leadership education and training that we see in other fields, such as education and social work. This is why it's acutely important that LIS take an interdisciplinary cue from other disciplines that cultivate leaders and don't just install managers.

To be fair, there are many LIS leaders doing this real and difficult leadership work, but because librarianship, especially public librarianship, is so firmly rooted in and espoused as a service profession, it has a hard time recognizing itself as a leader in the social justice and equity movement. And until we can see ourselves as such, no one else will.

Recommendations

As social justice theory and practice continue to proliferate in library and information science, significant gaps exist in scholarship and practice, especially in regard to leadership in the profession. A distinct LIS definition of social justice is necessary for building a more holistic approach to social justice practice in libraries. Social justice must be a thoughtful and purposeful leadership practice that impacts the inner workings of the library and the outward work with the community. LIS practitioners, especially administrators, must engage theory along with practice to support and sustain an intentional, reflective, and sustainable social justice practice in their libraries.

The Social Responsibility of Museums

Spencer R. Crew

In 1971, the director of the Brooklyn Museum, Duncan Cameron, wrote an essay entitled "The Museum, a Temple or the Forum," wherein he argued that museums were suffering an identity crisis because they fluctuated between different roles that he believed were incompatible. As temples, museums were churchlike places of contemplation and thoughtful reflection. Staff members had sifted through the available artifacts and determined which ones were worthy of exhibition and admiration. Placing them on exhibit signaled the end of any discussion about their value to society. Museums that followed the path of a forum created a different atmosphere. In forums, ideas and new perspectives were the coin of the realm. Debate was central to the process: the conversation itself was important, and reaching a unanimous decision about the functions of museums was no longer the end goal. This emphasis on exchange made such institutions into lively, engaging spaces. Cameron firmly believed that the temple and the forum could not coexist in the same space and that any effort to integrate the two functions was a mistake to avoid.

While I do not necessarily agree with Cameron, I find the dichotomy he describes worth examining. His essay defines two extremes of a spectrum on which museum institutions can be viewed. On one end of the spectrum, museums view themselves as repositories for important materials, where their primary function is to preserve, research, and exhibit objects. The role of the public is minimized in this process. Staff members, as "experts," determine what is best and then share it with the public. The public is expected to passively accept the staff's decisions and take in the intrinsic value of the materials on display. There is no exchange in this setting. Museum professionals who see their role in this way have been described by scholars like Mark O'Neill as "essentialists," believing in beauty and knowledge for their own sake and not for other purposes (96).

On the other end of this spectrum are museums and employees who see their institutions' primary role as that of a forum, where ideas are explored and traditional ways of doing and seeing things are challenged. They raise questions of interest for their visitors and attempt to stimulate critical thinking. The objects they collect and uplift are not just beautiful or significant items but also vehicles for exploring the world and seeing it from new perspectives. The visitor, rather than the artifacts, is the focus in these circumstances. These institutions also emphasize building a strong, positive connection with the communities they serve. O'Neill sees them as operating under an adaptive model where focusing on the needs and interests of the people is their ultimate responsibility (97).

While these models exaggerate the realities of museum operations, they still capture the different views that permeate and cause friction within the field forty years later. In 2019, the International Council of Museums (ICOM) brought forward a new definition of museums for consideration: "Museums are democratizing, inclusive, and polyphonic spaces for critical dialogue about the pasts and the futures. Acknowledging and addressing the conflicts and challenges of the present, they hold artefacts and specimens in trust for society, safeguard diverse memories for future generations and guarantee equal rights and equal access to heritage for all people" ("ICOM"). For many in the field, this point of view expanded the vision for the role of museums too far. As one museum worker wrote, the definition "pushed at the edges of past practice to suggest a more activist role of museums as contributors to their cultures, redressing past wrongs, and aspiring to leadership for a more inclusive and environmentally responsible global culture" (Fraser). Other aspects of the fuller definition offered by the ICOM Standing Committee on the Museum Definition have sparked disagreement, but this particular section bears further discussion in the context of this essay. Is it improper for museums to take a social activist role? Should museums remain neutral and focus their attention on the preservation, presentation, and study of the materials under their control? How one responds to these questions is important in the context of the turmoil—some would say the social revolution—currently occurring in the United States and other parts of the world. Is it the role of museums to join in the fray, using the tools at our command to contribute to the conversation? Or is it our role to remain neutral, without interjecting ourselves into the debate?

An important aspect of this discussion within the museum profession in recent years is the responsibility of cultural institutions to provide value and positive contributions to the communities they serve and that surround them. Museums that welcome interaction and regular visitation from nearby residents are an asset to their communities. The status of this ongoing relationship shapes the role a museum can play during a time of social unrest. If the institution has not built trust with an immediate community, it will be difficult to find connection and resonate in a moment of heightened tension. Even with well-formed relationships, there are various ways that museums can increase their value and cultural capital during these moments.

Museums must proactively seek engagement and conversation with nearby communities to accurately gauge their perceived value. Institutions must not make uninformed assumptions about what communities need or about what will and will not resonate with said communities. Community feedback from "nonexperts" can be uncomfortable for professionals to receive, but the opportunity to learn and internalize community needs and perspectives is invaluable in building and sustaining relationships. Fully engaging in this type of practice can transform an institution from an imposing, uninviting presence to a place that values the viewpoints and contributions of its neighbors. Actions that result from these conversations must also be more than a one-time effort and must demonstrate an ongoing commitment to dialogue and engagement. For museums that have not connected to their respective communities, our current social and political moment is precisely the time to begin to build these bridges. As many institutions are intensifying their commitments to equity, museums that have not historically been viewed as community partners have an opportunity to improve local relationships.

One museum that has recently modeled this practice of reconsidering community engagement is the Virginia Museum of History and Culture (VMHC), in Richmond, Virginia. Under the leadership of Jamie O. Bosket, appointed in 2017, the museum acknowledged that it had not built a strong relationship with African Americans in Richmond and launched a series of initiatives to strengthen dialogue and connection. They sponsored meetings with community members to better understand how the museum was perceived and what the museum might do to improve that perception. These dialogues prompted the museum to assemble a group of advisers to continue the relationship and to assist in the creation of an exhibition: *Determined: The Four-Hundred-Year Struggle for Black Equality*. This exhibition commemorated the four hundredth anniversary of the arrival of the first enslaved Africans in colonial North America, focusing on African American history in Virginia and Richmond.

The process of collecting for the exhibition allowed the museum to increase their community contacts as well as improve the representation of African American history and culture in their collections. For the institution, the exhibition represented "the museum's commitment to representing *all* Virginians and their diverse stories" ("Virginia Museum") and was judged a success by the larger Richmond community. *Determined* also increased African American appreciation for and visitation to the museum. A ceremony to dedicate Arthur Ashe Boulevard in collaboration with the city of Richmond drew the largest number of visitors—seven thousand—VMHC had ever hosted in a single day. In a speech at the ceremony, Ashe's nephew, David Harris, remarked that "for a long time," he had felt that "this museum was not a place for people like him." Now that had changed (Kollatz).

The museum's commitment to this communal lens for their work went beyond a single exhibition. Previously known as the Virginia Historical Society, the institution advocated to change their name to Virginia Museum of History and Culture to signify their commitment to access and inclusion to the surrounding communities. VMHC hosted programs and lectures in conjunction with *Determined* and created a corresponding online exhibition to increase access during and after the initial show. Most importantly, the museum continues to interact with African American community members through other museum projects such as hosting a "State of Black America" town hall in the museum's auditorium and developing an agreement with the Black History Museum and Cultural Center of Virginia to house and digitize its collection for use by both institutions. Bosket sees these actions as a long-term relationship that will remain central to the work of this museum. He hopes the museum will be "the place where you go not only to understand but to feel and absorb why these past events, people, and their decisions matter today" (Kollatz). His efforts have made VMHC a trusted community partner that exemplifies the immense benefits of a committed effort to changing the perception and place of an institution within a community.

Reimagining a museum's role going forward is also the task of institutions that have established relationships with their communities. The Smithsonian's National Museum of African American History and Culture (NMAAHC) has sought unique ways to connect with a global contingent of visitors as well as the regional Washington, DC, communities. One of the program series that developed, A Seat at the Table, brings together individuals from a cross-section of communities for a family-style dinner and evening of conversation. Registration is open to the public, and the low participation fee is subsidized by the program sponsor. Program topics have uplifted dialogue around social justice and religion, culture, identity, and community ("Seat"). While a speaker or panel is featured during the meal, all tables (to which participants are assigned at random) are encouraged to discuss the topic at hand and then share their reflections with the larger group, creating a forum where all voices can be heard and new ideas and perspectives can be exchanged. The outcome for this program goes beyond convening community members; it decenters our institution as the single source of knowledge and value and shares that power with each person who participates. It has continued to encourage productive dialogue across lines of difference and provides space for healing in moments of local or national crisis.

In response to the global COVID-19 pandemic, NMAAHC provided an outlet for users to express their reactions to the events around them. Since anger, confusion, fear, and other emotions are natural reactions to extraordinary moments in time, we offered space to share these feelings by providing opportunities for participants to understand that they were not alone in whatever they were feeling and experiencing. One effort we initiated in spring 2020 was the creation of our *Community Curation* platform (see "Learn More"). This digital space attracted contributors from across the nation and creatively captured the impact of the pandemic during a time when the community did not have physical access to the museum space. We were and are particularly interested in the ways in which African Americans have navigated this health crisis, and we reached out especially to communities where we had established ties and good relationships. The project offered real-time reactions from those who responded to this opportunity and will be invaluable to the museum and to researchers in the future. It also encouraged participants to recognize the historical importance of their experiences and to consider how their material culture has possible historic importance and can be shared with a local museum in their area or with NMAAHC.

The same principle applied to capturing the energy of participants in recent protests against racism across the United States. In many ways, these actions generated a possible watershed moment in US history and the world. In collaboration with the National Museum of American History and Anacostia Community Museum at the Smithsonian, NMAAHC curators were on the streets of DC, talking to protesters and collecting the posters, signs, and art that people were using to effect social change. The members of our staff approached this gathering and collecting process with sensitivity, understanding that these materials have tremendous emotional meaning and value for their creators, who may not have wished to have their objects removed and taken to a museum. Curators took time to talk with participants to build rapport so that they were comfortable with our collecting effort. We also conducted and recorded oral interviews of consenting participants to capture their thoughts as to why they were protesting and what outcomes they wanted. This collecting process had value both for the people from whom we were collecting and for the museum's project of recording this unprecedented historic moment.

Museums' educational role also adds value to their communities. In their capacity as educational institutions, museums can provide tools that capture critical issues of the moment and offer pathways for users to address them and create tactics to overcome them. We have found digital platforms to be among the most effective and far-reaching vehicles for fulfilling this responsibility. A digital platform can reach beyond the walls of the museum and connect with interested parties who wish to make use of it. This was the principle underlying the "Talking about Race" portal created by NMAAHC over the past year and shared publicly in June 2020. The goal was to construct what our education staff called a "brave space" that offered ways to constructively engage a critical issue facing American society—race. It emerged from a decade of work and learning by the museum's education department. Before the doors of the museum ever opened, the staff began offering workshops titled "Let's Talk: Race in the Classroom" to help educators sensitively navigate issues of race with their students. Through trial and error in the workshops, museum staff members identified the worries and challenges faced by many educators. Some of these issues were external, but others were internal baggage carried by the teachers. To craft strategies to get past these impediments, our staff consulted outside experts on how to effectively navigate discussions about race and tested and refined their guidance over time. They saw this work as a core responsibility of the museum and an important tool to provide classroom educators.

While our staff members were pleased with the effectiveness of the subsequent workshops, they understood that only workshop attendees benefited directly from the experience. Seeking to create a means of increasing the impact, reach, and usefulness of what our educators had accomplished, the museum organized a team to broaden the reach of the workshop material. The result was the carefully crafted multimedia portal "Talking about Race." It provides tools to support more conversations about racial identity, racism, and the historical and current impact of these topics on American society. The platform acknowledges how challenging these discussions can be and creates helpful entry points for generating exchanges and learning. The belief is that the more the issue is squarely faced and understood, the more likely actions can increase to lessen racism's negative impact.

The platform employs several techniques to increase its effectiveness. Most importantly, it encourages participants to be reflective, self-reflective, and thoughtful during the process. At the start, the portal directly confronts the reality that we are all aware of race, both our own and one another's. Even children are aware of these differences at a very young age. Rather than ignoring or denying the reality of race and racism, the platform encourages participants to engage and understand its impact. Specifically, it offers pathways for three sectors of society—educators, parents or caregivers, and individuals committed to equity—to wrestle with the historic role of racism in US history and its negative impact through to the present day. Embedded in each pathway are activities, multimedia presentations, questions and actions, and steps designed to facilitate learning and insights. We encourage users to think, talk, and then act in opposition to racism. Users are challenged and encouraged to embrace the responsibility to resist racism with the understanding that not doing so is to allow it to flourish.

The goals of this portal are ambitious but an appropriate task for our museum to accept. A commitment to social justice is a long-standing core principle of NMAAHC. It is also a position that museum supporters have come to expect of us. Consequently, creating the portal and continuing to add new learning as well as guidelines for additional sectors of society represent a logical step for the museum.

A similar commitment to social justice and equity, specifically concerning the repatriation of Native patrimony, guides the work of the National Museum of the American Indian (NMAI). The foundation for the initial holdings of NMAI was the George Gustav Heye collection. Heye, over the course of several decades beginning at the turn of the twentieth century, acquired materials from Native groups across the Americas through archeological excavations and purchase. In 1922, Heye created the National Museum of the American Indian, through which he continued acquiring additional material. At the time of his death in 1957, the holdings numbered nearly 700,000 items. However, the museum suffered financial difficulties, and in 1989, the Smithsonian Institution assumed control. The acquisition of the collection brought with it controversy about the contents of the collection and concerns expressed by Native American tribes about how artifacts had been obtained. Determined to respond appropriately to these concerns, NMAI affirmatively embraced the question of repatriation. An important part of the NMAI Act of 1989 committed the museum to the return of Native human remains and associated funerary items (United States [Public Law 101-185] sec. 11–14).

The Smithsonian Institution's repatriation office leads this effort for the museum and has expanded its actions to include the repatriation of sacred objects and objects of cultural patrimony. It takes seriously the expectation of the NMAI Act as well as the guidelines set out in the 1990 Native American Graves Protection and Repatriation Act (United States [United States Code]). To this end, it sponsors the travel of Native representatives to the museum to view materials of concern to them and to encourage discussions about their future disposition. This commitment has resulted in the return, in collaboration with other Smithsonian units, of more than 250,000 objects to the appropriate tribal groups. One recent illustration of this commitment was the repatriation of a Prairie Chicken Society headdress and a Weather Dance robe to Siksika Nation, located in Alberta, Canada. The action embodied a basic operational principle of NMAI as noted by its acting director, Machel Monenerkit, who emphasized at the ceremony, "Our repatriation policy embodies our mission and vision" ("National Museum"). From its inception, NMAI has sought to work closely with Native communities, whom it sees as its most important constituency. Failing to do so undermines any hope it may have of forging partnerships of value with Native peoples. NMAI, NMAAHC, and other cultural institutions that see social responsibility as an important part of their mission are obliged to provide tools and programs in times of social change that acknowledge and speak to the needs of our constituents.

Museums are part of larger communities and society. They collect, perform research, and share their work through exhibitions. However, it is not enough to create experiences for visitors that are enjoyable to observe but do not offer food for thought. Our programs and presentations must do more than that. We are socially irresponsible if our work does not recognize and respond to the everyday issues around us. Such a lack of engagement will cause members of the communities in which we reside to see us as detached and unconcerned about things of importance to them. It will reinforce the view of our organizations as imposing and uninviting places disconnected from the communities to which we want to link. More importantly, to quote the civil rights activist and social critic Eldridge Cleaver, "There is no more neutrality in the world. You either have to be part of the solution, or you're going to be part of the problem" ("Eldridge Cleaver").[1] If museums are to remain valued partners in our communities, we cannot be viewed as part of the problem.

NOTES

A condensed version of this article, entitled "Being Part of the Solution," originally appeared in the September-October 2020 issue of *Museum*, a publication of the American Alliance of Museums.

1. The expression famously used by Cleaver was coined by an advertising agency owner, Charles Rosner, as part of a campaign for the federal program Volunteers in Service to America, or VISTA, in 1967 (Goodheart).

WORKS CITED

Cameron, Duncan F. "The Museum, a Temple or the Forum." *Curator: The Museum Journal*, vol. 14, no. 1, Mar. 1971, pp. 11–24.

Determined: The Four-Hundred-Year Struggle for Black Equality. Virginia Museum of History and Culture, virginiahistory.org/exhibitions/determined-400-year-struggle-black-equality.

"Eldridge Cleaver Quotation." *Roz Payne Sixties Archive*, U of Nebraska, Lincoln, Center for Digital Humanities, rozsixties.unl.edu/items/show/567.

Fraser, John. "A Discomforting Definition of Museum." *The Museum Journal*, vol. 62, no. 4, 29 Oct. 2019, pp. 501–04. *Wiley Online Library*, https://doi.org/10.1111/cura.12345.

Goodheart, Adam, et al. "Paul Ryan, Black Panther?" *The New York Times*, 12 Aug. 2012, archive.nytimes.com/campaignstops.blogs.nytimes.com/2012/08/12/paul-ryan-black-panther/.

"ICOM Announces the Alternative Museum Definition That Will Be Subject to a Vote." *ICOM*, 25 July 2019, icom.museum/en/news/icom-announces-the-alternative-museum-definition-that-will-be-subject-to-a-vote/.

Kollatz, Harry, Jr. "Changing History." *Richmond Magazine*, 21 Oct. 2019, richmondmagazine.com/news/features/changing-history/.

"Learn More." *Community Curation*, National Museum of African American History and Culture, www.communitycuration.org/home/learn-more. Accessed 31 Oct. 2023.

"National Museum of the American Indian Repatriates Two Objects to the Siksika Nation." *Smithsonian*, 9 July 2021, www.si.edu/newsdesk/releases/national-museum-american-indian-repatriates-two-objects-siksika-nation.

O'Neill, Mark. "Essentialism, Adaptation and Justice: Towards a New Epistemology of Museums." *Museum Management and Curatorship*, vol. 21, no. 2, 2006, pp. 95–116.

"A Seat at the Table." *National Museum of African American History and Culture*, 2017, nmaahc.si.edu/events/series/seat-table.

"Talking about Race." *National Museum of African American History and Culture*, 2020, nmaahc.si.edu/learn/talking-about-race.

United States, Congress. Public Law 101-185. 28 Nov. 1989. *National Museum of the American Indian*, americanindian.si.edu/sites/1/files/pdf/about/NMAIAct.pdf.

United States, Congress, House. United States Code. Title 25, chapter 32, Office of the Law Revision Counsel, 16 Nov. 1990, uscode.house.gov/view.xhtml?path=/prelim@title25/chapter32&edition=prelim.

"Virginia Museum of History and Culture Announces Advisory Committee and Collecting Initiative for a New Exhibition on Four Hundred Years of African American History." Virginia Museum of History and Culture, 6 Mar. 2018, virginiahistory.org. Press release.

Rethinking Systems

Absent Justice

Dontá McGilvery

PROFESSOR BLACK IN AMERICA, *speaking to a diverse group of students seated at their desks in a predominantly white institution in Anytown, USA.*

So, I ask you, where in the world can *we* go for safety? Speaking of safety, where the hell is JUSTICE, because every time I call the roll, JUSTICE is absent. Wait, let me try looking at the attendance sheets of the other courses taught here at American Humanities Institute of Greatness; maybe JUSTICE is a no-show in everyone else's course as well.

(*The professor grabs the attendance sheets and begins reading aloud the names of each course to see if* JUSTICE *was present or absent.*)

"There's a Stranger in My Nice Neighborhood"? JUSTICE was present for that class . . . OK, fine. Ah, let's check this one out: "Karen's Crying for Help"? Oh, JUSTICE was present for that class as well. Hmm, moving forward. "Law Enforcements and the 'Fear for My Safety'"? Ugh, JUSTICE was present for that course, too.

(*Feeling uncomfortable, the professor readjusts their body and addresses the class.*)

Well, exactly what classes has JUSTICE not shown up for? (*Looks at the other attendance sheets and slowly begins to say the course names.*) "The Color of Death in the American Civil Rights Movement"? Well, JUSTICE was a no-show for that one. (*Keeps reading.*) The next class I see here is entitled "Botham Jean: Blackness, Home, Ice Cream, and Dallas." Wow, that's an interesting title . . . uh . . . JUSTICE was a no-show again. Ah, here we go, finally. (*Brightens up.*) "Philando Castile, His Fiancée, and Their Daughter: A Family Image": I know JUSTICE has to love families. (*Skimming across the paper.*) JUSTICE was (*a disheartening look*) again a no-show. Well, let's look at the class that's gathered here today. (*Brightens up again.*) Let's see who is present and who is absent, shall we? My classes know how to represent well. For this semester's class, entitled "No Knock at Midnight: The Life and Death of Breonna Taylor," is JUSTICE present? (*Looks at the class as no one says a word.*) JUSTICE? (*Still no response.*) No JUSTICE here to represent Breonna? Why has JUSTICE withdrawn from every BIPOC-centered course? Better yet, was JUSTICE ever really enrolled in BIPOC-centered courses to begin with? All of you (*pointing to the students*), who are all of you here? What's your names?

(*Each individual, one by one, turns over the name tag that sits on their desk. Written on each student's tag is the name* AMERICA. PROFESSOR BLACK IN AMERICA *takes a moment to look around at the names.*)

So, I realize I need to change my original question: If AMERICA is as diverse as this class, with whom, then, does JUSTICE's allegiance lie? Who is the AMERICA that has stolen JUSTICE's heart?

Five Things about the Concept of Justice

Jane Elliott

After fifty-two years of doing the Blue Eyes / Brown Eyes exercise in discrimination with people of all ages, in several different countries, and in most of the states in the United States of America, I have learned some interesting things about the concept of justice. In the exercise, I separated participants by the color of their eyes, a physical characteristic over which they have no control, which is determined by the same chemical, melanin, that also determines skin color, and then treated them negatively or positively based on the color of their eyes. Much of what I have learned may be objectionable to many, but I hope readers will try to find a kernel of truth here to which they can respond positively—one that may make it easier to recognize and to furnish justice to those who are other than white.

The first thing to know and understand is that society denies justice in the twenty-first century by using ignorant, racist language from centuries past. To carry this ignorance into the twenty-first century is to be determined to speak of justice, to promise justice, to preach about justice, and to teach about justice while practicing injustice based on skin color, on a national scale.

The second thing to know and understand is that society bases its provision of justice on the terms used to refer to those it considers deserving or undeserving of justice. As long as people are identified by the color of their skin, people will be treated unjustly. This is partly because of the associations attached to the colors so broadly assigned. Does anyone really think that "white" people are white? Of course not. People use the word *white* because, although it's totally inaccurate, it's what they are accustomed to saying and hearing—yet its use reinforces the idea that people classified as such are clean, pure, unsullied, and therefore deserving of the power to decide who is or is not entitled to be treated justly. In the United States, we have not adopted a term commensurate with *African American* or *Asian American*, such as *Euro American*. Such terms are used for othering while "whiteness" retains its power.

The third thing to remember is that words are indeed the most powerful weapon devised by humankind, and we use them to destroy or to elevate people every minute of the day. The eye-color exercise is all about words, and I have watched people of all ages live up to, and down to, my judgment of them, simply based on the words they are exposed to for the duration of the experience. If I can turn a reader into a nonreader, and a brilliant student into someone who acts like an ass, in the space of a few minutes by describing them in defamatory ways for a short time, what can we do to members of the human race, with whom we use the skin-color exercise for a lifetime?

The fourth thing I remember every day is that we will not have a just society until we have education in the schools instead of indoctrination. As long as communities continue to employ and pay teachers instead of choosing and encouraging educators, we will not have justice in our society. Until citizens insist that the schools provide social studies instead of antisocial studies, we will turn out graduates who are ignorant of the true history of this country and the people who live here. As long as cultures continue to encourage students to believe in the lie of more than one race of people on the face of the earth, we will have racism and the dislocations that it causes.

The fifth thing I have learned is that what is often called "white privilege" is really white ignorance, and it will not be cured until we educators start teaching that we are all members of the same race, which evolved in sub-Saharan Africa between 300,000 and 500,000 years ago. Until we in the twenty-first century have begun to realize the brilliance of those first modern human beings, who were able to travel to and populate every landmass on the face of the earth without any modern technology, we will not fully appreciate how badly we have been taught and how poorly we have been educated. And until we understand that we, whatever our skin tone, are all descendants of those first modern, dark-skinned people, we will not have a truly just society.

Social Justice Required? Faculty and Student Engagement with University-Wide Learning Objectives

Andrea E. Brewster, Phyllis R. Brown, and Jennifer Merritt Faria

In 2009, Santa Clara University, a Jesuit and Catholic university in California's Silicon Valley, implemented new core curriculum requirements aimed at fostering intentional and engaged learning related to the university's mission, vision, and values. Experiential Learning for Social Justice (ELSJ), one of two core requirements that make social justice an explicit goal, specifies that all students must complete a course requiring them to reflect on connections between their learning in a community placement and learning related to the subject matter of the discipline-specific course.

Courses approved for ELSJ are offered by many departments in the College of Arts and Sciences, the Leavey School of Business, and the School of Engineering so that students may complete the requirement with courses in or closely related to their majors. In this essay, we analyze and reflect on ways classroom instruction in different disciplines integrates community-based learning and disciplinary learning to address the ELSJ learning objective that calls for students to "[r]ecognize, analyze, and understand the social reality and injustices in contemporary society, including recognizing the relative privilege or marginalization of their own and other groups" ("Integrations").[1] Direct assessment of learning and reexamination of syllabi and assignments revealed avenues for improvement of teaching and learning that proved effective across the different disciplines of these required courses. We had been concerned that even though assignments in each of the courses mapped to this learning objective, course materials rarely specified or required students to think about what social justice is or what they could do to fight injustice. Therefore, our investigation set out to clarify whether a shared understanding of social justice would enhance student learning and whether disciplinary differences would result in different definitions of social justice as well as different understandings of what can be done and is being done to fight injustice. While assessment data did indicate that students will benefit from more attention to what social justice is and what the desire to achieve justice demands of practitioners, it also suggested that faculty development related to transparent assignment design can have an even more positive effect on our social justice efforts. Our provisional conclusion is that student and faculty reflection on what social justice is and faculty development related to transparent assignment design are more important than agreement on what social justice is.

Literature Review

Scholarship relevant to our investigation focuses on assignment design and learning related to community placements and social justice.

Transparent Assignment Design

The Office for Curricular Effectiveness at Washington State University provides a web page that identifies three especially important elements of transparent assignment design ("clearly communicating the purpose, task, and criteria" for each course assignment) and provides a toolkit "intended to help faculty and programs seeking to design or refine assignments to be more transparent" ("Transparent Assignment Design"). Another valuable resource, the National Institute for Learning Outcomes Assessment (NILOA), provides curated resources relevant to antiracist teaching, learning, and assessment of student learning (learningoutcomesassessment.org). The home page of the *TILT Higher Ed* website specifies that the Transparency in Learning and Teaching (TILT) project

> aims to advance equitable teaching and learning practices that reduce systemic inequities in higher education through two main activities:
>
> 1. Promoting students' conscious understanding of how they learn
> 2. Enabling faculty to gather, share and promptly benefit from current data about students' learning by coordinating their efforts across disciplines, institutions and countries

And the winter-spring 2016 issue of *Peer Review: Emerging Trends and Key Debates in Undergraduate Education*, published by the Association of American Colleges and Universities (AACU), provides examples of ways colleges and universities have applied NILOA and TILT practices to enhance learning by underserved students (McNair, *Transparency*).

How Learning Works: Seven Research-Based Principles for Smart Teaching, by Susan A. Ambrose and colleagues, aims to enhance student learning by assisting faculty members in understanding ways they can apply the science of learning to their teaching practices. The authors present research by the National Research Council and other scholars of learning in ways that are accessible for faculty members teaching in a variety of disciplines. They begin with a definition of learning:

> 1. Learning is a *process*, not a product. However, because this process takes place in the mind, we can only infer that it has occurred from students' products or performances.
> 2. Learning involves *change* in knowledge, beliefs, behaviors, or attitudes. This change unfolds over time; it is not fleeting but rather has a lasting impact on how students think and act.
> 3. Learning is not something done *to* students, but rather something students themselves do. It is the direct result of how students interpret and respond to their *experiences*—conscious and unconscious, past and present. (3)

Their seven principles of learning are grounded in

> recognition that (a) learning is a developmental process that intersects with other developmental processes in students' lives, and (b) students enter our classrooms not only with skills, knowledge, and abilities, but also with social and emotional experiences that influence what they value, how they perceive themselves and others, and how they will engage in the learning process. (3–4)

Community-Based Learning and Social Justice

A 2019 special issue of *The Journal of Experiential Education* draws attention to the centrality of social justice to experiential learning. Although the experiential learning Karen Warren writes about in her introduction to the journal issue is different from community-based learning, her reminder is important to our analysis of ways community-based learning incorporates and advances social justice. Warren writes, "The articles in this issue represent a rich array of the kind of conceptual and empirical work needed to develop experiential education further as a means of promoting social justice." She reminds readers that a program's uses of experiential activities can perpetuate injustice even when the intention is to foster social justice and concludes that the authors "in this issue invite more questions than provide answers, as is the case in any important dialogue." She hopes that "the past and present ideas about social justice in the *Journal* [will] serve as a rallying cry for critical pedagogy and structural reform to achieve equity, accessibility, and liberation in all aspects of experiential education" and invites readers "to use these conversations as a foundation for re-creating just action in the practice of experiential education" (Warren, "Reflections" 5). However, the special issue does not define social justice beyond specifying the need for structural reform for equity, accessibility, and liberation (Warren, *Social Justice*); apparently, the authors assume that a shared understanding of what social justice is makes definition unnecessary.

In contrast, two recent textbooks begin with definitions. The preface to the second edition of *Is Everyone Really Equal? An Introduction to Key Concepts in Social Justice Education*, by Özlem Sensoy and Robin DiAngelo, includes a section called "What Is Critical Social Justice?" The coauthors note the challenges of agreeing on a definition but—after emphasizing that social justice requires "recognition that society is *stratified*" and inequality is "deeply embedded in the fabric of society (i.e. structural)"—then list six principles related to the need for change and relevant to multiple disciplines:

> All people are individuals, but they are also members of social groups.
>
> These social groups are valued unequally in society.
>
> Social groups that are valued more highly have greater access to the resources of a society.
>
> Social injustice is real, exists today, and results in unequal access to resources between groups of people.
>
> Those who claim to be for social justice must be engaged in self-reflection about their own socialization into these groups (their "positionality") and must strategically act from that awareness in ways that challenge social injustice.
>
> This action requires a commitment to an ongoing and lifelong process. (xx)

Sensoy and DiAngelo emphasize that the responsibility of critical social justice practice is to align actions with values aimed at reducing stratification and inequality (xx). They define four responsibilities, beginning with recognition "that relations of unequal social power are constantly being enacted at both the micro (individual) and macro (structural) levels" and understanding of "our own positions within these relations of unequal power." Recognition and understanding make it possible to "think critically about knowledge; what we know and how we know it" and to "act on all of the above in service of a more socially just society." Subsequent chapters address "key concepts necessary for beginning to develop critical social justice literacy" (xxi). These principles and responsibilities provide a framework capacious enough to work for courses in multiple disciplines.

The textbook *Teaching for Diversity and Social Justice* presents a definition similar to the one provided by Sensoy and DiAngelo. Lee Ann Bell begins the first chapter with the heading "What Is Social Justice?" She describes social justice as "both a goal and a process" that "involves social actors who have a sense of their own agency as well as a sense of social responsibility toward and with others, their society, the environment, and the broader world in which we live. These are conditions we not only wish for ourselves but for all people in our interdependent global community" (3). She specifies that the process should be

> democratic and participatory, respectful of human diversity and group differences, and inclusive and affirming of human agency and capacity for working collaboratively with others to create change. Domination cannot be ended through coercive tactics that recreate domination in new forms. Thus, a "power with" vs. "power over" paradigm is necessary for enacting social justice goals. Forming coalitions and working collaboratively with diverse others is an essential part of social justice. (3)

This chapter also provides a definition of social justice education that "includes both an *interdisciplinary conceptual framework* for analyzing multiple forms of oppression and their intersections, as well as *a set of interactive, experiential pedagogical principles and methods/practices*" (4). Thus, the definitions here are particularly apt for our ELSJ requirement.

Bell then gives an overview of the book, which aims to "help readers make sense of, and hopefully act more effectively against, oppressive circumstances as these arise in different contexts" (4). She explains ways theory contributes to understanding of the restrictiveness, pervasiveness, and cumulative effects of oppression as well as the influences of socially constructed categories, power hierarchies, and a status quo that is hegemonic, normalized, internalized, and intersectional but at the same time both durable and mutable, with consequences for all (6). Bell concludes with the importance of working for social justice because "oppression is never complete; it is always open to challenge." To do so, she suggests that it is important to develop a critical consciousness, deconstruct binaries, draw on counternarratives, analyze power, look for interest convergence, make global connections, build coalitions and solidarity, and follow the leadership of oppressed people as accountable and responsible allies (16–17). The chapter is rich in references to the work of other scholars who have contributed to Bell's understanding of social justice and social justice education.

Not all researchers report on the positive contributions of community-based learning to social justice education. Laura Finley and Kelly Concannon introduce their essay "Social Justice Education in Higher Education" with examples illustrating that many colleges and universities express pride in their growing emphasis on social justice, but they also note that "the rhetoric far exceeds [higher education's] actual performance regarding its commitment to civic engagement, social justice, and preparing students to better their communities" (243). Sections defining social justice and progressive pedagogy, reviewing literature related to "enacting social justice education inside the college classroom," and describing social justice education outside the classroom lead to a section on challenges, with a particular emphasis on the pitfalls of service learning projects. The coauthors are particularly concerned about projects designed by educators without consulting the community groups to be served, because such projects can perpetuate injustices rather than advance social justice (244–49). The essay ends with a summary of best practices followed by the conclusion that "social justice education is messy, complex, and oftentimes . . . difficult to codify in terms of intended outcomes and results, particularly when we are placing value on both the epistemological *and* ontological aspects of what we do in our classrooms in general, and in higher education in particular." Therefore, Finley and Concannon argue, social justice education should encourage students to understand "the social roots of inequalities," to reflect "deeply on our own role in sustaining or reducing those inequalities," and to take "action in and *with* communities to promote a peaceful and more just world" (251).

Dan W. Butin and Randy Stoecker devote entire books to critiques of service learning. In *Service-Learning in Theory and Practice: The Future of Community Engagement in Higher Education*, Butin is particularly concerned that institutionalized service learning undermines itself through "internal subversion" (48). He argues that the limits of service-learning "are inherent to the service-learning movement as contemporarily theorized and enacted. As such, there may be a fundamental and unbridgeable gap between the rhetoric and reality of the aspirations of the present-day service-learning movement" (23). To close that gap, he suggests that service learning practitioners think of community engagement as a "methodology and focus of inquiry" rather than a solution to problems of injustice (74).

In *Liberating Service Learning and the Rest of Higher Education Civic Engagement*, Stoeker also expresses concern about the institutionalization of service learning but even more concern about the disconnection he sees in his own work between service learning and political engagement:

> The lack of an explicit theory guiding service learning practice . . . allows it to drift without rudder or paddle on the currents of dominant neoliberal theories about class, race, gender, ability and power in this country. And because the dominant theories are constrained in the narrow swath of liberal-conservative thinking within neoliberalism, the lack of an alternative explicit theory that can provide such direction has led to a consequently system-maintaining practice. Thus, liberating service learning is about making its current theory explicit, deconstructing it, and then building a new theory that can lead to new practice to produce better results. (8)

One such practice Stoeker hopes to see is a reorientation of service learning from an emphasis on assessment of what service learning achieves to a focus on ways social change is achieved (146).

The Experiential Learning for Social Justice Requirement

To meet our goal of high-impact community-based learning (as defined by George D. Kuh) for all undergraduates, all ELSJ courses must allow students to apply direct community engagement experiences to their in-class learning and reflect deeply on the impacts of their community-engaged learning. Central to this goal is the integration of these community-based learning experiences into rigorous academic courses across the disciplines. For instance, students can take an ELSJ course in religious studies that allows them to consider community engagement from the vantage point of religious theory and practice; other students can take an ELSJ course in engineering that brings engineering concepts into communities and community wisdom into the classroom. A business professor arranges for their students to teach small community groups about microlending and to receive zero-interest loans for projects they suggest. Regardless of discipline, however, to be approved, all ELSJ courses must have syllabi that embed three learning objectives into the curriculum and include assignments that allow assessment of learning related to the objectives. Rooted in a "critical service-learning" orientation described by Robert A. Rhoads and by Tania D. Mitchell, these objectives address learning related to civic engagement, diversity, and social justice. For the social justice objective, students must demonstrate an understanding of the structural underpinnings of social injustice, including their own and others' relative privilege and marginalization. For the diversity objective, students must demonstrate that they appreciate the value of alternate perspectives and worldviews. For the civic engagement objective, students must demonstrate that they recognize the importance of civic engagement that benefits underserved populations.

Implementing this requirement for all undergraduates was possible because of ongoing community partnerships maintained by our Ignatian Center for Jesuit Education (ICJE), especially the Thriving Neighbors initiative. The ICJE website explains:

> Rooted in a faith that does justice, the Ignatian Center for Jesuit Education partners with local community organizations whose members and clients serve as co-educators for Santa Clara University students. Informed by and in conversation with Catholic social tradition, the Center facilitates community-based learning opportunities that underscore commitments to the common good, universal human dignity, justice as participation, and solidarity with marginalized communities. ("Arrupe Engagement")

Community-based learning is a teaching method that allows students to enhance their knowledge of an academic subject by engaging in "authentic" work in real-world settings to reinforce the learning objectives embedded in the discipline-specific curriculum for the course with the goal of promoting social justice in our neighborhoods and beyond.

Community Partnerships

Because students are encouraged in these courses to consider the knowledge and skills of community members involved in the partnership and the social systems that impact their lives and livelihoods, they often emerge not only with enhanced perspectives on privilege and power but also with reverence for the people most challenged by the unequal distribution of socioeconomic, sociocultural, and sociopolitical advantages. Since at least one ELSJ course is required of all undergraduates, by 2016 SCU's community-based learning program had grown to support approximately 1,200 students enrolled in sixty academic courses annually by matching each student with an appropriate community placement at one of over fifty-five local partner agencies such as Estrella Family Services, Catholic Charities' Focus for Work, Independence Network, and many K–12 schools ("Community Partners"). Adding to the need for growth is the fact that many students choose to enroll in additional community-based learning opportunities after they complete the core requirement. Whether for an ELSJ class or an independent community-based learning opportunity, every placement experience is designed to reinforce the cognitive, affective, and participatory objectives of coursework. Course planning aims to provide our community partners with consistent support and engagement.

To do this work, the Arrupe Engagement program requires that students participate in an orientation before beginning their community placement. Facilitated by staff members from ICJE and from the partner agency, the orientation encourages in students a disposition that reflects specific attitudes and values, including

commitment to solidarity, mutuality, and reciprocity in their relationships with community members;

respect for communities themselves;

awareness of the dimensions of power and privilege that can either impinge upon or undergird their own experiences of resilience in the face of struggle or vulnerability;

desire to recognize and probe integral connections between course content and the community context; and

willingness to participate in authentic reflection on their own experiences of citizenship and belonging in local and global communities, moral development, and vocational discernment.

Over the following eight weeks, in cooperation with members of the SCU faculty and the community partner agency staff, the community-based learning program introduces college students to individuals living on the margins and invites them to recognize and understand the ways in which social structures can either perpetuate or dismantle systems of discrimination. Individuals in the partner programs share expertise that comes from their own lived experience to engage students in meaningful conversations on issues of equality, opportunity, and more.

As the manager and curator of this learning experience, the ICJE embraces a pedagogical perspective grounded in the Ignatian intellectual tradition that underscores the connection between students' experiences, their reflections on those experiences, their resulting actions, and the creation of a more just and humane world. In other words, the ICJE asserts that one can teach cognitive ideas and theoretical concepts, but if students do not have authentic, affective, and participatory experiences that allow them to better understand human suffering and resilience, and have opportunities to reflect on those experiences such that they might inspire action grounded in contemplative discernment, our programs will not achieve our goals. Clearly, the ICJE Arrupe Engagement program shares the definitions of social justice articulated in the textbooks described above, but at the time of our study, the introduction for students did not include a definition of social justice. Moreover, our investigation has revealed that, like the examples in the special issue of *The Journal of Experiential Education*, syllabi for Santa Clara's ELSJ courses do not define social justice or include readings that define it, apparently assuming a shared understanding of what social justice is. However, rather than articulate a definition to be shared by all faculty members, providing opportunities for faculty members and students to develop their own understandings of social justice and how to foster it from different disciplinary perspectives may be more advantageous.

Thriving Neighbors

Beyond the traditional community-based learning program, the ICJE has created a place-based initiative that allows all of the university and community stakeholders previously mentioned to continue these unique relationships over an extended period. This neighborhood-centered program, known as the Thriving Neighbors initiative, fuses engaged teaching and learning with collaborative scholarship, service, and solidarity. Thriving Neighbors supports individual faculty members, students, and community residents who then design, develop, implement, evaluate, and sustain community capacity-building programs in areas of mutual concern ranging from K–12 education to public health promotion, legal justice, access to economic opportunities, environmental sustainability, food security, and more ("Thriving Neighbors").

The hallmark of the Thriving Neighbors model is leadership that shifts back and forth between university and community stakeholders: college students and neighborhood leaders, university faculty members, and institutional partners from schools, social service agencies, churches, and more, such that the overarching partnership can work to dismantle injustices by creating capacity-building programs anchored in "right relationship." In this model, the university as a whole adopts the values and dispositions expected of students so that, together with community partners, SCU can build a broad-scale authentic partnership focused on promoting social justice. At its prepandemic peak, in 2018, the Thriving Neighbors initiative logged approximately fifteen thousand hours of university-community engagement involving approximately fifteen ongoing community-based programs.

At times, the challenges faced by people living on the margins can seem too abstract or unfamiliar to elicit understanding, empathy, or collective social action from some students. Nevertheless, when disciplinary-specific coursework draws on community-based learning principles and engagement with community members, and students and community members walk side by side for sixteen hours over the course of eight weeks, many students do adopt a spirit of humility and sincere interest in hearing others' stories and sharing their own stories. The results can be life-changing for individuals in the partner organizations and for our students. The classroom components of ELSJ courses can create a fertile, relevant, and safe space wherein students meet to share thoughts, ideas, hopes, and dreams, thereby allowing real social change to germinate. Rather than entering communities paternalistically, university students and faculty are encouraged to identify as equals with community members such that together they may achieve their stated mutual goals, which might in fact include developing a shared understanding of social justice as well as a shared commitment to working for positive social change.

Additionally, community-based work, rather than merely serving the academy's need for research venues and subjects, enacts a desire for critical dialogue, described by the Brazilian educator and scholar Paulo Freire as a means to facilitate authentic changes for the privileged and the oppressed.[2] This critical dialogue requires those with power and privilege to accept that they have much to learn from those who experience marginalization; in this way, both parties can serve as equal partners in the process of developing creative solutions to social ills. The Ignatian term for this process is "walking in accompaniment," because it involves walking side by side with community members and opening to opportunities for transformation. The eventual goal of this process is to move together toward a type of solidarity that allows students and community members to be genuine partners creating social change, not only in their own lives but also in the communities that surround them.[3]

In the spring quarter of 2020, Santa Clara University swiftly shifted all undergraduate courses to remote learning in response to state and county mandates related to the COVID-19 pandemic. The need to adapt quickly was particularly challenging for ELSJ courses, since a direct, face-to-face community-based learning pedagogy is elemental to high-impact student learning in these courses and supports the long-standing community partnerships facilitated through the Arrupe Engagement and Thriving Neighbors programs. Nevertheless, we were acutely aware that health had to come first—that of our partners and their clients, many of whom are members of groups most vulnerable to and disproportionately impacted by COVID-19.

Instead of canceling the ELSJ courses, we decided to focus on ways our programs and students could continue to connect with our partner organizations and engage authentically, albeit virtually, with community members. We reached out to community partner organizations to learn about their most pressing needs and invested in faculty development by meeting one-on-one with each spring ELSJ faculty member to flesh out how virtual engagement activities might still support the course learning objectives and the ELSJ-specific learning objectives, offering regular online ELSJ faculty group meetings, and collecting and sharing best practices in remote community-based learning. This helped us work with community partner organizations to identify ways that we could still connect with them, for example, through live or recorded conversations with community leaders and interviews with partner organizations about community impacts of COVID-19. These online encounters provided additional context for students about the mission and purpose of the partner organization and brought into stark relief the social injustices heightened within these communities by COVID-19.

Assessment of Student Learning: Description of Data Sources

Our assessment of student learning in ELSJ core courses draws on program-level direct assessment conducted in 2014 and student responses on quarterly self-assessment surveys (2017–18 and 2020) in relation to the three learning objectives common to all ELSJ courses.

Student Work

For our 2014 direct assessment of student learning in ELSJ core courses, all faculty members teaching these courses provided work from a randomly selected sample of students. The assignments they provided, usually reflection essays, allowed students to demonstrate their proficiency in the three ELSJ learning objectives. Student work products were collected from a randomized sample of 114 students across ten different majors.

To score student work, seven faculty members convened and used a rubric designed to measure learning related to the three course learning objectives. In order to align their approaches to scoring using the rubric, faculty members participated in a norming session and discussion. Each learning objective was scored separately on a four-point scale, where "1" indicated the student had not provided evidence of meeting the learning objective, "2" signified the student learning was approaching the standard expected, "3" meant the learning met the standard, and "4" referred to work that had exceeded the standard. Each faculty member then individually scored a sample of student work.

Student Self-Assessment

All students enrolled in ELSJ courses are asked to complete an online survey about their learning experiences in the course during week eight of a ten-week quarter. The survey includes closed- and open-ended items related to social justice, diversity, and civic engagement objectives and asks students to reflect on the integration of learning in their community placement and in the course. Further, the survey asks students to report their learning gains on a five-point scale on several social-justice-related learning objectives. Data reported below include all three quarters of student survey feedback from the 2017–2018 academic year. The survey response rate was thirty-five percent over the year (forty-four percent in the fall, twenty-seven percent in the winter, and thirty-two percent in the spring), and 402 survey responses are analyzed here. Results from spring 2020 are also discussed below in relation to the additional challenges posed by online teaching and learning.

Assessment of Student Learning: Social Justice Objectives

As noted above, fulfillment of the three ELSJ learning objectives is assessed using defined requirements. For the civic engagement objective, students must demonstrate that they recognize the importance of civic engagement that benefits underserved populations. For the diversity objective, students are expected to demonstrate that they appreciate the value of alternate perspectives and worldviews. And for the social justice objective, students must demonstrate an understanding of the structural underpinnings of social injustice, including their own and others' relative privilege and marginalization.

Student Work and Syllabus Design

Since 2014, faculty members have used a four-point analytic rubric to measure learning related to all core course objectives and score student achievement in assignments aligned with those objectives. The Office of Assessment at SCU set a target of approximately eighty percent of the students meeting or exceeding the objectives set in the core areas. For ELSJ, results came closest to that on our diversity learning objective, which seventy-eight percent of students met or exceeded in the 2014 assessment. About two-thirds (sixty-six percent) of students met or exceeded the civic engagement learning objective. However, students appeared to find the social justice learning objective the most challenging; only sixty percent met or exceeded the goal (table 1).

Specifically, analysis of student work in ELSJ courses showed that sixty percent of the work demonstrated understanding of the complexity of group differences that lead to privilege, marginalization, or social injustice (including re-

Table 1. Performance on Learning Outcomes (percent/*n*)

Learning objective	1 Does not meet	2 Approaching	3 Meets	4 Exceeds
1.1/1.4 (civic engagement / civic life)	8% (9)	26% (30)	40% (45)	26% (30)
1.2 (perspective)	4% (4)	18% (19)	55% (58)	23% (25)
1.3 (social justice)	14% (15)	26% (27)	34% (36)	26% (27)

Source: "Highlights from ELSJ Assessment of Winter 2014 Classes" 1.

lated underlying causes, such as social, structural, economic, ideological, political, historical, cultural, or other relevant factors). Another twenty-six percent demonstrated a surface understanding of group differences leading to these objectives, and fourteen percent showed no awareness of group differences that lead to privilege, marginalization, and social injustice.

After reviewing these findings, the Office of Assessment and Undergraduate Studies staff reevaluated the alignment between course assignments in these ELSJ course syllabi and the students' achievement of the learning objectives. In courses where the assignment was judged to be fully aligned (i.e., clearly and explicitly asked students to demonstrate their learning related to the social justice objective), seventy-eight percent of the student work was rated as proficient in social justice understanding. This indicated to us that, in addition to developing students' social justice learning in ELSJ courses, we needed to focus on faculty development and curriculum design. This is particularly important in the light of the research that shows that assignment design can level the playing field for students.

As noted above, the TILT project provides a plethora of resources "including assignments, curricula, assessment and strategic initiatives, all toward the goal of enhancing student success equitably" ("TILT Higher Ed"). Amy B. Mulnix's article "The Power of Transparency in Your Teaching" emphasizes the importance of "making obvious the intellectual practices involved in completing and evaluating a learning task." Not to teach those practices gives advantages to students whose high school education provided strong preparation. But making those practices transparent is not easy. As Ambrose and colleagues explain, faculty members have often arrived at a point where they are largely unconscious of their competence, while students may be unconscious of their incompetence (95–99). Teachers must help students move from unconscious incompetence to conscience incompetence and then to conscious competence. Transparent assignment design helps students recognize and acquire component skills fundamental to assignments, practice integrating the component skills, and know when to apply the skills (96–97).

Tia Brown McNair, AACU's vice president for diversity, equity, and student success, reports,

> AAC&U's recent national survey of chief academic officers found that "85% of AAC&U member institutions report that they have a common set of intended learning objectives for all undergraduate students . . . [but] fewer than one in 10 (9%) indicate that almost all students understand those intended learning objectives, and [only] 36% think that a majority of students understand them." ("Designing" 3)

Various organizations, including AACU, NILOA, and the UNLV TILT initiative, seek to increase student understanding. Mary-Ann Winkelmes and colleagues describe one teaching intervention supported by the TILT initiative as "a simple, replicable teaching intervention that demonstrably enhances students' success, especially that of first-generation, low-income, and underrepresented college students in multiple ways at statistically significant levels, with a medium to large magnitude of effect" (34). Underrepresented and low-income students in the seven participating schools reported that their learning benefited from knowing the purpose of each assignment, being given assignments that explain how they relate to learning objectives, being given help with steps required to complete the assignments, and being given tools that allow them to assess the quality of their work (34). Fortunately, between 2017 and 2020, the university offered faculty members opportunities to participate in faculty learning communities focused on transparent assignment design, and many ELSJ instructors participated.

Student Self-Assessment

The student feedback survey administered to all students taking community-based learning courses contained three items that relate to social justice. The first item asks students to indicate how they rate their gains in understanding some of the causes of social, economic, or political inequality facing their community placement. The second question asks students to report their gains in understanding appropriate and impactful ways of taking social action to address inequalities. The third question asks students to evaluate their gains in commitment to using their own gifts and abilities to benefit underserved populations. In addition to giving a numeric score for each question, students are asked to explain their selection with a written response.

According to the 2017–18 self-assessment data, students reported they were making gains in understanding some of the causes of the inequality they encountered through their academic coursework and community-based learning experience. Sixty-seven percent of students reported good or great gains (rated 4 or 5 on a five-point scale) in understanding some of the causes of social, political, or economic inequality facing the community in their placement. One student described their experience this way: "I am definitely more aware now of the social issues that the communities surrounding my school face. It really surprised me because it's almost as if I was blind to these issues prior to this course and my Arrupe experience." Another student reported, "I have learned many new ways to look at injustices around me and have learned to identify injustices that I may not have noticed before." These deepening insights are the intent and the result of ELSJ courses.

Students who rated their gains as a three or lower (thirty-three percent of students) on this metric often described characteristics of their site or their personal experience there but tended to report that they had not come to understand causes of social inequities through their community experiences. For instance, one student at a K–12 school placement stated, "[The placement] has been more about learning how to connect with the kids for me, not about how they were put in a situation of inequality." Another student at a placement with seniors expressed a better understanding of inequality but not of its causes. The student wrote, "I'd say I was able to see more of the effect of the inequalities rather than the causes as the marginalization of the elderly has been going on for so long I think it is hard to pin down its exact causes."

In addition to rating their understanding of the causes of inequality, students rated their understanding of ways of taking action to address community inequalities. Fewer students self-identified as having made strides; only fifty-five percent rated themselves as making good or great gains in understanding ways of taking action to address these inequalities. One student described the intended objective: "The placement as well as my ELSJ class together have made me realize the need for social change and how to start working towards it." In contrast, students who rated their gains as three or lower (forty-five percent of students) on this metric often expressed frustration with a lack of awareness of how to take transformative action to address inequalities. One wrote, "Being a so-called role model has been a great experience, but I haven't learned any concrete ways to take social actions to address the inequalities in a given community." Another commented, "I feel like I know how to help those who face inequality but not how to address or minimize the inequality."

While two-thirds of students reported good or great gains in understanding the causes of social inequality and fifty-five percent reported good or great gains in understanding ways to take social action to address these inequalities, over two-thirds of students who participated in an ELSJ course (and accompanying community-based learning experience) *want* to participate in social change. Sixty-nine percent of students reported feeling a commitment to using their abilities and gifts to benefit underserved populations. According to one student, "I had little idea of the impact I could have but now have the desire to help in whatever ways I can." Given this expressed sense of purpose, it is even more critical that students understand the complexities of social justice and learn more transparently about appropriate and impactful ways to take social action.

In response to our new, virtual community-based learning options, students reported learning gains slightly (but not significantly) lower for our social justice learning objective than students in the prior three quarters and significantly lower gains on the diversity and civic engagement objectives. This suggests that the civic engagement and diversity learning objectives are most impacted by the presence or absence of direct, face-to-face contact in community activities—contact that was not possible in the remote instruction modality of spring. One student specified, "I completely understand that this is an unprecedented time—I just would have liked more time with the community." These results from spring 2020 emphasize the value of Arrupe's regular community-based learning engagement model and also gave us direction about where to concentrate our efforts with faculty and students in the following academic years.

This study clarified the authors' vision for social justice action at SCU. As of 2020 we had already begun to ensure that all faculty members who taught ELSJ courses were aware of the research on transparent assignment design and of opportunities to participate in a faculty learning community focused on increasing pedagogical equity for our students. Current administrative leaders responsible for the core curriculum have proposed to share our work with all faculty members teaching ELSJ and to facilitate opportunities for us to discuss our research and recommendations with all faculty and staff members interested in social justice.

In the meantime, ELSJ curriculum leaders continue to collaborate with Arrupe Engagement leaders, encouraging faculty members to include discipline-specific definitions in their course materials. We are encouraged by faculty development programs, even during the pandemic, aiming for anti-racist pedagogies. Notably, in summer 2020, fourteen of twenty-nine faculty members who had taught ELSJ courses in the spring or would teach them that fall 2020 participated in the Association of College and University Educators' Creating Optimal Online Learning (COOL), a program designed to support more effective and equitable online instruction.

Sharing our study more broadly with colleagues, including librarians, undergraduate studies and faculty development administrative leaders, the director of educational assessment, and faculty members who teach core religion, theology and culture, civic engagement, and diversity courses (since diversity courses share the explicit goal of social justice with ELSJ courses, while social justice is implicit in learning goals for religion, theology and culture, and civic engagement courses) will help dissolve barriers inadvertently created by silos in educational structures similar to the separate categories of research reflected in our literature review.

NOTES

1. Another goal addressed by our ELSJ courses is civic engagement; the ELSJ learning objective mapping to this goal is "Recognize the importance of life-long responsible

citizenship and civic engagement in personal and/or professional activities in ways that benefit underserved populations" ("Integrations"). A main goal of each community placement is to ensure that the recognition specified in the learning objective is associated with action as well as reflection.

2. These ideas permeate Freire's writings (beginning with his dissertation) but are central to *Pedagogy of the Oppressed*, which has circulated widely in English translation. Richard Shaull summarizes two interrelated points in his foreword: an assumption "that man's ontological vocation (as he calls it) is to be a Subject who acts upon and transforms his world, and in so doing moves toward ever new possibilities of fuller and richer life individually and collectively" and "that every human being, no matter how 'ignorant' or submerged in the 'culture of silence' he or she may be, is capable of looking critically at the world in a dialogical encounter with others" (32).

3. For more information about the ways Thriving Neighbors works for social justice, see Merritt et al. Since 2021, Thriving Neighbors placements have focused exclusively on children's education and not on economic development.

WORKS CITED

Ambrose, Susan A., et al. *How Learning Works: Seven Research-Based Principles for Smart Teaching.* Jossey-Bass, 2010.

"Arrupe Engagement." Ignatian Center for Jesuit Education, Santa Clara U, www.scu.edu/ic/programs/arrupe-weekly-engagement/. Accessed 2 Nov. 2023.

Bell, Lee Ann. "Theoretical Foundations for Social Justice Education." *Teaching for Diversity and Social Justice*, edited by Maurianne Adams and Bell, with Diane J. Goodman and Khyati Y. Joshi, 3rd ed., Routledge, 2016, pp. 3–26.

Butin, D. *Service-Learning in Theory and Practice: The Future of Community Engagement in Higher Education.* Palgrave Macmillan, 2010.

"Community Partners." Ignatian Center for Jesuit Education, Santa Clara U, www.scu.edu/ic/programs/arrupe-weekly-engagement/community-partners/. Accessed 3 Nov. 2023.

Finley, Laura, and Kelly Concannon. "Social Justice Education in Higher Education." *Leadership, Equity, and Social Justice in American Higher Education: A Reader*, edited by C. P. Gause, Peter Lang, 2017, pp. 242–52. Higher Ed 23.

"Highlights from ELSJ Assessment of Winter 2014 Classes." *Rubrics, Reports, and Guidelines*, Santa Clara U, 15 Dec. 2014, www.scu.edu/media/offices/provost/institutional-effectiveness/assessment/ELSJ-Core-Assessment-2013-14.pdf.

"Integrations." *Santa Clara University: Office of the Provost*, www.scu.edu/provost/core/integrations/. Accessed 27 Dec. 2023.

Kuh, George D. *High-Impact Educational Practices: What They Are, Who Has Access to Them, and Why They Matter.* American Association of Colleges and Universities, 2009.

McNair, Tia Brown. "Designing Purposeful Pathways for Student Achievement through Transparency and Problem-Centered Learning." McNair, *Transparency*, pp. 3–5.

———, editor. *Transparency and Problem-Centered Learning.* Special issue of *Peer Review.* Vol. 18, nos. 1–2, winter-spring 2016.

Merritt, Jennifer C., et al. "The Sacramental Nature of Community." *Catholic Identity in Context: Vision and Formation for the Common Good*, edited by Stephen K. Black and Erin M. Brigham, U San Francisco P, 2018, pp. 95–115.

Mitchell, Tania D. "Traditional vs. Critical Service-Learning: Engaging the Literature to Differentiate Two Models." *Michigan Journal of Community Service Learning*, vol. 14, no. 2, spring 2008, pp. 50–65.

Mulnix, Amy B. "The Power of Transparency in Your Teaching." *Faculty Focus*, 12 Nov. 2018, www.facultyfocus.com/articles/course-design-ideas/power-transparency-teaching/.

National Research Council. *How People Learn: Brain, Mind, Experience, and School*. Expanded ed., National Academy Press, 2000.

Rhoads, Robert A. *Community Service and Higher Learning: Explorations of the Caring Self*. State U of New York P, 1997.

Sensoy, Özlem, and Robin DiAngelo. *Is Everyone Really Equal? An Introduction to Key Concepts in Social Justice Education*. 2nd ed., Teachers College Press, 2017.

Shaull, Richard. Foreword. *Pedagogy of the Oppressed*, by Paulo Freire, translated by Myra Bergman Ramos, 30th anniversary ed., Bloomsbury, 2014, pp. 29–34.

Stoeker, Randy. *Liberating Service Learning and the Rest of Higher Education*. Temple UP, 2016.

"Thriving Neighbors." *Santa Clara University*, 2024, www.scu.edu/ic/programs/thriving-neighbors/.

"TILT Higher Ed Examples and Resources." *TILT Higher Ed*, tilthighered.com/tiltexamplesandresources. Accessed 2 Nov. 2023.

"Transparent Assignment Design." *Office of Assessment for Curricular Effectiveness*, Washington State U, 2024, ace.wsu.edu/assignment-design/transparent-assignment-design/.

Warren, Karen. "Reflections on Social Justice in Experiential Education: Expanding the Dialogue." Warren, *Social Justice*, pp. 3–6.

———, editor. *Social Justice in Experiential Education*. Special issue of *The Journal of Experiential Education*, vol. 42, no. 1, Mar. 2019.

Winkelmes, Mary-Ann, et al. "A Teaching Intervention that Increases Underserved College Students' Success." McNair, *Transparency*, pp. 31–34.

A Pedagogy of Solutions: Promoting Problem-Solving in Social Justice Teaching

Leigh Ann Litwiller Berte

Teaching for social justice objectives often centers on understanding social problems. Helping students understand how contexts and structures produce systems of social relations is perhaps the most valuable contribution we educators can make to their intellectual evolution into engaged, active community members. A range of terminology can describe this deep understanding of social issues, but one concept—systems thinking—demonstrates the ability to span a range of disciplines, from environmental science to urban planning, computer science, engineering, and psychology (Bishop 8). Beyond promoting an understanding of the elements that define a lived reality, systems thinking encourages a focus on the interconnections, relationships, and feedback loops among those elements that perpetuate a system or pattern of behavior (Meadows 2–5).

This systems thinking approach is one that we have undertaken at Spring Hill College in a series of radically interdisciplinary courses (with the participation of professors from as many as ten different disciplines), each of which addresses a social issue from diverse local, national, and global perspectives. In this format, we have organized courses around themes such as food, water, petroleum, technology, garbage, migration, protest, and terrorism.[1] Our first course of this nature was developed in response to the 2010 BP oil spill in the Gulf of Mexico; as a school on the Gulf Coast, we aimed to understand how petroleum shaped the economy, environment, and lives of those in our region alongside how it impacted, for example, Africa's Niger Delta and Europe's North Sea. Exploring how these diverse case studies are shaped by the interplay of similar multinational corporate, governmental, and nongovernmental institutions allowed a systems understanding of petroleum and its related problems to emerge.

While accurate, ambitious, and intellectually sound in terms of modeling this problem, this systems approach had an unintended consequence: despair. By the end of the first class, our students were overwhelmed and discouraged. They now understood all too well the structures and institutions that define the system of petroleum extraction and exchange. The problems that system produced seemed intractable. A classroom activity introduced by a professor teaching in the course alerted me to what the class was missing. Jamie Franco Zamudio, a psychology professor, organized students into small groups and gave them a scenario: "You are competing for grant funding to address a petroleum-related problem; come up with a proposal and defend it." The energy, creativity, and knowledge students demonstrated in those impromptu presentations made us realize what students needed: they needed a chance to formulate and weigh potential solutions to the problems they were studying.

In fact, this focus on solutions is a part of systems theory itself; one might even say it is the ultimate goal of understanding systems. Donella Meadows writes in *Thinking in Systems: A Primer*:

> Once we see the relationship between structure and behavior, we can begin to understand how systems work, what makes them produce poor results, and how to shift them into better behavior patterns. As our world continues to change rapidly and become more complex, systems thinking will help us manage, adapt, and see the wide range of choices we have before us. It is a way of thinking that gives us the freedom to identify root causes of problems and see new opportunities. (1–2)

At its best, systems thinking helps us to identify "leverage points for change" (6). We had designed our course to foster understanding of a system—an essential step for engaging an issue but not empowering in and of itself. If we want to educate students to be action-oriented problem-solvers, we have to make space for solutions in our classrooms. We need a pedagogy of solutions.[2]

Solutions require a different sort of pedagogy because they are, by nature, speculative. They are proposals of what might be rather than analysis of what is. As such, they raise particular pedagogical challenges. In academia, we often feel on firmer ground when tracing established patterns that we have the data and historical record to support. To invite students to speculate—to be creative in an informed, engaged way—is to invite them to consider the unknown and untried, which can exceed our areas of expertise and complicate processes of evaluation. Assignments have to be carefully designed to balance students' creativity and idealism with an understanding of constraints and contexts. Further, students who are not often asked to think this way can overlook issues or problems that may seem obvious to faculty members. The problems that students explore have been addressed in countless white papers, dissertations, and studies, so the solutions they develop will be partial, fledgling, and limited. However, despite these drawbacks, students need practice developing problem-solving skills, and a college classroom is a good incubator for their ideas and efforts. A well-crafted solutions project as a capstone in a social justice course can be an important step in developing the skill of problem-solving beyond and outside a classroom.

The centrality of problem-solving to creating engaged and efficacious community members is key to approaches such as the American Association of Colleges and Universities (AACU)'s signature work initiative and problem-based learning (PBL). The AACU, which funded the grant team at Spring Hill that developed the idea for our systems thinking courses, defines signature work and "integrative learning" as students "[s]olving complex real-world problems," using "concepts learned inside and outside the classroom," through projects "related to a significant issue, problem, or question" ("Integrative Learning").[3] Relatedly, the goal of PBL is for students to become "engaged problem solvers" and "self-directed learners" as they grapple with "ill-structured" problems—the PBL term for the type of intractable issues that society faces (Savery 8). However, because so much of problem-solving depends on having a sufficiently complex understanding of the problem, much of this literature focuses on how instructors can better model and promote understanding of problems themselves. While the end goal of both signature work and PBL is problem-solving, these final steps of the process get less attention. Articulating a pedagogy of solutions shifts the focus from enhancing problem knowledge to considering the solution-oriented elements of the process. Rather than adopting the vocabulary from either signature work or PBL initiatives, this essay employs the vocabulary developed by our cross-disciplinary teaching teams in the construction of solutions-based projects in a liberal arts context. Because so much of the work on PBL is cross-disciplinary—having evolved out of graduate school approaches, particularly those used in medical school—it is useful in articulating a pedagogy of solutions for social justice undergraduate teaching.

At Spring Hill, we have taught eight iterations of this course format, which means we have had seven opportunities since that original petroleum course to adjust the trajectory of the classes to incorporate solutions in meaningful and productive ways. Our various attempts to do so have centered on two main types of assignments: action projects and analytical projects. Direct action solutions assignments require that students design and implement a solution in their local—typically campus—community; analytical solutions assignments prompt students to design potential solutions that they present rather than implement. Both assignment types develop problem-solving skills, but they hone different aspects of that skill set. Analysis of our successes and failures with these varied approaches reveals some basic principles that may guide others' development of a pedagogy of solutions that is intentional and productive.

Action versus Analytical Solutions

To develop an intentional pedagogy of solutions, instructors need to match solutions activities with learning objectives. That means reflecting on the skills and competencies that specific solutions activities promote rather than considering activities under broad categories of "problem-based learning," "community engagement," or "service." The test of a solutions activity is whether or not it promotes the skills and competencies necessary for students themselves to become problem-solvers. In terms of learning and skill objectives related to a solutions pedagogy, two objectives are integral to all problem-solving approaches: problem definition and creativity. The first relates to deciding where to engage: What aspect of the problem will you focus on? Or, in Meadows's terminology, what leverage point will you choose? This first objective requires knowledge of the system itself that has to be cultivated prior to a solutions project. The second necessary element of a solutions pedagogy relates to the generative, creative element fundamental to problem-solving. At the basis of problem-solving is an ability to assess the state of things and then create something new: to think outside the box or to modify or recombine existing elements, building on promising developments. A solutions pedagogy that creates problem-solvers has to make space for students to go through the process of defining an area of focus and then generating a creative solution.

We learned the importance of foregrounding such skills and competencies early in the progression of these courses. Because the courses include a local component, we always take field trips to community sites that relate to the topic, and sometimes, those have been linked to service days. For example, in the food course, after touring the Bay Area Food Bank, we volunteered there for an afternoon, sorting food and organizing fresh vegetables into packages for distribution in food deserts within the city. At first, we considered this a "solutions" activity; however, at best, this service day reinforced course content while encouraging volunteerism. While this type of service activity "felt good," it did little to prompt students to consider leverage points for change or to develop the actual skills needed to make change. Students were merely inserted into an organization that, while it may be doing systemic work for change, has already made those assessments. I can imagine alternative approaches to a service day that would promote systemic analysis—such as asking students to research community organizations that work on a specific issue and then argue for why and how the class might serve at one of those organizations over others—but for professors to make arrangements for students to tour and serve, even for a more extended period of time, has a limited impact on developing problem-solving capacities in students.

This awareness pushed our teaching team toward different types of activities that more directly cultivate the skills and competencies required for solution development. We have employed two major types of solutions projects that cultivate very different skill sets in students: action projects and analytical projects. An action project requires implementation. Examples of this type of project in our courses include art installations, campus education projects, one-day protests, flyer campaigns, letters to the administration or to community entities, and articles in the campus newspaper. We have also typically designed these as group projects, since successful community action requires collaboration. Beyond collaboration, action projects emphasize skill sets such as logistics, planning, and communication, including awareness of audience; group members cultivate efficacy and agency alongside these skills. This type of project is often favored as supplying "real world" experience because the students actually implement their plans. It would be more accurate to think of these projects as "enacted," because they allow students to gain experience carrying out a solution within a smaller community—typically the campus community—which offers a manageable scope for a course capstone project.

In contrast, analytical solutions projects offer a more conceptual experience. In these projects, students develop a more wide-reaching solution, and while the solution is not implemented in the "real world," it is subject to a more complex planning process wherein students consider the opportunities and constraints—funding, stakeholders, allies, opponents, and such—that relate to their solution. Learning to think through solutions at this macro level is as important for students as enacting their solutions and is a logical outgrowth of systems thinking. Examples of this type of project in our classes have been group presentations that highlight a solution or set of solutions. For example, in the water course, students proposed a solution to a water-related problem and defended their solution as sustainable; in the terrorism course, they presented three solutions to a specific ongoing conflict involving terrorism and weighed the merits of the solutions for the class. Analytical solutions emphasize a different set of skills: research, stakeholder analysis, and systems understanding and engagement.

We have typically offered all solutions assignments in our courses as collaborative or group projects. Both require an interactive planning process in which students negotiate their focus, determine their approach, assume different roles, divide work, and manage implementation (be it real or hypothetical). Collaboration adds an additional "real world" component to this approach, since solutions are not developed or implemented in a vacuum. In either case, to develop a pedagogy of solutions, instructors must be conscious of their objectives and the types of skills that different solutions approaches promote and develop assignments accordingly. The remainder of this essay addresses what we at Spring Hill have learned about how to best support and structure learning experiences of this kind.

Assignment Design

Our various successes and failures with solutions projects have produced insight into elements of assignment design that promote better outcomes. It appears that action projects work best when objectives are articulated for students and then the instructor steps back and lets them figure out how to get there. Analytical projects require specification of some of the analytical categories to consider when formulating a solution.

Action Projects

If the goal of an action project is to develop solutions behaviors in students—from problem definition to solution development and implementation—then professors need to stay out of the way as much as possible. Our biggest mistake in this vein occurred in the water course as we designed an awareness campaign about water and single-use plastics as well as global water issues, such as the link between access to water and girls' educational opportunities in developing nations. We planned and executed what we thought was a beautiful and unified campaign: two graphic design majors in the class produced excellent visuals, and the class fanned out to blanket campus water sources—such as bathrooms, water fountains, and cafeteria water dispensers—with the designed flyers, each stating a specific, arresting water-related fact. However, orchestrating a unified project created several problems. First, the expertise required of the graphic design majors placed an unfair load on them in the execution of this project as they reworked their design in response to class critique, fit the messaging to the design, and facilitated color printing. Second, the coordinated blitz of campus required scheduling and assignment of dorms and buildings to different students. Packets had to be assembled with printouts and locations "covered." And all this was unfolding at the end of term—a busy time for everyone. Ultimately, the graphic design professor who taught along with the course coordinator stepped up to play too large a role. Although the class as a whole shaped the design, content, and physical distribution of the flyers, too much of the solutions process—especially the logistics planning—was in the hands of professors.

These deficiencies were largely corrected in the campus education projects produced in our technology class. After studying Adam Alter's *Irresistible: The Rise of Addictive Technology and the Business of Keeping Us Hooked*, which addresses the tech sector's strategic development of addictive technology, students were concerned about the issue of technology overuse. For this action project, instead of participating in a unified class campaign, students worked in groups of five or six, an arrangement that gave them more ownership of the focus of their project. One group wanted to address the issue of binge-watching on *Netflix*, another group wanted to conduct a survey and use its results to raise awareness about technology usage patterns, and another wanted to highlight the consequences of technology overuse. Groups determined their focus and came up with creative approaches on their own. The design of the flyers and their dissemination across campus was entirely their job. To document their campaign, students uploaded pictures of their flyers from around campus; judging by the range of photos, they covered quite a bit of ground without a need for central planning. Although we sacrificed the impact of a visually unified and strategically timed effort, students gained the experience of working with a small team to conduct an awareness campaign, experiencing the full process from focus definition to implementation.

We concluded that instructors can best support student learning in action projects by laying out the elements of the process—problem focus, solution development, expertise identification, task breakdown, and implementation logistics—and then allowing students the freedom to innovate in those areas. Depending on student ability level, instructors can adjust the timing and frequency of progress reports as groups move through these steps. However, the most important learning objective for a solutions pedagogy is that students experience the process themselves.

Analytical Projects

Analytical projects require that students think through the complexities of a solution rather than experience those complexities. While some of the steps included in the above-described action project sequence are somewhat intuitive—many would emerge organically from a highly motivated group given a broad assignment—the types of considerations necessary to propose a strategic solution in an analytical project are not intuitive. They are learned.

The problem-solving process we developed in our classes is consistent with a blend of frameworks from educational psychology. James Voss and Timothy Post have identified the behaviors expert problem-solvers employ when addressing the types of social problems our courses investigate. Problem representation—understanding concepts and factors related to the problem—is the first step. Subsequent steps are directly solutions-related: (1) identifying solutions that eliminate the causes of the problem, (2) developing procedures to implement the solutions, and (3) justifying the proposed solution—explaining why it would work and considering the problems that might arise through implementation (see Xun and Land 8). Xun Ge, a professor of educational psychology, and Susan Land, a professor of educational learning and design, build from these observations and identify four major processes for problem-solving: "(a) problem representation, (b) generating and selecting solutions, (c) making justifications, and (d) monitoring and evaluating goals and solutions" (8). The first two steps in both processes—understanding the problem and developing, selecting, and justifying solutions—are fundamental to any concept of problem-solving. But we have found Voss and Post's emphasis on implementation is an important third step in the process, while Xun and Land's emphasis on monitoring and evaluating solutions is vital for closing the loop on the process.

Ideally, analytical solutions assignments elaborate on these stages—problem representation, articulation of solution concept, implementation, and evaluation. We scaffold learning for students in the form of questions that help them move toward articulating a well-developed solution. Strategic questions are the perfect scaffolding element to foster problem-solving skills because they alert students to factors to consider without providing an answer. Xun and Land advocate for a mixture of "question prompts and peer interactions" for developing problem-solving capacities in students; they offer excellent suggestions for additional questions—particularly in the proposal and evaluation phases—that scaffold this learning (16 [table 1]). Taken together, these suggestions provide a useful road map of how solutions-oriented analytical assignments might be developed and enhanced.

Our most successful analytical solutions projects have been scenario-based. Typically, students form groups of three to five people and compete for either grant funds or seed money, depending on whether their group decides it will operate as an NGO or as a corporation. As a first step, students are required to explain the problem they are addressing with references to appropriate contexts that demonstrate an awareness of the system in which the problem is situated. Their explanation will serve as an introductory or background element of their presentation. The groups then work through three stages: proposal, implementation, and evaluation of the solution they are promoting.

In the proposal stage, students bring together their capacity for creativity with real-world knowledge. Their solution must be innovative but not unrealistic—meaning they have to have support for the feasibility of their idea from a study, a pilot program, or other corroborating evidence related to their concept. We have had good luck with using the following questions to scaffold student learning:

> Why did you select this particular point of intervention into the system?
>
> Is your solution proposal technological, behavioral, or policy-oriented?
>
> Why did you choose that solution type?
>
> What are the benefits of your proposal to a specific population?

Additional questions that might be asked at this stage include:

> What is your chain of reasoning for selecting that solution?
>
> Do you have evidence to support your solution? (Xun and Land 16)[4]

Hearing students articulate their answers to these types of questions demonstrates their understanding not only of course content but also of means of applying that knowledge in the real world to create practical solutions. For example, in our water class, one group advocated for sanitation improvements as their point of intervention after learning that open human defecation is a major source of water contamination in developing nations. They analyzed the system to determine a key leverage point and designed a solution to target it. Their specific solution was a program to expand Arborloos—composting toilets that become sites for tree planting when full.

The implementation aspect of a project is often difficult for students, since they are usually unaccustomed to considering the logistics or timeline for launching a project. It is important to have realistic expectations in this phase; the implementation schemes will not necessarily be comprehensive. However, it is useful for students to think through and articulate this vital aspect of the solutions process. Some questions that we have used to enhance their implementation plans include:

What resources are necessary (in terms of staffing, materials, or publicity) to make this project happen?

What are you going to use the grant or seed money for?

What steps or phases would be included in implementing your proposal?

Are there partners or allied organizations you might work with to ensure or improve implementation?

The question of funding is notably absent from this list because it is often one of the most difficult for students to answer. Because it is not necessarily fair or realistic to expect students to be conversant with grant or government funding sources or to understand how much certain elements of their project will cost, we design a project scenario in which they are competing for funding so that this element of implementation is, to some extent, neutralized. However, one could add questions—such as "Are there additional funding sources that you plan to combine with the grant/seed money?" or "Are there actions you can take (for example, community building) that do not require money?"—that would invite them to explore this pertinent question without requiring it.

The final stage of the solutions process—evaluation—was the most difficult one for us to discern. Having included it as a logical rather than intentional element of our first analytical solutions assignment, described below, we only later recognized the necessity of integrating it into all such assignments. Our water class required students to assess the sustainability of their proposed solutions as part of a framework introduced by an outside speaker for the course. Jim Chamberlain, codirector of the University of Oklahoma's Water Center, who has also worked with Engineers without Borders, spoke about his work on multiple continents and emphasized the importance of sustainable solutions, judged by the intersection of three main factors: a successful engineering technology (using local materials and appropriate to the problem), an entrepreneurial element that ensures economic sustainability beyond installation, and cultural awareness to facilitate necessary behavioral changes. For example, the benefit of a future fruit tree helps facilitate the cultural or behavioral shift to consistent indoor defecation so that the Arborloo mentioned earlier does not sit unused. By requiring students to assess their solutions in terms of this three-part check on sustainability, we were challenging them to evaluate their solutions in response to a clear set of goals. Students need such a framework provided for them because they do not have the experience or knowledge to be able to judge their solutions on their own. They need a measuring stick. Otherwise, their solutions come across as pie-in-the-sky panaceas rather than as reflective, complex, and nuanced proposals.

Clearly, a sustainability matrix only works with a specific type or set of projects. Xun and Land offer a set of general questions that could be used to scaffold learning at what they call the "monitoring and evaluating" stage:

> What are the pros and cons of this solution?
> Have I identified all the constraints?
> Have I considered the perspectives of different stakeholders?
> What would be the side effects of this solution? (16)

We might also include Voss and Post's question "What problems might arise in implementation of this solution?" (qtd. in Xun and Land 8). Our teaching team added a modified version of this sustainability question: How will you involve the people impacted by the solution to ensure success? These questions encourage students to think critically about their own solutions, considering the costs and benefits of their proposed course of action.

The last question suggested above incorporates a stakeholder approach, which we have learned is the best way both to foster deep content knowledge about an issue and to encourage evaluation of solutions. While experts can provide valuable awareness of stakeholders involved in an issue, identifying stakeholders—those who have a vested interest in an issue—is also a relatively easy skill that students can cultivate. One fundamental framework is teaching students to consider four major categories of stakeholders: governmental entities, businesses, nongovernmental organizations, and individuals. Highlighting the major subdivisions in these categories helps students recognize and connect actors and impacts:

> Governmental entities (legislative, executive, judicial, military, law enforcement)
> Businesses (small business, multinational corporations, start-ups, entrepreneurs)
> Nongovernmental organizations (local, national, and international nonprofits)
> Individuals (consumers, employees, residents, community members)

Experienced systems thinkers often employ these terms and are aware of some of the patterns involved in relationships among these entities. Stakeholders are a transferable framework for systems understanding. Enabling students to identify these actors and place them in relationship to each other deepens their awareness of context for issues and offers perspectives from which to consider solutions.

This stakeholder approach plays a key role in the students' analytical presentations. By giving students a scenario that requires that they act as either a nonprofit or a corporation, we give them a specific perspective from which to enter into solutions development. In each presentation, students must identify the organization or corporation they have adopted and explain that organization's or corporation's mission. Solutions originate from a perspective, and the scenario reinforces this. In fact, we learned a good deal from our failure to assign a specific perspective in the iteration of the assignment used in the terrorism course. We asked students to identify four different stakeholder perspectives involved in their selected terrorist event (for example, perpetrators, victims, first responders, and media), but we did not assign the presenters an identity—they were outside the situation, like an omniscient narrator, rather than embedded in it. Afterward, we realized that we should instead have asked the presenters to articulate a solution and then explain how three or four different stakeholder groups would view that solution. That would have deepened their understanding of the complexity of peacemaking, demonstrating how solutions have to be evaluated from the perspective of multiple stakeholders.

These analytical projects give students experience in the full span of the solutions process as they model problems, develop and weigh solutions, consider implementation, and evaluate their solutions. Training students to think in this way and allowing them to practice these skills is critical to their evolution into problem-solvers. I emphasize the term *evolution* here because students are often just beginning to identify themselves as potential agents for change who have efficacy in the world. They are just beginning to practice these skills. For that reason, our evaluation of student work on solutions is the final element of a solutions pedagogy that requires reconsideration.

Evaluation

Evaluation of solutions work is complicated for multiple reasons. First, students typically lack experience with problem-solving at the level of social issues. Even students who might be approaching expert levels in their ability to analyze an issue or problem are typically novices in the area of constructing solutions and considering the many facets of implementation and evaluation that solutions thinking requires. They have not done this before. Further, instructors—even if we are evaluating solutions work that is out of our field—have knowledge frameworks that relate to stakeholders and base knowledge of current events and the realities of implementation that are generally more advanced than what students possess (Voss and Post 276). That differential is often invisible to us. Finally, we often grade from a perspective of looking for gaps or omissions in student work, holding as a standard a product that would be "complete" or would demonstrate "mastery" over a body of knowledge. Solutions development puts students in the realm of educated speculation. There are infinitely many things that students could include in their solutions. If we evaluate what is not there in a solution, we are setting students up for failure and ourselves for disappointment. Hence, evaluation of solutions work requires a significant paradigm shift.

Grading novices requires a unique approach. The students in our courses are often juniors and seniors whom the professors know as stars in their major field of study and may have difficulty recognizing as solutions novices. Focusing on what was not covered in a solution, or on what the graders themselves have deep knowledge of, rather than giving credit for what was addressed can result in grading that seems inordinately harsh. After deep reflection, I understood that our evaluation rubric needed to be tailored to this situation. Our initial rubric asked graders to assess the solutions presentations in the four main areas mentioned above (documented explanation of the problem, clear and thorough explanation of the solution, logistics of implementation, and assessment of sustainability); however, the categories offered for evaluating students' performance in these areas were traditional. Graders could choose "excellent," "satisfactory," or "weak." These categories had always seemed adequate before, roughly overlaying on *A*, *B*, or *C* work, but they play directly into the mastery concept of evaluation.

Indeed, rethinking and thus improving our evaluation rubric required a paradigm shift. Categories more appropriate to grading novices in their evolution as problem-solvers are articulated in the Dreyfus model of skill acquisition, formulated by Stuart Dreyfus and Hubert Dreyfus, brothers and University of California, Berkeley, professors of industrial engineering and philosophy, respectively. The model outlines a trajectory for the full skill-acquisition process: "novice, advanced beginner, competent, proficient, and expert" (Peña).[5] These categories do much to help us understand the evolution of complex skills and to give us a vocabulary to conceptualize realistic student outcomes. Students in a college course who are just beginning to practice these skills will likely not be approaching mastery or expertise but might realistically aim for competence. With this in mind, I determined that the evaluation options on our rubric should be "competent," "emergent," and "not present/observed." This scale can more accurately and realistically frame evaluator assessment of novice work.

Finally, instructors must keep in mind their relative expertise and how it impacts their perceptions of student problem-solving. Instructional research on the impacts of the expert/novice divide highlights some of the aspects of expertise that become invisible to instructors, often because their schema are so well ingrained. Adam Persky and Jennifer Robinson, pharmacy professors at University of North Carolina Chapel Hill and Washington State, respectively, explain: "Experts have built substantial knowledge bases that affect what they notice, and how they organize, represent and interpret information. These adaptations lead to better problem solving and performance" (72). Further, instructors are often frustrated specifically by evaluating solutions work: "The problem-solving process also may frustrate instructors since they tend to take deeper approaches to understanding the problem where novices may take a more superficial approach" (77). Understanding that novice solutions work is going to be beginner work—demonstrating fledgling understanding of problem modeling and solutions elements such as implementation—helps to reduce this frustration. Our responsibility as instructors is to move students toward competence and proficiency by providing scaffolding for appropriately pitched problem-solving tasks rather than to approach students with preconceived and unrealistic expectations.

Ultimately, a pedagogy of solutions places the focus on what we instructors can do to promote solutions-oriented skills and habits of mind in students. By being more specific about our goals and objectives for solutions activities and what skills and competencies they develop, we can be more intentional about designing useful experiences for students. We need to scaffold solutions work constructively, providing structure and stepping back in the optimal combinations to develop competence and proficiency. We must also acknowledge the unique aspects of solutions development work in order to accurately frame both tasks and evaluation processes for students. Such an approach will help cultivate problem-solving skills in students that reap real benefits both in and beyond the classroom.

NOTES

1. As a professor of English and a member of the Shared Futures AACU grant team that developed the original course, I have continued to coordinate these courses, convening the teaching team for planning in the fall and then providing support for the course in the spring when it is taught. While this team-taught endeavor has had many contributors from our faculty, I am fortunate to have had the perspective of coordinating these courses over the past eight years.

2. The term *solutions* is used in this essay to emphasize the movement toward resolution that occurs in the later stages of the problem-solving process rather than to suggest that sweeping amelioration of intractable problems is possible. Solutions do not necessarily completely solve a problem—they chip away at root causes, try to motivate change, and begin an intervention that can help correct larger structural injustices within a system.

3. With Margaret Davis, a professor of English and grant team member at Spring Hill, and Tiffany Thomas, a student involved in one of the early courses I describe here, I gave the keynote presentation at the Liberal Education and America's Promise (LEAP) Challenge Forum at AACU's Diversity, Learning, and Student Success conference in 2015 (Litwiller et al.), testament to the mutual relevance of signature work and our courses in systems thinking.

4. Xun and Land include these questions in the next phase, which they call the "justification" of solutions.

5. See Peña's article on the limitations of the Dreyfus model, particularly of the idea that experts move toward "intuition" rather than taking an analytical approach. While I am aware of the limitations of the model and of the detailed explanations of what types of skills and reasoning are employed at each level, I am chiefly interested in the evolutionary nature of this model and its useful terminology.

WORKS CITED

Alter, Adam. *Irresistible: The Rise of Addictive Technology and the Business of Keeping Us Hooked.* Penguin Books, 2017.

Bishop, Peter. "Teaching Systems Thinking." *Futures Research Quarterly*, vol. 24, no. 2, summer 2008, pp. 7–38.

Chamberlain, Jim. "Global Water Outreach." Global Water course, 24 Mar. 2014, Burke Library, Spring Hill College, Mobile, AL. Lecture.

"Integrative Learning and Signature Work." *American Association of Colleges and Universities*, 12 Feb. 2024, www.aacu.org/office-of-global-citizenship-for-campus-community-and-careers/integrative-learning.

Litwiller, Leigh Ann, et al. "Contexts for Signature Work." LEAP Challenge Forum. AACU Conference on Diversity, Learning, and Student Success, 27 Mar. 2015, San Diego, CA.

Meadows, Donella H. *Thinking in Systems: A Primer.* Chelsea Green Publishing, 2008.

Peña, Adolfo. "The Dreyfus Model of Clinical Problem-Solving Skills Acquisition: A Critical Perspective." *Medical Education Online*, vol. 15, 14 June 2010, https://doi.org/10.3402/meo.v15i0.4846.

Persky, Adam M., and Jennifer D. Robinson. "Moving from Novice to Expertise and Its Implications for Instruction." *American Journal of Pharmaceutical Education*, vol. 81, no. 9, 2017, https://doi.org/10.5688/ajpe6065.

Savery, John R. "Overview of Problem-Based Learning: Definitions and Distinctions." *Essential Readings in Problem-Based Learning: Exploring and Extending the Legacy of Howard S. Barrows*, edited by Andrew Walker et al., Purdue UP, 2015, pp. 5–15.

Voss, James F., and Timothy A. Post. "On the Solving of Ill-Structured Problems." *The Nature of Expertise*, edited by Michelene T. H. Chi et al., Psychology Press, 1988, pp. 261–85.

Xun Ge, and Susan M. Land. "A Conceptual Framework for Scaffolding Ill-Structured Problem-Solving Processes using Question Prompts and Peer Interactions." *Educational Technology, Research and Development*, vol. 52, no. 2, 2004, pp. 5–22. *JSTOR*, www.jstor.org/stable/30221193.

The Evolutionary Science of Social Justice

Joseph L. Graves, Jr.

The scientific method is an important tool for understanding the natural universe; indeed, no other tool has performed as well with regard to delivering useful information about natural phenomena. Examples of how well the scientific method works exist in its grand theories, such as Newtonian and relativistic motion, the conservation of matter and energy, and evolution by the means of natural selection. The applications of such grand theories impact the lives of virtually all the people on this planet, both positively and negatively. For example, the biology of vaccination utilizes an evolutionary principle. Viruses are allowed to undergo adaptation to nonhuman cells, and then the attenuated (weakened) virus is introduced back into human populations. The attenuated viruses stimulate recipients' immune responses to strengthen them against infection from the ancestral wild strain. The improved methods that utilize only a portion of the viral genetic code and thus allow more rapid production of vaccines would have been impossible without prior evolutionary insights. These technologies have saved the lives of millions. On the other hand, the knowledge that allowed the invention of vaccines can also be used to produce biological weapons, as Shiro Ishii did for the empire of Japan (Williams and Wallace). Similarly, the physics of nuclear energy has been employed to generate electrical power for millions but, utilized in atomic weapons, has the potential to destroy all human life on this planet.

What, then, is science? Science, narrowly defined, is a system of acquiring knowledge based on methods of observation, hypothesis, and experimentation. This system results in an organized body of knowledge gained through research that allows repeatable and verifiable investigations into the natural world. Moreover, science is a continuing effort to discover and increase human knowledge and understanding through disciplined research (Spellman and Price-Bayer). Natural processes govern all life on this planet (including human life); therefore, it is important to understand how these processes work and don't work. In modern nations, science literacy impacts scientific innovations, technological developments, markets, democratic processes, public policy, access to health care, media understanding, cyber security, and even reception of religious dogma (Allen).

Despite the significance of science, the American public is poorly prepared to understand it. Both the K–12 and university systems have done a terrible job teaching science across the curriculum. Indeed, while terms like "writing across the curriculum" exist, I have never encountered the idea that all students graduating with university degrees should have a working capacity to reason scientifically or numerically. General education programs typically deal with science or mathematics competencies by requiring students to take one or two general nonmajor science or math courses. By the time they attend university, many students have developed a true dislike of science and math and are unengaged in these nonmajor courses. This means they graduate without any alteration in what may be an actively or passively nonscientific worldview.

The lack of science literacy allows false claims about nature to proliferate and in part explains how and why some vested interests advance anti-scientific agendas. Examples of anti-scientific movements currently being propagated globally include denial of climate science, anti-vaccination campaigns, special creationism, and flat-earth theories. During April 2020, President Donald Trump advanced unscientific claims concerning the efficacy of the antimalarial drug hydroxychloroquine as a treatment for COVID-19 (Bump). He continued to adhere to this claim despite clinical studies demonstrating that the drug is ineffective and increases heart attack risks (Molina et al.). Worse than Trump's pseudoscientific virus cures are the ongoing claims that he won the 2020 election, one of the greatest dangers to our democracy in the United States. This unfounded claim was subsequently taken up by conspiracy theorists who proposed that voting machines had been massively tampered with to favor Joe Biden. We have since learned that Trump had plans to seize voting machines in disputed states and replace state electors with others who had pledged loyalty to him (Cohen et al.; Feuer et al.).

A less understood issue is how a lack of scientific literacy contributes to the persistence of racist ideology (Graves, *Race Myth*). For example, surveys show that between 1993 and 2004, fifty-two percent of Americans surveyed (N=4,888) did not accept the evidence that modern humans evolved from earlier species of animals. This question is considered the litmus test for the acceptance of the scientific fact of evolution (Berkman and Plutzer). A consequence of evolution is descent with modification. This means that all organisms on this planet are descended from a common ancestor and also that within individual species, such as modern humans, all members share common ancestry. Furthermore, scientific evidence shows that for modern humans, that ancestry began in sub-Saharan Africa. Thus, European American creationists tend to reject evolution not just because of its evidence for shared human ancestry but because that ancestry began in Africa (Graves, "Out of Africa").

In addition to rejecting the shared ancestry of modern humans, there has been a resurgence of white supremacist racist ideology. Europe has seen the rise of far-right, racist, anti-immigrant parties such as the Danish People's Party, the French Front National (now National Rally), Golden Dawn, Jobbik, Lijst Pim Fortuyn, and the Polish Law and Justice Party (Mushaben). Such sentiments have also been observed in Israel. Recently, an Israeli television station released recordings of two rabbis at a religious school in the West Bank saying, respectively, that Adolf Hitler was "the most correct person there ever was and was correct in every word he said . . . he was just on the wrong side" and that Arabs are genetically inferior:

> All around us, we are surrounded by peoples with genetic problems. Ask a simple Arab, "Where do you want to be?" He wants to be under the occupation. Why? Because they have genetic problems, they don't know how to run a country, they don't know how to do anything. Look at them. . . . Yes, we're racists. We believe in racism. . . . There are races in the world and peoples have genetic traits, and that requires us to try to help them. The Jews are a more successful race. (Pilleggi)

This sort of unscientific bigotry concerning human biological variation is widespread around the globe (Graves, "Out of Africa" and *Emperor's New Clothes*; Dikötter).

What Evolution Can Tell Us about Human Beings

In my foreword to *The Evolutionary Psychology of Violence*, edited by Richard Bloom and Nancy Dess, I decry the separation of psychology and sociology from evolutionary biology. The separation exists despite the inescapable fact that our species, anatomically modern humans, evolved from previous species of hominids whose morphology and behavior were shaped by natural selection. This is a fact whose impacts on social structures we continue to underestimate. In an apocryphal story, a supposed contemporary of Charles Darwin, Lady Ashley, upon being told that modern humans were descended from apelike ancestors, responded, "Let's hope it's not true; but if it is true, let's hope that it does not become widely known!" (Buss). This anecdote, even though invented, gets across an important sentiment concerning human anthropomorphism. Much of what is believed about human culture is premised on the idea that we are unique among all animal species on this planet. This belief is false. We know that other mammals are capable of quite sophisticated thinking; for example, rhesus macaques can utilize probability to predict future events (De Petrillo and Rosati). This should not be that surprising, since humans share ninety-eight percent of their genome with chimpanzees and the chimpanzee and human lineages diverged only 6.4 +/– 1.5 million years ago (Stauffer et al.). Given how much of our genomes are shared in common, it is highly unreasonable to think that our behaviors are so drastically different. Traits formerly thought to be unique to humans, such as walking upright, culture, use of fire, reduced body hair, complex tools, and communication with language, are also present in other large-brained organisms, differing only by a matter of degree. That difference in degree is perhaps most evident in the categories of language and complex toolmaking, and there is evidence that these neural circuits overlap in our brains (Stout and Chaminade). On the other hand, some traits not unique to humans and that also play a large role in the societies we have produced are inclusive fitness, intergroup hostility, and our predisposition to accept authority (Fishbein and Dess).

The concept of inclusive fitness explains how altruism, once believed a paradox of evolutionary theory, can evolve in any species. In a system of natural selection that acts to improve the differential reproductive success of individuals, scientists had been at a loss to explain how altruism (behavior that benefits other individuals) could have evolved. The evolutionary biologist William D. Hamilton proposed a model wherein a gene that promotes altruistic behavior could spread within populations if the benefit to the recipient (B) times the relatedness to the actor (r) were greater than the cost (C) to the actor:

$$(B \times r) - C > 0$$

The cost is measured in units of evolutionary fitness (or differential reproductive success, which is composed of both the probability that an individual lives and their reproductive success). Hamilton's model solved the problem of how insects such as bees and ants could evolve a system of sterile castes with one reproductive queen. In this case, the sterile females are contributing care to their sister's (the queen's) offspring. The mating system of these insects ensures that the sterile females are actually more closely related to the queen's offspring than they would be to their own.

In the context of our human species, inclusive fitness means that human altruistic behavior is most evolutionarily rewarded by acts that we direct toward our genetic kin (siblings, children, and cousins). For example, one study of women in Los Angeles examined costly instances of giving and receiving help (e.g., picking up a sick friend's kids or lending money for a house down payment). The study tested two inclusive fitness theory predictions: first, that among kin, helping increases as a function of genetic relatedness, and, second, that among kin, helping increases as the recipient's reproductive value increases. The women described 2,520 instances of giving help and 2,651 of receiving help. Most of the help given and received was between individuals who were not related (~71%). However, the study showed that far more help was given and received by kin who shared half their genetic material (parents, full siblings, and children; ~23%) than by those who shared one-fourth of their genes (half siblings, grandparents, aunts, and uncles; ~4%) or less (cousins, children of half siblings, etc.; ~2%; Essock-Vitale and McGuire). A strong test of inclusive fitness theory (and one that is relevant to social justice struggles) is provided by life-and-death scenarios. In a cross-cultural study in the United States and Japan, participants were asked to select one person from among several family members they could save from a burning house. This scenario allowed for only one person to be saved; those who remained in the house would die. The persons in the house shared with the participant either one-half, one-fourth, or one-eighth of their genetic material. In another aspect of the experiment, these individuals also varied by age (<1, 10, 18, 45, and 75 years). In both Japan and the United States, the results followed the prediction of inclusive fitness theory. The propensity to save individuals declined linearly with genetic relatedness and, within genetic relatedness groups, declined linearly with age, which is related to an individual's ability to reproduce (Burstein et al. 23).

Inclusive fitness theory is also related to reciprocal altruism, a theory that explains how altruistic behavior can be beneficial to persons who are not closely related. A series of experiments by Herbert Gintis and his collaborators showed that strong reciprocity—a strong form of reciprocal altruism that refers to a predisposition to cooperate with others and punish those who violate the terms of cooperation even when it is unlikely that the personal costs of these actions will be repaid—is entirely consistent with inclusive fitness theory. In reciprocal altruism, costly cooperation occurs between two unrelated individuals. The proviso here is that this altruism benefits both partners in the sense of "you do for me and I will do for you" (Silk). In the case of reciprocal altruism, the evidence for its widespread existence is weak in nonhuman animals but much stronger in humans. Arguably, unique human traits, especially language, make reciprocal altruism easier to sustain (Clutton-Brock). Gintis and colleagues proposed that strong reciprocity played a role in helping to evolve the moral capacity within our species that values freedom, equality, and representative forms of government.

Intergroup hostility is a constant feature of our species. This may be part of the evolutionary heritage we share with other primates. Many behaviors related to social interaction, such as forming groups to seek out and attack outsiders or to stake out and defend territory, are shared between orangutans, gorillas, chimpanzees, and humans, suggesting they are inherited from a great ape ancestor (Mathew et al.). Yet traits characteristic of each species also evolved over time, a process known as descent with modification. Anatomically, modern humans evolved in Africa (East, Central, or South is still debated). Modern human behavior as measured by technology and art had certainly appeared in humans before they began their migration out of Africa (Pickrell and Reich). Our ancestral social behavior was characterized by moderately large communities, coalitions of males linked by kinship, unrelated females attached to a specific male (or males), and some intergenerational lineal patterning. Lineal patterning refers to genetic inheritance from humans' direct ancestors or relatives, and its features resulted from life history evolution changes in humans as compared to other primates (slower growth, later maturation, and longer life span; Mathew et al.).

Patriarchy is not considered an ancestral trait of humans but rather something that developed in association with the domestication of animals. The dominance of males in these early societies is consistent with the predictions of social dominance theory (Sidanius et al.). Social dominance theory focuses on both individual and structural factors that contribute to various forms of group-based oppression. Oppression in modern societies results in part from the inherited evolved behavior of our primate ancestors. Behaviors that may have been beneficial for differential reproductive success of these ancestors in their environments but are maladaptive in the modern world are examples of a phenomenon called "evolutionary mismatch." Evolutionary mismatch has been demonstrated for a variety of behaviors in modern humans that have been made possible by our recent and rapid technological and cultural evolution. Examples of these recent cultural and technological innovations include modern food surplus, concentrated drugs, and tools such as smartphones (Sbarra et al.).

Probably the most unfortunate of these evolutionary mismatches resides in our brains. The human brain is not an exquisitely designed reasoning machine, as is claimed by the special creationists. Rather, it is the result of descent with modification and is therefore quite imperfect. Gary Marcus describes the human brain as a "kluge," meaning a haphazard construction resulting from selection for specific cognitive tasks. Some of these tasks are in concert with each other, whereas others result from trade-offs. These tasks are ultimately related to the differential reproductive success of individuals (Marcus)—which does not mean they ensure our psychological and social well-being. Indeed, in some cases, it produces quite the opposite, or what we call mental illness (Nesse; Hidaka).

Our brain fails in so many arenas that could help us achieve social justice that it is worth reviewing these faults. Because these failings are predictable (Ariely), they can be and are manipulated for particular social ends. For example, while "belief" is ubiquitous in humans, our brain is not automatically an objective-truth-finding machine that provides us with reasons for what we believe. Indeed, our beliefs are contaminated by our moods, desires, goals, and, often, self-interest. This is why we are vulnerable to superstition, manipulation, and fallacy (Schick and Vaughn). An example of this that has come to social significance recently is the use of fake news in social media platforms to influence politics. In the last three months of the 2016 electoral season, fake news stories generated more shares, reactions, and comments on *Facebook* than the top real stories (Pennycook et al.). However, the influence of these sites was hard to measure, and data suggest that people consuming the most fake news content were about ten percent of the most conservative Americans (Silverman). This would suggest that these fake news stories played the role of reifying beliefs already held by this segment of the population. The lesson of these vulnerabilities is that the default position for human thinking about virtually everything is irrational, meaning that we must train our minds to work in a rational manner. Here, *rational* refers to thinking that follows the principles of critical reasoning. Examples of such reasoning are recognizing forms of basic logic, logical fallacies, arguments, credibility of sources, and the difference between subjective and objective claims. Rational thinking requires work because our human brain operates on two primary mental pathways: one that is fast, automatic, and largely unconscious (ancestral), and one that is slow and deliberate (derived; Marcus). The ancestral automatic system is shared by many large-brained organisms, whereas the derived deliberative system is something found primarily in primates (hominids; Marcus). The greatest strategy of all despotic societies is to make it as difficult as possible for people to learn how to use their deliberative system to think rationally and, when that fails, to simply remove the rational thinkers—as in the assassinations of Rosa Luxemburg, Medgar Evers, Malcolm X, and Martin Luther King, Jr., as well as the imprisonment of Antonio Gramsci, Nelson Mandela, and many others.

Cultural Evolution and Mismatch

While what we know about human social behavior in the Pleistocene epoch (2,580,000–11,700 years ago), when the earliest humans appeared, is open to debate, we know a great deal more about the Holocene period (from 11,650 years ago to the present). Generally accepted is the belief that the amount of intergroup hostility and social hierarchy dramatically increased with the coming of agriculture. Agriculture allowed human groups to produce social surplus—that is, more food than is required to meet the caloric needs of a society's population. The existence of such surplus represented a novel environment for brains that had evolved under the condition of hunter-gatherer subsistence. Domestication of plants and animals required that humans intentionally take control of the life cycle of the target plant or animal population and assume responsibility for that population's care to meet specific and well-defined objectives serving human needs. Domestication involved a fundamental change in human socioeconomic organization in which successive generations of domesticates became integrated into human societies as objects of ownership (Ingold). Melinda Zeder has presented a model of the incorporation of domesticates into human socioeconomic organization as being involved in the origin and evolution of notions of property in human societies (see table 1). Similarly, a recent study explains how the domestication of cereal plants and the creation of social surplus played a major role in the development of social complexity and inequality for early Holocene societies throughout the Mediterranean (Leppard). This analysis places the economic growth observed in these early civilizations in the context of Thomas Piketty's model positing a rate of return on capital that exceeds the rate of general economic growth as a major force for the divergence of wealth. Over approximately six thousand years, this process transformed a planet without social complexity, cities, and institutionalized inequality into one in which the habitable planet was covered by complex, territorially discrete, and hierarchical urban societies (Cherry).

Table 1. Incorporation of domesticates into human socioeconomic organization

Before Upper Paleolithic (~300,000–200,000 YBP[a])	Upper Paleolithic (~50,000–12,000 YBP)	[Time period unknown]	[Time period unknown]	Widespread by Bronze Age (~6,200–2,300 YBP)
No notions of property	Group rights to territories containing resources	Group rights to resources	Individual rights to resources by means of producing them	Evolved notions of property
Small groups; kin networks tight	Small groups; kin networks tight	Small groups; kin networks tight	Larger groups; kin networks tight	Larger groups; kin networks more diffuse

Source: Data from Zeder.
a. YBP = years before the present day.

These hierarchical societies continued to evolve through phases of political economic systems: slave societies, in the ancient world; feudalism, from the Middle Ages to the early twentieth century; capitalism, from the early sixteenth century to the twentieth century; and monopoly capitalism, from the late twentieth century to the present. A consistent feature of these political economic systems is patriarchy, although racism in particular is associated with the growth of capitalism (Wilson; Scott; Graves and Goodman). Some social movements in the nineteenth and twentieth centuries aimed to devise and implement alternative forms of political economy that redressed social hierarchy. Anarchism, socialism, and communism share the common notion of class struggle. While anarchism never presented a unified or clear picture of how society should be governed after the fall of capitalism, socialist and communist ideology proposed that the working class, or proletariat, should initially dominate the state. In the early to mid twentieth century, the working class represented the majority of people living in the industrialized nations. Since the latter portion of the twentieth century, however, the traditional notion of the working class has changed. Under neoliberal capitalism, a growing number of people has transitioned into "structural unemployment." Structural unemployment refers to the amount of unemployment required in an economic system in order to maintain a pool of potential workers willing to compete for and accept low-wage jobs (Overbeek). Nevertheless, the core idea of socialism is to place the government in the hands of the majority of people, as opposed to the way governments currently operate—in the interests of the capitalist class, which constitutes an ever-shrinking proportion, about one percent, of the population of the United States. Socialism is also premised on the notion that economic production, instead of being driven by supply-demand principles, should be planned to meet the well-being of the majority of a nation and eventually the world. A socialist society would therefore ask questions concerning the cost-benefit ratio to society in relation to the production and sale of goods that are detrimental to a population's health. For example, the ultraprocessed food industry has contributed to an increase in a variety of metabolic disease in the twentieth century (Rauber et al.).

The most significant attempts to bring socialism or communism into existence have been the Bolshevik revolution (1917–24); anti-capitalist revolutions in China, Korea, Cuba, and Vietnam (1949–73); and general anti-colonial revolutions in India, Africa, and Latin America in those same periods. However, capitalism has been resilient to these challenges. Of course, the champions of capitalism claim that its resilience originates in human nature—specifically, that capitalism is based on meritocracy and that it provides all individuals with an opportunity to achieve either meaningful and satisfying employment or the ownership of their own business. Thus, capitalism is a political-economic system consistent with individual self-interest. So long as this is true, individuals will think it harmful to replace this system with some other way of doing things. Furthermore, humans are more likely to cling to existing institutions even when it is in their self-interest to change them. Indeed, the more people feel threatened, the more likely they are to stick with the familiar. This behavior results from a fundamental error of reasoning that is inherent in the human brain (Marcus). Further, proponents of capitalism claim that socialism and communism have utterly failed to show that they can adequately serve individual self-interest. Prime examples of that failure are the fall of the Soviet Union as well as the backsliding of China into capitalism. On the face of it, these events appear to support the case for capitalism. Yet a more nuanced examination of history proves otherwise.

Karl Marx outlines his ideas for the coming of communist society in a letter eventually published as *Critique of the Gotha Programme.* Marx saw socialism developing out of capitalism and thought that its best chance of succeeding would be in highly industrialized nations that had a history of democratic principles and hence a generally high level of education and literacy in the working class. The first stage of the transition would be the "dictatorship of the proletariat." By this phrase, Marx meant that the apparatus of the state and the productive forces (namely, industries and agriculture) would be taken over by, and employed in the interest of, the working class (i.e., the vast majority of people in the society). Marx made no prediction regarding how this transition would occur; in a democratic society, it could conceivably occur by an election of working-class party representatives to the national parliament or congress. In a despotic one, it would have to occur by a revolution against the government and the establishment of a new one. The duration of the proposed "dictatorship" was never made clear, but generally the idea was that it would usher in the period of socialism: "each according to his abilities, each according to his needs." Everyone's basic needs would be met under socialism by a high level of production. Local and national democratic bodies would determine allotments of material goods according to need, considering factors such as household size. All people would require adequate housing, access to healthy food, clean water and air, and safety from violence. Finally, communism would come into existence after the complete capacity to meet everyone's needs was achieved. In such a society, the state would no longer have reason to exist.

Clearly, Marx's idea of the transition from capitalism to socialism was never realized in practice. The Bolshevik revolution of 1917 briefly implemented the "dictatorship of the proletariat," but by 1924 this had been destroyed by a combination of external and internal forces (Deutscher). The primary external force was the attack on the infant Soviet state by many nations, including Britain, the United States, and France, that aided the former czarists (White Russians) and precipitated a civil war estimated to have cost two million lives and destroyed important infrastructure (Markevich and Harrison). Shortly after the Civil War, an internal coup occurred within the Bolshevik Party. The death of Lenin in January 1924 left the future of the Soviet Union in the hands of the party's greatest theoretician, Leon Trotsky, who realized that the Soviet Union could not expect to outproduce the capitalist nations, particularly in the aftermath of the war. His idea for the triumph of socialism was the notion of "the permanent revolution." This meant the spread of socialist ideas, particularly into the industrialized West, in countries such as Germany (Trotsky). However, to facilitate this triumph, the gains of the revolution in Russia had to be consolidated. To achieve this, Trotsky relied on his New Economic Policy (NEP), which would allow some reversion of capitalism in agriculture. To get the NEP passed, he needed the aid of Joseph Stalin and conspired to have Lenin's last testament, which implored the party to remove Stalin as general secretary, suppressed over the vigorous opposition of Lenin's wife, Nadezhda Krupskaya. The statement was never read to the party, and in return, Trotsky thought he would receive the support for his NEP from Stalin.

Stalin, on the other hand, had a strategy premised on "socialism in one country." He was strongly anti-Semitic, valued the interests of "white" Russians above the non-European members of the Soviet Union, and detested both Trotsky's intellectualism and his Jewish heritage. He used both nationalism and anti-Semitism to maneuver Trotsky out of the leadership in the party and to have him expelled from the Soviet Union on charges of being an "agent of the bourgeoisie" (Deutscher). Stalin then consolidated his hold on the Soviet Union by purging all opposition to him within the party (1929–36). The purges began with removals from the party, imprisonment, and finally executions. During the Great Purge (the most intense period, from 1936 to 1938), it is estimated that four million party members were executed (Getty). In addition, the forced collectivization of agriculture in the Ukraine is estimated to have caused five million deaths through the execution of people resisting the policy and through starvation resulting from dramatic losses in agricultural productivity (Rosefielde).

Finally, one must also consider the carnage visited upon the Soviet Union by the Nazi invasion. This was in part facilitated by Stalin's foolish trust of Adolph

Hitler and his previous purges of some of the most accomplished military officers in the Red Army. This left the USSR completely unprepared for the Nazi invasion. It is generally unappreciated in the West that the bulk of the fighting and death in the European theater of World War II took place in the Soviet Union, killing approximately 13.5% of the total Soviet population—25 to 26 million people (Brainerd)—and reducing the ratio of males to females within the Soviet Union from approximately 1.0 in 1930 to 0.6 in 1945. In comparison, the United States experienced about 418,500 military and civilian deaths, representing about 0.2% of the total population. Taken together, these historical tragedies and the US Cold War strategy of forcing the Soviet Union to prioritize national spending on nuclear and conventional armaments (at the cost of consumer goods) guaranteed the fall of the Soviet Union (Lieber and Press).

In the aftermath of the Second World War, the capitalist nations, led by the United States, conducted all-out attempts to stop the spread of socialist or anticolonial revolutions. This translated to violence against primarily non-European people in Africa, Asia, the Pacific Islands, and Latin America. For example, the United States dropped approximately 2.5 million tons of munitions on Vietnam and Laos during the Vietnam War (1955–75). This was the largest bombing campaign in the history of warfare (Miguel and Roland). The use of military power to deny others the fundamental human right of self-determination did not stop with Vietnam but continued into the new millennium and can be seen in operation in the current US policy in the Middle East.

The Possibility of Social Justice

To explore the possibility of social justice, we must define "social justice." One definition of social justice is promoting a just society by challenging injustice and valuing diversity. In this definition, diversity refers to various aspects of human identity (socially defined race, ancestry, gender, sexual orientation, national origin, and others) that are the subjects of social subordination. Accepting this definition suggests that we believe that all people have a right to equitable treatment, support for their human rights, and a fair allocation of community resources. (It is legitimate to ask in models of social justice what exactly community resources should include. For example, should everyone be guaranteed employment at a living wage, health care, adequate education, clean water and air, and healthy food?) In addition, this definition suggests that individuals should not be discriminated against, nor their welfare and well-being constrained or prejudiced, on the basis of any of these identity features or any other characteristic of background or group membership (Rawls).

At present, we have no evidence that supports the notion that our species is capable of originating and maintaining "just" societies. If such societies ever existed, they did so before the establishment of agriculture some ten to twenty thousand years ago—that is, before the social surplus that created an evolutionary mismatch both in terms of our general health and in terms of our behavior. It is clear that our brains do not operate well under conditions of social hierarchy. Indeed, the more unjust our societies, the worse the dysfunction becomes. This dysfunction occurs in both the oppressor and the oppressed. Oppressors experience the stress of maintaining unjust social institutions as well as their financial costs. For example, in the United States, the belief in white supremacy has created conditions that increase the sickness and mortality of poor persons of European descent (Metzel). The oppressed suffer even more. Abundant evidence exists that low social status harms individual physical and mental health and that this is a condition inherited from the common ancestor of the great apes (Snyder-Mackler et al.). Indeed, recent studies make clear the molecular effects of social status and the various insults that result from social dominance hierarchy on the human body. For example, one study examined the pattern of gene expression in pro-inflammatory, neuroendocrine, and antiviral transcription pathways in individuals who were surveyed to determine how much racial discrimination they had experienced in their lives. The study found that relative to European Americans, African Americans showed increased activity of two key pro-inflammatory transcription control pathways (NF-κB and AP-1) and two stress-responsive signaling pathways (CREB and glucocorticoid receptor). The results suggest that differences in experiences of racial discrimination can potentially account for more than fifty percent of the total race-related difference in pro-inflammatory transcription factor activity. This is significant because so much of complex disease in humans is driven by inflammation (Thames et al.).

The key question we must ask ourselves is this: Are unjust societies sustainable? The global carnage of the twentieth century suggests that they are not. In our current century, studies suggest that the capitalist economic systems driving this injustice may have already pushed our species past the tipping point (to extinction; Moore). An example of this sort of analysis claims that the complete collapse of human civilization could occur as early as 2050 as a result of climate change (Spratt and Dunlop). Therefore, when people think about how to prevent or slow anthropogenic climate change, they must also question if such an effort could succeed under capitalism. I argue that such reforms are impossible to achieve in this social system.

Socialism or Barbarism is the title of the collected writings of the German Marxist Rosa Luxemburg. Luxemburg was murdered in 1919 by protofascists after a failed attempt at socialist revolution in Germany. The barbarism she warned of came to pass in the form of World War II, and specifically the Holocaust in Germany. Now, more than one hundred years later, we stand at the threshold of similar events; for example, there is a global rise of authoritarian parties and leaders (as in Russia, Israel, Brazil, and the United States). In 2024, despite the fact that Donald Trump currently faces over ninety criminal indictments, he is more popular now with his political base than he was in 2020 (Weiner et al.). The wars between Russia and Ukraine and between Israel and Hamas have the potential to morph into global confrontations. Developments such as these have placed the fate of our entire species at stake. The COVID-19 pandemic is just a taste of what we can expect if we do not address ongoing social injustice. Indeed, the spread of the SARS-COV2 virus was facilitated by exotic meat markets in Wuhan frequented by the wealthy, leading to exposure and infection of the poor who worked there (Pagani et al.). We must apply our evolutionarily mismatched minds to the urgent task of social justice. Indeed, the degree to which we see prosocial behavior is very much premised on the social systems that we live in (Penner et al.). We cannot move humanity from the brink of the abyss without it. What is certain is that either we replace capitalism with new systems that have the potential to allow for more just societies, or extinction of our species will follow.

What Can Be Done

Many think that social revolution is distant water for a near fire. History propels itself at its own pace, and nothing we can do will rush it along. However, we can have a vision of what we want to achieve and commit ourselves to working toward those ends. Having an evolutionary understanding of human social behavior can provide tools to help make that future, and there are immediate things that we can achieve to advance such understanding in our society. First, we must recognize that our brains are evolved quantities originally only useful for promoting individual reproductive success in environments that have little resemblance to those we currently live in. This is why they are flawed organs, mismatched to the social and cultural challenges we now face. Therefore, it is crucial that we promote strategies to ensure that all students are immersed in critical thinking training very early in their education. Those critical thinking skills should be organized around core competencies such as effective oral and written communication, basic logic, numeracy, and scientific literacy as well as cultural and historical literacy. Students with these skills would immediately realize that most of the existential issues we face are inter- and transdisciplinary in nature.

Such students would also be able to immediately recognize why the teaching of evolutionary science and climate change is currently under attack. This is a general attack on reason that has spread to attempting to prevent an accurate telling of US and global history and our current social conditions by demonizing critical race theory. Because white supremacy and its supporting institution of racial capitalism are not sustainable, they are fighting, in the manner of all doomed systems, to preserve themselves, in this case through a racist attack on anti-racism. The problem, of course, is that systems perform as they were designed to perform. In the case of capitalism, that means the greater concentration of wealth into even fewer hands. This growing gap between haves and have-nots cannot be tolerated in the evolved minds of the latter group. This means that this system will become even more unstable. It is imperative that we act now to dismantle this economic system, or we will find ourselves living in a completely totalitarian society rigidly structured by class, race, gender, and sexual orientation. This means in immediate terms that we must defeat the candidacy of Donald Trump for the presidency of the United States. However, achieving that will not be enough. What is required is that we develop a new political party that goes beyond the simplistic divide in policies illustrated by the Democrats and Republicans. Such a party would prioritize the needs of the underserved populations in America, move for a rational economy that is not simply driven by profit, and take seriously imminent existential issues, such as climate change.

In this regard, understanding the biology of human beings provides guidance for our liberation. While our brains are inherently irrational, they can be trained. We are motivated by self-interest, but self-interest is best fostered by altruism (kin and reciprocal). There is no reason to continue to construct society in a series of zero-sum games. Preventing catastrophic global climate change will benefit everyone, preventing the spread of lethal pandemics will benefit everyone, deploying science and engineering to develop sustainable renewable energy will benefit everyone, and designing economies that provide meaningful employment and just standards of living will benefit everyone. Not everyone understands that yet, but it is our charge as scholars to provide a road map to help people reach those conclusions.

WORKS CITED

Allen, Henry Lee. "Science Literacy and the Future of Ethnic Minority Groups in the United States: The Unfinished Civil Rights Movement." *Athens Journal of Social Sciences*, vol. 5, no. 2, 2018, pp. 133–50.

Ariely, Dan. *Predictably Irrational: The Hidden Forces that Shape Our Decisions*. HarperCollins, 2008.

Berkman, Michael, and Eric Plutzer. *Evolution, Creationism, and the Battle to Control America's Classrooms*. Cambridge UP, 2010.

Bloom, Richard W., and Nancy Dess, editors. *The Evolutionary Psychology of Violence: A Primer for Policymakers and Public Policy Advocates*. Greenwood Publishing Group, 2003.

Brainerd, Elizabeth. "The Lasting Effect of Sex Ratio Imbalance on Marriage and Family: Evidence from World War II in Russia." *The Review of Economics and Statistics*, vol. 99, no. 2, 2017, pp. 229–42.

Bump, Philip. "Trump's Promotion of Hydroxychloroquine Is Almost Certainly about Politics Not Profits." *The Washington Post*, 7 Apr. 2020, www.washingtonpost.com/politics/2020/04/07/trumps-promotion-hydroxychloroquine-is-almost-certainly-about-politics-not-profits/.

Burstein, E., et al. "Some Neo-Darwinian Decision Rules for Altruism: Weighing Cues for Inclusive Fitness as a Function of the Biological Importance of the Decision." *Journal of Personality and Social Psychology*, vol. 67, no. 5, 1994, pp. 773–89.

Buss, David M. *Evolutionary Psychology: The New Science of the Mind*. 6th ed., Taylor and Francis, 2019.

Cherry, John F. "Sorting Out Crete's Prepalatial Off-Island Interactions." *Archaic State Interaction: The Eastern Mediterranean in the Bronze Age*, edited by William A. Parkinson and Michael L. Galaty, School for Advanced Research Press, 2010, pp. 107–40.

Clutton-Brock, Tim. "Cooperation between Non-kin in Animal Societies." *Nature*, vol. 462, 2009, pp. 51–57.

Cohen Marshall, et al. "Trump Campaign Officials, Led by Rudy Giuliani, Oversaw Fake Elector Plot in Seven States." *CNN*, 20 Jan. 2022, www.cnn.com/2022/01/20/politics/trump-campaign-officials-rudy-giuliani-fake-electors/index.html.

De Petrillo, Francesca, and Alexandra G. Rosati. "Rhesus Macaques Use Probabilities to Predict Future Events." *Evolution and Human Behavior*, vol. 40, no. 5, Sept. 2019, pp. 436–46, https://doi.org/10.1016/j.evolhumbehav.2019.05.006.

Deutscher, Isaac. *The Prophet: The Life of Leon Trotsky*. 1954–64. Verso Books, 2015. 3 vols.

Dikötter, Frank. *The Discourse of Race in Modern China*. Oxford UP, 2005.

Essock-Vitale, Susan M., and Michael T. McGuire. "Women's Lives Viewed from an Evolutionary Perspective: II. Patterns of Helping." *Ethology and Sociobiology*, vol. 6, no. 3, 1985, pp. 155–73.

Feuer A., et al. "Trump Had Role in Weighing Proposals to Seize Voting Machines." *The New York Times*, 31 Jan. 2022, www.nytimes.com/2022/01/31/us/politics/donald-trump-election-results-fraud-voting-machines.html.

Fishbein, Harold D., and Nancy Dess. "An Evolutionary Perspective on Intercultural Conflict: Basic Mechanisms and Implications for Immigration Policy." Bloom and Dess, pp. 157–202.

Getty, J. Arch. *Origins of the Great Purges: The Soviet Communist Party Reconsidered, 1933–1938*. Cambridge UP, 1987.

Gintis, H., et al. "Explaining Altruistic Behavior in Humans." *Evolution and Human Behavior*, vol. 24, no. 3, 2003, pp. 153–72.

Graves, Joseph L., Jr. *The Emperor's New Clothes: Biological Theories of Race at the Millennium*. Rutgers UP, 2005.

———. Foreword. Bloom and Dess, pp. vii–ix.

———. "Out of Africa: Where Faith, Race, and Science Collide." *Critical Approaches to Science and Religion*, edited by Myrna Perez Sheldon et al., Columbia UP, 2023, pp. 255–76.

———. *The Race Myth: Why We Pretend Race Exists in America*. Dutton Books, 2005.

Graves, Joseph L., Jr., and Alan Goodman. *Racism, Not Race: Answers to Frequently Asked Questions*. Columbia UP, 2022.

Hamilton, William D. "The Genetical Evolution of Social Behavior." *Journal of Theoretical Biology*, vol. 7, no. 1, July 1964, pp. 1–16.

Hidaka, Brandon H. "Depression as a Disease of Modernity: Explanations for Increasing Prevalence." *Journal of Affective Disorders*, vol. 140, no. 3, Nov. 2012, pp. 205–14, https://doi.org/10.1016/j.jad.2011.12.036.

Ingold, Tim. "Growing Plants and Raising Animals: An Anthropological Perspective on Domestication." *The Origins and Spread of Agriculture and Pastoralism in*

Eurasia, edited by David R. Harris, Smithsonian Institution Press, 1996, pp. 12–24.

Leppard, Thomas P. "Social Complexity and Social Inequality in the Prehistoric Mediterranean." *Cultural Anthropology*, vol. 60, no. 3, 2019, pp. 283–308.

Lieber, Keir A., and Daryl G. Press. "The Rise of US Nuclear Primacy." *Foreign Affairs*, vol. 85, no. 2, Mar.-Apr. 2006, pp. 42–54.

Luxemburg, Rosa. *Socialism or Barbarism? Selected Writings*. Pluto Press, 2013.

Marcus, Gary. *Kluge: The Haphazard Construction of the Human Mind*. Houghton Mifflin, 2014.

Markevich, Andrei, and Mark Harrison. "Great War, Civil War, and Recovery: Russia's National Income, 1913 to 1928." *Journal of Economic History*, vol. 71, no. 3, 2011, pp. 672–703.

Marx, Karl. *Critique of the Gotha Programme*. 1875. *Selected Works*, by Karl Marx and Friedrich Engels, vol. 3, Progress Publishers, 1969, pp. 13–30.

Mathew, Sarah, et al. "Human Cooperation among Kin and Close Associates May Require Enforcement of Norms by Third Parties." *Cultural Evolution: Society, Technology, Language, and Religion*, edited by Peter J. Richerson and Morten H. Christianson, MIT Press, 2012. Strüngmann Forum Reports 12.

Metzel, Jonathan M. *Dying of Whiteness: How the Politics of Racial Resentment Is Killing America's Heartland*. Basic Books, 2019.

Miguel, Edward, and Gerard Roland. "The Long Run Impact of Bombing Vietnam." National Bureau of Economic Research, 2006, www.nber.org/papers/w11954. Working Paper 11954.

Molina J. M., et al. "No Evidence of Rapid Antiviral Clearance or Clinical Benefit with the Combination of Hydroxychloroquine and Azithromycin in Patients with Severe COVID-19 Infection." *Médecine et Maladies Infectieuses*, vol. 50, no. 4, June 2020, p. 384, https://doi.org/10.1016/j.medmal.2020.03.006.

Moore, Jason W., editor. *Anthropocene or Capitalocene? Nature, History, and the Crisis of Capitalism*. PM Press, 2016.

Mushaben, Joyce Marie. "A Spectre Haunting Europe: Angela Merkel and the Challenges of Far-Right Populism." *German Politics and Society*, vol. 38, no. 1, Mar. 2020, pp. 7–29.

Nesse, Randolph M. *Good Reasons for Bad Feelings: Insights from the Frontier of Evolutionary Psychiatry*. Dutton Books, 2019.

Overbeek, Henk. "Globalization, Neo-liberalism, and the Employment Question." *The Political Economy of European Employment: European Integration and the Transnationalization of the (Un)Employment Question*, edited by Overbeek, Routledge, 2003, pp. 13–28, www.taylorfrancis.com/chapters/edit/10.4324/9780203010648-3/globalization-neo-liberalism-employment-question-henk-overbeek.

Pagani, Isabel, et al. "Origin and Evolution of SARS-CoV-2." *The European Physical Journal Plus*, vol. 138, no. 2, 2023, article 157. *SpringerLink*, https://doi.org/10.1140/epjp/s13360-023-03719-6.

Penner, L. A., et al. "Prosocial Behavior: Multilevel Perspectives." *Annual Review of Psychology*, vol. 56, 2005, pp. 365–92.

Pennycook, Gordon, et al. "Prior Exposure Increases Perceived Accuracy of Fake News." *Journal of Experimental Psychology: General*, vol. 147, no. 12, 2018, pp. 1865–80, https://doi.org/10.1037/xge0000465.

Pickrell, Joseph K., and David Reich. "Toward a New History and Geography of Human Genes Informed by Ancient DNA." *Trends in Genetics*, vol. 30, no. 9, Sept. 2014, pp. 377–89, https://doi.org/10.1016/j.tig.2014.07.007.

Pilleggi, Tamar. "Embracing Racism, Rabbis at Pre-Army Yeshiva Laud Hitler, Urging Enslavement of Arabs." *The Times of Israel*, 30 Apr. 2019, www.timesofisrael.com/embracing-racism-rabbis-at-pre-army-yeshiva-laud-hitler-urge-enslaving-arabs/.

Rauber, Fernanda, et al. "Ultra-processed Food Consumption and Risk of Obesity: A Prospective Cohort Study of UK Biobank." *European Journal of Nutrition*, vol. 60, no. 4, 2021 pp. 2169–80. *SpringerLink*, https://doi.org/10.1007/s00394-020-02367-1.

Rawls, John. *Justice as Fairness: A Restatement.* Edited by Erin I. Kelly, Harvard UP, 2001.

Rosefielde, Steven. "Excess Collectivization Deaths 1929–1933: New Demographic Evidence." *Slavic Review*, vol. 42, no. 1, spring 1984, pp. 83–88, https://doi.org/10.2307/2498736.

Sbarra, David A., et al. "Smartphones and Close Relationships: The Case for an Evolutionary Mismatch." *Perspectives on Psychological Science*, vol. 14, no. 4, July 2019, pp. 596–618, https://doi.org/10.1177/1745691619826535.

Schick, Theodore, and Lewis Vaughn. *How to Think about Weird Things: Critical Thinking for a New Age.* 5th ed., McGraw-Hill, 2008.

Scott, Helen. "Was There a Time before Race? Capitalist Modernity and the Origins of Racism." *Marxism, Modernity, and Postcolonial Studies*, edited by Crystal Bartolovich and Neil Lazarus, Cambridge UP, 2002, pp. 167–82.

Sidanius, Jim, et al. "Social Dominance Theory: Its Agenda and Method." *Political Psychology*, vol. 25, no. 6, 2004, pp. 845–80.

Silk, Joan B. "Reciprocal Altruism." *Current Biology*, vol. 23, no. 18, 2013, pp. R827–R828, https://doi.org/10.1016/j.cub.2013.03.052.

Silverman, Craig. "This Analysis Shows How Viral Fake News Stories Outperformed Real News on Facebook." *BuzzFeed News*, 16 Nov. 2016, www.buzzfeednews.com/article/craigsilverman/viral-fake-election-news-outperformed-real-news-on-facebook.

Snyder-Mackler, Noah, et al. "Social Status Alters Chromatin Accessibility and the Gene Regulatory Response to Glucocorticoid Stimulation in Rhesus Macaques." *Proceedings of the National Academy of Sciences of the United States of America*, vol. 116, no. 4, 11 Dec. 2019, pp. 1219–28, https://doi.org/10.1073/pnas.1811758115.

Spellman, Frank R., and Joan Price-Bayer. *In Defense of Science: Why Science Literacy Matters.* Government Institutes, 2011.

Spratt, David, and Ian Dunlop. "Existential Climate-Related Security Risk: A Scenario Approach." Breakthrough: National Centre for Climate Restoration, May 2019, docs.wixstatic.com/ugd/148cb0_b2c0c79dc4344b279bcf2365336ff23b.pdf.

Stauffer, R. L., et al. "Human and Ape Molecular Clocks and Constraints on Paleontological Hypotheses." *Journal of Heredity*, vol. 92, no. 6, 2001, pp. 469–74.

Stout, Dietrich, and Thierry Chaminade. "Stone Tools, Language and the Brain in Human Evolution." *Philosophical Transactions of the Royal Society B*, vol. 367, no. 1585, Jan. 2012, pp. 75–87, https://doi.org/10.1098/rstb.2011.0099.

Thames, April D., et al. "Experienced Discrimination and Racial Differences in Leukocyte Gene Expression." *Psychoneuroendocrinology*, vol. 106, Aug. 2019, pp. 277–83, https://doi.org/10.1016/j.psyneuen.2019.04.016.

Trotsky, Leon. *The Revolution Betrayed: What Is the Soviet Union and Where Is It Going?* 1936. Pathfinder Press, 1973.

Weiner, Rachel, et al. "Republican Loyalty to Trump, Rioters, Climbs in Three Years after Jan. 6 Attack." *The Washington Post*, 2 Jan. 2024, www.washingtonpost.com/dc-md-va/2024/01/02/jan-6-poll-post-trump/.

Williams, Peter, and David Wallace. *Unit 731: Japan's Secret Biological Warfare in World War II.* The Free Press, 1989.

Wilson, Carter A. *Racism from Slavery to Advanced Capitalism.* Sage Publications, 1996.

Zeder, Melinda A. "Central Questions in the Domestication of Plants and Animals." *Evolutionary Anthropology*, vol. 15, 2006, pp. 105–17.

Actorvism = Actor + Activism

Harry Lennix

There has never been a time in the history of our republic that the concept of social justice has been as well financed, politically endorsed, or popularly championed. Public figures, including actors, athletes, and the like, are making a point of associating their private identities with social activism. In turn, there is a novel tendency for movement leaders to eagerly interpolate a celebrity's political opinion into the public sphere. This essay considers the particular case of a professional actor in this recent trend.

Actors are behaviorists whose chief methodology is mimesis. How then can anyone other than the individual autonomous actor ever know what deeply held convictions, ideals, or principles are inherent to an actor or are carryovers from an actor's study or assignment? Indeed, how can actors, whose chief duty is to manifest the position of alternative psyches, ever be certain what position they personally hold? To undertake the vocation of acting is therefore to forego, as a conscious choice, any credibility in the promotion of social or political agendas as an autonomous entity. However, by their very function, actors are activists, influencers, and agents provocateurs. I use the term *actorvist* to indicate actors who voluntarily relinquish their own wills to the wills of the spectators at the point of engagement with any particular cause that aims to power change and progress with a social system. Since an actor will be judged for the persuasiveness of their acting rather than for the reason they are acting, their best hope for propagating social justice is through utilizing the machinery of craft in which they are engaged rather than self-expression.

Though examples abound in classical philosophy to illuminate the unique paradox of an actor's function in society, perhaps there is nothing that is so apt as one in religious history. I use as premise for this exploration of actors engaged in social justice work the case and cause of Genesius of Rome. As related in Acts of the Martyrs, Genesius received a divine revelation while performing a comedy ridiculing the rite of baptism for the Christian-hating Emperor Diocletian. The actor's reward for announcing his real-time conversion was torture and beheading ("Saint Genesius"), which almost certainly would not have happened had he simply stuck to the script.

In theory, such a fatal critique would not likely happen today in the so-called free world. Hard-won tolerance of religion, self-identification, and self-direction is to a large extent codified into the laws of Western societies, and some actors have been compelling populist figures on both sides of the political spectrum. Still, actors must tread soberly into any fray where they actively dare to undermine governmental or capital-based power systems (frequently coterminous). Yet a true crusade for justice must include within its definition and mandate the absolute disruption of such oppressive systems.

In spite of Immanuel Kant's categorical imperative, one wonders why actors, who make their living in commercial entertainment, would ever take on the burden of participating in activities that are at odds with the aims of the culture industry upon which their efficacy relies ("Culture Industry"). After all, part of Kant's method is conditioned upon the interrogatives "What ought I to do?" and "What may I expect?" Actors could reasonably predict damage to their popular reputations and a decrease in lucrative work while in the pursuit of self-limiting causes such as justice. Further, how can an actor, whose obligation it is to submit their will and ego in a process to achieve a fusion of identification with a narrative figure—and not to be "actually" themselves—be considered reliable in promotion of a social cause? Finally, per the moral argument—which this matter ultimately is—why might anyone hope to achieve, even anticipate, a widespread and desirable response to their engagement with social causes?

In what follows, I demonstrate that any realistic aspiration to bring about social justice while engaged in commercial endeavors is bound to arrive at frustration in one or both areas. Yet there may be a way to transcend this quandary. Examples from our recent and distant past inspire a rational hope in the objective of progress and change, but, in the age-old methodology of making our case, we must first set the stage.

What Is Social Justice?

For that matter, what do we mean by *justice* itself? This is a concept perhaps better left to the poet than to the polity. Contained within its definition is the idea of an objective and universal treatment of a citizenry. Its meaning involves the idea of a proportional and deserved response to an action, claim, or condition of being. Within the US system of government, justice is positioned as a cardinal virtue endowed to us by "Nature" as an aspect of its law ("Declaration of Independence"). Notwithstanding this precept, we note that the west pediment of the Supreme Court building positions justice as secondary to law in its architectural inscription, "Equal Justice under Law." Social justice, then, if it is to be, must be endorsed and enacted by—indeed represented within—the laws of the local and national governments.

Objectionable policies at the heart of the social unrest of recent years are once again before the United States Congress and Supreme Court. As of this writing, however, no coherent definition of the nature or agenda of social justice has found consensus. To some, social justice consists of reparations to the descendants of enslaved people. To others, addressing social justice means defunding police departments of state and local governments, setting international environmental mandates, enshrining 2SLGBTQIA+ rights, limiting the restrictions resulting from the COVID-19 pandemic, and other actions. Social justice is, in effect, an extension of the ideals of the civil rights movement. Whereas the civil rights movement sought to correct the articles and enforcement of existing laws as practiced, social justice takes aim at correcting the very definition of the language that composes the law. Hence, much of the philosophy that underpins the general aims of social justice is indistinguishable from critical race theory (see "Critical Race Theory").

From this vantage, one may understand the concept of social justice as equal treatment through the unbiased application of law, the equitable distribution of the commonly held material resources of a nation, and absolute fairness of representation in the governmental, financial, and cultural systems that hold dominion over a population. Justice must be, then, a civitas; that is, political inclusion determined by common agreement and, to a lesser extent, by common definition ("Civitas"). *Common* cannot, however, be synonymous with *majority*, as it was in the Jim Crow era or post–World War I Germany, where an empowered polity denied the personhood of those outside its ethnicity. Decisions by a privileged group outnumbering those whom Howard Thurman deemed the "Disinherited" cannot be presumed to be justice (Winn). Notwithstanding, justice can exist in a consensus. Courage cannot. As Frederick Douglass reminds us,

> Power concedes nothing without a demand. It never did and it never will. Find out just what any people will quietly submit to and you have found out the exact measure of injustice and wrong which will be imposed upon them, and these will continue till they are resisted with either words or blows, or with both. The limits of tyrants are prescribed by the endurance of those whom they oppress.

In the case of the United States, even with its history of unequally applied laws, the government stipulates in its Declaration of Independence that the "consent of the governed" is the inarguable precondition to deriving the "just" powers that tolerate their existence.

Here, *consent* implies free choice, an essential precept in the achievement of any form of justice. The argument is largely one of the entitlements due from one segment of the society to another or, rather more optimally, from one human-made system of power to the populace.

No accurate recipe of the ingredients of social justice can leave out the principle of economic reforms that would benefit the politically marginalized and financially vulnerable masses. Lorraine Hansberry renders this point in *A Raisin in the Sun* with an exchange between Mama and Walter, mother and son:

> *Mama: (Quietly)* Oh—*(Very quietly)* So now it's life. Money is life. Once upon a time freedom used to be life—now it's money. I guess the world really do change . . .
>
> *Walter:* No—it was always money, Mama. We just didn't know about it.
>
> *Mama:* No . . . something has changed. *(She looks at him)* You something new, boy. In my time we was worried about not being lynched and getting to the North if we could and how to stay alive and still have a pinch of dignity too [. . .] You ain't satisfied or proud of nothing we done. I mean that you had a home; that we kept you out of trouble till you was grown; that you don't have to ride to work on the back of nobody's streetcar—You my children—but how different we done become. (74)

Hansberry's dialogue illustrates the inevitable evolution of the cause of social justice from generation to generation. Mere freedom cannot be considered a great accomplishment in a society where that freedom is guaranteed by right. Life and liberty, after all, are granted as inalienable rights, along with the pursuit of happiness. Arguably, this third pillar is the de facto raison d'être of this movement, that is to say a material and financial manifestation of full inclusion into a capitalist society. The most salient elements of social justice are contained within the law already. Constitutional amendments 14, 15, and 19, along with the Civil Rights Acts of 1964 and 1968, are matters of settled law. Indeed, the Constitution, if it were ever put into full effect, requires not one more amendment to achieve a truly just society. To the credit of the structuralists and philosophers from whose work the current movement draws its most potent ideas, the entire proposition rests upon redefining, or rather expanding, the field of players who populate these intersecting and interlocking systems.

The insoluble paradox is that branches of our society are built upon and caused to thrive on account of the inequities within these unjust systems. More specifically, in a culture industry, relative ideals such as beauty, physical fitness, charm, and skill are designed to create conditions of a hierarchy where distinctions are preferred. In the currency of our contemporary cause célèbre, the distinction is not one of material or physical standards but of adoptions of internal or moral virtues: Who do you support politically? What causes do you promote outside your profession? What do you eat, and to whom do you owe your moral duty?

The answers to such questions are scrutinized with as much zeal as is the devotion to one's vocation. Much of this is largely played out on social media, where, from behind a screen, people may reveal their true thoughts as private individuals—or cannily promote a public persona, or both. In this virtual space, actors can break away from their professional roles and take up credible causes as themselves. Although there is no foolproof way to determine the level of sincerity of an "actorvist" or any social media user, we can measure the level of consistency between the expressed and promoted position over time and the individual's behavior. That is, do the private and public identities conflict or harmonize?

If anything, public pronouncements most often demonstrate what justice is not. It is not, for example, sermonizing and condescension. It is not empty rhetoric or platitudes put forth by vacuous politicians whose public statements and private behavior frequently conflict. It is not a promise of good intentions. Nor is it achieved by printing banalities on a football pitch or basketball court or on the Internet. It cannot power itself by its mere existence as an ideal, structuralism aside. Justice is not something that multinational corporations or state-sponsored organizations tend to promote without first redefining it and then controlling its terms. Governments, and those who operate the media by their sanction, inevitably define the parameters of what is permissible with regard to justice.

Justice employs legislation and policy to equitably promote a sense of well-being and a sense of security, and our concern for justice must always be to ensure the immutable requirements that demonstrate justice in action. What this might look like in practice relies upon an agreed-to set of conditions and a commitment to a code of ethics that unseats systems that oppress those on the fringes of power who have been denied access to the full benefits of the US social contract.

Still, new and traditional modes of ethical shifts will not result in a natural development of a just nation by themselves. Justice depends upon advocates who champion its aims, articulate its cause, and model its effects. It requires living and breathing models as proof of its viability—an actualization of its plausibility. To this end, an actor, one who operates within these systems as an insider who frequently represents themselves as an everyperson, or even an outsider, might well suffice.

What Is the Actor?

Cypher, in *The Matrix*, offers a common material definition of an actor as one with stature and an ability to forget or ignore one's own personal and communal histories in embodying another's real or imaged reality: "I don't want to remember nothing. Nothing . . . you understand? And I want to be rich. You know, someone important, like an actor." In the strictest sense of the word, an actor is someone who does something. That is to say, an actor is an individual participating in an event. For our purposes, it is an individual taking part in a public performance, though it can also be something more. There are occasional cases where the actor *becomes* the event.

Western history ascribes to Thespis the distinction of having been the first actor. Legend holds that while taking part in a religious festival (here again the sacred aspect is present), Thespis launched into the recitation of poetry, transforming his location into a performance space, carrying within himself the story in the form of the characters who related the events. He literally embodied the narrative in character and description for the first time in a moment of inspired improvisation, thereby initiating the idea of "acting" as we have come to understand it. This is a stirring history and, in its own way, a heroic discovery of human potential. The metamorphosis must have been startling to the spectators, something akin to a magician's performance as both source and object of a magic trick.

However, if the profession of acting is ever to gain the credibility it deserves, the craft of acting will have to be approached as more of a science. The leap to science need not be so arduous. Acting as a field of study is but a subset of anthropology. Anthropology has termed our earliest human predecessor Homo habilis, meaning "handy man." We might reasonably assume that Homo habilis was doing more than making and using tools for some self-motivated reason; the tools must have served a need in the community. But Homo habilis might also have been named Homo narratoris—a teller of stories.

As researchers in a scientific, cultural field, actors are obligated to refrain from unduly impacting the area in our purview of observation. The Hawthorne effect, however flawed, suggests that our study alone of the subjects we portray, without action to further influence the object of observation, is already a burden to overcome for a conscientious actor ("Hawthorne Effect"). By our very definition, actors are already activists. Nonetheless, an actor of integrity has a duty to the scientific method. While in the process of study or performance, there must be no intrusion of our opinion upon the figures we embody or their actions lest we agitate the field under observation. To breach this protocol would subject the offender to justifiable condemnation. Actors, in action, are a medium only—even when portraying themselves. Actors presenting themselves as themselves and not in service to the character they embody are unworthy of their craft, or so the theory goes.

On the other hand, differences exist between artists and scientists. A scientist is expected to be conscientious, while most artists feel compelled to have a conscience. As private beings, actorvists have a right to opinions about the characters they portray. They have, even, a debt as independent citizens to the society in which they live. The primary issue to the actorvist of conscience becomes this question: Where does my sacred obligation lie—with my vocation (acting) or to a social cause (activism)? How the actor answers this question determines the degree and manner of inner struggles to be assumed.

Special consideration is and should be given to the ethical expectations we have of artists. There has always been a more relaxed boundary allowed to accommodate an artist's need for more and deeper human experiences. It is permissible, even encouraged, to "lie" while one is acting, for example. We are unavoidably taking part in a form of identity theft or fraud. Our dispensation from requirements such as honesty is granted in our assignments. At best, we are living examples of the "liar's paradox" of classical philosophy.[1]

In establishing our duty to the vocation of acting, we must first consider what the expectations are. William Shakespeare's works are a good place to start. Hamlet has strong words about this specialized category of person, how they show up in society, and how they ought to be treated: "let them be well used, for they are the abstract and brief chronicles of the time. After your death you were better have a bad epitaph than their ill report while you live" (2.2.503–06). In these terms, players are not persons: they "are" (not "are like") the "abstract and brief chronicles of the time." They embody and impersonate an abstract reality made flesh. They are, effectively, epiphenomena of actual human beings or personifications of metaphysical attributes.

In *The Tempest*, Shakespeare doubles down on the theme of the gossamer nature of the actor's substance: "These our actors, as I foretold you, are all spirits / And are melted into air, into thin air . . ." 4.1.148–50). Macbeth alludes to

> . . . a walking shadow, a poor player
> That struts and frets his hour upon the stage,
> And then is heard no more. It is a tale
> Told by an idiot, full of sound and fury,
> Signifying nothing. (5.5.24–28)

To the extent that seismology registers impacts of earth-moving events, or that an aftershock results in measurable consequence, an actor is best understood as the resulting fallout from these initial causalities. Actors, in fact, have no claim to an ontology while engaged in the execution of their professional duty. Indeed, by choice, actors are "nonbeings" granted admittance to a community in an effort by that community to find contracted delegates to represent it—something akin to a war correspondent or the now omnipresent videographer. That is, they are exposed and subject to the effects of the field of observation but are professionally prohibited from affecting it.

These are ways of thinking about the duty of the craft, the deontology that undergirds our profession. Under these conditions, we as actors are held to a standard of accountability that involves our dependability, bankability, and, as it were, word of honor. Our code is a commitment to the artful representation of human experience. Our competence lies in our ability to divert, misdirect, and elude detection as soldiers of fortune. Our chief means of doing so is the audience's pleasure in a dramatic presentation (mise-en-scène) and in our delivery of messages, be they platitudes, programming, or agitprop. As actors, our private being may be in perfect harmony with our professional duty as long as we accept that our sacred assignment is, even in tragedy, to provide a form of pleasure. As Theodor Adorno clarifies, "Pleasure always means not to think about anything, to forget suffering even where it is shown. Basically it is helplessness. It is flight; not, as is asserted, flight from a wretched reality, but from the last remaining thought of resistance" (Adorno and Horkheimer 144). There is seldom any conflict in the devotion to such principles as long as we do not make moral judgments as private persons. Morality in execution of the craft is left to a producer and patron, never to a performer. Once undertaken, the assignment itself takes precedence. All consideration of ethics is to be contained within the aesthetics of the presentation. It is to this that an actor is ultimately committed.

To achieve the level of expertise requisite for a career in acting, an actor must endeavor to master every aspect of the set of skills that enable their employment. These skills include, but are not limited to, a seamless integration of character with a self-contained psyche who agrees to turn over to the cause and effects of a mimetic event their very will and agency. An actor's professional duty is to engage their own persona, their gestures, and their utterances to become an agent in a representative event that advances narrative events. Any breach of this trust is a desecration of the craft. Actors bind their autonomous and private selves to any positions associated with their duties as paid performers within a narrative. Professional players dedicate their individual ontology to the projects and ends of a cause or enterprise from which they derive their value (material or otherwise). To breach this divide of the two states of the sacred (performance) and profane (private life) by presuming to "awaken" the social and moral consciousness of the people is to be willing to risk self-immolation. It would be difficult to imagine, for example, an action film star who personally abhors gun violence publicly urging audiences not to see their movie.

As professional pretenders, we may arrogate to ourselves a dispensation from ethical culpability since aesthetics is separate from ethics and exists as a cause unto itself. Once again, Adorno argues:

> The work of art still has something in common with enchantment: it posits its own, self-enclosed area, which is withdrawn from the context of profane existence, and in which special laws apply. Just as in the ceremony the magician first of all marked out the limits of the area where the sacred powers were to come into play, so every work of art describes its own circumference which closes it off from actuality. (Adorno and Horkheimer 19)

Whether the performer accepts as true what they are saying or doing is of no importance; theirs is not to believe but, rather, to persuade. They may convince their observer of the ethical rectitude of an agenda, a course of action, or an emotional response. Through their expertise, they persuade their subjects to believe in *them*—the final reward for their mastery. This achievement is sufficiently noble in itself, presuming that a presentation has aesthetic merit. In essence, a performance *is* a social statement.

A plausible claim to ethical virtues such as advancing social justice causes, then, can be made only when there is total consistency between an actor's complete commitment to a cause and their performance in service of the same cause. Hence, we have arrived at the unavoidable dilemma with which we began: To what does an actor owe their chief obligation—to their vocation or to the society to which they belong? Can it be both? And, if so, which takes primacy?

What Has an Actor to Do with Social Justice?

The cause of social justice carries with it a demand on the very celebrity status of an actor. It is a ponderous demand. How much involvement as private citizen will an actor's career abide before the ability to disappear within a role is compromised? To combine citizen activism with professional acting would be to jeopardize both the integrity of the work and that of the actor taking it on. To adopt an acting career is almost to forgo any credibility in the promotion of social or political agenda as an autonomous entity. Attempts to appease both professional and private agendas are fraught with peril. One inevitably takes precedence. To accomplish the integration of both would be to accomplish something akin to the mystery of the hypostatic union, a claim unique to Christ, who put it more clearly: "And if a house be divided against itself, that house cannot stand" (*Holy Bible*, Mark 3.25).

Abraham Lincoln applied this principle to the United States in recognition of the imminent catastrophe of the American Civil War. If it applies to the whole of the polis, then it must certainly apply to an actor employed as a representative thereof. When there are moral demands made by society that are at variance with the nature of an artist's duty, both systems of principles are compromised and doomed to fail. Those in the social sphere will correctly make the claim that the actor is engaged in virtue signaling as self-promotion, currying favor by appeasing the zeitgeist while profiting as a private citizen from a corrupted system built upon elitism. Alternatively, the heads of the industry where the artist is benefiting can make the plausible claim that an actorvist is unreliable, a shameless hypocrite biting the hand that feeds them.

Unquestionably, the advent of social media has exacerbated the dilemma of the actorvist as public figure and private citizen. It is now possible to know instantaneously what actors think of any number of social or political issues. Opinions may be offered with no prompting or editing, defining the moral positioning of anyone, famous or "Internet famous." Such social media activity can effectively extend the lifespan of movements and events. For instance, in the aftermath of the murders by police officers of Mike Brown, in Ferguson, Missouri, and George Floyd, in Minneapolis, Minnesota, at least two dynamic actorvists emerged as voices for the cause of Black Lives Matter (BLM): Kendrick Sampson and Jesse Williams. Much of their credibility in speaking to the frustrations of life in Black America in the pursuit of justice for the killing of unarmed Black men by the police stemmed from the fact that they were risking their personal and professional livelihoods. Fortunately, the results demonstrated a successful use of their public profiles and digital platforms. Indeed, the BLM movement as a phenomenon demonstrated the power of social media to sustain attention and to withstand the inevitable scrutiny that follows when the results do not line up with the call to justice.

Personal statements on social media do not always carry high risk, particularly when they espouse opinions that are both popular and sanctioned by those who run the platforms. Bravery is not a precondition of justice, and the absence of it in such cases does not preclude the ultimate goal of achieving it. Integrity, though, is a function of justice, and transparent hypocrisy undermines it. There is no exception for the professional hypocrites otherwise known as actors. Instead, as Lincoln went on to suggest, the actor of true virtue must make a choice for one or the other or risk exile from both sides. On the one hand, expulsion from the fellowship of actors carries with it damage to the actor's reputation as a skillful artisan. On the other, society may brand the actor as a meretricious faker (as their profession dictates they must be) seeking public praise for personal humility along with the trappings of fame. The sole remedy for this conflict is in adherence to the wisdom of Otto Ludwig's aphorism: "The highest that he could rise to then was to die gloriously for something; now he rises to the greater, to live humbly for something" (qtd. in "Mark"). Arguably, this was not an option for Genesius. Undoubtedly, he would have been willing to live humbly for his newly adopted faith, but in a moment of true bravery, he abandoned his craft. As a believer in the faith and a former Catholic seminarian, I admire his fortitude in the critical moment. I can also imagine understanding the emperor's outrage, even if I cannot endorse his response.

Genesius had breached the code of the magi, as it were, and revealed his inner soul—a soul pure but doomed to be short-lived. We actors revere our patron saint as a zealot, a true believer, a martyr, and, as one might view it, the very first "method actor"—that is, one who interpolates or conflates their own emotional and spiritual reality with that of the character being presented. Genesius, then, is an exemplar of combining personal and civic action. How astonishing it must have been to see a player admonish a tyrant in public during a performance. This action is the very essence of speaking truth to power, one of the bedrock components of being an actorvist.

In Genesius's time, Christians used the structures of Roman dominance—namely, the physical infrastructure of roads—for the propagation of faith. The groundwork has always to be laid before the message can successfully be delivered. In our new age, that pathway is no longer stone or asphalt but an industry built upon ethereal media superstructures or platforms. The pathways for delivering justice have, therefore, necessarily changed, and with them, God—the initial inspiration of the cardinal virtue of justice—has been redefined. This replacement of moral compulsion with purely personal or even societal benefit needlessly dooms the causes of actorvists to futility.

Nietzsche posited that "God is dead," killed by the arrival of an enlightened time (167). But he did suppose that the pillars of His existence remained as self-sufficient ends unto themselves. The humanism that informs the current social justice era is nevertheless a matter of moral urgency, at least to those who take on the burden. In the final piece of Kant's imperative, we must consider what awaits those actors in our new millennia who choose to pick it up. What may an activist expect?

What Case Studies Show

In a time where commercial viability is in itself the chief form of currency, even actorvists who are not subject to a despot's wrath are gambling the exposure of their total beings. The more they promote their personal agendas outside of their professions, the thinner the veil becomes between them and their dramatic creations.

At the close of the Civil War, John Wilkes Booth was the epitome of the actorvist, a point underscored by the fact that his murderous treason took place in a theater. He fatally shot President Lincoln, then leapt to the stage—breaking his leg—and denounced the greatest US president as a tyrant. Perhaps Edwin Forrest's jingoism from a generation earlier provided inspiration for Booth and the nationalistic propaganda of John Wayne. In 1849, the American actor Forrest and the English actor William Macready's respective patriotism (a "social cause") with regard to performance styles resulted in the loss of at least twenty-two souls during the Astor Place Riot ("Astor Place Riot"). John Wayne, a century later, was a dependable patriot on and off screen. Whatever our opinions of his personal ethical standards (eluding military service, for example), his social identity never deviated from the principles he advocated in his performances; John Wayne, the actor, appeared consistent with John Wayne, the private citizen.

Ronald Reagan began his executive career as the head of the Screen Actors Guild, a labor union whose purview involved rights and, therefore, justice for actors. His visible activism helped him advance to the presidency of the United States.

Arnold Schwarzenegger, an actor who became the governor of California ("Governorship"), likewise remained consistent on- and off-screen as a warrior and US patriot—even though he was not born in the United States—until he left public office, at which time he began to tack along a more liberal course on some issues. His inclusion here illustrates the irreconcilable dichotomy between the presentations and public functions that made his fortune and the positions he now takes as a private citizen.

Jane Fonda, in contrast, politicized and circumscribed her career by taking socially motivated stances for which she was scrutinized and labeled a traitor, a hypocrite, and the like. Whatever truth there is to her public reception, in Fonda's ascendancy, she took stances that were daring and unlikely to be to her personal advantage. Her career suffered unquestionably from her political advocacy, but her work was not inconsistent with her personal positions. In the current politicized climate, when calls for action, justice, and entitlements have created categories of groups and subsets clamoring for recognition and material support, the expression of personal opinions is virtually de rigueur for every actor in the industry, and Fonda's positions would be more a matter of marketing in which less consequential risk would be involved.

Black actors who were contemporaries of the aforementioned stars represented a political position just by showing up to work. Writ large, they had little to say about the social causes of the time. They frequently embodied those causes themselves. They carried with them, by their very presence as dramatis personae, a statement of position within the world. The fact that they were actors at all was evidence of a courage, fortitude, and resistance to commonly held expectations. Few Black actors who had achieved wide industry prominence and acclaim thus dared or bothered to weigh in on matters outside of the boundaries of their profession. Two twentieth-century performers who were not satisfied with their mere acceptance by the culture industry, however, were Sidney Poitier and Harry Belafonte. Poitier was a superb performer whose career was a giant leap for industry acceptance of Black people at the center of a cinematic event. Belafonte never had quite the same level of opportunity in the discipline of acting, but he made up for it in his laudable commitment when compared to Poitier's rather quiet advancement of the cause of social justice. Both men were active in the civil rights movement.

Through their performances within the medium itself, Poitier, Belafonte, Eartha Kitt, Ossie Davis, Diana Sands, and others contributed to the social standing, recognition, and (aspirational) acceptance of a historically rejected people. Advocacy for a virtuous cause can only be successfully accomplished and sustained when the cause is in the work itself. Thereby all who engage in the work and all that needs to be conveyed to achieve the objectives of this cause are in complete synthesis. In the feature film *The Greatest*, wherein he played himself, Muhammad Ali became the apotheosis of the actorvist. Here was the sublime integration of self-expression, social agenda, and narrative. No stronger metaphor can exist than a prizefighter who is also fighting systemic injustices such as religious persecution, racial discrimination, war, and hostile attitudes from his fellow combatants in the ring. Because of his standing as a literal and figurative fighter, Ali achieved a perfect fusion.

A compelling exception, however, exists with the case of Kim Kardashian. In spite of a thin acting résumé—in the sense of portraying figures apart from herself—she has achieved substantive progress on prison sentencing reform by leveraging her extraordinary social media profile and presence. In this case, she has influenced actual legislative reform despite critics' dismissal of her actions as virtue signaling (Phelps). Danny Glover has eluded any claims of self-serving, pursuing activism not through social media but through a lifelong commitment to empowering those on the margins here and abroad (Putnam-Walkerly).

Ultimately, however, the most enduring legacy for an actorvist is the work they produce as cocreators of the roles they take on. The ideas and causes propagated through our craft is perpetual in a way that our bodies, opinions, and personal ideas can never be. Even when not filmed or otherwise captured, the characters we choose to play endure beyond our mortal coil and remain for the living to inhabit. In the consistent, eternal, enduring performance of characters outside of ourselves, we are at our most convincing.

The Personal as Political as Professional

My interest in the potential for a socially motivated metanarrative extends beyond my love of acting. Very early in my life, I had what I still consider to be the noble intention of becoming a Catholic priest. In those formative years at Archbishop Quigley Preparatory Seminary, the idea of service to others as a way of life became a very real obligation—in fact, an inexorable duty of a life with any worthwhile meaning. I left the sanctuary of my environment to pursue a career in the muddied spiritual waters of the entertainment industry with the hope of bringing about a spiritual reawakening to as many people as possible through a more inclusive field of endeavor. The overall objective of providing joy, self-revelation, accurate representation of human experience, truth, and skillful execution has remained, even through my explorations of other religions or no religion at all.

Now, I have embraced again my former faith, and it has occurred to me that like the early evangelists, the Roman road system, meant to subjugate the empire's peons and collect their taxes, was perhaps the very best tool to promulgate the good news. My method is not to proselytize but to dramatically and truthfully represent the consequences of taking or avoiding the less-traveled road. This, I believe, is the highest aim of the artistic endeavor—to find the extraordinary in the everyday, to reveal the uniqueness in the uniform, and to allow an observer a path to aspects of a divine truth. It is my belief that this truth, once revealed, will impel those who receive it to act on behalf of all humankind.

Yet I also believe that throughout the history of civilization, aesthetics has been sufficient in or through itself to bring about social progress. The persuasive narrative has full power to transform individuals or the entire demographic from within by inspiring—indeed, provoking—the will of the subject into action through the process of imaginative expression of truth and beauty. Marred by the inherent limitations and contradictions of the medium that carries it, a perfect truth can make whole the medium itself or, at least, the vessel which exists within it.

NOTE

1. In the liar's paradox, a liar states that he is a liar and that he is lying, raising questions about how we might come to discern truth (that is, whether the liar is lying or telling the truth); see Beall et al.

WORKS CITED

Adorno, Theodor W., and Max Horkheimer. *Dialectic of Enlightenment.* 1947. Verso Books, 1997.

Ali, Muhammad. *The Greatest.* Directed by Tom Gries, Columbia Pictures, 19 May 1977.

"The Astor Place Riot: Shakespeare as a Flashpoint for Class Conflict in 1849." *Folger Shakespeare Library*, 9 May 2017, www.folger.edu/blogs/shakespeare-and-beyond/astor-place-riot-macbeth-new-york/.

Beall, J. C., et al. "Liar Paradox." *The Stanford Encyclopedia of Philosophy*, edited by Edward N. Zalta, spring 2011, Stanford U, plato.stanford.edu/archives/spr2011/entries/liar-paradox/.

"Civitas (Roman)." *A Dictionary of Greek and Roman Antiquities*, edited by William Smith, New York, 1872, pp. 260–62.

"Critical Race Theory." *Wikipedia: The Free Encyclopedia*, Wikimedia Foundation, 8 Nov. 2023, en.wikipedia.org/wiki/Critical_race_theory.

"Culture Industry." *Wikipedia: The Free Encyclopedia*, Wikimedia Foundation, 6 Oct. 2023, en.wikipedia.org/wiki/Culture_industry.

"Declaration of Independence: A Transcription." *America's Founding Documents*, National Archives, 2023, www.archives.gov/founding-docs/declaration-transcript.

Douglass, Frederick. "(1857) Frederick Douglass, 'If There Is No Struggle, There Is No Progress.'" *BlackPast*, 25 Jan. 2007, www.blackpast.org/african-american-history/1857-frederick-douglass-if-there-no-struggle-there-no-progress/.

"Governorship of Arnold Schwarzenegger." *Wikipedia: The Free Encyclopedia*, Wikimedia Foundation, 21 Oct. 2023, en.wikipedia.org/wiki/Political_career_of_Arnold_Schwarzenegger.

Hansberry, Lorraine. *A Raisin in the Sun.* 1959. A Raisin in the Sun *and* The Sign in Sidney Brustein's Window, by Hansberry, edited by Robert Nemiroff, New American Library, 1987, pp. 5–151.

"Hawthorne Effect." *Wikipedia: The Free Encyclopedia*, Wikimedia Foundation, 5 Oct. 2023, en.wikipedia.org/wiki/Hawthorne_effect.

Holy Bible. King James Version, Thomas Nelson Publishers, 1990.

Kant, Immanuel. *The Moral Law: Groundwork of the Metaphysics of Morals.* Translated by Jonathan F. Bennett, Psychology Press, 2005.

"The Mark of the Immature Man . . . ." *Quote Investigator*, 24 Nov. 2018, quoteinvestigator.com/2018/11/24/mature/.

The Matrix. Directed by Lana Wachowski and Lily Wachowski. Warner Brothers, 1999.

Nietzsche, Friedrich Wilhelm. *The Gay Science: With a Prelude in German Rhymes and an Appendix of Songs.* Translated by Walter Kaufmann, Vintage, 1974.

Phelps, Jordyn. "Kim Kardashian West Meets with Trump, Recently Commuted Ex-Prisoners at White House." *ABC News*, 4 Mar 2020, abcnews.go.com/Politics/kim-kardashian-west-meet-trump-recently-commuted-prisoners/story?id=69386103.

Putnam-Walkerly, Kris. "Danny Glover's Social Justice Secret: Organizations like Barrios Unidos Make the Difference." *Forbes*, 21 May 2021, www.forbes.com/

sites/krisputnamwalkerly/2021/05/21/danny-glovers-social-justice-secret-organizations-like-barrios-unidos-make-the-difference/.

"Saint Genesius." *Roman Catholic Saints*, 2011, www.roman-catholic-saints.com/saint-genesius.html.

Shakespeare, William. *Hamlet. The Norton Shakespeare: Based on the Oxford Edition*, Stephen Greenblatt, general editor, W. W. Norton, 1997.

———. *Macbeth.* Classic Books Company, 2001.

———. *The Tempest.* Classic Books Company, 2001.

Winn, Christian Collins. "Jesus and the Disinherited: Howard Thurman Still Speaks to the Church." *Christianity Today*, 11 June 2020, www.christianitytoday.com/ct/2020/june-web-only/jesus-and-disinherited.html.

Burning It Down Means Building Community

Multicultural Solidarity Coalition

Students who struggle to make a meaningful impact and to organize where they are must grapple with the contradictions of working within the university as an institutional structure and yearning to destroy it and to create something altogether different. Administrators lead students down a degrading path of co-optation, gaslighting, and other strategies of erasure used to silence us as key stakeholders. This essay explores our experience organizing as the Multicultural Solidarity Coalition (MSC). We are university abolitionists working in, with, through, around, and against the university as a means to an end (i.e., learning, an experience with truth that entails our commitment to the end of the university as we know it). In working within the university, we are repurposing its resources to self-radicalize (Kelley 154). While we acknowledge the value of education, we call for an end to its traumatic and oppressive institutionalization by lighting our matches and "burning it down" so that even the colonial roots of the university are scorched and we can rebuild our educational system on the foundation of liberation and justice.

Our use of the phrase "burn it down" acknowledges fire as a generative source. Historical and current images of cities being "burnt down" by grieving communities have been employed to indicate an uncontrolled threat. This perceived threat is used to justify the violent repression of the masses by the police and other institutions tasked with law enforcement and to justify increasing these forces' presence in our lives through containment policies of law and order. We see a connection between advancing the white supremacist colonial project and the need to stamp out the supposed chaos of fire: "That many of us have come to see fire as loss rather than renewal, destruction rather than creation, is bound at once to Western ideas of ecology and economy" (Clark and Yusoff 8). We use the words *fire* and *burning* intentionally to reference not only a process of generative destruction of the cisheteropatriarchal white supremacist settler order but also a practice of tending to the ecological cycles of the Earth (Kimmerer and Lake 39): a creative process of unleashing energy and an opportunity to change the landscape, recycle matter, and reconsider relations involved in core concepts like "learning." In this instance, the language of "burning it down" is also anarchistic in calling for the university to be reconstructed as a life-affirming endeavor rather than to continue as a violent apparatus of the state.

Broken Promises

On 4 April 2019, our university, located in the southwestern United States, held a career fair in which Customs and Border Patrol (CBP) was invited to recruit students on campus. In response to the threat that many undocumented students felt knowing that CBP was present on campus, a Latinx and Chicanx student group organized a protest outside the event. Carla Salazar,[1] an undergraduate student present at the protest, recalls that day as the first time she felt unsafe on campus and began to recognize the university as a violent space for students from marginalized communities. She remembers students yelling racist comments and throwing drinks at the protesters from the second floor of a nearby university building.

After this event, organizations for Chicanx, Latinx, and undocumented students met with university administrators several times to express concerns about the trauma and fear experienced by undocumented students as a result of the presence of CBP and Immigration and Customs Enforcement (ICE) on campus. Figures 1–3

Figure 1. Patriot Front flyer posted on the campus of Arizona State University (ASU), Tempe, in 2018.

Figure 2. "Stand your ground" flyer, featuring an image of Nicholas Sandmann, posted at ASU, Tempe, in 2019.

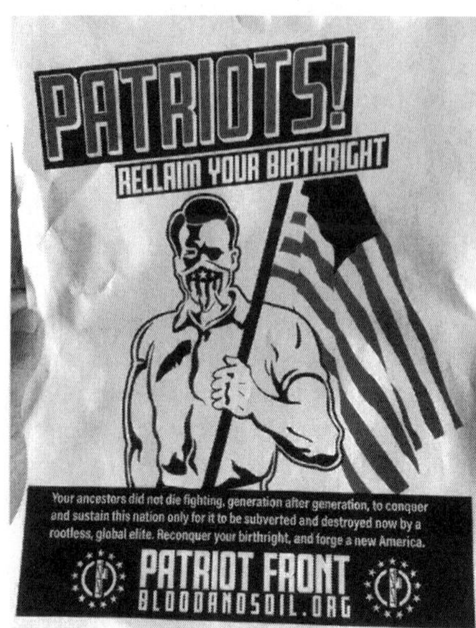

Figure 3. Patriot Front flyer posted at ASU, Tempe, in 2018.

provide some examples of the hostile messages posted around campus prior to the event. Carla remembers an administrator responding to their concerns by saying, "Well, you know why ICE was created, right? It was after September 11th to protect the country from terrorists. You can critique the agency, but it's to stop terrorism," ignoring the blatant weaponization of this government agency against migrants and the resulting criminalization of Black and Brown bodies. Claiming an inability to block ICE and CBP from recruiting at a public university and an obligation to cooperate with government agencies, the administration was only willing to agree to alert the student groups forty-eight hours in advance of CBP or ICE coming to campus.

In November 2019, only seven months later, the administration broke this promise when a Republican student group invited an ICE agent as a guest speaker without advance warning to the affected students. The student activists held another rally, this time alongside Palestinian students protesting the presence of the Israeli Defense Force (IDF) on campus (Quaranta and Nano). The result of this protest was not discourse leading to policy change but rather an investigation into student activists based on accusations of anti-Semitism. As witnesses to the intimate relationship that our university maintains with government institutions like ICE, CBP, and IDF at the cost of their students' mental health and well-being, we challenge the very design of the university and its entanglements with the state. We are students because we believe there is value in education, and we organize because we believe that real learning is anathema to corporatization, privatization, and militarization.

Inherent Violence

Thinking in terms of exploitation and the accumulation of capital allows us to bring history, politics, and economics to bear on our circumstances. We borrow from Cedric Robinson's argument that "[t]he development, organization, and expansion of capitalist society pursued essentially racial directions, so too did social ideology. As a material force . . . racialism would inevitably permeate the social structures emergent from capitalism. I have used the term 'racial capitalism' to refer . . . to the subsequent structure as a historical agency" (4). Expanding upon the relationship between racialization and the accumulation of capital, Jodi Melamed notes:

> Capital can only be capital when it is accumulating, and it can only accumulate by producing and moving through relations of severe inequality among human groups—capitalists with the means of production / workers without the means of subsistence, creditors/debtors, conquerors of land made property / the dispossessed and removed. These antinomies of accumulation require loss, disposability, and the unequal differentiation of human value, and *racism enshrines the inequalities that capitalism requires.* (1; emphasis added)

Thus, the university, as one of the social structures of capitalism, and one tasked with training future workers, is entirely permeated by racial-economic exploitation. To be a citizen of the university means to pay the price of admission, which is more than an exchange of currency. However, the price for students of color, 2SLGBTQIA+ people, and historically marginalized communities is elevated, and the tax is conformity to violent norms. In this way, those who continue fighting the battle from within must pay their pound of flesh. This tribute, claimed historically through extractionism and devastation of the land, is also exacted through the erasure strategies described below, including gaslighting, co-optation, and epistemic violence.

We name the university as an inextricable part of the maintenance—through violence—of racial capitalism and settler colonialism. Racial capitalism requires a human "surplus" that consists of "excess" populations who are ripe for extractable labor, profit, and disposability (Gilmore).[2] The modern university was not constructed with underserved populations in mind but rather to train wealthy, white boys to be the next generation of elites (Berlin 20–31). As Edwin Mayorga, Lekey Leidecker, and Daniel Orr de Gutierrez note, "The university . . . , birthed by colonialism, is an essential agent of extant colonial violence, both materially, in extracting, accumulating, and withholding resources from marginalized communities, and epistemically, in monopolizing legitimate knowledges" (9). Essentially, the university facilitates the "colonization of knowledge," a mission whose violence it must in turn conceal (7).[3]

Institutional Landscape

This essay documents our experiences as organizers within a specific sociopolitical context: Arizona State University (ASU). As one of the largest public educational institutions in the country, ASU is known for having been named "#1 in Innovation" by *US News and World Report* for several consecutive years ("ASU Named the Nation's Most Innovative University") and has gained notoriety for its New American University model. At the heart of this model is the 2014 university charter, which alleges ASU's success as measured "not by whom it excludes, but rather whom it includes and how they succeed" ("ASU Charter"). While this message may seem to connote an ideology of acceptance and tolerance, "[t]he system by which the college is funded means that it literally cannot afford to exclude students, even if it wanted to" (Fisher 23). Neoliberalism encourages the university to allow everyone in, but the intention is not to ensure students' success but rather to extract their intellectual property (i.e., research) for the benefit of the university. Fred Moten and Stefano Harney explain this idea further, stating that the university is "a credential-granting front for finance capitalism and a machine for stratification" ("The University: Last Words" 3). ASU promotes the New American University as an "innovative" business model and project. This project, like other neoliberal institutions, depends on severe worker precarity, a corporatized hierarchy of relational violence, and practices of monopolizing the economy of the Greater Phoenix area. For example, Arizona State University Enterprise Partners, the 501(c)(3) nonprofit dedicated to revenue generation, consists of five entities that identify new revenue opportunities ("About"). ASU sees the increase of revenue and the educational fulfillment of the charter as intimately imbricated. Embedded within the nonprofit structure of ASU Enterprise are for-profit ventures that illustrate the ways in which the public neoliberal university has become enmeshed in the private sector.[4]

To further contextualize ASU, one must understand the history of Arizona as a history of both Spanish and US colonization. ASU is a part of that history. Of the five ASU campuses, we focus on the Tempe campus, which is occupying part of the land of the Akimel O'odham and Piipaash peoples. The Tempe campus is situated between Apache Boulevard, Mill Avenue, Rural Road, and University Drive. The names of these roads hark back to the five *C*'s taught in Arizona public schools as the foundation of Arizona's statehood: copper, cattle, citrus, cotton, and climate. In more recent history, Arizona has made itself known for passing racist anti-immigration laws like Senate Bill 1070, banning bilingual education and ethnic studies with Proposition 203 and House Bill 2281, and forcing undocumented students to pay out-of-state tuition with Proposition 300 ("AZ Prop 300"). Considering the campus's proximity to the US-Mexico border and the fact that Indigenous languages and then Spanish were spoken here before English, it takes a great deal of enforcement through violent policies to enact and uphold these laws that run counter to the very makeup of the region. ASU, their police, and their ever-expanding presence in Arizona work to enforce these policies. ASU's reluctance to denounce hate speech on its campuses, citing the First Amendment as a reason to let neo-Nazis speak, and the fact that undocumented students are charged out-of-state tuition are both indicators of the university's deeply problematic ideological stance.

While we point the finger at ASU, we must also acknowledge that we, as students, are currently reluctant participants in this neoliberal project. We know that universities do not exist to support us, but we fight from within to create a liberated educational environment (Kelley 156). Although our experiences have taken place here, in a particularly right-wing, particularly corporate environment, we acknowledge and affirm that our experiences are not unique. We invite you, the reader, to replace our university name with your own to interrogate the ways in which all US universities are entangled with the neoliberal state. Our struggle is shared with student organizers across the country who fight against oppression.

School Stinks

For centuries, rote memorization, standardized testing, and disciplining students' bodies and minds have been deployed as pedagogical tools. Considering these traditional methods, we understand that teaching and schooling are not inherently transformative or liberatory. We cannot assume that teachers, even with the best intentions, are the vanguard of the revolution simply by virtue of their role as educators. In fact, teachers, because of their position within institutions, often operate as agents of the state whose aim is to build human capital, only to have that human capital exploited by the students' current and future employers. We are thus alienated from our work both as students and as teachers. We ponder whether the degrees, knowledge, and experiences we seek are worth the violence we are subjected to by the university. We offer this essay to document our movement, the violence of ASU as an apparatus of the state, and our hope that the lessons we have learned can be used by communities in struggle both in and outside the academy.

The many authors of this essay came together (on *Zoom*) in the summer of 2020 as proponents of the MSC. Our main purpose was to finalize a proposal for a multicultural center, coauthored over the course of two years by marginalized undergraduate and graduate students at our predominantly white institution. The MSC campaign seeks the implementation of our proposal in its entirety, including our demand to defund the ASU police department. Our campaign is led by Black, Indigenous, and other femmes of color. From our intersecting positionalities as BIPOC, 2SLGBTQIA+ and mostly femmes, we consider our university, like all other institutions in this country, as designed to disempower our communities—namely, women, BIPOC, neurodiverse people, folks with disabilities, 2SLGBTQIA+ people, migrants, the working class, and families in poverty. The primary aim of the university is to teach students how to be agents of the state, a socialization process that in many cases discourages critical thought and liberatory practices. One of the main goals of any university is to regulate, produce, and accumulate legitimate knowledge as a commodity. As we move through the university system, we are, in ways that are both immediate and slow, incorporated into the very institution we should despise. The system tries to train us, the oppressed, how to best serve the cisheteropatriarchal white supremacist state and the capitalist system. However, our role in the university is to be a part of the engine of social transformation (Kelley 157).

The Multicultural Center They Closed

In many ways, the university relies on the impoverishment of institutional memory. Students depart a few years after they arrive, and our transitory nature provides the conditions for a history that can be adjusted and rewritten by administrators to fit their rhetorical needs. For this reason, constructing our own historical memory of our institution—one that takes into account the reality of violence against marginalized communities—has been crucial to our organizing in helping us understand where to begin, where and how we fit in, and what demands were necessary to even attempt to address this violence. We learned that before the MSC campaign, which began in 2016, there was a group called Students against Discrimination (SAD), who embarked on a similar journey in the 1990s. The university newspaper reported that SAD's proposal was approved in 1996 and was in operation by 1998 (Anderson; L. Cruz). One of the spaces was known as the Intergroup Relations Center (IRC), meant to be an "instrument to expand the understanding of multicultural issues on this campus" (Anderson). The IRC disappeared sometime after 2008 for reasons unknown to us, but perhaps influenced by the economic recession occurring at that time. In addition to the IRC, there was a multicultural center housed in a separate physical space, meant "to combat the sense of dissociation from the university; the center dedicate[d] itself in enhancing the experience of minority students by providing services that assist[ed] in the successful transition, retention and graduation of minority students" (L. Cruz).

Lucía Obando, a student attending ASU from 2007 to 2011, remembers spending time in the multicultural center, located on the top floor of the student services building. She was active in student groups and remembers the space feeling safe and being the center of student activism. The student groups hosted multicultural events and study sessions where meals were also provided. Lucía remembers volunteering on campus to collect signatures to get the DREAM Act on the ballot and being met by hostile students who made her feel rejected and afraid as an undocumented student herself. The multicultural center was the only place she felt comfortable disclosing her undocumented status, because many of the students were going through similar experiences.

Despite Lucía's full-ride scholarship funded by a private donor to circumvent the Proposition 300 restrictions around federal funding for undocumented students, ASU threatened to take her funding away at the end of each semester, because it was contingent on the willingness of the private donor and not from a guaranteed funding source. Without this scholarship, Lucía would have been forced to pay out-of-state tuition that she could not afford. The multicultural center was the physical and political space where undocumented students, who do not have access to Free Application for Federal Student Aid (FAFSA), Pell Grants, or any other kinds of federal help, came together to organize fundraisers to pay each other's tuition and fees. At the multicultural center, Lucía and other undocumented students felt safe enough to share their status with one another and to get the support they needed rather than having to live in secret. Lucía's story, and the story of many others, are why we continue fighting for a multicultural center.

See Us

The first demand of the MSC proposal is "to recognize race and other marginalized identities" (*Executive Summary* 1). Ideologies that purport not to see race perpetuate racial inequalities by superficially erasing our identities without addressing the real oppression we face. These race-neutral ideologies ignore structural racism and undermine any effort to combat it. Equity does not mean treating everyone the same; equity means allocating more resources to those who are structurally disadvantaged. This means tracking retention and graduation rates of students of color, tailoring services and programs for these populations, and supporting these students to ensure their success. Throughout the researching and writing of the proposal, it was incredibly difficult to find retention and graduation rates of students of color at our institution. To identify the areas where students are struggling, demographic surveys must disaggregate race. At ASU, Middle Eastern students are tracked as white but face increased discrimination linked to Islamophobia and xenophobia. They should be disaggregated from the "white" racial category to better track their success. African international students and African American students have vastly different backgrounds and trajectories. However, they're also aggregated in the racial data that's publicly available to undergraduate students ("Facts"). We cannot see how students are really doing from data organized in such broad categories. How will any university become more equitable if it refuses to see us?

In the university, we are customers and laborers first, students second. We are viewed as empty vessels (Freire 79) to be filled with knowledge, because what we've learned in our communities and through our own lived experiences is not valued within academe. Not only our ways of relating to research but also our ways of theorizing are devalued. As Barbara Christian points out, "[P]eople of color have always theorized—but in forms quite different from the Western form of abstract logic. And I am inclined to say that our theorizing (and I intentionally use the verb rather than the noun) is often in narrative forms, in the stories we create, in riddles and proverbs, in the play with language, because dynamic rather than fixed ideas seem to our liking" (68). The university claims ownership over knowledge and has the power to determine which knowledges are acceptable and which are not. What we learn in our communities is deemed folk knowledge, and we are taught to refer to our community members as "laypeople" who possess no expertise. We experience this when our ancestral or Indigenous knowledge is discredited by academic demands for objectivity, evidence, and quantitative data that may not be easily extracted from the qualitative storytelling that is present in our communities (see Chilisa).

We are not treated as autonomous social subjects but rather as workers whose task is to produce knowledge for the university to own and accumulate like any other product on the capitalist market. As student workers, teaching assistants, and research assistants, we are underpaid not only metaphorically, in terms of the meager academic acknowledgment we receive, but also literally in the form of low wages. We are doubly exploited by the university, and many of us will spend our lives being forced to work to pay off our student loans. As an apparatus of the state, the university does not consider our humanity but rather our productivity. How else does a phrase like "publish or perish" become a common saying within academia?

Because our academic success depends on our adaptation to the university, we are essentially forced to compete to be the most exploited and most assimilated student to fulfill the expectations of the university and the larger society. When we labor under the delusion that the university exists as a neutral and benevolent site of learning, or falsely believe that the university operates as a site of subversion or counterintelligence production against the state, we may insist that the university cannot be thrown away, that the university is, in fact, one of our most precious tools. This lesson is inculcated in students, who experience their academic success as a personal, emotional, authentic expression of themselves.

Support Us

Our demand that the university "provide increased services for marginalized communities" seeks to combat the exploitation we describe (*Executive Summary* 1). This demand includes, but is not limited to, federal TRIO programs, the Louis Stokes Alliances for Minority Participation program (LSAMP), and Students Taking Action Reaching Stars (STARS).[5] We also outline the concept of a community learning fellowship that would provide an alternative to the traditional teaching assistant and research assistant positions, where graduate students are exposed more acutely to the scrutinizing and disciplining gaze of the academy and are asked to reproduce it as our job (3–5). Graduate students shouldn't be limited to scholarship based on knowledge claims made in the academy and for the academy. Knowledge production and claims to knowledge in our communities should be valued equally: "Our production of knowledge begins in the bodies of our mothers and grandmothers, in the acknowledgement of the critical practices of women of color before us. The most profound and liberating politics come from the interrogations of our own social locations, a narrative that works outward from our specific corporealities" (C. Cruz). Conforming to the rigid standards of academic knowledge production alienates us from the knowledge we have gained through our embodied experience of the world.

Because we are currently in an urgent moment of multiple crises, including a political uprising surrounding racial injustice, a global pandemic, exacerbated inequality, the further degradation of democracy, and environmental destruction, we are compelled to do work aimed at community liberation and not the economic development of the university.[6] The community learning fellowship would allow us to work side by side with communities directly impacted by the various exigencies we face. Because the people closest to the problem are the people closest to the solutions, we need to be working in our communities. Teaching and research assistantships as currently structured direct time and energy toward the reproduction of the university from the classroom rather than toward community goals. The assumption that all graduate students want to continue our academic research as scholars to become professors is a very limiting view of our potential to effect radical change in the world and in our communities.

While the community learning fellowship outlined in our proposal may fall under the larger umbrella of service learning or, more generally, social justice pedagogy, we reject the notion that these concepts are inherently liberatory. Social justice as a signifier is all but neutralized. We know social justice pedagogy only as it has existed or been imagined within the constraints of our colonial education system—which is to say, we don't actually know social justice pedagogy. It appears before us as a contradiction. Moving successfully through the university requires a disciplining of the self into a legible subject of the university by doing studenthood or branding oneself as a public intellectual.[7] There is a line of authority from the state legislature to the university president to the program director to the professor. We must pass through this gaze, not only in the structures of programs and hierarchized space between different levels of bosses but also as it appears in our classmates, in our curriculum, in our students, and in our professors. The logics of this ideology and its inflections thus show up in our classrooms, students, teachers, mentors, mentees, and administrators. Without an articulation against such manifestations and an explicit positioning toward liberation, the anti-Black logic of racial capitalism will continue to appear and constitute large roles in our structures and relations. Against the militarization and industrialization of the university, we argue that learning, and therefore our education, should center around healing and community building instead of carcerality. We want epistemic justice more than we want "successful" careers. We propose the community learning fellowship as one way to survive the violence and create loopholes through which we can begin reclaiming and redistributing the stolen wealth of the university.

Abolish Campus Police

We further confront university administrators' entanglement in the settler colonial project in our demand for noncooperation with ICE and CBP and the abolition of campus police. This demand recognizes "the need to address the hostility towards marginalized communities through trainings, services, and a safer environment" (*Executive Summary* 1). We know the police do not keep us safe. Students, faculty members, and staff members of color have been attacked and threatened by the militarized police force on college campuses.[8] Defunding the police is a first step towards the abolition of the carceral state. We echo abolitionists like Angela Y. Davis, Ruth Wilson Gilmore, Alexis Pauline Gumbs, and Mariame Kaba in contending that defunding and abolishing the police force is not a destructive process but rather a constructive process in which we imagine, reimagine, and implement systems of community-oriented safety and justice that do not take the form of retributive violence.[9] In this spirit, we ask that funds from the campus police department go directly to the multicultural center.

Rather than engaging with the true intention of our demand, our university administration responded by publishing a twenty-five-point plan, now known as the LIFT (Listen, Invest, Facilitate, Teach) Initiative, which states that "ASU commits to an ASU police force on which all officers have a baccalaureate degree or the opportunity to earn a baccalaureate degree if they do not have one" (Crow). The administration not only made it look as if they were considering our demand but also found a way to profit from it by turning their eighty-seven police officers into potential student-customers. While this does nothing to further our demand of abolishing the police, it appeases the general public, generates income for ASU, and increases the police budget: a real win-win-win situation except for us, the students, who were quickly exhausting the official channels without our proposal having been approved in its entirety.

Our understanding of the university has allowed us to anticipate the administration's moves to quell our movements and co-opt our demands. They wear us down to burn us out. In response, we strategize and we reorient. Our proposal includes a note on implementation that anticipates inaction and evasion tactics by making clear that

> [w]e call upon the university administration to show real intent to make the contents of this proposal a reality. We cannot accept the burden of producing all the plans for implementation. . . . When the time comes to implement the contents of this proposal, we intend to be present; we intend to hold to our vision and ensure that, in making it a reality, we do not become lost. (*Executive Summary* 17)

The Multicultural Solidarity Coalition has been a public-facing campaign precisely because we know that the meetings behind closed doors are meant to get us exactly nowhere.

Give Us a Place

On the surface, it may seem a contradiction to make demands of an institution we want to abolish, but the university will never be undone unless the patriarchy is, unless capitalism is, unless white supremacy is; and so we organize wherever we find ourselves. We recognize the need to be able to live well now, which is why we demand the creation of "a physical space for marginalized communities" (*Executive Summary* 1). The MSC campaign has held multiple public events, asking students about the university campus climate for students of color and other marginalized populations—religious, sexual, and gender minorities. We have heard repeatedly from marginalized students that they feel isolated, unheard, and unsafe on campus. There is no place for us to go where we feel safe and supported. Many students drop out of college, transfer, or become online students due to this hostility and sense of unbelonging.[10] A physical space for marginalized students would create a space of relative safety and solidarity.

Because education is not politically neutral, neither are educational spaces. Desmond Tutu has said, “If you are neutral in situations of injustice, you have chosen the side of the oppressor” (“Desmond Tutu”). In our case, the supposed neutrality of the university only reinforces violent power dynamics that marginalize our communities. It’s not just the campus police who have the capacity and willingness to punish us but also the administrators, professors, and classmates who wield their carceral ideologies against us. It’s a common belief of political and social conservatives that the university is the bastion of liberal ideology, responsible for radicalizing the youth. It is not.

Here, we have found each other and have begun to build trust and community through the work of demanding that our university provide a refuge where we can survive and navigate a hostile environment. The MSC has already become a space wherein community learning is taking place. While a traditional university constructs a hierarchy of power based on level of education (for example, undergraduates, graduate students, faculty members, and administrators), the MSC is a space where individuals with shared political commitments engage in collaborative dialogue to tackle the structural problems present at our university. This space, by design, acknowledges and affirms the importance of the unique contributions that all campaign members bring. This collaborative approach seeks to question and ultimately dismantle the hierarchies we have been trained to respect in exchange for horizontal learning. Why do we make any demands at all if we don’t expect them to be realized in a way that resembles our dreams of dismantling the university entirely? Because “we can begin the process of making community wherever we are” (hooks 143) and “in and through community lies the salvation of the world” (Peck 17). In essence, we are asking for fundamental changes to how our university engages with marginalized students, and our proposal provides a blueprint for how to begin addressing inequity more authentically. The multicultural center, however, is by no means the end goal of our work to abolish the university as an institutional structure.

Circular Meetings Going Nowhere

In June 2020, we hosted a virtual town hall to garner more community support and to put pressure on the ASU administration. This event was hosted on *Facebook* by the Black Graduate Student Association (BGSA) and the Graduate Women’s Association (GWA), because the presidents of those organizations were also members of MSC. In response to that event, the administration emailed the students who were presidents of BGSA and GWA along with the faculty supervisors of those groups. Because ASU only recognizes, and therefore reserves the right to control and punish, official student groups, MSC made the deliberate choice to maintain its status as an unofficial student organization to preserve our autonomy. However, in this instance, members' participation in officially recognized groups gave ASU an avenue to try to rein us in by alerting our faculty advisers, who were not a part of MSC, that they should attend a meeting with administrators to discuss the town hall we had held. We responded by email on 4 July 2020, requesting that the administrators meet with MSC in its entirety "so that you can hear from us all and that we can remain transparent and accountable to our coalition." A *Zoom* meeting with administrators was set up (when asked to provide the names of everyone who would be attending the meeting, we refused to provide this list to avoid any potential retaliation). In this meeting, we were told by an administrator that the university could not designate spaces specifically for marginalized communities on campus because "the entire campus should be perceived as a multicultural center." The meeting was ultimately unproductive except that one administrator agreed to speak to the university president about the proposal and to meet with us again in two weeks.

At our second meeting with administrators, we were told that our proposal was one of 200 responses that the university president had received in response to his 1 June 2020 email sent to the entire university asking for "new ideas" on how to address racial inequality in the midst of widespread racial justice protests. We were essentially told that all proposals matter, so to speak, and that it would be given equal consideration with the 199 other responses. This approach ignored the fact that our proposal was the product of extensive and in-depth research, campus focus groups, protests, a petition, press conferences, and five years of student-led struggle. The administrators reported on what they had done in the two weeks since our previous meeting, which included unnecessary summaries of other meetings we had attended with them and a slew of other unrelated items, such as updating a website that did nothing to further our cause. We demanded a "yes" or "no" answer to our proposal. They evaded this direct question throughout the meeting and agreed to meet with us again without having said "yes" or "no." When MSC followed up by email to schedule yet another meeting, we received no response.

We continued looking for other avenues and found collaborators in other ASU student organizations and the cultural coalitions.[11] They invited us to meetings that they were able to convene—as official ASU student groups—with administrators, where we were told that our demands to become a sanctuary campus and to defund the university police would not be implemented or even considered. This rejection deepened our relationship with the students in these groups, as they were now in full support of our proposal and ready to position themselves against the administration. In response to the clear dismissal of these two key components of our proposal and the refusal to meet with us directly, we continued hosting virtual town halls to make this university response public.

Direct Action

As days went by without our hearing anything from administrators, we decided that it was time to march. Shortly after we released a flyer with our community partners, our comrades in a Black-led student organization were threatened with expulsion if they participated in the march; as a registered student organization, they could be punished by the university. Administrators justified these threats by citing COVID-19 concerns about gatherings, even though the university was holding in-person classes at the time. The student organization was forced to rescind their sponsorship of the event. Just weeks before this incident, several videos of white ASU students drinking alcohol and slip-and-sliding in large groups had gone viral (Baxter). To our knowledge, these students were not held accountable for their reckless behaviors. We observed that even COVID-19 precautions and disciplining mechanisms, in an echo of the university's racist history, were disproportionately aimed at Black and Brown students.

We marched on 30 August 2020 (fig. 4). We rallied at a park near campus, loudly blasting N.W.A.'s "Fuck the Police," capturing the rage of the moment and punctuating a long sentence of injustice. Among the participants were community organizations like Black Lives Matter Phoenix Metro, ASU student athletes, professors, students, and community members. After initially gathering to talk about social distance practices, we marched, chanting, "When Black (trans/queer/undocumented) lives (students/athletes) are under attack, what do we do? Stand up, fight back."

At our university police headquarters, we talked about the history of policing, its origins in slave patrols, and the anti-Blackness of local, state, national, and international jurisprudence. We called for the defunding of the university police. We marched across the Tempe campus to the stone bearing the inscription of the overglorified university charter so we could point out its false claims of

Figure 4. Demonstration outside the ASU police department demanding that the department be defunded and disarmed, 30 August 2020.

inclusion (fig. 5). Several students spoke about the violence and sustained exclusion they had experienced on campus and how the charter did not reflect their lived experiences. After marching, we returned to the park. Feeling intimidated by the presence of the police, we departed quickly after saying just a few words upon returning to the park. As we drove away, we observed bike cops lined up at the park's edge and police vehicles waiting at each corner.

Divide and Conquer

The university's "list of twenty-five actions" to support "Black students, faculty and staff" (Crow) was published on 2 September 2020, exactly two days after our march. Several of these action items were stolen from our proposal. We say "stolen" because, although we are the authors of this proposal, we continue to be shut out of the deliberative processes. In October 2020, two students from MSC were selected to participate in the ASU Advisory Council on African American Affairs (ACAAA). In addition to the university-sanctioned committees, students organized parallel working groups as an attempt to hold administrators accountable. This effectively divided the students into multiple levels of hierarchical committees involving seemingly endless meetings and no action. As of December 2020, it was still unclear whether and how these committees and working groups would be interacting with one another. In preparation for the 4 November 2020 meeting of the ACAAA, a list was shared that had an administrator's

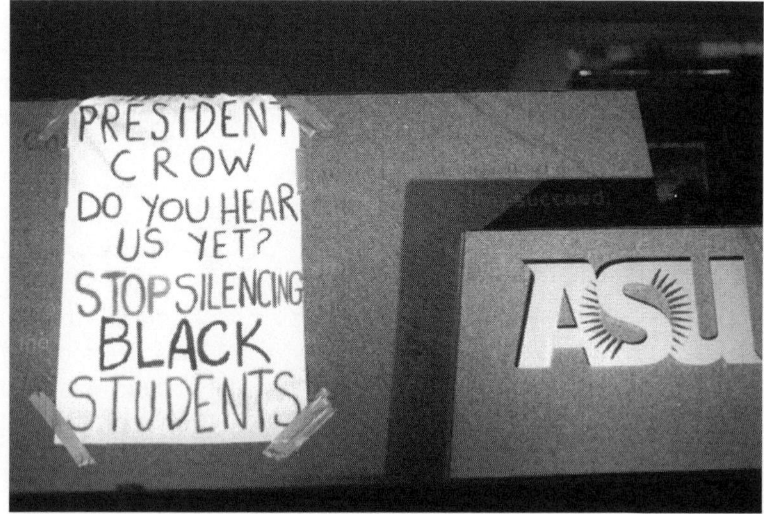

Figure 5. Poster taped over ASU's charter during protest of ASU police department, 30 August 2020.

name next to each of the twenty-five points. The list was only shared with members of the ACAAA, who were told not to share that information with anyone else. Privately assigning administrators, with a small group of students, as leaders determining how to implement each of the twenty-five items proved that the administration was not open to hearing from anyone that they hadn't personally invited to the table. This meant that the parallel student-led working groups would be necessarily ignored throughout the process.

We also note that the ACAAA asked anyone who was not Black to leave the committees, except for the committee on the multicultural center. While we agree that Black voices must be centered when addressing issues of inequality, we don't believe that the work of dismantling the white-supremacist-capitalist-cis-hetero-patriarchy is to be done by Black people alone. That is especially true if the university does not compensate the Black students and faculty who are now essentially working as university consultants for free. This is exploitation, not liberation; expecting those most harmed by this oppressive system to bear the heaviest burden of dismantling.

In fall 2021, a small room on the third floor of the student pavilion on the Tempe campus was labeled, without student input, a "Multicultural Communities of Excellence" room (fig. 6). It has no resources, programming, or staff, and students have been told that they cannot reserve the space, use the offices, or leave any art in the space. That same semester, students from MSC were invited to participate in an aesthetic committee and a hiring committee. Since neither of these committees ever met, students were excluded from any decisions that would have come before these committees. For example, the mural added to the room was installed without consulting or notifying students (fig. 7).

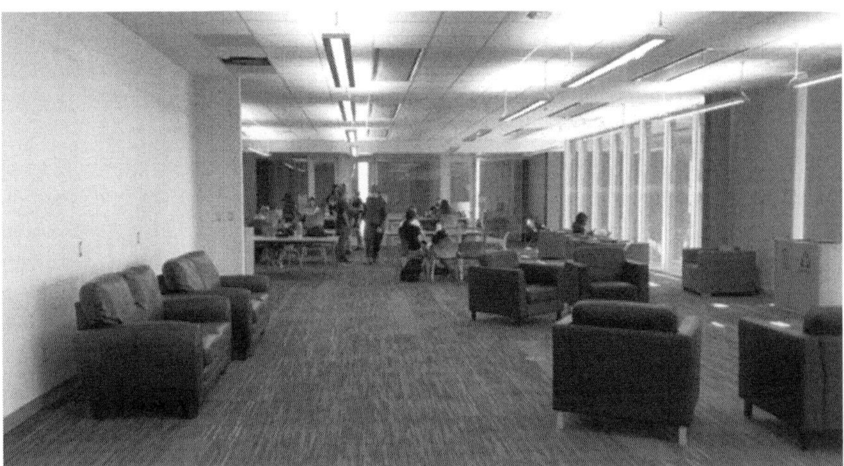

Figure 6. "Multicultural Communities of Excellence" room at ASU.

Figure 7. Mural installed in ASU's "Multicultural Communities of Excellence" room.

The University Will Not Abolish Itself

One problem with a solutions-based or social justice approach to teaching and learning is the assumption that there are easy solutions to complex problems that individual students can solve within a semester, within a course, or by completing certificates. Framing social justice issues in these terms shifts the focus away from a long-term systemic approach and gives students the false hope that they alone are somehow capable of fundamentally changing our society. The framing of social justice issues as existing simply because people in power are somehow unaware of their own role in maintaining an oppressive system is what leads students, faculty, and staff to spin their wheels until they burn out and give up. The term *social justice* "has come to be a proxy for heteropatriarchal racist logics of individuality, a project that cannot dismantle coloniality because it was created to foment it" (Patel 90). Solutions-based or social justice pedagogy is the imposition of reformist politics on potentially radical students—an institutional strategy to channel students into writing op-eds, "creating awareness," and attending endless meetings with committees intended to maintain the status quo and increase the profit margin.

It is not in the university's best interest to sanction its own dissolution, because the university is a business, and profit is its purpose. Any other outcome is purely coincidental and certainly secondary to the work of accumulating wealth and power. Universities teach revolutionary histories and social justice pedagogy without actively practicing or supporting such endeavors and "thus the critical academic is made complicit in the institution's negligence, locked into the university's attempts to become amenable to those it oppresses. To be critical of the university traps one within settler futurity" (Mayorga et al. 95). Ultimately, social justice pedagogy is beside the point, because administration and faculty either do not practice what they preach or what they preach is misinformed by university-sanctioned colonial epistemologies. However, being confronted with this hypocrisy can lead to politicization, which is where we find ourselves. By making demands, we see the true colors of this our university. It's the work of organized students to light the first sparks. With this as our foundation, we begin to understand that the classroom is not a revolutionary space unless the students are setting it ablaze.

We Shall Dance

Moten and Harney remind us that the only ethical relationship we can have with the institution of the university is one of theft ("The University and the Undercommons" 101). We can use the institutional resources of our university to invest in and strengthen our communities in order to heal, build power, and to accomplish the goals of abolition. As students at Swarthmore College also point out, we

> are responsible for moving [resources] back into the communities they came from, in an enriching and sustaining manner. This repatriation is not a "sharing" of university resources, which would engender relationships of dependency. Rather, it is theft, using the university's own property to enable communities to thrive independent of the institution. . . . [I]f you are not leveraging your position in some manner to contribute to this theft, you are helping to maintain the settler colonial university. That is why we say loot the bookshelves and burn the school down. (Mayorga et al. 11)

Because the university systematically extracts labor and intellectual property from us, our only ethical choice is to extract the university's material resources and redistribute them to our communities.

Our vision for the future of education emphasizes community learning, or what we see as colearning. While the multicultural center we outlined in our proposal does not yet exist, and we continue to be excluded from the decision-making process, we have successfully created an autonomous parallel space in which we are building community and truly learning. We have learned about one another's struggles and acquired skills needed to sustain grassroots movements, such as engaging ethically with others, meeting facilitation, honest communication, and even writing collectively to produce this essay. The MSC is a space that does not alienate us from our work, because our labor is not being exploited, nor are we investing in our own human capital to be exploited in the future. Through this collective engagement, we begin to unlearn what the university and the state have ingrained in us. Together, we actively reject the violent ways of our university. We do this to imagine new possibilities of learning, of growing, and of dismantling the systems of oppression that shape our lives.

Because we are using the space of the academy to unlearn our forced assimilation and corporate training, our proposal and our existence are a threat to our university. Our proposal demands that Arizona State University move from a command-and-control power structure to a more diffuse leadership structure. Our proposal demands a high level of autonomy and respect for student leadership.

Administrators have proven so committed to their approach that they have been unwilling to receive input from students regarding even agenda setting, unlocking office doors, putting art in the multicultural center, or the color of the furniture they are planning to purchase. Our proposal requires that our university stop marginalizing students. We imagine an educational experience in which the well-being of students is prioritized above profits and our student autonomy is respected. We imagine a community that is strong and cared for. What might happen if we learn together and build a community that facilitates the dismantling of the university as we know and experience it? What might happen if we kindle the flames needed to burn it to the ground? What if burning down the university is only the beginning? We envision a future in which we thrive and rejoice in community, dancing upon the ashes and never looking back.

NOTES

We want to first and foremost recognize the MSC as the collective author of this chapter. However, because of the pressure to publish, we also want to recognize the individuals who worked on this paper: Miriam Araya, Kelly Baur, Miranda Bernard, Jamal Brooks-Hawkins, Alex Gilbert, Ana Isabel Terminel Iberri, Ronae Matriano, Kierra Otis, Mastaani Qureshi, and Sarra Tekola.

1. Students named in this essay were interviewed by phone in 2021 and have been assigned pseudonyms.

2. For more information on racial capitalism, anti-Blackness, and carcerality, see Taylor; Jackson; Wang.

3. For more information on empire, domination, and the violence of modernity, see Lowe; Hartman and Campt.

4. The ASU Enterprise includes the ASU Foundation, an organization dedicated to gaining and working with private donors; University Realty LLC, a real estate company that advances commercial and residential real estate projects; SkySong Innovations, a corporation that works with ASU to coordinate its technological research with the private sector; ASU RealmSpark, an investor in education technology companies; and, finally, ASURE, an applied research division that offers consultations to "the defense and security industry" ("ASURE").

5. TRIO, LSAMP, and STARS are programs that can be used to support and increase retention of underrepresented minorities. TRIO programs (such as the McNair Scholars Program, which is funded at 151 institutions) are supported by the US Department of Education. LSAMP is a program designed to increase the number of underrepresented minorities receiving degrees in STEM disciplines, and STARS is a retention program for first-year African American students.

6. This moment is a product of age-old injustices; see Wynter: "all our present struggles with respect to race, class, gender, sexual orientation, ethnicity, struggles over the environment, global warming, severe climate change, the sharply unequal distribution of the earth resources (20 percent of the world's peoples own 80 percent of its resources, consume two-thirds of its food, and are responsible for 75 percent of its ongoing pollution,

with this leading to two billion of earth's peoples living relatively affluent lives while four billion still live on the edge of hunger and immiseration, to the dynamic of overconsumption on the part of the rich techno-industrial North paralleled by that of overpopulation on the part of the dispossessed poor, still partly agrarian worlds of the South)—these are all differing facets of the central ethnoclass Man vs. Human struggle" (260–61).

7. See Moten and Harney: "Professionalization is the privatization of the social difference through negligence" ("The University and the Undercommons" 34).

8. The ASU police department has had a violent history for decades (see, for example, "F.B.I.") and has been protested, during the most recent movement sparked by the death of George Floyd, by student leaders on ASU's campus (Miscenich).

9. When questioned in an interview about the distinction between abolition and transformative justice, Gumbs stated, "I learned both of those terms in the context of the organization Critical Resistance, and I learned abolition as a critical and generative term, and a movement with three main components: dismantle, change, build. That definition of abolition included the daily work of generating relationships, systems, and processes that produce peaceful, sustainable results that fully address the unaddressed fears, intergenerational trauma, and systemic violence that prisons, policing, and surveillance (the systemic external version, and the internalized versions) pretend to mitigate" (Imarisha et al.). For more information on the university and abolitionism, see Abolition University (abolition.university/).

10. Rape and sexual assault survivors have elected to go fully online because their rapists were not expelled from ASU.

11. The cultural coalitions consist of seven coalitions that represent different oppressed or marginalized communities. They are mainly tasked with celebrating heritage months and other events of their respective communities.

WORKS CITED

"About." *ASU Enterprise Partners*, www.asuenterprisepartners.org/. Accessed 17 Nov. 2023.

Anderson, Brian. "ASU Strikes Deal with SAD, OKs Group's Proposals." *The State Press*, 27 March 1996.

Arizona State, Legislature. House Bill 2281. *Arizona State Legislature*, 3 May 2010, www.azleg.gov/legtext/49leg/2r/summary/h.hb2281_05-03-10_astransmittedtogovernor.doc.htm.

Arizona State, Legislature. Proposition 203. *Arizona State Legislature*, 7 Nov. 2000, www.azleg.gov/legtext/54leg/1R/summary/S.HCR2026ED.pdf.

Arizona State, Legislature. Senate Bill 1070. *Arizona State Legislature*, 23 Apr. 2010, www.azleg.gov/legtext/49leg/2r/bills/sb1070s.pdf

"ASU Charter, Mission and Goals." *New American University*, Arizona State U, newamericanuniversity.asu.edu/about/asu-charter-mission-and-goals. Accessed 10 Dec. 2020.

"ASU Named the Nation's Most Innovative University for the Ninth Consecutive Year." *ASU Online*, Arizona State U, 17 Sept. 2023, news.asu.edu/20230917-university-news-asu-no-1-innovation-nine-years-us-news-world-report.

"ASURE." *Arizona State University*, asure.asu.edu/. Accessed 14 Dec. 2020.

"AZ Prop 300: Public Program Eligibility for All Terms Prior to Spring 2023 per Prop 308." *Office of the Registrar*, Northern Arizona U, in.nau.edu/registrar/citizenship/.

Baxter, Erasmus. "Parties, Basketball, Slip-and-Slides: ASU Student Employees Say Campus Is a Health Risk." *Phoenix New Times*, 26 Aug. 2020, www.phoenixnewtimes.com/news/arizona-state-university-covid-19-cases-parties-dorms-community-assistants-11489737.

Berlin, James. *Rhetoric and Reality: Writing Instruction in American Colleges, 1900–1985*. Southern Illinois UP, 1987.

Chilisa, Bagele. "Decolonising Transdisciplinary Research Approaches: An African Perspective for Enhancing Knowledge Integration in Sustainability Science." *Sustainability Science*, vol. 12, 2017, pp. 813–27.

Christian, Barbara. "The Race for Theory." *Feminist Studies*, vol. 14, no. 1, 1988, pp. 67–79. *JSTOR*, www.jstor.org/stable/3177999.

Clark, Nigel, and Kathryn Yusoff. "Queer Fire: Ecology, Combustion and Pyrosexual Desire." *Feminist Review*, vol. 118, no. 1, 2018, pp. 7–24.

Crow, Michael M. "Arizona State University List of Twenty-Five Actions to Support." *Office of the President*, Arizona State U, 2 Sept. 2020, president.asu.edu/commitment/news-and-updates.

Cruz, Cindy. "Toward an Epistemology of a Brown Body." *International Journal of Qualitative Studies in Education*, vol. 14, no. 5, 2001, pp. 657–69, https://doi.org/10.1080/09518390110059874.

Cruz, Lynda. "Center Helps Growing Minority Population." *The State Press*, 21 Jan. 2004, www.statepress.com/article/2004/01/center-helps-growing-minority-population.

Davis, Angela Y. *Are Prisons Obsolete?* Seven Stories, 2003.

"Desmond Tutu 1931." *Oxford Essential Quotations*, Oxford UP, 2017, www.oxfordreference.com/view/10.1093/acref/9780191843730.001.0001/q-oro-ed5-00016497.

Executive Summary of the Cultural Excellence Center and Scholars Program. Multicultural Solidarity Coalition, 2020, docs.google.com/document/d/1AAdd_jSvn3HIHjRuSiXtpza9IRT9n3PZqYcT2O6ANgU/edit.

"Facts at a Glance: Fall 2021." University Office of Institutional Analysis, Arizona State U, 2022, uoia.asu.edu/sites/default/files/asu_facts_at_a_glance_-_fall_2021.pdf.

"F.B.I. Examines Actions of Police at Arizona State." *The New York Times*, 2 May 1989, www.nytimes.com/1989/05/02/business/fbi-examines-actions-of-police-at-arizona-state.html.

Fisher, Mark. *Capitalist Realism: Is There No Alternative?* John Hunt, 2009.

Freire, Paulo. *Pedagogy of the Oppressed*. 30th anniversary ed., Continuum, 2000.

Gilmore, Ruth Wilson. *Golden Gulag: Prisons, Surplus, Crisis, and Opposition in Globalizing California*. 2nd ed., U of California P, 2018.

Hartman, Saidiya, and Tina Campt, editors. Special issue of *Small Axe: A Caribbean Journal of Criticism*. Vol. 31, no. 1, 2009.

hooks, bell. *All About Love: New Visions*. Harper, 1999.

Imarisha, Walidah, et al. "The Fictions and Futures of Transformative Justice: A Conversation with the Authors of *Octavia's Brood*." *The New Inquiry*, 20 Apr. 2017, thenew inquiry.com/the-fictions-and-futures-of-transformative-justice/.

Jackson, George. *Blood in My Eye*. Random House, 1972.

Kaba, Mariame. "Yes, We Mean Literally Abolish the Police." *The New York Times*, 12 June 2020, www.nytimes.com/2020/06/12/opinion/sunday/floyd-abolish-defund-police.html.

Kelley, Robin D. G. "Black Study, Black Struggle." *Ufahamu: A Journal of African Studies*, vol. 40, no. 2, summer 2018, pp. 153–68, escholarship.org/uc/item/8cj8q196.

Kimmerer, Robin, and Kanawha Lake. "The Role of Indigenous Burning in Land Management." *Journal of Forestry*, vol. 99, no. 11, 2001, pp. 36–41, academic.oup.com/jof/article/99/11/36/4614303?login=true.

Lowe, Lisa. *The Intimacies of Four Continents*. Duke UP, 2015.

Mayorga, Edwin, et al. "Burn It Down: The Incommensurability of the University and Decolonization." *Journal of Critical Thought and Praxis*, vol. 8, no. 1, 2019, pp. 87–106, works.swarthmore.edu/cgi/viewcontent.cgi?article=1152&context=fac-education.

Melamed, Jodi. "Racial Capitalism." *Journal of Critical Ethnic Studies*, vol. 1, no. 1, 2015, pp. 76–85. *JSTOR*, https://doi.org/10.5749/jcritethnstud.1.1.0076.

Miscenich, Sebastian. "ASU's Police Department Should Be Abolished." *The State Press*, 24 June 2020, www.statepress.com/article/2020/06/spopinion-asupd-should-be-abolished.

Moten, Fred, and Stefano Harney. "The University and the Undercommons: Seven Theses." *Social Text*, vol. 22, no. 2, 2004, pp. 101–15.

———. "The University: Last Words." *Are.na*, uploaded by tess murdoch, 2020, www.are.na/block/7921022.

N.W.A. "Fuck the Police." *Straight Outta Compton*, Priority/Ruthless, 1988.

Patel, Leigh. *Decolonizing Educational Research*. Routledge, 2015.

Peck, Scott. *The Different Drum: Community Making and Peace*. Touchstone, 1987.

Quaranta, Kiara, and Nellie Nano. "Students Protest against Events Hosting ICE and IDF." *The State Press*, 15 Nov. 2019, www.statepress.com/article/2019/11/sppolitics-students-protest-ice-and-idf-on-campus.

Robinson, Cedric J. *Black Marxism: The Making of the Black Radical Tradition*. U of North Carolina P, 1983.

Taylor, Keeanga-Yamahtta. *Race for Profit: How Banks and the Real Estate Industry Undermined Black Homeownership*. U of North Carolina P, 2019.

Wang, Jackie. *Carceral Capitalism*. Semiotext(e), 2018.

Wynter, Sylvia. "Unsettling the Coloniality of Being/Power/Truth/Freedom: Towards the Human, after Man, Its Overrepresentation—An Argument." *CR: The New Centennial Review*, vol. 3, no. 3, fall 2003, pp. 257–37.

Project Humanities: Modeling Community Engagement

Neal A. Lester

Since 2011, Project Humanities has been bringing Arizona State University (ASU) and local communities together to talk, listen, and connect through critical conversations, lectures, panels, performances, film screenings, festivals, contests, symposia, conferences, trainings, and service to enact community development as both "an outcome and a process whereby communities act collectively for self-empowerment" (Quimbo et al. 591). The short, student-intern-produced video "What Is Project Humanities?" on the Project Humanities *YouTube* channel introduces our program this way: "What if there was an organization that could unite communities through their differences? What if there was an initiative that could teach us to be better humans? This is Project Humanities."

An academic unit that is not a department, a center, or an institute with majors, minors, certificates, and faculty members, Project Humanities nevertheless touches and impacts every aspect of ASU—students, staff members, administrators, faculty members, alumni, emeriti, potential students, and retirees—and the greater public with its programming, activities, and events. A unique collaborative entity with no known counterpart at other colleges and universities, Project Humanities coordinates and cosponsors thirty to fifty events and activities annually across all four ASU campuses and at community venues across Arizona. By the end of spring 2023, more than 32,000 people had participated in Project Humanities activities and events. From March 2020 through October 2021, though COVID-19 protocols necessitated curtailing most in-person outreach, Project Humanities offered approximately 140 unique, mostly virtual events. Since the peak of COVID, we have continued programming in hybrid formats for inclusion and accessibility and to remain connected to the robust national and international online following we developed while solely online.

Though Project Humanities events and programs are always informed by scholarly research and facilitated by researchers, clinical experts, and community practitioners, this model of community engagement and development recognizes that knowledge is gained not just through traditional disciplinary means but also from expertise that comes in many forms and from multiple diverse perspectives. Globally, community development involves educator-researchers and the public working together to ensure the economic, social, environmental, and cultural strength and stability of local communities. As a practice-based activity, community development focuses on "promoting participative democracy, stable development, human rights, equal opportunities, and social justice, through . . . organizing, educating, and empowering people" ("Community Development"). Aware that "[p]olicy-makers, practitioners, and academics . . . benefit from better understanding . . . what community development is from a conceptual and . . . an applied perspective," Project Humanities at Arizona State University (ASU) demonstrates the importance of humanities education and its direct implications for community empowerment and growth in the twenty-first century (Matarrita-Cascante and Brennan 303). Our vision is one of inclusion and reciprocity such that we are learning from our attendees and we know our attendees are learning from us.

Project Humanities' community engagement underscores "community development as the process of creating or increasing solidarity and agency," solidarity in the sense of "building a deeply shared identity and a code of conduct," and agency in relation to "the capacity of a people to order their world" (Hustedde and Ganowicz 3). Responding to moral, ethical, political, social, and communal disconnection and inaction, Project Humanities, in 2012, created a signature program, the Humanity 101 Movement, to address the perennial question "Are we losing our humanity?" ("Humanity 101"). Building "shared identity and a code of conduct" rooted in the social justice focus of humanities study, the Humanity 101 Movement promotes and challenges all to live by seven non-faith-based principles posited as foundational and endemic to strong, sustainable relationships, communities, and organizations: empathy, compassion, forgiveness, integrity, kindness, respect, and self-reflection. A virtual and experiential toolbox of programs, activities, databases, resources, and strategies, Humanity 101—while promoting these values that represent humanity and human interactions and engagements at their best—has become the framework undergirding all of Project Humanities' justice, equity, equality, and diversity programming.

By multiple measures, Project Humanities is an academic success, and that success is largely attributable to its partnerships with over three hundred ASU, local, national, and international entities.[1] Individuals and communities within and beyond ASU know Project Humanities because of its social justice and equity work and acknowledge Project Humanities as a model and leader for humanist entrepreneurship, community engagement, and community development. By taking humanities conversations and practices beyond campus classrooms and by engaging with communities both inside and beyond our university, Project Humanities was doing "public humanities" before it became the academic buzzword that it is now. This model fundamentally challenges the artificial Western separation of *public* and *humanities*, subscribing instead to the notion that the humanities *are* the public and that those who study and practice the humanities are members of multiple communities simultaneously. In the same way that humans acknowledge and comprise intersectional identities simultaneously, Project Humanities embraces and promotes the fact that people are not single-identity individuals, as Audre Lorde, like so many other "radical" (and most often female) thinkers of color, reminds us: "There is no such thing as a single-issue struggle because we don't live single-issue lives" (138). As a university entity, Project Humanities is an intentional disruption of static and even restrictive "traditional" ways of understanding, engaging, and experiencing the humanities and community.

Boundary-crossing and boundary-challenging human experience within the context of a university education and experience, Project Humanities embodies entrepreneurial thinking and practices. It attracts new and diverse audiences and challenges what teaching and learning are—and the sources of each—while intentionally practicing and learning reciprocity rather than the "savior" model of engagement associated with the university as ivory tower. Further, Project Humanities invites and challenges humanists to step outside disciplinary, research, pedagogical, and engagement silos. The very existence and presence of Project Humanities at the largest public Research I university in the United States challenges mainstreamed voices perpetuating cultural sirens around the "crisis in humanities" narrative such as Frank Bruni's "The End of College as We Knew It?" and Bruce Abramson's "The Humanities Are Dead." Both opinion pieces share similar laments for similar reasons, using similar examples of what constitutes learning and authority. Abramson states his intellectual and creative panic and concern:

> The humanities are indeed dead in America. It's long past time to stop funding the institutions that pretend to study them, subsidizing students who pretend to study them and paying the faculties who've failed to teach them. Once we have cleared away the detritus, perhaps we can invest in a humanities education that teaches the value of *our rich cultural legacy*. (emphasis added)

Bruni's references to "we" and Abramson's to "our" signal and perpetuate a "traditional" racialized, gendered, elitist, and exclusionary angst and clamoring to hang onto a dying way of thinking and being. As Project Humanities' founding director and foundation professor of English, I offered a response to the alleged crisis narrative by insisting that humanists "reframe how we [are] talking about the work that we do. We have to talk about intersectionality. Even though somebody may be a business major or a kinesiology major doesn't mean that they can't engage in these conversations about humanist principles and about how we are human. . . . You don't need to major in the humanities to talk about being human" (Lester, "Are the Humanities Really in Crisis?"). People—whether or not they are students and scholars—experience, read, and engage life through talking, listening, and connecting beyond disciplinary boundaries. Hence, Project Humanities' innovation and entrepreneurship embody varied multidisciplinary, multiprofessional, and multicommunal approaches and strategies of imagining and practicing social justice and the necessity of human connection.

Background: Planting Seeds

When Project Humanities launched as a week of multidisciplinary events to promote and celebrate the humanities as a discipline in spring 2011, the vision was to grow the program into a local and national leader advancing the understanding, study, and public practice of the humanities broadly. As dean of humanities in ASU's College of Liberal Arts and Sciences, I was tasked by the university president to "make humanities more robust." I came to understand that this meant creating energy and excitement through humanities research, teaching, and collaboration for students, faculty members, staff members, and community stakeholders. Too often, individuals and communities see the humanities as synonymous with the arts and do not easily demonstrate an understanding of how humanities work goes beyond the artificial disciplinary boundaries that for traditional institutions of higher education still characterize a paradigm of knowledge creation, institutional operation, and excellence. Modeling community engagement for Project Humanities means that stakeholders imagine and witness the humanities as a locus for generating new ideas about social issues and as a field that attracts new resources and audiences. Humanities practitioners, through this lens, see this work as a respected and much-sought-out intervention in matters of diversity, equity, and justice. The humanities, by raising questions, critiquing, and self-critiquing, are disruptive in the same way that Martin Luther King, Jr., calls for social disruption in his speech "The Other America": "large segments of . . . society are more concerned about tranquility and the status quo than about justice and humanity." Project Humanities is indeed a constructive and conscious disruptor in the quest for "justice and humanity."[2]

Organizationally, Project Humanities' conceptual and operational task was and continues to be to move away from the typical disciplinary approach to the humanities within the academy. The National Endowment for the Humanities announces its mission on its website: "NEH enables individuals and institutions across the United States to study, preserve, and share the best of America's history and culture" ("Our Work"). Despite the multidisciplinary and inclusive understanding of the purpose and practice of the humanities evidenced by this national organization, a 2021 Whiting Foundation grant call for humanities work at the high school level shows this common tendency to resort to listing disciplines, failing to acknowledge that disciplines themselves are not rigid or static in their methodologies or approaches:

> The Whiting Foundation seeks to support proven interventions that bring students into the heart of the humanities. The [$20,000–$35,000] grants are

> intended to support organizations undertaking interventions such as teacher training, enrichment activities in or outside of school, or the development or dissemination of curricular resources. The work funded . . . must be based in the *core humanities disciplines of history, philosophy, or the study of literature and other arts, or in fields like classics that combine those disciplines* [emphasis added]. The program excludes literacy per se, language learning, and the *practice* of arts (e.g., creative writing). ("Proposals")

Project Humanities' pedagogical, disciplinary, and community engagement approach to humanities is not limited to traditional methodological borders, the very borders that separate humanities from the public, as in the call for proposals' emphasis on disciplines. The philosopher Lewis R. Gordon argues that once academicians acknowledge that the very construct of methodology is influenced by the history of white supremacy and the global movement to delegitimize Black and Brown people as producers of knowledge, they realize that adhering to these artificial borders and boundaries that constitute and restrict humanist thinking and action is itself an act of colonization. Hence, Project Humanities' theoretical, philosophical, pedagogical, and community engagement position is that social justice work is at the core and foundation of humanities. Acknowledging this truth is not only a matter of decolonizing knowledge; this position also creates a platform for more historically marginalized knowledge producers and more intentional bridge-building between humanities and the public.

Project Humanities calls for and embodies a more nuanced understanding and value of humanities research and study, as the humanities scholars cited here indicate. Cathy N. Davidson and David Theo Goldberg suggest:

> The humanities engage three broad sets of questions: those of meaning, value, and significance. Meaning concerns interpretation of data, evidence, and texts. Value ranges over the entire field of cultural, aesthetic, social, and scientific investments. Significance, implicating both the former two, raises questions of representation, in the sense of accounting for (explanation) and of capturing, in the sense both of offering a faithful rendition (description) and of making broad claims (generalization).

Challenging what Marjorie Garber identifies as the faulty assumption of an inherent "dichotomy between the humanities and the world" (qtd. in Byrne A4),[3] Project Humanities further subscribes to the new way of thinking about and "doing" humanities proposed by Jennifer Summit:

> Most definitions of "the humanities" will tell you that they study "what it means to be human." But this is a relatively recent definition, arising only in the last century, when "the humanities" were defined against "the sciences."

> Areas of study such as philosophy, literature, and history were grouped together shortly after the Cold War, when members of the American academy submitted postwar policy recommendations on education to the US government. The newly defined "humanities" bolstered the incorporated disciplines but at the same time created a scholarly divide. . . .
>
> The "studia humanitatis" emphasize "humanity," understood as civility, kindness, and generosity, over the elevation of the "human" per se. Through a combination of knowledge, skill, and practical wisdom students would be prepared not only to work for themselves but to contribute to the common good. This model of education emerged in response to dramatic shifts of the European Renaissance, including increased access to education, advancements in printing technologies, and the development of knowledge-based workers, like civil servants and lawyers. ("Stanford Scholar")

As does Project Humanities, Summit calls for "a new education philosophy. To address the changing needs of the world," she says, the academy needs "a new definition of the humanities . . . that's as radical and as forward-thinking as the one invented by our Renaissance ancestors" ("Stanford Scholar"; see also "Humanities"). Project Humanities is this new definition in its conception, goals, mission, range, and impact.

With local, national, and international acknowledgments and accolades from diverse organizations, Project Humanities—as a model of community engagement and development—has substantially raised ASU's profile as a research institution that values "public-facing" humanities and humanities research in its myriad forms in its pursuit of excellence and innovation. A celebrated model of "doing humanities" innovatively and accessibly (see "Awards and Accolades"), Project Humanities has been looked at by colleges and universities across the country who want to emulate some form of this model.[4]

One of the hallmarks of Project Humanities' programming as a new definition of humanities theory and praxis—these are not necessarily separate—is its ability to keep its proverbial fingers on the social, political, and communal pulse. In 2020, for example, during the COVID-19 pandemic lockdown, Project Humanities transitioned in-person programming to a virtual format and even created a new podcast club, which held biweekly online meetings to discuss podcast episodes with links to Project Humanities event topics. Our ongoing Vital Voices series of facilitated discussions attracted a nationwide audience in fall 2020 with the program "The Uses of Anger." Community members participated virtually by sharing "a poem, passage, visual art, artifact, or story that connects them with anger" ("Vital Voices"). While for many complicated reasons, most of Project Humanities' supporters are white women, for this event, mostly Black women participants from across the nation shared two-to-three-minute performances of original material and other poems, songs, and passages that documented and legitimized creative expressions of and responses to anger. With me facilitating as founding director, the cofacilitating psychologist, Michelle Melton, explained that anger is a response to feelings of hurt, fear, disappointment; anger itself is not an emotion. Somehow, participants breathed a sigh of relief in this ninety-minute celebratory moment of emotional and psychological validation after the murders of George Floyd, Breonna Taylor, Ahmaud Arbery, and, disturbingly, too many others to name here. Politically and socially engaged Black folks' tempers were high, and many mostly white folks—some self-proclaimed allies—were questioning why rioting and looting had taken place during recent protests. Another discussion, "White Women Dismantling White Supremacy," was also a response to the summer of alleged racial reckoning that found folks across the racial spectrum "talking about white supremacy now in ways they wouldn't before," as I explained, continuing, "White women are asking what they can do, and looking for ways to hold each other accountable. . . . These are hard conversations to have, but if people are really interested in dismantling social injustice, they have to happen" (Trimble). Virtual attendance at this event was one of the project's highest.

Project Humanities' virtual research-informed and facilitated community conversations on topics pulled from current news headlines have brought in the organization's most engaged local, national, and international participation. As part of ASU's research enterprise, since 2018, every Project Humanities event registrant—whether they attended or not—has received within a week of each program an emailed list of selected resources compiled from participant *Zoom* and *Facebook Chat* discussions, facilitators' and panelists' recommendations, and Project Humanities staff research in preparing for and marketing the specific event. In recent years, Project Humanities has further extended its programming beyond event attendance by creating three-to-five-minute event highlights recap videos for each event ("Event Recap Videos") in addition to the longer recorded programs. In the last three years or so, we have learned that even recap videos may be too long for people's attention spans, so we are creating shorter reels, modeled on *Instagram* and *TikTok* postings, to promote and market upcoming and past events.

Another distinguishing characteristic of Project Humanities is that it hosts programs in venues as varied as the audiences, participants, and attendees it attracts. In addition to ASU classroom and online environments, venues include local churches, museums, community centers, high schools, community colleges, banks, arts spaces, libraries, restaurants, parks, and other outdoor spaces. In 2014, Project Humanities received the inaugural Phi Beta Kappa Award of Excellence for making liberal arts accessible to multiple communities.[5] At the award reception, Brenda Thomson, the executive director of Arizona Humanities, a state public humanities entity affiliated with the National Endowment for the Humanities, commented on Project Humanities as an engagement catalyst:

> [T]here has never been a program quite like Project Humanities. . . . The topics . . . are wide-ranging. They provoke you—invite you to participate, invade your creative imagination. . . . You can't be at a Project Humanities event without feeling something, . . . meeting people you've never met before. You may find yourself happy. You may find yourself crying. But you will find yourself. . . . [T]he space will be a safe space that makes for difficult conversations . . . about topics you never explored before. . . . [For example,] Professor Neal Lester took Project Humanities to a local church to discuss the topic of the N-word. . . . [B]ombs and guns and knives can kill, but so can words. . . . [A] young man who thought the N-word was cool . . . quoted another young high school student who said, "It's not cool to be loved and hung with the same word," and he said after attending that event, he would never use that word again.
>
> ("Project Humanities Community Testimonial")

Realizing the relevance of education beyond academic boundaries, student volunteers often discuss the meaningful cross-pollination that occurs between their Project Humanities involvement and the scholarly and creative work in their formal education. While taking an undergraduate introduction to literature course with me, Austin Davis attended the on-campus Project Humanities event "Vital Voices: Social Justice" and read one of his poems. About that first experience, Davis recalls, "It filled me with . . . [s]ome sort of connectedness I hadn't felt in college before." As a senior, Davis produced a jazz album of spoken word poetry about homelessness; he also started an outreach program, AZ Hugs for the Houseless, under the auspices of Arizona Jews for Justice. About his connection to Project Humanities, Davis explains:

> Project Humanities makes people feel like they are a part of something that is really meaningful. . . . [I]t just fills people with love. That's always what I feel when I'm around . . . the team or any of the events. . . . I . . . feel more at home in our humanity. . . . It makes people gravitate towards each other, and have these open conversations. . . . And it's so natural too, nothing's forced. It's just very organic. And it's beautiful. I'm grateful and lucky to be a part of it, even in a small part. ("Ten Years")

Project Humanities' successes are linked directly to moments when participants, stakeholders, supporters, and investors admit to becoming enlightened and more aware, having greater clarity, and desiring to move to some action. To affect and change participants' view of themselves and of their place in the world is to witness those "magic moments" that transform, encourage, and connect people. In "Strange Bedfellows: Community Development, Democracy, and Magic," Esther Farmer explains this unchoreographed occurrence:

> "Magic moments" are experienced when people are transformed by feelings of surprise and delight, . . . that collective "aha" feeling, or experience the joy of connection with a group. These moments allow people to temporarily suspend their belief systems and feel a collective openness to something new and transformative. They can sometimes be life changing. . . . [P]ractitioners often have to facilitate the creation of environments in which they can happen. Community developers in this field strive to engage citizens holistically, including their emotional and creative assets . . . [to] challenge traditional models that often reflect class, race, and gender biases. The process of creating environments for magic to happen can promote a culture of democracy, where principles of inclusion and participation are manifest. (294)

Project Humanities acknowledges that community engagement and community development are inherently about relationships between individuals, across communities. The organizational successes of Project Humanities, then, embody collaboration, reciprocity, and dialogue. Further centering community engagement, Project Humanities facilitated in 2017–18 the grant-funded series Aridity and the Desert: A Moveable Feast for Positive Community Engagement (Bunning). The title was based loosely on the novelist Ernest Hemingway's description of Paris as a "moveable feast": "Wherever you go for the rest of your life, it stays with you." Those who live or have lived here find that Arizona and the Southwest stay with them for the rest of their lives, so it is important that Arizonans—and by extension all folks through the Project Humanities lens—build positive relationships by talking, listening, and connecting within communities, across cultures, disciplines, professions, and generations. "Community" can be defined as "a place where people associate and create meaningful relationships" (Matarrita-Cascante and Brennan 298). John R. Owen and Peter Westoby make clear that community development is fundamentally about relationships:

> A critical first step in community development work involves initiating and responding to contact with others. Contemporary approaches rely heavily on the ability of practitioners to communicate effectively with the people with whom they are working. Prior to "facilitating" "good public processes," or "mobilizing" "common pool" resources, or even "empowering communities" to "do it themselves," practitioners must first build good local-level relationships. . . . Given that the objective of that [interpersonal] communication is to bring parties together, we focus our attention on the use of dialogue in building a developmental process between individuals. (306)

This Project Humanities series included the events "Perspectives on Place" and "Place and Place-Making," focused on the Sonoran Desert of southwest Arizona—where Arizona State University and Project Humanities are located and where dustiness and heat can represent metaphorically a lack of and need for better connections and understandings of individual lives within an ever-changing world. Conversations were both locally and nationally necessary to demonstrate that the almost hourly news stories of divisiveness, violence, inhumanity, and misunderstanding need not overwhelm or disempower individuals and communities committed to effecting positive and impactful social change. Hence, Project Humanities' focus was not on the dryness and moisture that characterize and too often center conversations about desert dwelling but rather on the aridity that emerges from such natural elements. The four Moveable Feasts each brought together fifty to sixty-five individuals to share a meal and catalyze positive engagement among Arizonans around the topics "Community, Place, and Progress," "Politics and Politicians," "Pride and Prejudice: Intersectionalities within LGBTQIA+ Communities," and "The Future of Innovation, Technology, and Humanity."

In order to assemble the most diverse participants for the Moveable Feast conversations, Project Humanities requested personal registration information from each applicant. This included asking participants how they identified racially, religiously, and politically, and even asking about their likes and dislikes. To ensure new and varied participation, interested participants could attend a single event in the series. Project Humanities created and orchestrated these opportunities and interactions intentionally to better ensure that learning would be a positive experience. Attendees overwhelmingly praised each of the four events. Feedback included praise for the facilitators, the delicious meals, and the pleasant venues, but, most importantly, attendees expressed gratitude for having been brought together simply to talk about human connections in an increasingly divided time and requested that we continue to offer these kinds of events.

By multiple measures for this series—formal and informal feedback surveys, attendance, the quality of the conversations, and the fact that attendees became regular supporters of subsequent Project Humanities events, activities, and programs—Project Humanities broadened audience perspectives and showed the interconnectedness of the humanities within and across disciplines and communities. Project Humanities demonstrated its ability as a leader and a catalyst for community- and bridge-building, demonstrating that "a community can transform its belief about the common good to build a stronger sense of unity and to take appropriate action steps rather than feel powerless" (Hustedde and Ganowicz 17). The Moveable Feasts encouraged mindful listening—that is, listening to understand rather than listening to respond. The events humanized strangers who became acquaintances and friends, attendees feeling heard even if they did not always agree with one another's views.

Critical Partnerships and Collaborations

At the heart of Project Humanities' impact and successes are the many strategic collaborations and partnerships we have created and sustained. Academicians, community groups, and individuals increasingly seek the initiative's guidance, partnership, and support. In 2019, for instance, the leaders of the Arizona African American Christian Clergy Coalition invited Project Humanities to be a critical partner in conceptualizing, organizing, implementing, and facilitating the sole Arizona historic commemoration of 1619, the year the first enslaved Africans were forcibly brought to what is now the US. Attracting nearly four hundred attendees, this multidimensional educational experience, hosted at the predominantly Black congregation of the First Institutional Baptist Church in Phoenix, offered statewide recognition of "the historical implications of slavery and how Africans and African Americans have moved forward . . . beyond enslavement" ("Four Hundred Years").[6] This commemoration invited participants into a public discussion of chattel slavery in the diaspora and a celebration of music, food, and culture despite the physical, psychological, and economic shackles in present-day Black Americans' experiences. Food, music, dance, libations, prayers, and chants became communal homage to a time and place that is both present and future, both here in Arizona and far in these diasporic traditions. Project Humanities welcomed this Arizona celebration as an opportunity to leverage place to generate a new narrative to counter Arizona's reluctance until 1993 to make Martin Luther King, Jr., Day a national holiday (see Warren).

Hosting several events and programs at local churches—programs that are not religious per se, such as film screenings of documentaries on local homelessness and on toxic masculinity—has attracted many supporters who continue to participate in Project Humanities programming. For instance, in 2018, Project Humanities facilitated a partnership between the First Congregational United Church of Christ Phoenix, whose membership is predominantly white, and the oldest Black church in Arizona, the Historic Tanner Chapel African Methodist Episcopal Church, to host a three-day men's conference coordinated by Project Humanities. The conference covered such topics as Black men navigating the law, Black men and mental health, Black men and sexual harassment, and Black men and spirituality. Sessions were facilitated by experts on and practitioners of these topics. Attendees have gone on to join other Project Humanities activities—such as our homeless outreach—and continue to recall this event in conversations about the range and impact of Project Humanities' community engagement programming.

Another important partnership thrives between Project Humanities and the Public Broadcasting Service (PBS) Indie Lens Pop-Up documentary film and discussion series. Working to create more critical audiences, Project Humanities hosts film screenings with discussion before these documentaries are broadcast publicly. These screenings are facilitated by panelists of experts from a range of backgrounds and experiences. The PBS and Project Humanities cobranding means that attendees expect high-quality documentary films with provocative conversations on a range of topics: modern-day lynchings of Black men veiled as suicides; romance and sexuality among individuals on the autism spectrum; the history of historically Black colleges and universities (HBCUs); the scarcity and poor quality of healthcare in the rural US; Indigenous children and US boarding schools; Indigenous rock music; children's television and the social impact of the popular show *Mister Rogers' Neighborhood*, which ran for thirty years; bias in technology; grassroots community organizing; cheerleaders, athletes, and the gender wage gap; environmental justice and Easter Island; gender and arranged marriages in India; the US government's use of drones during wartime; and the history of the 9to5 women's labor movement. This ongoing partnership has forged other partnerships with hosting venues such as the Tempe History Museum and the Burton Barr Phoenix Public Library, both public humanities and justice spaces that bring together individuals from disparate parts of the Phoenix metro Valley of the Sun and various socioeconomic groups.

Community partnerships further underscore Project Humanities' social embeddedness. Our Service Saturdays homeless outreach program, for instance, led to U-Haul's donation of a seventeen-foot truck to transport outreach items to and from an outdoor distribution site in downtown Phoenix every other Saturday morning for the last ten plus years ("Homeless Outreach"). Additionally, a couple who manage a local running store and volunteer with our program have donated nearly five hundred pairs of gently used returned running shoes to this cause. Project Humanities' outreach is as much about community-building and community-sustaining as about offering human kindness to individuals and underrepresented populations too often denied such support and visibility within the greater society. Over the years, hundreds have volunteered for weekly Friday two-hour sorting sessions—where we take in donations, sort them, label them, size them, and pack them in bins for biweekly Service Saturdays distributions. Coming from across the Valley, multigenerational volunteers (from middle-schoolers to retirees)—including professionals, students, faculty members, staff members, administrators, and police officers—work together as "personal shoppers" for two hours, supporting over two hundred adults experiencing homelessness. Since beginning in 2012, Project Humanities' homeless outreach—which distributes clothing, shoes, and toiletries—has supported over 18,000 nonunique clients and hosted some 9,900 nonunique volunteers, who have clocked just over 18,600 total volunteer hours. For several years, this ongoing, year-round outreach has benefited from a robust partnership with the Keys to Change Campus in downtown Phoenix, a hub of services for those experiencing homelessness, where our volunteers set up a free marketplace of donated goods from which our clients can select with the assistance of volunteers as their "personal shoppers." In turn, partnering with the Keys to Change Campus has stopped the constant threat and criminalization by the City of Phoenix Police Department of Project Humanities and other such organizations offering various humanitarian support to those who are unhoused. Such threats and criminalization demonstrate the risks involved in promoting basic humanity and disrupting the status quo that says that the work groups like ours do is not ending homelessness as a national crisis. Our minimal time spent interacting with our clients signals that kindness, respect, and compassion can go beyond other tangible measures of impact and success for our clients. This outreach experience has also led to volunteers' understanding and practicing language used when talking about this outreach to others—such as leading with "people experiencing homelessness" instead of "homeless people"—and to intentional efforts to steer clear of "poverty porn"—exploiting intentionally or unintentionally others' vulnerabilities for personal gain and social capital—in posting about and promoting our volunteer efforts.

Organizations dedicated to the humanities have also been critical partners in bringing Project Humanities together with other advocates interested in community service, engagement, and development. For instance, after I gave an invited high school keynote on Project Humanities' Humanity 101 Movement for a Rho Kappa National Social Studies Honor Society induction ceremony in 2017, Linda Burrows, then a specialist in social studies and world languages at the Arizona Department of Education, invited me to speak as founding director at the Arizona Civics Coalition's seventh annual Civic Learning Conference, offering this context:

> This year's theme [is] "Our Sputnik Moment: Revitalizing Civic Learning and Community Engagement throughout our Civic Spaces." I instantly thought of you and your students. My daughter was one of the officers at that [honor society] ceremony and participated in a few Service Saturdays. Of all the service she did, Service Saturdays was one of the most meaningful to her and helped to shape her world view. . . . I witnessed how impactful your message was on my high school students years ago and would love to share that same message at our conference with pre-K through grade 12 educators and administrators, plus our adult education community from all over the state. (Personal communication with author, 2 Dec. 2019)[7]

For the 2020 annual convention of the Modern Language Association (MLA), the premier North American professional humanities advocacy organization, the executive director, Paula Krebs, invited me to serve on a plenary panel with humanities leaders from the Simpson Center, the American Council of Learned Societies, the National Endowment for the Humanities, and the National Humanities Center to discuss the future of humanities research and public humanities and to highlight exemplary local initiatives.[8] The impact of the model of Project Humanities as community engagement and development resonated with faculty members and students who attended the plenary. One doctoral candidate in cinema and media studies at the University of Washington, Richard Boyechko, expressed this to the director:

> It was very fulfilling to hear your views about the future of humanities and, perhaps even more importantly, to see how you actually implemented that vision in the here and now. What you said regarding scholars not seeing them-

> selves as saviors coming down from the hill to educate the masses deeply resonated with me. That has been a source of frequent "scholarly existentialist" struggles for me, since I cannot reconcile our purported values as humanists on one hand and the kind of specialization and siloed scholarship that we do on the other. It seems to me that to make our knowledge serve the communities that support us, we need to be engaged with the kind of culture that people in those communities respond to rather than discounting it as inferior to what we have chosen to study. Your clearly, accessibly, and enthusiastically articulated convictions have done much to steady my shaken faith in the discipline and reaffirmed my plans to do more participatory research for my dissertation . . . (Personal communication with author, 11 Jan. 2020)

The overwhelmingly positive reactions to the national presentation at the MLA convention launched additional responses to the Project Humanities model. Following the 2020 MLA plenary, I was interviewed by the *Chronicle of Higher Education* (Lester, "Are the Humanities Really in Crisis?" and "Humanity 101 in Action"), which in turn led to subsequent invitations to speak about Project Humanities as a community engagement model from four US universities who acknowledged seeing the *Chronicle* coverage. Presented in my October 2020 feature keynote, "Humanities and Entrepreneurship; or, the Entrepreneurial Humanist," given as part of the Mellon Foundation–funded "Engaged Humanities" initiative at the University of Illinois, Chicago (UIC), the model of Project Humanities shifted attending humanities undergraduates' ideas about the possibilities of humanities research, study, and engagement, as evidenced in their anonymous feedback shared with me by Ellen McClure, the professor leading this initiative. One student in response to the keynote commented on

> [t]he lack of intersectional identity in everyday products like Rice Krispies cereal, children's literature, and junk mail. I had never recognized the lack of diverse characters as a reflection of exclusion. These ubiquitous products teach us early on who [does] and who doesn't belong or fit the picture. What surprised me the most . . . was the first activity. . . . When picturing Cinderella, most of us imagined the blonde, blue-eyed white princess. Seeing her and other fairy tale characters portrayed as black or simply nonwhite significantly subverted my expectations and that says a lot about the culture I live in. (McClure, personal communication with author, 26 Oct. 2020)

McClure, a professor of French and history and then director of UIC's Engaged Humanities Initiative, had this to say about the Project Humanities model and how her thinking about engaged humanities had changed as a result of my talk:

> The feedback was overwhelmingly wonderful—the Provost found the talk "exciting and inspiring," and one of our second-year seminar professors wrote

> asking whether we had any plans to do some similar activities at UIC. It's also led me to think much more boldly and creatively about the Initiative. . . . It's really about exactly what you're describing—how to lead/work/teach in a way that involves "letting go" (including of our ideas of what the humanities should be) and "letting come"—responding to students, situations, a rapidly changing world. The fact that your incredible talk arrived just as I was starting the course in earnest seems like some sort of sign.
>
> (Personal communication with author, 17 Oct. 2020)

In a subsequent communication, McClure added, "Once again, profound thanks for the talk and for the work you're doing. I know that for me personally, it dovetailed with a lot of other things I'm doing and thinking about right now, in the best possible way—you've altered my own trajectory" (26 Oct. 2020).

The 2020 MLA plenary and subsequent events led to an invitation from Krebs to moderate a discussion on faculty and media interactions key to community development efforts at the 2022 MLA convention. Project Humanities as a model of diversity and technology was the focus of my presentation at the October 2021 conference "Diversifying Tech Leadership," hosted by the World's Best Connectors, a Phoenix-based resource for senior executives. Such presentations and press coverage have furthered the visibility and impact of Project Humanities, thus enabling it to continue to expand its student, corporate,[9] and community engagement.

What Project Humanities Does to Promote and Build Community

Project Humanities' thirteen-year-plus track record demonstrates the humanities' strong interrelationships across disciplines, and its programming contributes to the positive and affirmative experience of diversity at ASU. That Project Humanities brings individuals and communities together to talk, listen, and connect across boundaries—professions, generations, and cultures—aligns with ASU's "New American University" ideal as a model for institutional and communal commitment to diversity, engaging the whole university—students, faculty members, staff members, and community members—and providing a unique lens through which to experience and engage diversity, inclusion, and belonging. Project Humanities' programming and outreach underscore the ASU institutional charter, which centers inclusion, collaboration, and reciprocity: "ASU is a comprehensive public research university, measured not by whom we exclude, but rather by whom we include and how they succeed; advancing research and discovery of public value; and assuming fundamental responsibility for the economic, social, cultural, and overall health of the communities it serves" ("ASU Charter"). In a 2018 case statement for investment in Project Humanities, Margaret Dellow, then program manager in the Office of Knowledge Enterprise at ASU, commented:

> Our world's challenges require a multidisciplinary approach. . . . In this complexity, communication can be difficult, especially when such diverse voices are speaking from different perspectives and with different motivations and understandings. The Humanity 101 principles create a common language through which we all can speak and relate regardless of our disciplines, backgrounds, and live[d] experiences.
>
> Project Humanities contends that it is through observance of these Humanity 101 principles that we begin to understand one another, resolve contentious issues, and heal rifts that divide us so that we can grow as a society and be better people. (*Project Humanities* 2)

An anonymous Arizona State University student organizer says that their engagement with Project Humanities as an undergraduate student has given them a more holistic understanding of humanities beyond the trite association of humanities with teaching critical thinking—which the humanities alone cannot claim as their sole purview. The student comments, "I realized humanities was more than just a major—it is part of life" (Mueller 41). What better way to see our impact than reflected in this integrated student perspective?

Humanity 101

Since 2012, Project Humanities' signature Humanity 101 Movement has been responding to the question, "Are we losing our humanity?" and offering seven Humanity 101 principles as foundational to diversity, inclusion, and human achievement: compassion, empathy, forgiveness, integrity, kindness, respect, and self-reflection ("Humanity 101"). With a focus on values critical to both an individual's and an organization's growth, confidence, and responsibility, Humanity 101 is a virtual and experiential toolbox of programs, activities, databases, and strategies that promote those values, which represent humanity at its best and are integrated into all that Project Humanities does, including the Service Saturdays homeless outreach program, the Hacks for Humanity annual hackathon, the Indie Lens Pop-Up PBS film screening and community discussion, the Humanity 101 in the Workplace: Lessons in Privilege and Bias workshops, and various community dialogue series, including Vital Voices, Dispelling the Myths, Aridity and the Desert, and the grant-funded Conscious Parenting community conversations, which we called Humanity 101 on the Homefront.[10]

Community engagement takes many forms under the Humanity 101 umbrella, as in the 20 October 2021 outdoor public event "Beyond Books: The 'Stuff' of Racial Representation," which I facilitated and based on my research on and teaching of African American literature and culture (see Terrill, "Interactive Exhibit"). My campus office is filled with several hundred racist US and global Black Americana artifacts that supplement my teaching of print texts in my courses. This "colored museum," which travels to my many community workshops on privilege and bias, the N-word, and cultural appropriation, was for the first time made available as a pop-up museum on my campus's Student Services lawn, enabling more public access. I talked about the creation of the collection—dolls, posters, commercial packaging, figurines, music boxes, toys, games, and magnets—as a tool for teaching social justice. Passersby entered the space, took photos, made video recordings, and spoke with the Project Humanities team about its justice programming. As in the Vital Voices series, some of the 150 attendees brought artifacts related to social justice, taking the opportunity to "do humanities" by looking at the history of racial representations, systemic racism, and white supremacy across cultures. One undergraduate student, Savannah Stewart, commented in a class assignment:

> It was . . . remarkable when the other attendees got up to share their experiences and displayed things that they have found during their travels from other countries. It shows that the disturbing tradition of mocking darker skin is one that happens all over the world, not just in the USA. All of these items really work together to show through vision and touch the reality [of] racism . . .

Eve Johnson, an ASU staff member, offered this response to the event in a personal message to me: "Very interesting items and conversation. Thank you for educating and opening our eyes to racial representation" (20 Oct. 2021). Another ASU staff member, Suzanne Wilson, shared during the session that before seeing the children's card game "Old Maid" on the display table, she had not considered the implications of a children's card game that mocks unpartnered and aging women. She later commented in a personal email communication that she had appreciated the hands-on humanities experience as "a very thoughtful and evocative event. Great demonstration of how to recenter narratives around race and gender" (21 Oct. 2021). Thanks to such enthusiastic feedback, this inaugural pop-up has become an annual presence that introduces new content to new people passing through and by the Student Services lawn, who get an unexpected lesson in humanities across disciplines and communities. The pop-up social justice museum has also become a regular traveling exhibition that challenges the academy's and society's privileging of books as the primary marker of teaching and learning. In the same way that this exhibit engages attendees, Project Humanities programming challenges and engages beyond the purely theoretical and the scholarly.

Signature Lectures

In addition to convening and facilitating critical community conversations, Project Humanities also brings to campus leading scholars, activists, and artists for Signature Lectures—extensive interactions and engagement with ASU communities. Since 2011, Signature Lectures have included Bernice A. King, the daughter of the slain civil rights leader Martin Luther King, Jr.; the transgender professional athlete Veronica Ivy; the author and blogger Nora McInerny; the anti-racism educator Jane Elliott; the American Indian Movement cofounder Clyde Bellecourt; the musician and producer Bobby Taylor; the rhythm and blues singer Ruth Pointer; the former Phi Beta Kappa secretary John Churchill; the poets Nikki Giovanni and Rita Dove; the humor columnist Gustavo Arellano; the feminist scholar bell hooks; the former MLA executive director Rosemary Feal; the former NEH chairs James Leach and William Ferris; the author Sherman Alexie; the activist Angela Y. Davis; and the author Carolivia Herron. Visits by these cultural and academic luminaries, in addition to facilitating what many folks deem difficult and courageous conversations, have become hallmarks of our success and impact. In addition to a presentation generally open to the public and university stakeholders, speakers meet our Project Humanities investors in a VIP reception; some, such as Jane Elliott, have special sessions with high school students or with select research and teaching faculty members who read the guest's work and discuss it among themselves and with their students before the visit.

All Project Humanities events are informed by scholarly research and facilitated by researchers, clinical experts, and community practitioners, often in combination. Project Humanities recognizes that expertise comes in many forms and that knowledge is not always gained through traditional disciplinary means. Some of Project Humanities' most engaging topics over the years have been on these topics: rape culture, menstrual equity, transgender identities, transgender athletes and sport, youth and mental health, missing and murdered Indigenous women, toxic masculinity, the N-word, call-out culture, body positivity, privilege and bias (see "Humanity 101 in the Workplace"), cultural appropriation in the forms of blackface and Indigenous mascots (see "Cultural Appropriation"), and myths regarding atheism and polytheism (see Terrill, "Casting Out Demons"). Participants routinely describe their experiences in their anonymous feedback surveys as "educational," "enlightening," and "inspiring." Indeed, the educational component comes through in survey comments such as these:

"As a minority, low-income, and first-generation college student, I often feel not empowered based on what I experienced, saw, and learned concerning environmental injustice against minorities. After this event, I felt a spark of hope and a sense of reflection and connection." ("Environmental Justice: Indigenous Communities" panel, November 2020)

"I work in an education-adjacent field but never before thought about access to menstrual hygiene products in schools." ("Menstrual Equity" panel, March 2019)

"I never considered the connection of food to philosophy. I am leaving with an awareness of how food both unites us as well as divides us." ("Food, Identity and Politics" panel and community sharing, October 2019)

"As a dance department head, this work really helped me with a personal goal of creating a dance program that is accessible for all body types. . . . As a dance producer who often does not see people on stage of my race, I have created my own event to uplift others, dance makers of color and all bodies." ("Disrupting Body Standards" panel, February 2019)

"I'm a librarian at a public library and would like to be more inclusive of cultures and introduce more into our story times and programming." (*Rumble: The Indians Who Rocked the World* film screening and discussion, November 2018)

"I learned a lot about missing and murdered Indigenous women and in general about Indigenous cultures and beliefs." ("Gender and Violence" World Café, September 2018)

"Looking forward to sharing what I've learned with my circle and where I work and consider how to incorporate these concepts into the services I provide." ("Gender and Violence" World Café, September 2018)

With research tools and strategies, Project Humanities' community engagement inspires new thinking and prompts action related to individual, group, professional, K–12, and higher education. Our programming can also have a personal impact that moves beyond our stated objectives and impact metrics, as this anonymous lecture attendee offers: "Thank you. My mother is dying and so upset. [Nora McInerny's] talk is giving me permission to hurt and not be stoic" ("Toxic Positivity: The Good, the Bad and the Unpretty," March 2021).

High School Symposia

Project Humanities values engaging students—undergraduate, graduate, high school, and middle school students—in talking, listening, and connecting across communities. While the most regular involvement of secondary school students is through our homeless outreach, Project Humanities has hosted three high school symposia on cultural awareness, including such topics as cultural appropriation, the N-word, and interfaith belief systems. Finding the project's community work on cultural appropriation on our website, an eighth-grade Indigenous Boy Scout's mother reached out for advice and resources:

> I am Anglo, my son is Navajo. I have worked hard as an adoptive parent to make sure my son is connected with Navajo culture . . . and his experiences are authentic.
>
> My son is having a negative experience with the Boy Scouts and their use or misuse of Native culture. I have made a formal complaint to Boy Scouts of America's national office about appropriation of Native American culture within their honor fraternity Order of the Arrow. My complaint has been ig-

> nored. . . . Order of the Arrow's misuse of Native sacred objects, Native language, wearing of headdresses and other Native regalia, and performance of imitated pow-wows is a source of anger, frustration, and depression for my son. . . . I would . . . like more research . . . about the negative effects of misappropriation with Native youth. My son does not want to quit Boy Scouts, but wants [to] voice concerns and make changes within the Boy Scout culture. (Karen A., personal communication with author, 17 Nov. 2015)

Following Karen's letter, and one from Ezekiel himself, I developed a relationship with this family by providing education and cultural resources (see "Cultural Appropriation"). I even visited Zeke and his parents on a research trip to New Mexico. A year later, Ezekiel was the keynote speaker at a Project Humanities high school symposium, where his passion, his cultural perceptivity, and his confidence in challenging a national organization inspired listeners. I received this letter from the family on Zeke's progress educating his Scout peers and the organization:

> [Our son] is very close to achieving Eagle Scout rank with Boy Scouts of America (BSA), and he would like to continue to push for change with BSA. His Eagle Scout project is about telling the history at Bosque Redondo, which included an education component of taking his troop to Canyon De Chelly and the Navajo Nation Museum to learn the history of the Long Walk and assimilation. (Karen A., personal communication with author, 30 May 2018)

Ultimately, this local Scout chapter came to understand how their rituals were culturally problematic and insulting and pledged to address the concerns raised. Our efforts to provide resources and guidance led this mom and her son to reach out to the cofounder of the American Indian Movement, Clyde Bellecourt, at our suggestion because he had been a Signature Lecturer some time before. For this student, there was empowerment and validation in his concerns about how he felt his Native identity was being trivialized and even mocked. A budding activist, he was encouraged by me as Project Humanities director to register his concerns with the national Boy Scouts of America leadership. In part, his letter read:

> My name is Ezekiel . . . , a 14-year-old Navajo teen from Moriarty, New Mexico . . . a member of Edgewood, Troop 640. I am writing to make a complaint about Order of the Arrow and ask Boy Scouts of America to stop cultural appropriation. . . . [T]hey mistreated the drum, the war bonnet . . . items that are considered sacred to Native people. [We] Native Americans are human beings too, not an icon [or a] thing. We should be treated equally . . . with respect to our culture . . . which we are trying to preserve for future generations. (1 Dec. 2015)

For Project Humanities, diversity and justice are inextricable companions. A commitment to understanding and educating about American Indians manifests in the project's land acknowledgment statement, read at all events since May 2020; multiple community conversations about the harm of sports teams' Indigenous mascots; a film showing and discussion of the documentary *In Whose Honor?*; a film showing and discussion with Indigenous representatives as panelists on the PBS partnership documentary *Dawnland*, about the history of government boarding schools and American Indian children; a screening and discussion of the PBS documentary *Rumble: The Indians Who Rocked the World*, about Native American rock artists; a conversation on missing and murdered Indigenous women; a conversation about environmental justice and Indigenous communities; and other events, on topics such as food sovereignty, that engage Indigenous and other cultural perspectives.

Hacks for Humanity

Project Humanities defines and demystifies the humanities both inside and beyond academia through talking, listening, and connecting. This approach has allowed Project Humanities to take the humanities outside the classroom and into the lives of supporters, stakeholders, and participants. People often ask those who study and teach the humanities, "What do you do with the humanities?" and humanists find ourselves having to justify what we do. This is a good challenge to have. Since 2014, Project Humanities' annual hacking event, Hacks for Humanity: Hacking for the Social Good, has been one way to meet this challenge head-on by engaging diverse multidisciplinary and multiprofessional communities in employing innovation and creativity (see "What Is Project Humanities' Hacks for Humanity?" and "Hacks for Humanity 2020 Promo"). Hacks for Humanity attracts participants from different fields and backgrounds, as well as corporate sponsors. COVID restrictions led to virtual participation by individuals from around the world and across the US. Feedback demonstrates that team participants, mentors, volunteers, and judges appreciate the uniqueness of this event and experience, especially the chance to meet and work with new people on the randomly assigned teams.

A thirty-six-hour community-building opportunity for intense innovation that goes far beyond coding, Hacks for Humanity offers many ways for the 150 to 200 participants to connect. What makes our annual hackathon unique is that it is not just for techies. Team participants of at least sixteen years of age register according to their individual areas of expertise, interest, or experience (as artists, coders, designers, engineers, entrepreneurs, and generalists) and are algorithmically, for the sake of diversity and developing new collaboration skills, assigned to teams to build a technological solution to a problem and compete for prizes. Mentors are those of any age who support the teams through the entire process of developing, pitching, and presenting their products. Volunteers, sponsors, supporters, and judges are also key. The goal is to create any technology for the social good that is grounded in at least three of the seven Humanity 101 principles. Our event focuses on thematic categories to further guide participants, such as education, health care, and the environment. Hackathon conveners provide these tracks from which the teams may choose. Incorporating market research, business plan development, target audience identification, website creation, and pitching skills, this event is a consummate entrepreneurial experience that allows for networking, workshopping, mentoring, volunteering, and being part of something bigger than oneself. The teams' products are consistently impressive and far-reaching.

The momentum does not stop once the winning team claims their prize; Hacks for Humanity has generated significant change within the lives of several participants. One example of the hackathon's sheer transformative power is demonstrated through the continuing success of its 2014 winning team, ARKHumanity, who designed an app to identify tweets containing specific key phrases frequently used by people in crisis who are at risk of self-harm or suicide. Since their formation and victory at the 2014 hackathon, the group has gone on to win various social enterprise competitions, to present at major academic and professional conferences, and to launch their own business, called HumanityX. This team continues to lead the way in improving humanity by saving lives through new technologies. Each year, our handpicked judges, representing diverse areas of experience and expertise, are impressed with the results and with the participants' energies and synergies. One judge from October 2021 posted this commentary on their public *Facebook* page: "Today I was privileged to act as a judge for ASU Project Humanities' eighth annual Hacks for Humanity. . . . This powerful, inspiring event challenged participants across the globe to develop tech solutions for the social good. Congratulations to Team MeasSure for developing an app that measures water quality, provides analytics, and assists users with contacting their elected officials."

Homeless Outreach

Another Project Humanities signature ongoing activity, its Service Saturdays homeless outreach program, has expanded substantially since it began over ten years ago, attracting intergenerational volunteers, families, high school students and teachers, community college members, retirees, ASU visiting faculty members, community exchange students, and many others. Project Humanities' homeless outreach began with a few volunteers from the university and the surrounding Maricopa County going to the sidewalks just outside the Keys to Change Campus in downtown Phoenix to support 150 to 200 adults experiencing homelessness. Volunteers came from different parts of the Valley and initially collected and stored clothing and shoe donations in their respective garages. On alternate Saturdays, they placed the folded donations on tarps and hung garments from a chain-link fence to create a pop-up marketplace along the sidewalk at Twelfth Avenue and Madison where clients could shop for free. What initially was called "Spontaneous Day of Service" to support unsheltered individuals was so transformative to the handful of volunteers who went down those first few Saturdays for the two-hour block—from 6:30 a.m. to 8:30 a.m.—that many saw a need and wanted to continue. Continuing this outreach translated into a designated space on the Project Humanities website, a 400+ member Service Saturdays *Facebook* group posting local and national stories about homelessness as a national political and social crisis, and lots of word-of-mouth recruitment of additional volunteers.

Project Humanities' biweekly Service Saturdays, where intergenerational, multiprofessional, and multicommunal individuals, groups, and organizations gather to distribute shoes, clothing, and toiletries, are part of Humanity 101 in Action, an outreach built on collaboration, volunteerism, and partnerships. The Saturday morning outreach continues to meet a growing need in local communities across the Valley, as mirrored across the United States: the need to extend humanity—through compassion, empathy, kindness, and respect—to individuals denied fundamental dignity. Not only has this outreach offered witness to what a travel-size tube of toothpaste or deodorant or a pair of generic socks can do to lift the spirits of those who do not have these basics, but volunteers' attitudes toward those who are unsheltered have also changed. No longer do volunteers talk about the unsheltered as "homeless people" but now refer to clients as "people experiencing homelessness," thereby acknowledging that homelessness is not an identity but a circumstance, one with which anyone can be faced. For the hundreds of people who have volunteered with Project Humanities over these many years, Humanity 101 in Action is a welcome opportunity for deep self-reflection and critical reflections on class, race, gender, age, sexuality, ability, mental health, wellness, suffering, loss, and humanity.

This interpersonal community-building that characterizes Humanity 101 also demonstrates how "[h]uman development processes seek healthier and more educated individuals, with stronger bonds amongst each other, and with the capacity to lead local efforts through established purposive collective action" (Matarrita-Cascante and Brennan 296). Volunteers take this outreach into the realm of activism, attending city council meetings, posting letters to city officials, and intentionally seeking out new partnerships. One volunteer has cultivated a partnership with the Bra Recyclers, another local nonprofit organization, who in one donation provided 150 assorted gently used bras for our cause. A volunteer shared that one client had cried upon getting two bras that fit. The profound, empowering impact of these essential articles of clothing for this individual's physical and mental well-being was obvious. Another community group, Kindness Konnectors, saw a *Facebook* post about our service and our request for bras and donated over four hundred nearly new bras. And the bras keep coming from this source as our outreach continues. Says Ramona Ferrara, a homeless outreach core member, "At least once every trip, someone makes a point to come back and show off what they found. Full of gratitude. . . . [T]hat serious strut when you know you look good, or you got the winning ticket, is unmistakable: full of confidence and beaming with pride!" (Personal communication with author, 13 Oct. 2021). Another regular volunteer, Randy Horshok, of the Arizona Chapter of the Michigan State University Alumni Association, invited members of the chapter to volunteer as well, at one point leading the number of volunteers on any given Service Saturdays distribution with a total of seventy. About the meaning of this outreach to him, Horshok explains:

> That human connection really makes it rewarding. I think it makes all the difference in the world. As you drive down the street and you see somebody pushing a shopping cart with clothes, for ninety-nine percent of the population, that is their only connection with that person with a shopping cart. They don't know what put them there. They don't know what mindset that person has. . . . This one time, this fellow says, "I don't need anything." Kind of stopped me in my tracks and looked at me. He goes, "I want to thank you guys because I was here two weeks ago, picked up clothing that I wore to a job interview, and I got the job. Wow! So, I'm going to be renting an apartment. I'm going to be working full-time, and I wouldn't have been able to do that had it not been for this." So he went through the whole line and thanked all the volunteers that he encountered. . . . [T]here's not a Saturday that I don't walk away from there with a smile and at least one pleasant memory. So, yeah, that's what makes it worthwhile. That's what makes us come back.
>
> ("Homeless Outreach")

Individuals, groups, and organizations wanting to get involved in this outreach have several options: doing donation drives and competitions; doing personal or corporate solicitations within familial, communal, and professional networks; joining weekly Friday sorting sessions; being "personal shoppers" for our clients during Service Saturdays; making an online tax-deductible monetary donation; or purchasing toiletry items through an Amazon Wish List. Especially for those who are not local, these monetary options have been valuable and appreciated. From middle and high school students to community members to retirees, this outreach has an important role for everyone interested.

For its tenth anniversary in 2021, Project Humanities assembled a Donations Challenge Committee of community supporters and students, who created a monthly challenge calendar to keep supporters engaged and contributing meaningfully, especially while the homeless outreach had to be significantly modified during the global COVID lockdown. Acknowledging that the needs of our unsheltered clients did not go away during the lockdown, Project Humanities partnered with two organizations able to take Project Humanities–assembled care packages of toiletries, along with backpacks, shoes, clothes, blankets, and underwear, to individual clients. Such partnerships with Arizona Jews for Justice and AZ Hugs for the Houseless kept donations of clothing, shoes, and toiletries circulating safely and steadily.

Humanity 101 in Action has become its own community-building entity through its partnership with the Keys to Change Campus, a hub of services for unsheltered individuals in downtown Phoenix (see "Dr. Neal Lester"). One local high school volunteer, Andrew Basha, 2016–17 president of the Rho Kappa Social Studies Honor Society, commented on the importance of this work for him and his high school peers: "We met people . . . just like us; we learned their names, heard their stories, and sent them off . . . with a few more basic necessities. . . . Service Saturdays allowed students to directly help a disenfranchised demographic while dispelling the myths surrounding homelessness for young, impressionable students" (*Project Humanities* 4). Volunteers do not simply "do good" for people experiencing homelessness; they also develop their own understanding of and empathy for the issues affecting vulnerable populations so that they are better positioned to create and understand the need for lasting change. As Santiago Griffin Todd, a Service Saturdays high school intern, explains after four years of volunteering with his mother, sister, and grandfather (who drives two hours down and back from Prescott, Arizona, to participate with Santiago):

> [W]e bring humanity to people by allowing them to choose what clothing they get . . . which allows people to choose their style and really brings humanity back where [it] may have been lost. . . . Project Humanities and helping people who were experiencing homelessness . . . has really helped enrich my thought processes and . . . advance me as a person and my sense of morals. I have a lot more respect for every single person as a human after meeting people in a place I had never been before . . .
>
> ("Santiago Griffin Todd")

Podcast Club

While most of Project Humanities' initial programming occurred during a nine-month academic year, the project has for the past three summers created new programming to keep community conversations going year-round. Transitioning to virtual events amid the COVID-19 pandemic prompted Project Humanities to devise new strategies to engage and to stay engaged with others. In the podcast club Talking, Listening, and Podcasting, listening to a podcast and discussing it for an hour virtually allows people from all over the world to talk, listen, and connect regarding the topics and ideas that enrich lives and potentially challenge and embolden thinking and behaviors. Its audio format also allows listeners to multitask as they learn. The podcasts selected are accessible, provocative, and linked to topics related to past and future Project Humanities events. These virtual conversations are cofacilitated by a Project Humanities team member in partnership with other Project Humanities community members, supporters, and partners. Podcast discussions occur during the summer months every other Thursday evening and are broadcast on *Zoom* and *Facebook Live*. Topics of these discussions have included "whupping" and African American parenting, death and dying, youth mental health as related to academic pressures, menstrual equity, the court system and neglected rape kits, modern-day voter suppression, anti-speciesism, and decriminalizing the "War on Drugs." Importantly, about half of past podcast discussions have been cofacilitated by high school student interns, underscoring Project Humanities' commitment to intergenerational input and leadership development. The interns choose the topic, research the topic, choose a cofacilitator, and determine the major critical points of the discussion. About our June 2020 podcast, *Spare the Kids*, a discussion of "whupping" and Black parenting through the lens of violence and systemic white supremacy, an anonymous attendee wrote this feedback:

> It was quite honestly the most human I've felt in months. Discussing the complex facets of the human experience with such nuance and in-depth analysis, hearing so many different viewpoints, . . . allowed me to reflect on my own levels of self-awareness while educating me on points I've never considered. I felt such mental freedom I can't even put into words. All-in-all one of the best discussions I've ever been a part of in my life and looking forward to the ones that follow!

Impact

Project Humanities is sometimes misperceived as solely an "outreach organization." Too often within our university and across higher education, this perception is reductive because community service and outreach are undervalued relative to what is rigidly deemed research and teaching. Project Humanities not only embraces outreach but also integrates research, scholars, and experts into its ambitious programming. Facilitating critical conversations across diverse communities that broaden perspectives and building understanding through talking, listening, and connecting, Project Humanities continues to instill passion and knowledge of humanities study and humanist thought. This approach continues to embody a model of the humanities that is not simply a list of academic disciplines but rather a way to provide tools and strategies to explore ways for people to connect with one another and to make meaning of shared human experiences. Project Humanities is "humanities in action," a proven catalyst for positive change that transcends political, socioeconomic, geographic, and cultural boundaries. It is not unusual to have attendees speak about taking what they learn and experience from our programs into other aspects of their personal and professional lives, as in this anonymous feedback from our March 2019 menstrual equity community discussion: "I will write a column for a journal about this issue. It will be included in the course content for women's health in the nursing program." At this particular event, attendees brought menstrual hygiene products to support our homeless outreach.

Strategic Vision and Goals

Now in its second decade, Project Humanities fosters and maintains a wide range of community and ASU partnerships. It continues to engage and cultivate its volunteer base and community partnerships, increase and cultivate its investor and support base, grow its social media and digital presence, grow its programmatic student engagement, grow and enhance its media presence, and seek and secure philanthropic and other external funding to support its robust programming.

Through talking, listening, and connecting across communities, cultures, disciplines, professions, and generations, Project Humanities is changing national and local perceptions of Arizona and the southwest borderlands as intolerant, hostile, and reluctant to engage critically on matters of difference in civil discourse and dialogue. The realities of legislation like a proposed ban on the teaching of ethnic studies in public school classrooms (Barr) and Arizona Senate Bill 1070 (Soler), for instance, in addition to encounters with racism on campus (Hendley) and in law enforcement ("ASU Professor"), continue to structure the narrative of intolerance and unbelonging for too many people considering Arizona as a home. In this environment, an "initiative [that] brings people together to learn to understand each other" (Bordow) is finding support. In the words of one young avid supporter back in 2011, Project Humanities is making the study of, conversation about, and "doing" of humanities "cool." Investment in and support of Project Humanities demonstrates ASU's public commitment to programs beyond STEM, and the project's success in growing philanthropic investments; securing outside funding to support programming; establishing a substantial media and social media presence; demonstrating rising engagement with online resources; attracting a growing number of volunteers, interns, and strategic partnerships; and receiving overwhelmingly positive feedback on programs and events all evidence Project Humanities' significant impact at ASU and enhancement of ASU's reputation in humanities work locally, nationally, and internationally. *US News and World Report* has repeatedly cited ASU as first in innovation, a title it has now bestowed on the university nine years in a row (Fuller).[11] Project Humanities' Hacks for Humanity is listed in the university's 2015 annual report, underscoring this innovation activity: "Project Humanities hosted Hacks for Humanity to create technology solutions for social good" (*Learn to Thrive* 6).

Project Humanities maps its success and impact by various indexes: number of events per year, number of attendees, number of strategic community and corporate partnerships and collaborations, funding received to support programming, student engagement, awards and accolades, and development. Project Humanities' programming continues to expand its visibility and impact. In 2019–2020, Project Humanities hosted 3,051 in-person participants; in 2020–2021, there were 3,133 virtual participants and 7,188 total *Eventbrite* registrants (even those unable to attend in person receive follow-up research materials on each event topic). Registration signifies awareness of a particular event and a potential to explore Project Humanities further.

Project Humanities' model supports such exploration in community-building intergenerationally and cross-communally. Such is the example of Santiago Griffin Todd, who has volunteered with Project Humanities since he was in eighth grade and is now attending ASU in order to stay connected with Project Humanities longer. After Santi and his grandfather began volunteering, Santi's mother and sister joined the homeless outreach volunteer team as well. The Todd family is also a financial investor as Humanity 101 Founders (those who invest $1,000 or more in Project Humanities programming)—an example of intergenerational and familial involvement that invests time, talent, and treasure. Says Santiago in an interview on the occasion of Project Humanities' tenth anniversary:

> Project Humanities and not only their homeless outreach . . . makes me think a lot more highly of ASU as a public institution versus a lot of more rigorous schools. Some of these initiatives are really just making my opinion of [ASU] so much higher. . . . I could really help make more of a difference and become even more intertwined with the other volunteers. . . . It's developed my thinking about going to college a little more because it's not just going to the classes. It's what you can do on the campus and around the campus and especially in the Valley as a whole. ("Santiago Griffin Todd")

As a model of impactfully engaging communities, Project Humanities exists at the intellectual, social, and academic nexus of diversity, inclusion, humanity, and justice. Created and envisioned as a space for inclusive personal, professional, and communal development, Project Humanities continues to evolve and to witness others' being alongside us in this evolution. Such is the case for a high school student who reached out to me as Project Humanities director in the course of her work on the question, "Are we losing our humanity?" That student graduated from high school, came to Arizona State University as an undergraduate, participated in Project Humanities as a student worker during her entire undergraduate career, then applied for a Project Humanities staff position, where she stayed for three years before heading off to pursue a master's degree at another university. Rachel Sondgeroth's long connection with Project Humanities impacted her greatly, as she affirms in this testimonial she shared in 2018: "Project Humanities was one of the reasons I decided to attend Arizona State University. I was intrigued by the programs . . . and inspired by Dr. Lester's eagerness to challenge students with leadership opportunities. From day one at ASU, I started engaging in the Project, believing that if I invested in them, they would invest back into me. I could have never predicted just how right I was." In his video testimonial on the occasion of Project Humanities' tenth anniversary in 2021, the university president, Michael M. Crow, commented on the social impact that Project Humanities is making and has made for a decade, adding that Project Humanities—at least under his leadership—is here "for the long haul" ("Project Humanities Ten-Year Anniversary Video"). With such continued institutional support, we are simultaneously appreciative and challenged to do more and be more in community-building and community-sustaining.

NOTES

1. Project Humanities has 122 unique ASU partners, 333 unique community partners, 55 unique venue partners, and 477 media stories.

2. Project Humanities' Vital Voices series, which has long included programming honoring King, is itself disruptive, as it does not rely on traditional lecture or panel models. Instead, it invites and encourages a facilitated discussion based on what participants bring to share. For the past four years, Project Humanities has hosted Vital Voices as a partnership with the Black Theater Troupe, who provide free theater space on the evening of the national Martin Luther King, Jr. (MLK), holiday. A recent MLK holiday Vital Voices event, hosted by myself and the King scholar Charles McKinney, was focused around the "radical" King, about whom few King nonscholar enthusiasts talk (see "King We Don't Know"). Our anticipated discussion and my interview with this reporter became the focus of the *Arizona Republic* reporter Greg Moore's article "Stop Looking at the Candy-Coated Martin Luther King and See Him for What He Was." Such a more nuanced reading of King's life and legacy is especially significant now, given that King quotes are often misappropriated by those who allege he ignored racial and class differences in, for example, his "content of character" / "colorblind" trope. This same commitment to educating ourselves and the general public on the evening of the MLK holiday led Project Humanities to host another virtual 2024 community conversation about King's economic policies, facilitated by me with Dr. McKinney as a scholar panelist and a Project Humanities staff member, Rae Macias, as a grassroots union community organizer.

3. In an interview, Garber discusses having spoken at the Presidential Forum at the annual convention of the Modern Language Association "on the topic of 'The Humanities and the World.' Other speakers on the program talked about literature and law, about the making of films from literary works, about anthropology and society. Reflecting on the topic, I decided instead to insist that the classroom and the lecture hall were very much part of 'the world,' and that if we accede to the idea that the world is to be found only outside the classroom we will pretty much give up the central value and importance of 'the humanities' and their claim to our attention. . . . The humanities are not just in society; they are society. I sometimes joke to my scientist friends that the humanities are what they are saving the world *for*" (Kinch).

4. In large part, Project Humanities is able to do this community engagement work and have it validated because of the leadership of the university where it resides. Within the institutional context of ASU as a "New American University" with specific "design aspirations" and funded primarily through the university president's strategic investments, Project Humanities affords a new paradigm of intersecting education theory and praxis through which it leverages place, transforms society, values entrepreneurship, conducts

use-inspired research, enables student success, fuses intellectual disciplines, is socially embedded, and engages globally ("Design Aspirations"; *Project Humanities*).

5. The Phi Beta Kappa Society press release reads: "Project Humanities received unanimous support in our selection committee process for its leadership in local and national conversations about the breadth, depth, and value of humanities across disciplines. Project Humanities is successfully blending academic research, community outreach, student development, and interdisciplinary approaches in compelling frameworks created by and enjoyed throughout the community. We applaud the vision and believe their efforts deserve Phi Beta Kappa's national spotlight" ("Project Humanities Receives National Award"). For selection criteria that underscores higher education and its connections to public programming and community engagement, see "Key."

6. Other community partners for this event included the African American Christian Clergy Coalition, Arizona Opportunities Industrialization Center, *Arizona Informant*, Arizona Commission on African American Affairs, NAACP, Phoenix College, International Ministerial Council of Arizona, Greater Phoenix Urban League, African Association of Arizona, Liberian Association of Arizona, and a host of individual sponsors and contributors (see Montgomery).

7. Tracey Benson, the then executive director of the Arizona School Boards Association, posted to the ASBA "Voices That Matter Campaign" page unsolicited responses to my conference keynote that grounded justice and humanity following the George Floyd murder and the global racial justice reckoning ("Voices"). Benson recalls that a few vocal conference attendees were bothered by the straightforwardness of my talk about the urgency of calling out systemic racism and white supremacy. Some felt that it was "too much for the keynote." Benson responded, "Is what was said untrue?" Benson's point is that systemic racism must be called out and addressed before it can be dismantled for those committed to justice work.

8. I received the Francis Andrew March Award for distinguished service to the profession from the MLA's Association of Departments of English (ADE) in 2015 and was later invited by the then director of the ADE, Douglas Seward, to present on the topic of humanities and entrepreneurialism at the 2020 ADE-ADFL Summer Seminar South, whose meeting theme was "The Public Humanities."

9. The annual Hacks for Humanity hacking event has become self-sustaining because of corporate support from such groups as State Farm, Amazon, Silicon Valley Bank, PayPal, Celtic Properties, Honeywell, Avnet Integrated, and ADP. Additional grant support for other Project Humanities programming has been provided by the Come Rain or Shine Foundation and the Puffin West Foundation.

10. Funded for two consecutive years by the Come Rain or Shine Foundation, this parenting initiative has included research experts as panelists and facilitators on "'Conscious' Parenting," "Parenting across Cultures," "Parenting and Suicide," "Talking to Kids about the Bad, Ugly and the Inevitable," "'Toxic' Parenting Behaviors," and "Spare the Kids: 'Whupping' and Black Parenting."

11. While the term *innovation* is relative and the method of any such ranking can signal inherent biases in those doing the ranking and determining what warrants being ranked, fiscal support through the university president's strategic investment funding signals a value of Project Humanities to our university's goals and mission, thereby allowing and encouraging certain traditional operational boundary crossings. Project funding

covers student and staff salaries and general operations. Special activities like the ongoing homeless outreach and the annual Hacks for Humanity: Hacking for the Social Good are funded through tax-deductible philanthropic donations and through corporate sponsorships that I, as founding director, mostly solicit. Including myself as a faculty member with seventy percent of my faculty workload devoted to Project Humanities as "service," Project Humanities has three full-time staff members; four to five student workers doing graphic design, social media communications, and events; and anywhere from three to four high school or undergraduate nonpaid interns. We are not and never have been a large staff, despite our ambitious programming and impactful reach.

WORKS CITED

Abramson, Bruce. "The Humanities Are Dead." *Newsweek*, 2 July 2020, www.newsweek.com/humanities-are-dead-opinion-1514862.

"ASU Charter, Mission and Goals." *New American University*, Arizona State U, 2020, newamericanuniversity.asu.edu/about/asu-charter-mission-and-goals.

"ASU Professor Arrested, Thrown to Ground for Jaywalking." *YouTube*, uploaded by Scripps News, 30 June 2014, www.youtube.com/watch?v=k8GfTp1NMvc.

"Awards and Accolades." *Project Humanities*, Arizona State U, projecthumanities.asu.edu/awards. Accessed 4 Oct. 2021.

Barr, Andy. "Arizona Bans 'Ethnic Studies.'" *Politico*, 12 May 2010, www.politico.com/story/2010/05/arizona-bans-ethnic-studies-037131.

Bordow, Melissa. "Being Better Humans." *Impact: Stories of Generosity and Opportunity at Arizona State University*, no. 9, fall-winter 2019, pp. 18–19.

Bruni, Frank. "The End of College as We Knew It?" *The New York Times*, 4 June 2020, www.nytimes.com/2020/06/04/opinion/sunday/coronavirus-college-humanities.html.

Bunning, Rachel. "ASU Awarded Fund for Positive Engagement Grant." *ASU News*, 31 Oct. 2017, news.asu.edu/20171031-asu-awarded-fund-positive-engagement-grant.

Byrne, Richard. "How Can the Humanities Prove Their Worth?" *The Chronicle of Higher Education*, vol. 54, no. 18, 11 Jan. 2008, A4.

"Community Development: Definition, Approaches and Types." *NigeriaSummary News*, 12 Dec. 2018, nigeriasummary.com/legit/11648/community-development-definition-approaches-and-types.

"Cultural Appropriation." *Project Humanities*, Arizona State U, projecthumanities.asu.edu/archive/cultural-appropriation. Accessed 30 Dec. 2023.

Davidson, Cathy N., and David Theo Goldberg. "A Manifesto for the Humanities in a Technological Age." *Chronicle of Higher Education*, vol. 50, no. 23, 13 Feb. 2004, B10–B11.

Dawnland. Directed by Adam Mazo and Ben Pender-Cudlip, PBS, Nov. 2018, www.pbs.org/independentlens/documentaries/dawnland/.

"Design Aspirations." *New American University*, Arizona State U, newamericanuniversity.asu.edu/about/design-aspirations. Accessed 4 Oct. 2021.

"Dr. Neal Lester on The McQuaid Mission Episode 15: The Importance of Community Outreach." *YouTube*, uploaded by ASUProjectHumanities, 19 Aug. 2021, www.youtube.com/watch?v=X0X2vbHYEMw.

"Event Recap Videos." *YouTube*, uploaded by ASUProjectHumanities, 23 Apr. 2020, www.youtube.com/playlist?list=PL2CbXK2E2M0rRjc0WoGUdI5Q2bRjZQ5QM.

Farmer, Esther. "Strange Bedfellows: Community Development, Democracy, and Magic." *Community Development*, vol. 46, no. 3, 2015, pp. 294–306, https://doi.org/10.1080/15575330.2015.1023818.

"Four Hundred Years Forward: A Commemoration Event." *Facebook*, facebook.com/events/s/400-years-forward-a-commemorat/420026521950497/.

Fuller, Mary Beth. "ASU Ranked No. 1 in Innovation for Ninth Straight Year." *ASU News*, 17 Sept. 2023, news.asu.edu/20230917-university-news-asu-no-1-innovation-nine-years-us-news-world-report.

Gordon, Lewis R. "Disciplinary Decadence and the Decolonisation of Knowledge." *Africa Development*, vol. 39, no. 1, 2014, pp. 81–92, www.ajol.info/index.php/ad/article/view/113311.

"Hacks for Humanity 2020 Promo." *YouTube*, uploaded by ASUProjectHumanities, 23 July 2020, youtu.be/ITNtvEQOMF0.

Hemingway, Ernest. *A Moveable Feast*. Charles Scribner's Sons, 1964.

Hendley, Matthew. "ASU Discouraging Face Paint at Athletic Events over Blackface Concerns." *Phoenix New Times*, 16 Oct. 2014, www.phoenixnewtimes.com/news/asu-discouraging-face-paint-at-athletic-events-over-blackface-concerns-6627544.

"Homeless Outreach." *Project Humanities*, Arizona State U, projecthumanities.asu.edu/service-Saturdays. Accessed 22 Nov. 2023.

"The Humanities: What Are They, What Were They, and What Might They Become?" *Vimeo*, uploaded by Stanford Humanities Center, 2011, vimeo.com/31211731.

"Humanity 101." *Project Humanities*, Arizona State U, projecthumanities.asu.edu/initiatives#Humanity_101. Accessed 4 Oct. 2021.

"Humanity 101 in the Workplace." *Project Humanities*, Arizona State U, projecthumanities.asu.edu/archive/humanity-101-workplace.

Hustedde, Ronald J., and Jacek Ganowicz. "The Basics: What's Essential about Theory for Community Development Practice?" *Community Development*, vol. 33, no. 1, 2002, pp. 1–19, https://doi.org/10.1080/15575330209490139.

In Whose Honor? Directed by Jay Rosenstein, PBS, 1997, archive.pov.org/inwhosehonor/.

"Key of Excellence Award." *The Phi Beta Kappa Society*, www.pbk.org/Key-of-Excellence.

Kinch, Sean. "Profound Activities of the Mind: Prior to Her Memphis Appearance, Shakespearean Scholar Marjorie Garber Talks with *Chapter 16* about the Pleasures of Reading and the Value of the Humanities." *Chapter 16*, 20 Mar. 2014, chapter16.org/profound-activities-of-the-mind/.

King, Martin Luther, Jr. "The Other America." 1967. *Civil Rights Movement Archive*, www.crmvet.org/docs/otheram.htm.

"The King We Don't Know." *YouTube*, uploaded by ASUProjectHumanities, 22 Nov. 2022, www.youtube.com/watch?v=Tbd7G1KPmf4&list=PL2CbXK2E2M0rWFZTty1q3YqGDVfKV49Qt&index=6&t=95s.

Learn to Thrive. Arizona State U, 2015, live-asu-edu.ws.asu.edu/sites/default/files/2022-01/151229_asu_2015_year_in_review_single_pages_0.pdf.

Lester, Neal A. "Are the Humanities Really in Crisis?" Interview by Emma Pettit. *The Chronicle of Higher Education*, 9 Feb. 2020, www.chronicle.com/article/are-the-humanities-really-in-crisis/.

———. "Humanity 101 in Action." Interview by Emma Pettit. *The Chronicle of Higher Education*, vol. 66, no. 21, 14 Feb. 2020, pp. A6–A7.

Lorde, Audre. *Sister Outsider*. Crossing Press, 1984.

Matarrita-Cascante, David, and Mark A. Brennan. "Conceptualizing Community Development in the Twenty-First Century." *Community Development*, vol. 43, no. 3, 2012, pp. 293–305, https://doi.org/10.1080/15575330.2011.593267.

Montgomery, Elizabeth. "How Phoenix Marked the Four Hundredth Anniversary of Slavery in America." *The Arizona Republic*, 22 Aug. 2019, www.azcentral.com/story/news/local/phoenix/2019/08/22/phoenix-community-commemorates-400th-anniversary-slavery-america/2063474001/.

Moore, Greg. "Stop Looking at the Candy-Coated Martin Luther King and See Him for What He Was." *The Arizona Republic*, 16 Jan. 2021, www.azcentral.com/story/opinion/op-ed/greg-moore/2021/01/16/martin-luther-king-radical-stop-candy-coating-him/4166489001/.

Mueller, Tracy. "Right Sized Life: Project Humanities Helps ASU and the Community Reflect on the Big Questions." *ASU Magazine*, vol. 10, no. 2, 2011, pp. 38–44.

"Our Work." *National Endowment for the Humanities*, www.neh.gov/our-work.

Owen, John R., and Peter Westoby. "The Structure of Dialogic Practice within Developmental Work." *Community Development*, vol. 43, no. 3, 2012, pp. 306–19, https://doi.org/10.1080/15575330.2011.632093.

Project Humanities. Arizona State U, 2018, projecthumanities.asu.edu/sites/default/files/2024-01/project_humanities_case.pdf.

"Project Humanities Community Testimonial: Brenda Thomson." *YouTube*, uploaded by Phi Beta Kappa, 15 Feb. 2014, www.youtube.com/watch?v=J1vXR_c-iq8.

"Project Humanities Receives National Award in Washington, D.C." *ASU News*, 4 Dec. 2013, news.asu.edu/content/project-humanities-receives-national-award-washington-dc.

"Project Humanities Ten-Year Anniversary Video." *YouTube*, uploaded by ASUProjectHumanities, 16 Feb. 2022, www.youtube.com/watch?v=2fucNFaMW3w.

"Proposals for Humanities in High Schools." *Knowledge Enterprise: Research Development*, Arizona State U, 1 Apr. 2021, funding.asu.edu/philanthropic-opportunities/proposals-humanities-high-schools.

Quimbo, Maria Ana T., et al. "Community Development Approaches and Methods: Implications for Community Development Practice and Research." *Community Development*, vol. 49, no. 5, 2019, pp. 589–603, https://doi.org/10.1080/15575330.2018.1546199.

Rumble: The Indians Who Rocked the World. Directed by Catherine Brainbridge and Alfonso Maiorana, PBS, www.pbs.org/independentlens/documentaries/rumble/.

"Santiago Griffin Todd—Service Saturday Testimonial." *YouTube*, uploaded by ASUProjectHumanities, 6 Oct. 2021, www.youtube.com/watch?v=iaPnkkaYf6U&list=PL2CbXK2E2M0pCEfmfkRENcrr958fOAat8&index=23.

Soler, Alessandra. "SB 1070 Is a Failed, Costly Experiment." *AZCentral.com*, 20 Apr. 2014, www.azcentral.com/story/opinion/op-ed/2014/04/20/sb-failed-costly-experiment/7951255/.

"Stanford Scholar Calls for New Definition of the Humanities." *Stanford Humanities Center*, Stanford U, 31 Oct. 2011, shc.stanford.edu/stanford-humanities-center/news/stanford-scholar-calls-new-definition-humanities-0.

"Ten Years of TLC Testimonials: Austin Davis on Homeless Outreach Partnership." *YouTube*, uploaded by ASUProjectHumanities, 23 July 2020, www.youtube.com/watch?v=j_ZQM4StciM&list=PL2CbXK2E2M0rEL2-MLCMjsjz1szQzGWTb&index=4.

Terrill, Marshall. "Casting Out Demons, Myths and Stereotypes: ASU's Project Humanities Hosts Community Engagement Program Designed to Dispel Falsehoods Surrounding Religion." *ASU News*, 19 Sept., 2019, news.asu.edu/20190919-arizona-impact-casting-out-demons-myths-and-stereotypes.

———. "Interactive Exhibit Demonstrates the Effect 'Stuff' Can Have on Racial Representation." *ASU News*, 22 Oct. 2021, news.asu.edu/20211022-discoveries-interactive-exhibit-demonstrates-effect-stuff-can-have-racial-representation.

Trimble, Lynn. "How Project Humanities Is Creating Conversations about Social Justice." *Phoenix New Times*, 21 Aug. 2020, www.phoenixnewtimes.com/arts/project-humanities-tackles-social-justice-issues-11488989.

"Vital Voices: The Uses of Anger." *YouTube*, uploaded by ASUProjectHumanities, 25 Jan. 2021, www.youtube.com/watch?v=BxOlFfWKcJs.

"Voices That Matter." *Arizona School Boards Association*, azsba.org/voices/tracey-benson/.

Warren, Jamie. "The Long Road to Recognition: Arizona's Ricky History with MLK Day and the Super Bowl." *Arizona ABC 15*, 3 Feb. 2023, www.abc15.com/news/black-history-month/the-long-road-to-recognition-arizonas-rocky-history-with-mlk-day-and-the-super-bowl.

"What Is Project Humanities?" *YouTube*, uploaded by ASUProjectHumanities, 2018, youtu.be/f9KJ4-RAvwo.

"What Is Project Humanities' Hacks for Humanity?" *YouTube*, uploaded by AZCulture, 28 Sept. 2017, www.youtube.com/watch?v=G_eE7_hGfgU.

"White Women Dismantling White Supremacy: Recap." *YouTube*, uploaded by ASUProjectHumanities, 21 Apr. 2021, www.youtube.com/watch?v=sGgAj1W_aSA.

Notes on Contributors

Miriam Araya (Multicultural Solidarity Coalition) is dedicated to achieving social justice and Black liberation. She received her master's degree in justice studies from San Jose State University in 2017 and is currently a second-year PhD student in justice and social inquiry at Arizona State University.

Kelly Baur (Multicultural Solidarity Coalition) is a documentary filmmaker and community organizer who dreams of a future with no police and no borders. She is currently pursuing a PhD in linguistics and applied linguistics at Arizona State University.

Miranda Bernard (Multicultural Solidarity Coalition) is a PhD student in the School of Life Sciences at Arizona State University, studying the role of community engagement and perceptions in marine interventions.

Andrea E. Brewster is associate director of educational assessment at Santa Clara University. Between 2010 and 2021, she facilitated the Experiential Learning for Social Justice undergraduate core curriculum requirement, taught community-based learning courses, and engaged in related curriculum development, research, and assessment projects. Her current scholarly interests involve assessing high-impact practices in undergraduate education and addressing equity issues in student success initiatives.

Jamal Brooks-Hawkins (Multicultural Solidarity Coalition) is a second-year PhD student in the School of Social Transformation at Arizona State University. His research focuses on radical reimaginings of Black sexuality development and the importance of joy in social-movement-building and cultural labor.

Phyllis R. Brown is professor emerita of English at Santa Clara University. Before returning full-time to the English department in 2015, she served as associate provost for undergraduate studies (2010–15) and as director of the undergraduate core curriculum (2008–12). She publishes on learning, education, and medieval literature.

Nicole A. Cooke is the Augusta Baker Endowed Chair and a professor at the University of South Carolina. Her research and teaching interests include human information behavior, critical-cultural information studies, and diversity and social justice in librarianship. The 2019 ALISE Excellence in Teaching Award recipient, she has edited and authored several books, including *Information Services to Diverse Populations* (2016) and *Fake News and Alternative Facts: Information Literacy in a Post-truth Era* (2018).

Spencer R. Crew is Clarence J. Robinson Professor of History at George Mason University. He worked for twenty years at the Smithsonian Institution's National Museum of American History and has served as interim director of the National Museum of African American History and Culture and as president of the National Underground Railroad Freedom Center. He is a past chair of the National Council for History Education and trustee emeritus of the board of the National Trust for Historic Preservation and has served on the nominating board of the Organization of American Historians and the board of the American Association of Museums. Crew has published extensively on African American and public history. His most recent publication is *Thurgood Marshall: A Life in American History* (2019).

Austin Davis is a poet and recent undergraduate student activist at Arizona State University.

Sébastien Dubreil is teaching professor of French and francophone studies, second language acquisition, and technology-enhanced learning at Carnegie Mellon University. With a specialty in computer-assisted language learning, he researches the use of technology in fostering transcultural learning. His most recent research examines the notions of social pedagogies, linguistic landscapes and game-based language, and culture learning.

Jane Elliott is an anti-racism educator whose acclaimed Blue Eyes / Brown Eyes social exercise, adapted in 1968 on the day after the assassination of Dr. Martin Luther King, Jr., makes her a leading national and international voice on justice issues and allyship.

Ash Evans received her PhD in rhetoric and composition from the University of Wisconsin, Milwaukee. Her research interests include digital rhetoric, composition pedagogy, and writing program administration.

Jennifer Merritt Faria is senior director for academics at Santa Clara University (SCU)'s Miller Center for Social Entrepreneurship, where she designs globally engaged teaching and research initiatives focused on advancing women's economic power and climate resilience in collaboration with the Miller Center's international network of social entrepreneur partners, teaches the Miller Center Lewis Family Fellowship courses, and leads faculty workshops on assignment design for global social impact. She has also served as SCU's director of community-based learning and led the Arrupe Engagement and Thriving Neighbors programs.

Alex Gilbert (Multicultural Solidarity Coalition) is a PhD student in the English department at Arizona State University. They are a trans linguist and writer from Knoxville, Tennessee.

Nikki Giovanni is a poet and distinguished university professor emerita of English at Virginia Tech University.

Joseph L. Graves, Jr., is the MacKenzie Scott Endowed Professor of Biology at North Carolina Agricultural and Technical State University.

Josh Greene is a Phoenix-born, African American architect in training. He spent three years as a Global Health Corps fellow and designer with MASS Design Group in Kigali, Rwanda, and currently works at Kéré Architecture in Berlin.

Laurie Grobman is distinguished professor of English and women's studies at Penn State University, Berks, and has two single-authored books, one coauthored book, and four coedited collections. Her article "'Anti-racist Commemorative Intervention' at the Hopewell Furnace National Historic Site," coauthored with three undergraduates, appeared in *College English* (2022), and her article "'Engaging Race': Critical Race Inquiry and Community-Engaged Scholarship" received the 2018 Richard C. Ohmann Outstanding Article in *College English* Award from the National Council of Teachers of English. Grobman was the 2014 Carnegie Foundation for the Advancement of Teaching Outstanding Baccalaureate Colleges Professor of the Year.

Anthony Q. Hazard, Jr., is professor of ethnic studies and history at Santa Clara University. He has held a postdoctoral fellowship in science in human culture at Northwestern University and the Inclusive Excellence Postdoctoral Fellowship at Santa Clara University. He is the author of *Postwar Anti-racism: The US, UNESCO, and "Race," 1945–1968* (2012) and *Boasians at War: Anthropology, Race, and World War II* (2020).

Cynthia M. Landrum is a doctoral candidate at Simmons University and a former public library administrator. Throughout her twenty-plus-year career in public libraries, equity, diversity, inclusion, and social justice have informed her practice and leadership. Her research interests include the lived experiences and narratives of public library leaders of color and social justice leadership practice in public libraries. She has presented professionally in the areas of community-centered library experiences, community inquiry in public libraries, and public libraries' role in community development and change efforts.

Lore/tta LeMaster is associate professor of critical/cultural communication studies in the Hugh Downs School of Human Communication at Arizona State University. Her scholarship engages the intersectional constitution of cultural difference with particular focus on queer and trans of color life, art, and embodiment. Her pronouns are interchangeably she/her/hers and they/them/theirs.

Harry Lennix is a stage and film actor and producer. His films *Revival!*, *H4*, and *Troubled Waters* are currently in circulation. His direction of *A Small Oak Tree Runs Red* received the Audelco Award for Best Production in 2018. Lennix currently appears on the long-running NBC series *The Blacklist*. He is a former seminarian and Chicago Public Schools teacher of music and civics. At Northwestern University, Lennix served as coordinator of For Members Only, the Black student union. He is a frequent lecturer and ambassador for causes including literacy, men's health, and community-police relations.

Neal A. Lester is a foundation professor of English and founding director of the award-winning Project Humanities at Arizona State University. With expertise in African American literature and culture, Lester is a national leader on conversations about the N-word, public humanities and entrepreneurship, privilege and bias, cultural appropriation, the race and gender politics of hair, and African American children's literature.

Leigh Ann Litwiller Berte is associate professor of English at Spring Hill College. An original member of Spring Hill's grant team for an American Association of Colleges and Universities global learning award, she has coordinated a series of interdisciplinary courses on social justice issues. The course model has been featured in *International Educator* and *Inside Higher Ed*, and Litwiller has presented and published on the courses at conferences and in *Diversity and Democracy*.

Gabriele Maier is associate teaching professor of German studies and director of the MA program in global communication and applied translation at Carnegie Mellon University (CMU) in Pittsburgh. She is coeditor of Heimat *and Migration: Reimagining the Regional and Global in the Twenty-First Century* (2013) and *Outreach Strategies and Innovative Teaching Approaches for German Program Building* (2021) and author of *Deutschland im Zeitalter der Globalisierung* (*Germany in the Age of Globalization*; 2015), a textbook for upper-level German courses. From 2017 to 2020, she was a fellow of the How Well? project, funded by the Center for the Arts in Society at CMU, where she worked with various student groups to educate the public about food insecurity and how to improve well-being on the CMU campus.

Ronald Mason, Jr., is professor of law at the University of the District of Columbia and former president of three Historically Black Colleges and Universities (HBCUs).

Ronae Matriano (Multicultural Solidarity Coalition) is a PhD student in the family and human development program at Arizona State University. They study Asian American racial identity development and critical consciousness.

Heidi Mau is associate professor in the department of communications at Albright College, where she teaches courses in digital literacy, digital design, and communications. Her research is in media and communication, intersecting areas such as digital and popular cultures, gender and sexuality, and memory studies. Her work has been published in *The Journal of Short Film*, *Journal of Popular Music Studies*, and *Journal of Lesbian Studies*, among others. In 2020, Mau was awarded the Dr. Henry P. and M. Paige Laughlin Research Award for Faculty Scholarship at Albright College.

Nathan McCullough-Haddix is deputy director at the Louis J. Koch Family Children's Museum in Evansville, Indiana.

Dontá McGilvery is a theater educator, social justice adjunct professor, and activist. He is the first Black male to earn a PhD in theater from Arizona State University, where he helped establish the culture and access department within the Herberger Institute for Design and the Arts.

Dianne McIntyre is an internationally acclaimed dancer, choreographer, dance historian, and educator.

Cheryl L. Nicholas is associate professor of communication arts and sciences at Penn State University, Berks. Her research considers how symbolic activity constitutes and is constituted by cultural worldviews. Her research appears in such venues as *Sexuality and Culture, Storytelling, Self and Society, and Queer Identities / Political Realities.* Nicholas is a recipient of the 2014–15 Penn State University Commission on Lesbian, Gay, Bisexual, and Transgender Equity (CLGBTE) Award for Outstanding Service. In 2017, she was honored in the Teachers on Teaching series by the National Communication Association, and in 2019 she was named an Alumni Teaching Fellow at Penn State.

Simon J. Ortiz is an internationally acclaimed poet and regents' professor emeritus of English at Arizona State University.

Kierra Otis (Multicultural Solidarity Coalition) is a full-spectrum doula and gender studies doctoral student in the School of Social Transformation at Arizona State University. Their research is concerned with birthing and reproductive justice for queer and trans Black people, Indigenous people, and people of color.

David Pilgrim is university distinguished professor of sociology; vice president for diversity, inclusion, and strategic initiatives; and founder of the Jim Crow Museum of Racist Imagery at Ferris State University.

Anke Pinkert is associate professor of German and cinema and media studies and Conrad Humanities Scholar for the College of Liberal Arts and Sciences at the University of Illinois Urbana-Champaign. She is the author of *Film and Memory in East Germany* (2008) and *Remembering 1989: Future Archives of Public Protest* (2024) and has published on postwar and post-Holocaust memory, visual culture, and postcommunist literature as well as on the public humanities and prison education. A faculty affiliate of the Education Justice Project since 2010, she has taught college courses on the Holocaust and cofacilitated a mindfulness meditation group at Danville Correctional Center (2010–14). From 2016 to 2018, she codirected a campus-wide, multidisciplinary research and engagement initiative on the public humanities.

Mastaani Qureshi (Multicultural Solidarity Coalition) is an Urdu-speaking, Pakistani, Muslim American who identifies as a cis queer woman. She is a radical cultural feminist passionate about abolishing colonist narratives in her native women's culture.

Maureen T. Reddy, professor emerita of English at Rhode Island College, has written extensively about race, gender, mothering, and popular fiction in various combinations. Her books include *Traces, Codes, and Clues: Reading Race in Crime Fiction* (2002), *Crossing the Color Line: Race, Parenting, and Culture* (1994), *Everyday Acts against Racism: Raising Children in a Multiracial World* (1996), and *Race in the College Classroom: Pedagogy and Politics* (2002, coedited with Bonnie TuSmith).

Jess Roberts is director of Albion's Big Read and professor of English at Albion College, a small liberal arts college in Albion, Michigan. Her essays appear in *Callaloo*, *ESQ*, the *Cambridge Companion to Nineteenth-Century American Poetry*, *South*, and elsewhere. Her current work uses literature as a resource for creating and sustaining community.

Tara Roeder is associate professor and director of first-year writing at St. John's University. She is coeditor of the collection *Critical Expressivism: Theory and Practice in the Composition Classroom* (2015) and the author of multiple essays, chapbooks, and poems. Her current research focuses on veganism as a social justice issue.

Leslie Anne Singel teaches African American literature at Columbia College Chicago. Her research focuses on the literature of race, ethnicity, and immigration as well as Irish and Irish-American studies.

John Streamas is associate professor of ethnic studies and graduate director of American studies and culture in the School of Languages, Cultures, and Race at Washington State University. A Japanese immigrant, he has published on war films, Japanese American literature, racialized narrative temporalities, depression memoirs by writers of color, and race on campus.

Sarra Tekola (Multicultural Solidarity Coalition) is a PhD student in the School of Sustainability at Arizona State University, studying decolonization as a response to climate change. They are also a founder of the Multicultural Solidarity Coalition.

Ana Isabel Terminel Iberri (Multicultural Solidarity Coalition) is a PhD student in the Hugh Downs School of Human Communication at Arizona State University. Her research focuses on intersectional approaches to critical communication pedagogy outside the classroom.

Jami Proctor Xu is an internationally respected poet and translator.